ADVENTURING IN
BELIZE

D0191493

THE SIERRA CLUB
ADVENTURE TRAVEL GUIDES

Adventuring Along the Gulf of Mexico, by Donald G. Schueler

Adventuring Along the Southeast Coast, by John Bowen

Adventuring in Alaska, Completely revised and updated,
 by Peggy Wayburn

Adventuring in Arizona, by John Annerino

Adventuring in Australia, by Eric Hoffman

Adventuring in Belize, by Eric Hoffman

Adventuring in British Columbia, by Isabel Nanton
 and Mary Simpson

Adventuring in East Africa, by Allen Bechky

Adventuring in Florida, by Allen deHart

Adventuring in New Zealand, by Margaret Jefferies

Adventuring in North Africa, by Scott Wayne

Adventuring in the Alps, by William E. Reifsnyder
 and Marylou Reifsnyder

Adventuring in the Andes, by Charles Frazier with Donald Secreast

Adventuring in the California Desert, by Lynne Foster

Adventuring in the Caribbean, by Carrol B. Fleming

Adventuring in the Chesapeake Bay Area, by John Bowen

Adventuring in the Pacific, by Susanna Margolis

Adventuring in the Rockies, Completely revised and updated,
 by Jeremy Schmidt

Adventuring in the San Francisco Bay Area, by Peggy Wayburn

Trekking in Nepal, West Tibet, and Bhutan, by Hugh Swift

Trekking in Pakistan and India, by Hugh Swift

Walking Europe from Top to Bottom, by Susanna Margolis
 and Ginger Harmon

ADVENTURING IN
BELIZE

The Sierra Club Travel Guide
to the Islands, Waters,
and Inland Parks of
Central America's Tropical Paradise

ERIC HOFFMAN

SIERRA CLUB BOOKS   SAN FRANCISCO

Library of Congress Cataloging-in-Publication Data
Hoffman, Eric.
    Adventuring in Belize / Eric Hoffman.
        p. cm.
    Includes bibliographical references and index.
    ISBN 0-87156-592-7
    1. Natural areas — Belize — Guidebooks. 2. Wilderness areas — Belize — Guidebooks. 3. Scuba diving — Belize — Guidebooks. 4. Skin diving — Belize — Guidebooks. 5. Belize — Description and travel. 6. Belize — Guidebooks. I. Title.
    QH108.B43H64   1994
    508.7282 — dc20   93-5569
                                                                            CIP

Production by Robin Rockey
Cover design by Bonnie Smetts
Book design by Abigail Johnston
Maps by Hilda Chen

10 9 8 7 6 5 4 3 2 1

*To the intrepid adventurers
Greg Moon and Mike Larrabee*

CONTENTS

Acknowledgments ix

ONE: OVERVIEW **1**

Why Visit Belize? 3   *What's Special about this Book?* 6
History and Cultures 8   *Belize's Magnificent Ecosystems* 13
Adventuring Activities and Services 21   *Getting to Belize* 28
Getting Around Belize 31   *Basic Travel Information* 36
Basic Facts about Belize 44

TWO: BELIZE DISTRICT **49**

Overview 51   *Belize City* 52   *Crooked Tree Wildlife
Sanctuary* 72   *Bermudian Landing Community Baboon
Sanctuary* 78   *Altun Ha ("Rockstone Water") Ruins* 86
Belize Zoo and Tropical Education Center 89   *Monkey Bay
Wildlife Sanctuary* 93   *Gales Point (Manatee Lagoons)* 94
Ambergris Caye 101   *Changa Paz's Top Dive and Snorkel
Sites* 107   *Hol Chan Marine Preserve (snorkeling and
diving)* 113   *Caye Caulker (snorkeling and diving)* 115
Caye Chapel 125   *St. George's Caye (snorkeling and diving)* 126
Other Cayes (snorkeling and diving) 129   *The Atolls* 129

THREE: STANN CREEK DISTRICT **143**

Overview 145   *Dangriga* 146   *South Water Caye (snorkeling
and diving)* 159   *Tobacco Caye (snorkeling and diving)* 165
Garifuna Villages 166   *Sittee River Sugar Mill* 171
Sittee River Tour 173   *Possum Point Biological Station* 175
Cockscomb Basin Wildlife Sanctuary 177   *Placencia (snorkeling
and diving)* 198   *Brian Young's Top Dive and Snorkel Sites* 207

FOUR: TOLEDO DISTRICT 213

Overview 215 *Punta Gorda* 216 *Mayan Ruins* 222
Visiting with Today's Maya 229 *Blue Creek Cave Hike* 239
Temash and Moho River Areas 241 *Cayes of Port Honduras
(snorkeling and diving)* 247 *Sapodilla Cayes (snorkeling
and diving)* 248

FIVE: CAYO DISTRICT 255

Overview 257 *Guancaste National Park* 259 *Belmopan* 261
Blue Hole National Park 265 *Spanish Lookout and Other
Mennonite Communities* 268 *San Ignacio and Santa Elena* 272
Xunantunich ("Maiden of the Rocks") Ruins 275 *Other
Mayan Ruins* 278 *Mountain Pine Ridge Forest Reserve* 279
Garcia Sisters Museum 282 *Mountain Lodges* 284 *Ix Chel
Farm and Panti Mayan Medicine Trail* 290 *Caracol ("Snail")
Natural Monument* 292 *Chiquibul Forest Reserve and
National Park* 298 *Benque Viejo del Carmen* 300 *Tikal
National Park, Guatemala* 302

SIX: ORANGE WALK DISTRICT 317

Overview 319 *Orange Walk Town* 319 *Cuello Ruins* 321
Lamanai ("Submerged Crocodile") Ruins 322 *Rio Bravo
Conservation and Management Area* 326 *Chan Chich Lodge* 332

SEVEN: COROZAL DISTRICT 341

Overview 343 *Corozal Town* 343 *Crossing the Mexican
Border* 345 *Cerros Ruins* 346 *Santa Rita Ruins* 347
Shipstern Nature Reserve and Butterfly Breeding Centre 348

Bibliography 353

Index 359

Acknowledgments

First and foremost, thanks to Therese and Tony Rath for taking me under their wing and patiently guiding me on my journeys throughout Belize. And, when my travels were over, thanks to Therese and Tony for responding to numerous faxes and fact-checking some of the text. Editor Linda Gunnarson's talent, perseverance, and diligence to detail were equally as important to the outcome of this project. Her upbeat approach to getting the job done was also a source of inspiration to the author.

Alan Auil and Paul Mills are two other Belizeans who deserve special thanks for unselfishly giving of themselves and availing their businesses to me with no strings attached. Other people and organizations whose expertise and logistical support were indispensable in the making of this book are Tommy Thomson, Tropical Travel, and TACA, American, and Continental airlines.

Others who took time out to share their knowledge and expertise are: Gilbert Andrews, Bob Aukerman, James Azueta, Howard Benson, George and Corol Bevier, Jim and Marguerite Bevis, Barbara Boardman, Amy Bodwell, Dr. Hugh Bollinger, Tineke Boomsma, Barry Bowen, Nick Brokaw, Mickey Browne, Bill Burley, John Carr, Dahlia Castillo, Alex Chee, Papio Cubb, Meb Cutlack, Tony Diaz, Roger Dinger, Dr. Jerry Eberhart, Janet Finlayson, Mick and Lucy Fleming, Aurora Garcia (Lol Mesh), Janet Gibson, Emma Gill, Glenn Godfrey, Isabel Goldberg, Kevin Gonzalez, Dr. Victor Gonzalez, Joy Grant, Tom Greenwood, Johnny Grief, Gach Guerrero, Jerry Hall, Tom and Josie Harding, Charles Hope, Dr. Rob Horwich, Paul Hunt, Anna Jimenez, Rudy and Margaret Juan, Emory King, Bill Konstant, Lita Hunter Krohn, Janice Lambert, Pablo Lambey, Dean Lindo, Vera Lo, Mary Dell Lucas, Betsy Mallory, John Masson, Sharon Matola, Logan McNatt, Martin Meadows, Jan Meerman, Bart and Suzi Mickler, Bruce and Carolyn Miller, Matthew Miller, James Nations, Lou Nicolait, Hermino Novelo, Larry Parker, Catherine Paz, Melody and Changa Paz, Patricia San Pedro, George Price, Dr. Alan Rabinowitz, Ernest Reimer, Mariam Robinson, William "Chet" Schmidt, John Searle, Mary and Paul Shave, Caesar Sherrad, Hon. Winston Smiling, Harry Taylor,

Lascelle Tillet, Sam Tillet, Tony the boatman, Terri Valentine, Joy Vernon, Lydia Waight, Mike Wendling, Chris White, Bill Wildman, Michael Wright, Brian Young, and Rosella Zabaneh.

ONE
OVERVIEW

Why Visit Belize?

Just imagine. A skin diving mask is pressed snugly against your face as you roll backward from the side of a boat. Warm water rushes around you. Beneath you hundreds of colorful tropical fish dance above immense coral outcrops and gently waving sea fans. You blink in astonishment as a huge sea turtle glides past toward deeper water.

Just imagine. You're hiking deep in the rain forest on a trail that tunnels through dripping greenery and fragrant flowering plants. You marvel at vines as big around as telephone poles twisting skyward. A keel-billed toucan with a multicolored banana-size bill hops through the foliage croaking hoarsely. Suddenly there's a flash of yellow on the trail a few yards away. You find yourself looking into the eyes of an ocelot. In a blink and without a sound the exotic cat is gone.

Just imagine. You've wiped the sweat from your forehead after climbing to the top of the tallest human-made structure in Belize, the massive temple Caana at Caracol. Below lie the ruins of an ancient Mayan city that was home to 180,000 souls around A.D. 700. In all directions is rain forest. Monkey and bird calls drift across the stillness.

Just imagine. You've been walking through the rain forest to a remote Mayan village when suddenly you hear melodic laughter, splashing sounds, and an unfamiliar language. The trail opens onto a vine- and fern-draped pool where a half-dozen Mayan women and children are swimming and bathing. One woman, with a flower tucked behind her ear and standing waist high in the water, says in English, "Hello, the village isn't far. We're cooling off." She smiles and points to where the trail picks up again after crossing the stream.

Just imagine. You're nursing a beer as you stretch out in a hammock strung between two coconut palms on a sandy caye littered with conch shells. The sparkly aqua-blue water laps at the beach. Overhead two frigate birds with six-foot wingspans ride the breeze. They look more like pterodactyls than birds as they glide and twist effortlessly against the cloudless sky, watching for unsuspecting fish near the water's surface. In the distance an old wooden fishing sloop tilts in the breeze, its tired yellow sails bulging, its precious cargo of lobsters on its way to Belize City.

These are some of my memories from Belize.

Belize is for people who want to interact with unbridled nature in the tropics. There are few countries in the world, and no other place as close to North America, with the unfathomable richness of immense intact and unspoiled ecosystems that are home to thousands of species of plants and animals in settings of coral reefs, freshwater wetlands, and dramatic rain forests. Belize's rain forests are also a major repository of ancient Mayan ruins, some of which are just beginning to be recognized for their importance in understanding the ancient Mayan world. Belizeans themselves are truly unique. They are a mostly English-speaking polyglot culture made up of Mayans, Creoles, Garifunas, Hispanics, Mennonites, and people of European ancestry. Racial and cultural harmony is the rule.

Among its nature destinations Belize boasts the longest barrier reef in the Western Hemisphere; Hol Chan Marine Preserve, an underwater park enjoyed by snorkelers and scuba divers; isolated, palm-studded cayes; the Cockscomb Basin Wildlife Sanctuary, the first park anywhere specifically set aside to protect jaguars; Caracol, the immense Mayan archaeological site whose ancient leaders once ruled better-known Tikal in Guatemala; the Bermudian Landing Community Baboon Sanctuary, a black howler monkey sanctuary run by subsistence farmers; and scores of Mayan villages tucked away in quiet, green valleys.

In Belize's forests and vast wetlands are an incredible 520 species of birds, among them keel-billed toucans, scarlet macaws, and jabirus. The biggest cat in the Americas, the jaguar, roams through about 70 percent of the country. There are four other wild felines — ocelots, margays, mountain lions (pumas), and jaguarundis — plus other terrestrial and aquatic rarities, such as tapirs, kinkajous, howler monkeys, and manatees.

In the shallow seas of the reef and atolls the abundance of life explodes in a constantly rearranging kaleidoscope of species. Everything from delicate and luminously polka-dotted yellowtail damselfish to majestic and graceful spotted eagle rays cruise Belizean waters. Hundreds of cayes dot the waters of the Barrier Reef and atolls.

Belize is just two hours' flying time from Los Angeles, Houston, and Miami. Accessibility for North Americans is enhanced by the fact that most Belizeans speak English, making communication throughout Belize free-flowing and rewarding regardless of cultural background. There are few other places in the world where you can

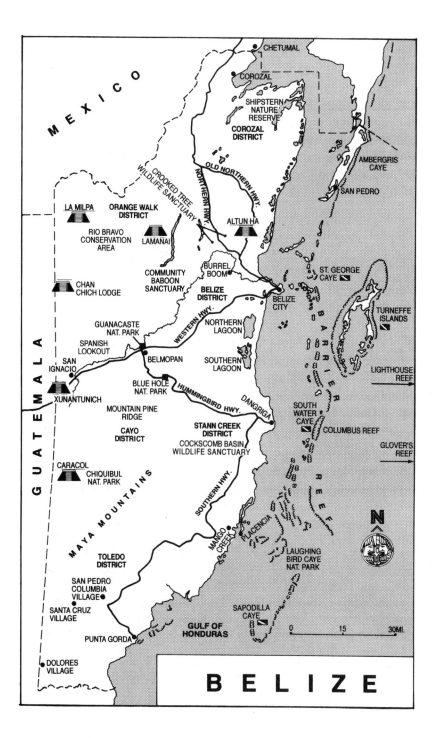

MEXICO

CHETUMAL

COROZAL

SHIPSTERN NATURE RESERVE

COROZAL DISTRICT

AMBERGRIS CAYE

SAN PEDRO

CROOKED TREE WILDLIFE SANCTUARY

NORTHERN HWY.

OLD NORTHERN HWY.

LA MILPA

ORANGE WALK DISTRICT

RIO BRAVO CONSERVATION AREA

LAMANAI

ALTUN HA

COMMUNITY BABOON SANCTUARY

BURREL BOOM

BELIZE DISTRICT

ST. GEORGE CAYE

BELIZE CITY

TURNEFFE ISLANDS

CHAN CHICH LODGE

GUANACASTE NAT. PARK

NORTHERN LAGOON

SPANISH LOOKOUT

SAN IGNACIO

BELMOPAN

WESTERN HWY.

SOUTHERN LAGOON

LIGHTHOUSE REEF

XUNANTUNICH

BLUE HOLE NAT. PARK

HUMMINGBIRD HWY.

DANGRIGA

SOUTH WATER CAYE

COLUMBUS REEF

GLOVER'S REEF

MOUNTAIN PINE RIDGE

CAYO DISTRICT

STANN CREEK DISTRICT

COCKSCOMB BASIN WILDLIFE SANCTUARY

CARACOL

CHIQUIBUL NAT. PARK

GUATEMALA

MAYA MOUNTAINS

SOUTHERN HWY.

PLACENCIA

MANGO CREEK

LAUGHING BIRD CAYE NAT. PARK

TOLEDO DISTRICT

SAN PEDRO COLUMBIA VILLAGE

SANTA CRUZ VILLAGE

SAPODILLA CAYE

PUNTA GORDA

GULF OF HONDURAS

0   15   30MI.

DOLORES VILLAGE

N

BARRIER REEF

BELIZE

speak in English with people from three non-European-based cultures.
There is one last reason why Belize is a worthwhile destination for anyone interested in preserving rain forest and reef ecosystems. Belize is a cash-poor country that has committed about one-third of its New Hampshire–size land mass to national parks and sanctuaries since 1981. The government, which is elected by its people, hopes to make Belize the number-one eco-tourism destination in Central America and believes its richness in natural treasures surpasses, or is competitive with, any country in the region. You can help preserve fragile ecosystems by simply visiting Belize. The money spent by eco-tourists strengthens the national resolve to forever protect immense biodiverse rain forests and reef ecosystems that have been set aside and aren't found in such a concentrated abundance anywhere else.

What's Special about this Book?

Adventuring in Belize was created to guide you on a personal adventure through one of the best nature destinations on Earth. My goal was to locate the best natural-history and nature-viewing areas in Belize, tell you how to get there, and indicate the costs involved. This book is different from other travel guides in that it goes beyond generalities about a region or an ecosystem to provide very specific information about everything from dive sites and hiking trails to the price ranges you can expect at individual restaurants, hotels, and dive and boat services. In particular the book contains enough detail to compete directly with any specialized books on scuba diving, snorkeling, or natural-history destinations in Belize. It includes descriptions of every readily accessible national park, dozens of islands, and scores of underwater dive and snorkel sites. Along with the description of each area there are specifics: the types of flora and fauna you are likely to see, listings of nature trails, recreational activities in the area, cautions, and essential information about the nearest accommodations and ways to access the area. The book provides more than 400 contacts throughout Belize plus information on tour operators, airlines, and Belizean government contacts in the United States and Canada.

My field research — and enjoyment — included scuba diving (more than forty dives) at a wide range of dive sites at depths ranging from 15 to 150 feet; snorkeling countless times; sailing on Belizean-made wooden sloops; exploring remote islands; walking the trails in every national park and wildlife sanctuary; staying in isolated Mayan villages; exploring remote river systems that can be reached only by boat; driving practically every road in Belize in all kinds of weather; exploring and researching more than twenty Mayan ruins, including Tikal in Guatemala; and interviewing more than 150 Belizeans and others who are involved in accessing and/or conservation of Belize's astounding ecosystems.

The views of experts — be they dive masters, archaeologists, or ornithologists — are offered to enrich the descriptions of the book's destinations. My intent was to merge my experience with the greater body of knowledge concerning each particular place. For example, even though I hiked every trail in the Cockscomb Basin Wildlife Sanctuary and recorded what I saw and experienced, the Cockscomb's director, Ernesto Saqui, supplied information about seasonal changes and which animals are most likely to be sighted on specific trails. In the process of interviewing these knowledgeable Belizean experts, I found that they were adding a special quality to this project beyond their particular expertise. I had begun the book ecstatic about getting to investigate some of the best rain forests, Mayan ruins, and reefs in existence and came home equally enraptured with the Belizeans themselves. Each individual was gracious and accommodating, and together they offered solid evidence that people from widely differing backgrounds, beliefs, and ethnic origins can get along. In these pages you'll hear from everyone from former Minister of Tourism and the Environment Glenn Godfrey and Belize Zoo director Sharon Matola to Belize Audubon president Therese Rath, Garifuna Council chairman Pablo Lambey, and dive master Changa Paz.

Lastly, this book provides information about recreational activities and makes distinctions between businesses offering similar services. From dive shop services to mountain-lodge tour packages, specific details are listed for each operator. For almost all activities, several businesses offering a similar service in an area are listed. This way you can shop around in terms of breadth and quality of service, as well as cost, and decide for yourself which one best suits your needs.

History and Cultures

While Europe entered the Dark Ages (around A.D. 500) great Mayan temples were glistening in the rain forests in today's country of Belize and elsewhere in Central America. The Mayans had started their ascent as one of the world's greatest and longest-lasting civilizations in 1500 B.C. Over the centuries they developed a highly ritualistic society. Their immense pyramids were adorned with friezes and plastered in bright colors. The smell of incense drifted through the sacred plazas from the inner sanctums of these temples, where astronomer-priests and members of the ruling elite lived and worshipped. Among the high-ranking members of society were mathematicians, architects, sculptors, generals, and a ruling noble class. The calendar they lived by was as accurate as any today.

The Mayan centers were highly organized, with outlying residential and crop-growing areas that covered dozens of square miles. At the civilization's zenith, between A.D. 300 and 900, more than 400,000 Mayans lived in what is now Belize. Caracol, Belize's largest ancient Mayan city, was home to 180,000 people. By the twelfth century A.D., most of the Mayan cities had collapsed, most likely due to a combination of factors that resulted in brutal warfare between centers and rejection of despotic rule within each center. By the time the Europeans arrived, most Mayans were found living in small, thatched-roof villages as they do to this day.

In 1502, Columbus sailed into and named the Bay of Honduras, which is part of the Caribbean Sea and immediately offshore from Belize's most southern sizeable town, Punta Gorda. Though Columbus saw the shore he never set foot on it.

The English arrived in about 1620, but not officially. These first non-native settlers were pirates who used the cayes and reefs as hideouts between raids on Spanish galleons. The pirates were later joined by shipwrecked British sailors and disbanded British soldiers who were driven from Jamaica when Spain wrested it from England in 1655. By 1705 some of these inhabitants began harvesting logwood (a bright red textile dye leeched from logwood became the rage of Europe). Later they would harvest mahogany as well. This "bastard colony" not claimed by England had a tough time of it for nearly a hundred years. It was subjected to numerous raids from neighboring Spanish settlements in today's countries of Honduras and Mexico. At the time, Spain claimed sovereignty over the entire New World, except for parts of South America assigned to Portugal by Papal decree. Despite the odds, the tenacious little colony of Englishmen persisted by extracting logwood and mahogany and avoiding the Spanish.

The early colony was centered primarily around today's site of Belize City. By 1720 African slaves had been brought into this settlement to work as loggers. About this time the English settlers became known as Baymen, a name that has stuck and carries romantic overtones. The settlement was known as the "River of the Bullys," because of the rough-and-tumble characters living in the swamps along both sides of Haulover Creek, where the settlement was located. The town took on a unique character. Unlike most of the Americas, where any vestiges of African culture were not tolerated in slaves, a degree of tribal identity was permitted in Belize, and the enslaved continued to practice beliefs from their homeland. Eventually, the River of Bullys became known as Belize Town. The name Belize is thought to be a mispronunciation of a Mayan word meaning "muddy water."

In 1763 Spain recognized the British colony in the Treaty of Paris, which allowed the British to harvest logwood in the region but did not address the issue of land ownership. The logwood concession was further extended in the Treaty of Versailles in 1783 and the Convention of London in 1786. Meanwhile, the colonial Spanish operating far from Europe continued to attack and harass the British settlement, freeing slaves and imprisoning English loggers from time to time. The Spanish tried to rid the area of the British once and for all on September 10, 1798, when they appeared on the waters off St. George's Caye (about five miles offshore from Belize Town) with an armada of fourteen ships crowded with soldiers prepared for a ground assault. A force of perhaps 200 English Baymen routed the Spanish with a few well-placed cannonballs and rifle fire. In the ranks of the Baymen were slaves shooting from fortifications on St. George's Caye and from a single English schooner. This incident, known as the Battle of St. George's Caye, ended Spanish claims to the region forever. The event assured that English parliamentary government, language, and culture would dominate the region, making the eventual nation of Belize decidedly English in character, not Latin, like every other country in Central and South America. St.

George's Caye Day is now celebrated every September 10 as a national holiday. It wasn't until 1862 that the settlement was officially declared British Honduras, a crown colony of Her Majesty the Queen of England. The boundaries were defined pretty much as they are today.

The British ruled the colony in a discriminatory manner toward people of color. However, they did encourage self-government for the colonists, setting a foundation for the parliamentary government adopted by Belize when it was finally granted independence in 1981.

During the period in which the English grip tightened on the region, other groups settled in what would become Belize. The European practice of bringing enslaved Africans to the Americas played heavily in the ethnic makeup of Belize. Slavery amounted to a death sentence for most slaves, whose life expectancy was about seven years throughout the region. Slavery was also as degrading in Belize as in other places, but in the logging camps there was more autonomy than in other places in the Americas. Slave owners often worked alongside their "property" in isolated camps. Englishmen often took slave women as their common-law wives, producing a "coloured class" that enjoyed many of the rights of free white men. Compared to North America and other places in the Caribbean, a greater percentage of the slave population was granted freedom here. The colony's "coloured class" was the beginning of the Creole culture that dominates Belize to this day, making up about 40 percent of the population. By the time slavery was abolished throughout the British Empire in 1838, half the population of the unofficial English colony was free black or "coloured" and about 10 percent was white. The percentage of white Belizeans in the general population then was practically the same as it is today.

Perhaps the most amazing group to emigrate into what would become Belize are the Garifunas, also known as Garinagus or Black Caribs. Today they make up about 10 percent of the population. Their beginnings in the region date back to 1635 when two Spanish ships filled with male African slaves broke up in a storm on the Caribbean island of St. Vincent, disgorging their human cargo on the rocky shore. The escaped Africans took Carib and Arawak Indians as their wives. Eventually a new culture, called Garifuna, developed. Its language was a mixture of African and Carib and Arawak Indian. To this day the Garifuna language has feminine words that are Arawak and Carib in origin and masculine words that are African in origin, demonstrating the gender-linked roots of the culture. Though most of today's Garifunas are nominally Christian, much of their traditional belief system is centered around *dugu*, which includes communicating by spirit mediums with long-dead relatives. Music, particularly the use of drums, is central to Garifuna ceremonies. The drum is still a symbol of the culture and is used for both religious observances and entertainment.

Defeat brought the Garifunas to Belize. They had governed most of St. Vincent independently of European powers for more than 125 years until 1796, when they were defeated by the British and removed to the Bay Islands off the coast of Honduras. From there they migrated to the coast of what would become British Honduras, where they set up isolated villages accessible only by boat. They made a living by fishing, farming, and trading. Today, the town of Dangriga is known as the heart of Garifuna culture. It is the place where famed Garifuna Alejo Beni settled with a large number of Garifunas on November 19, 1832. November 19 is now a national holiday known as Settlement Day. The Garifunas never enjoyed full citizenship rights and acceptance under the British. Today they are an integral part of Belizean society. Garifunas have improved their plight through ingenuity and the public education available to all Belizeans. Though many Garifunas are living in their traditional manner, many of today's Garifunas are teachers and civil servants and also are known as artists and musicians. Punta rock, a distinctive form of music that makes use of traditional Garifuna drums blended with reggae and amplified with modern electronic equipment, got its start among today's Garifuna musicians.

During the nineteenth and twentieth centuries, other important groups became woven into Belize's social fabric. From 1847 to 1863 the Caste Wars in the Yucatán sent thousands of Hispanic refugees into northern Belize. The war was a Mayan revolt against Mexican rule that resulted in ruthless slaughter on both sides. Today about 30 percent of Belize's population can trace its ancestry to the refugees from the Caste Wars. Most of these people live in the northern Corozal and Orange Walk districts, where sugar cane farming is practiced in earnest. Sugar cane production is Belize's number-one source of foreign revenue today. Sugar cane arrived in Belize with immigrants from the Caste Wars, and sugar cane farming was further entrenched by Confederates from the U.S. Civil War who arrived soon after with capital and expensive processing machinery.

A few hundred Chinese, Lebanese, and East Indians made their way to Belize to work in the sugar cane industry. Mayans fleeing repressive rule in Guatemala and Mexico settled in central and southern Belize during the 1940s and 1950s, supplementing the small numbers of Mayans still living in Belize. The Mayans now number about 12,000.

The Mennonites, a European religious sect dating back to Germany at the time of Martin Luther, emigrated to Belize in 1958 from Mexico and Canada, where they had established colonies to escape persecution for their beliefs. The Mennonites number about 5000 and have created many settlements in Belize where they have cleared hundreds of acres for dairy, beef, and chicken farming. They are now the backbone of Belize's poultry and dairy business. Belize has proven hospitable to the Mennonites, who have locked horns with governments over the centuries because of their unwillingness to serve in the military, vote, attend public schools, and bank outside their communities. The Belizean government has not stood in their way.

The latest influx of immigrants to Belize are uneducated Hispanic subsistence farmers and hunters. They have arrived at an alarming rate. Estimates run as high as 40,000 new immigrants since 1985, most of them undocumented. Most are fleeing tyrannical and murderous conditions that plague many of the people occupying the bottom of the pecking order in Belize's neighboring countries. Considering that Belize's entire population is only 200,000, this group represents a significant percentage of the entire population. There is a sense of compassion and foreboding about these immigrants, whose lack of education and understanding of democratic and ecological principles dear to most Belizeans is increasingly apparent. The sheer number of these latest immigrants concerns many Belizeans and was an issue in the 1993 general elections.

Present problems aside, voter turnout in the last national election was nearly 90 percent, proving that democracy is healthy and strong in Belize. Unlike some of the large Western democracies where cynicism and apathy have eroded voter participation, the average citizen in Belize believes his or her vote counts and exercises the franchise at every opportunity.

Belize's Magnificent Ecosystems

Throughout history, national treasures often have been thought of in terms of human-made structures such as the Taj Mahal, the Great Pyramids of Giza, and the Sydney Opera House. Part of the appeal of these treasures is found in their uniqueness and scarcity. Belize's national treasures include its share of mysterious Mayan ruins, but its truly outstanding treasures are its magnificent ecosystems.

Belize has a wealth of intact biodiverse ecosystems while those of neighboring countries have been squandered. This reality was not planned but was the outgrowth of benign neglect of Belize by its colonizers. During the period of colonialism, much of the world experienced blind exploitation of resources, rapid population growth, and highly invasive land use. Wild areas and indigenous cultures were destroyed so quickly that much of this went unrecorded. British Honduras (later to become Belize) became a colonial backwater of the British Empire, which always had bigger fish to fry. The colony was a place forever on the back burner. British futurist Aldous Huxley may have summed up the British view of British Honduras when he derisively observed: "If the world had any bookends British Honduras would certainly be one of them. It is not on the way from anywhere to anywhere else. It has no strategic value. It is all but uninhabited."

Huxley saw the colony as a useless dead end. In his time, the concept of a nation's wealth did not include swamps, mangroves, coral reefs, and wild cats. No gold, oil, or precious metals had been found in British Honduras. There was no gold rush, land stampede, or schemes to resettle shiploads of Great Britain's convicts as had been done in the colonies in North America and Australia. The population never skyrocketed. To this day Belize is one of the least densely populated countries in the world. Logging of selected trees (logwood and mahogany) occurred sporadically for centuries, but this pursuit was not on a grand scale and did not result in the kind of deforestation that has destroyed biodiversity throughout much of the tropics.

By comparison, nearby El Salvador, which is roughly the same size as Belize, is home to 7 million people. Scant rain forest remains, and such delightful jungle creatures as the common green iguana have disappeared. Ironically, due to benign neglect by the British, British Honduras remained a land swathed in rain forests. Belize's Barrier Reef, which extends offshore for the entire length of the country, created a natural barrier that to this day has blocked the creation of a deep-water port that would have dramatically contributed to the exploitation of the country's forests. Such were the conditions when Belize moved slowly toward nationhood in 1981.

By the time Belizeans mustered the will to create their own nation and the British were willing to grant them independence, new ideas about nature were at work in the world. The concept of "ecotourism" had come of age. In Belize, regardless of differing opinions as to what constitutes eco-tourism, the general concept fits like a glove. The Barrier Reef was the first natural feature to become known and visited by people from outside Belize. With the arrival of scuba divers and recreational fishermen, tourism became a big moneymaker, transforming places such as San Pedro Town on Ambergris Caye from sleepy fishing villages to bustling resorts. As time went on, the rich biodiversity of Belize's rain forests became known. Belize's founders realized that what had been seen in the past as useless swamp and hostile jungle was actually one of the last bastions for thousands of species of plants and animals that had been wiped out or were on their way to extinction in other places.

An ecosystem is a complex matrix of life made up of communities of plants and animals and their common environment. The health of a particular ecosystem affects all living things that dwell in it. Two ecosystems are especially well represented in Belize: coral reef systems and tropical rain forests. Belize has the most extensive coral reef system in the Western Hemisphere and vast, pristine stands of rain forest, home to more than 400 kinds of birds and a great diversity of wildlife, including the jaguar, the biggest cat in the Americas. Mangroves, wetlands, and pinelands and savanna comprise Belize's other ecosystems.

Barrier Reef, Atolls, and Cayes: When it comes to reef systems, nothing else in the Caribbean comes close to Belize's Barrier Reef and atolls in terms of size and variety of underwater topography. Only the Great Barrier Reef of Australia and several other South Pacific reefs are more massive. A scuba diver could spend several lifetimes exploring the reef systems in Belize and never make the same dive twice. The reef ecosystem of Belize is an unfathomably complex and bountiful environment that is intricately tied to nutrients produced by the rain forest. Belize's many watercourses deliver the nutrients to the sea.

The Barrier Reef is 180 miles long. It touches the shore on northern Ambergris Caye and drifts seaward as it heads south more than 10 miles from shore at the Sapodilla Cayes in the Gulf of Honduras. When the circumference of Belize's immense atolls (Lighthouse Reef, the Turneffe Islands, and Glover's Reef) are added up, the total comes to 140 miles. When added to the length of the reef itself there are more than 320 miles of coral reef in Belize to explore.

The formation of coral reefs is a tropical seas phenomenon that dates back at least 500 million years. Most Belizean reefs are mere babes, perhaps 6500 years in the making. The essential building block is the coral polyp, which occurs in colonies of countless millions and comes in many colors and configurations. Polyps are tiny, stationary animals that eat plankton. The veneer of the reef is composed of living coral and sponges sitting atop the skeletal remains of previous generations of coral that date back thousands of years.

Much of the Barrier Reef's underwater topography is called spur and groove. This is typified by pronounced coral ridges divided by deep trenches with flat, sandy bottoms, often with dramatic overhangs and tunnels embellishing the spur walls. This varied underwater environment allows such diverse reef residents as eels, nurse sharks, stingrays, groupers, parrotfish, porkfish, trunkfish, and damselfish to live in close proximity to one another. The diversity and volume of fish can be astounding. It is not uncommon to sight 50 different species in numbers too vast to count on a single dive. More than 230 species of fish live on the reefs.

Belize's Barrier Reef features dozens of kinds of coral, ranging from bulbous brain corals to spectacular forests of elkhorn and staghorn corals. Living with the corals are different kinds of tube and barrel sponges, undulating green and purple sea fans, crustaceans including lobsters, spectacular orange-red gorgonian soft coral, and, of course, myriad fish.

Out past the Barrier Reef lie the atolls. They are sort of an ultimate destination for divers: farther from shore, more isolated, and in many places virginal. Belize's atolls are unique. The common perception that an atoll gets its start from a shallow platform created by an underwater volcano doesn't hold here. The Belizean atolls grew from gargantuan fault blocks that tilted toward the surface from great depths. The drop-offs from the atolls are awesome. From coral formations lying a few feet beneath the surface a reef can be sitting on a wall that plummets straight down for 10,000 feet. This is why wall dives on the atolls are visually so exciting. Divers descending to eighty or ninety feet stand a good chance of seeing the entire continuum of life found in the tropical ocean — everything from giant tube sponges and staghorn coral to tiny, colorful damselfish, groupers, schooling yellow grunts, and spotted eagle rays gliding a few yards beneath the surface in an unforgettably graceful underwater flying demonstration, plus the powerfully streamlined open-water predators such as bluefin tuna, large barracudas, and sharks.

Dive sites in Belize offer an unending variety that allows divers to contemplate and appreciate fish, corals, sponges, crustaceans, and the Byzantine geology that combines forces to create an ever-changing panorama of formations and colorful creatures. Snorkelers and scuba divers can access the shallow, rich-in-fish "cut" through the Barrier Reef that is now the mainstay of Hol Chan Marine Preserve, offshore from Ambergris Caye. Along the coast and on the atolls are many cuts, other types of shallow sites, plus deep wall dives, immense twisted cathedral-like formations, deep cuts, patch reefs, spur and groove formations, and tunnels leading to underwater caverns. The best known of the caves is the Blue Hole, a deep but relatively straightforward place to visit for its car-size stalactites 150 feet below the surface. Other caves require greater expertise, careful judgment, a guide, and perhaps a touch of lunacy to visit.

Dotting the reefs and atolls are stunning little jewels of bright green mangrove islands or sandy, palm-studded cayes. Among the most spectacular are Half Moon Caye Natural Monument, Laughing Bird Caye National Park, Tobacco Caye, and the Sapodilla Cayes. There are more than 200 cayes in all, most of them uninhabited by humans, but important nesting sites for sea turtles and magnificent open-ocean birds, such as the blue-footed booby.

Conservation of the reef system is a perplexing priority facing the Belizean government. No other ecosystem in Belize is under such pressure of rapid development backed by "big bucks" and increasing use as is the northern Barrier Reef. Significant moves by the government to protect the reef ecosystem began in 1987 when the Hol Chan Marine Preserve was set aside. The reserve includes not only reef but the supporting sea grass and mangrove communities within its boundaries. Other recent government decisions include outlawing spear fishing, setting aside Laughing Bird Caye as a national park, attempting to control lobster and conch fisheries by setting seasons, protecting sea turtle rookeries, and meeting with managers of the Great Barrier Reef in Australia to learn about comprehensive reef management. These moves are seen as well intended but piecemeal. The Belize Audubon Society is advocating an overall management plan for the entire coast and reef that designates protected areas, fisheries, development areas, and special-use areas with a balance in mind that ensures that Belize's reef ecosystem will remain healthy.

Mangroves: Mangroves are an important and little understood ecosystem in Belize. Mangroves are uniquely adapted plants that can filter salt water and stabilize emerging islands, sandbars, and riverbanks with their unique root systems. They function as filters to the offshore reef and buffers against wave action and hurricanes. Mangroves are vast nurseries to young fish and nesting areas for birds. Some of the most exciting predatory fish behavior I've witnessed has been while snorkeling among mangrove islands near Placencia. Belize has red, white, and black mangroves. Some excellent mature stands of red mangroves can be found near Belize City and on Ambergris Caye. Black mangroves are the least common throughout the country. Large stands of white mangroves line the coast between Punta Gorda and the Temash River.

Unfortunately, development activities around Belize City reflect little understanding of or respect for the role mangroves play in the natural scheme of things, which includes protecting coastal building sites from being swept into the sea during hurricanes. Wildlife Conservation International marine biologist and primary creator of Hol Chan Marine Preserve Janet Gibson has expressed concern about the destruction of mangroves in coastal areas where increases in tourism have led to larger and larger development schemes.

Wetlands: Moving and standing fresh water is a big part of the natural world in Belize. The Belize River, New River, Temash River, Moho River, Stann Creek, Sarstoon River, and Río Hondo are among Belize's largest river systems. These rivers are fed by smaller rivers, such as the Macal and Mopan, and myriad watercourses with origins deep in the Maya Mountains and elsewhere. As the water heads toward the coast, much of it collects in flat areas that may cover as much as 30 percent of Belize's land mass during the wet season. These wetland ecosystems are biologically rich areas, creating homes for hundreds of wetland bird species that mass by the thousands during certain seasons. Some of these birds are endangered, such as the jabiru, with its nine-foot wingspan, and the peregrine falcon, which finds easy pickings among lily-walking northern jacanas, ducks, and other birds. The wetlands also are home to the hikatee (a large freshwater turtle), Morlet's crocodile, and manatee, each of them an endangered species but living here in substantial numbers. Wetlands with particularly special appeal are Crooked Tree Wildlife Sanctuary (primarily birds), the Southern Lagoon (manatees and birds), New River, and Shipstern Nature Reserve.

Pinelands and Savanna: This ecosystem can occur at different elevations. Its primary feature is a spindly pine tree known generically as Caribbean pine, which really covers two closely related species. The pines occur in combination with small, palmlike trees called palmettos. Craboo and calabash trees, grasses, and occasional standing water typify this environment. Soils poor in nutrients and drainage are the underlying feature.

Pinelands are dominant in the northern Maya Mountains in a region known as Mountain Pine Ridge. In this setting, which is about 3300 feet in elevation, the ground cover includes ferns and orchids. With rushing creeks transecting it, this habitat has the incredulous feel of being both tropical and subalpine. In lower elevations, such as along much of the Southern Highway, New Road, and Western Highway in the area near the Belize Zoo, the pinelands and savanna areas have a more classic look. The sparse pines and small palms dot vast grasslands, creating a Serengeti-like appearance, often with the bright green backdrop of the Maya Mountains. In the pine environment wildlife is harder to find and somewhat limited compared to other habitats in Belize. Because the area is so exposed, many creatures are active only under the cloak of darkness. Generally, the ancient Mayans moved across the pine and savanna areas but did not live in them permanently. They found the rain forest and coast more bountiful and able to sustain their densely populated cities.

Tropical Rain Forest: About 60 percent of Belize is covered in different kinds of tropical rain forest, most of which is uninhabited by humans. Significantly, too, much of the 33 percent of Belize that has been designated as sanctuaries, national parks, and conservation areas is characterized by a rain forest ecosystem. Three ingredients identify a tropical rain forest: plenty of rain, a great variety of trees, and warm temperatures. Belize's rain forests receive between 60 and 170 inches of rain a year. The temperature never drops below 50° F, but is usually around 80° F. The combination of water and warmth nurtures a nonstop, slow-motion explosion of more than 4000 species of plants. Trees dominate tropical rain forest, with more than 700 species living in Belize. Some of the larger trees, such as the Mayans' sacred ceiba (or silk cotton) tree and the mahogany tree, reach heights of 150 feet.

Even though the forests of Belize have been mined for centuries, the logging has generally been low impact and species specific. Mahogany and logwood trees kept the early British and their African slaves busy for two centuries. Other trees, such as the cohune palm, provided roofing material and cooking oil to the ancient Mayans as well as today's Mayan and mestizo milpa farmers. The trees are the foundation and umbrella for the rain forest, in which more than 3000 nontree species of plants flourish, many of them bromeliads and orchids that require narrowly defined micro-environments in order to survive. Air plants grow in the massive trunks and limbs of the buttressed older trees. A large old tree may support twenty-five air plants in its branches. Belize has more than 250 kinds of orchids, many species of colorful heliconias, and plants North Americans think of as indoor plants, such as poinsettias and philodendrons.

Within a rain forest are plants that produce flowers and fruit on a rotating basis. Insects, birds, and mammals change their diets accordingly. Lack of food is rarely a problem. It's no wonder there are more than fifty kinds of bats (most of them fruit and nectar eaters), hundreds of species of birds, and thousands of kinds of insects living in Belizean rain forests. The rain forest is a fortress for Belize's five kinds of predatory cat, as well as the tapir, Central American river otter, two species of monkey, kinkajou, tayra, and a plethora of small mammals. To the human visitor the flowering trees offer a visual display not usually associated with the common stereotype of a dank rain forest. Trees such as the buttercup tree, which produces a profusion of yellow flowers, or the bookut, with rich pink blossoms, are unforgettable.

Though all rain forests have trees and prodigious amounts of rain

Scarlet macaw, the largest
parrot in Central America.
Photo by Eric Hoffman.

as their common denominator, there are many kinds of rain forests
in Belize. The tropical deciduous forest is fairly prevalent. This kind
of forest is distinguished from other types by the predominance of
trees that shed their leaves during the dry season to conserve water.
Cohune palm forest is another type that is clearly distinguishable
within the larger rain forest. Regardless of the individual types of
forest, together they are a powerful force in nature. Rain forests create their own climate. About 75 percent of the rain that falls in a
rain forest evaporates through the leaves of its trees, which helps
create clouds for more rainfall.

As a focus for conservation efforts, "save the rain forest" is not
a hollow slogan. It is incredibly important. Wildlife Conservation
International ornithologists Bruce and Carolyn Miller, who have
been working in Belize for years attempting to inventory and understand the complex systems, point out that rain forests worldwide
take up only 7 percent of the land but contain almost half the species of animals and plants in the world. Current predictions put the
amount of Central American rain forest surviving by the year 2000
at about 10 percent of what was there when the Mayan civilization
flourished. It's not alarmist to say that rain forests worldwide are under attack. With the disappearance of forests in neighboring coun-

tries, the efforts to preserve as much of Belize's rain forest as possible will become more important in the years to come.

Among the best places in Belize to experience the rain forest are the Cockscomb Basin Wildlife Sanctuary, Chan Chich Lodge, the Rio Bravo Project, and the remote Chiquibul National Park, location of the magnificent Mayan ruins known as Caracol.

Adventuring Activities and Services

Experiencing the best Belize has to offer is accomplished through a wide range of activities and services. This section presents essential information and identifies businesses offering the following services: scuba diving, snorkeling, indigenous boat hires, yachting, sea kayaking, canoeing, rafting, windsurfing, fishing, exploring Mayan ruins, and visiting rain forest parks and sanctuaries.

Scuba Diving: There is no shortage of dive operators in the commonly visited areas of Ambergris Caye (San Pedro), Caye Caulker, St. George's Caye, and Belize City. You can basically show up, present your PADI or NAUI card, rent the equipment, and join a group for a half-day or full-day dive trip to any of an endless number of excellent sites. Most island hotels either organize or direct snorkeling outings for their guests, who can rent mask, snorkel, and fins for a nominal fee at most major hotels or dive shops. The water runs between 80° F and 84° F. Most divers forgo a wetsuit, though if you prefer, you might use a Lycra or thin three-quarter wetsuit. Occasionally, snorkelers can be accommodated on an outing with scuba divers—for example, at Hol Chan Marine Preserve, which has relatively shallow water and is a short boat ride from shore. Visibility will range between 25 feet and 150 feet depending on location and conditions.

Farther offshore are three atolls: the Turneffe Islands, Lighthouse Reef (with its well-known Blue Hole and the Half Moon Caye Natural Monument), and Glover's Reef. Operators from Ambergris Caye,

Caye Caulker, St. George's Caye, Caye Chapel, Belize City, and other points in the region can reach most northern reef and atoll destinations in half- or full-day trips. However, some of the dive sites on Glover's Reef and northern Lighthouse Reef and points south, starting with Tobacco Caye (and including South Water Caye, Placencia, Laughing Bird Caye, and Port Honduras) and ending at Sapodilla Cayes, are accessed from Dangriga and Punta Gorda, or by buying a dive package that includes transportation from Belize City and a stay at an island lodge for three to seven days.

For this book, great effort was made to locate and experience the best dive sites along the entire Barrier Reef and the three atolls. The text includes descriptions of dive sites and how to get to them, plus the recommendations of leading dive masters who operate from Ambergris Caye, Caye Caulker, South Water Caye, Northern Caye, the atolls, Placencia, and Punta Gorda. Details of day-boat dive operations serving these and other areas are also given.

Considerations for divers and locating a dive master: There are well over thirty dive operations in Belize. Overall, service is good to excellent. Dive masters are supposed to be certified by either the NAUI or PADI. However, there is continual turnover in personnel in some operations while in others the same dive masters have been in place for years, which is pretty much the standard worldwide. The turnover rate makes recommending a particular business difficult because often the quality of the service is contingent upon the expertise and personality of the dive master. Many dive sites are in very remote areas, which means hours from help if something should go wrong. The one recompression chamber in Belize is on Ambergris Caye.

Some dive operations are part of the many recreational services offered by island or mainland hotels. Typically, without knowing the particulars of the dive shop or dive masters, you are whisked from your hotel room to a dive site and back in a matter of hours. Other set-ups consist of diving lodges on remote cayes. Having completed more than forty dives myself in Belize, I found significant differences in the quality of the services and dive sites, and I have made efforts to identify specific dive operators who are well known for their quality of service, which includes equipment, adherence to international safety standards, and selection of dive sites.

The information shared in this text is based on my experiences and, because of the nature of scuba diving, does not necessarily mean your experiences will be the same. You must make your own judgments in assessing if a particular dive operation meets with your idea of professionalism, and you alone are responsible for the risks you take while scuba diving. Dive operations I most enjoyed were Changa Paz, Amigos del Mar, San Pedro, Ambergris Caye, Belize, C.A. (phone 026-2706; fax 026-2648); Larry Parker, Reef Divers, P.O. Box 13, San Pedro, Ambergris Caye, Belize, C.A. (phone 026-2371); Cottage Colony, St. George's Caye, P.O. Box 428, Belize City, Belize, C.A. (phone 02-77051; fax 02-73253); Blue Marlin Lodge, South Water Caye, P.O. Box 21, Dangriga, Belize, C.A. (phone 05-22243; fax 05-22296) (see also the "Dangriga" section of the Stann Creek District chapter for Pelican Beach Resort, which has accommodations on South Water Caye with ties to Blue Marlin's dive operation); Lighthouse Reef Resort, Northern (Two) Caye, P.O. Box 26, Belize City, Belize, C.A. (phone 02-31205), or P.O. Box 1435, Dundee, FL 33838 (phone 1-800-423-3114 in the United States and Canada); Blackbird Caye Resort (Turneffe Islands), 81 West Canal Street, Belize City, Belize, C.A. (phone 027-7670; fax 02-73092).

If you find that a dive operation listed in the text is no longer in business, has sky-high rates, or responds unsatisfactorily, you can obtain the most up-to-date list of dive operations by contacting the Belize Tourist Board, 415 Seventh Avenue, New York, NY 10001 (phone 1-800-624-0686), or P.O. Box 325, Belize City, Belize, C.A. (phone 02-77213/73255).

Live-aboard dive boat services: There are a half-dozen live-aboard dive boats operating in Belize. For dive package details offered by these operators, shop around by contacting the boat and tour companies offering trips to Belize and your local dive clubs. Boats operating in Belizean waters include *Belize Aggressor,* P.O. Drawer K, Morgan City, LA 70381 (phone 1-800-348-2628 and 504-385-2416); *Manta IV,* Indigo Belize, P.O. Box 450987, Sunrise, FL 33345 (phone 1-800-468-0123 and 305-473-1956); *Reef Roamer II,* Triton Tours, 1111 Veterans Boulevard, Suite 5, Kenner, LA 70062 (phone 1-800-426-0226 and 504-522-3382); *Wave Dancer,* Peter Hughes Diving, 1390 South Dixie Highway, Suite 2213, Coral Gables, FL 33146 (phone 1-800-932-6237 and 305-669-9391); *Christy Ann* and *Blue Yonder,* Belize Scuba Cruise, P.O. Box 459, Belize City, Belize, C.A. (phone 02-52002).

In general, these packages are expensive compared to land-based dive operations, for which you pay U.S. $25 to U.S. $125 per outing, stay in budget accommodations, and economize on meals by choosing inexpensive restaurants. However, to a diver with the single intent of accessing the best scuba sites, rather than getting to know Belizeans and visiting the national parks on the mainland, the live-aboard experience may be most appealing.

Snorkeling: Snorkeling is excellent at selected sites in Belize, though most underwater activities are geared to scuba divers. You can rent fins, mask, and snorkel in any coastal or island area where diving and snorkeling are enjoyed. With the exception of a few cayes that are directly on top of the Barrier Reef or an atoll, many of the good snorkeling sites require a short to moderate-length boat ride to reach them. Snorkeling sites on Ambergris Caye, Caye Caulker, St. George's Caye, Caye Chapel, Northern (Two) Caye, Half Moon Caye, South Water Caye, the Sapodilla Cayes, and other areas are described in the text. Hol Chan Marine Preserve on Ambergris Caye is probably the most popular snorkeling site in Belize.

Yachting, Power Boating, Windsurfing, Canoeing, and Kayaking: Motor yachts and sailcraft are available for rental in Belize. However, considering the bare-boating (renting a boat without a skipper or crew) and sail charter potential in Belize, this is a much underdeveloped recreational activity. The largest facility for recreational, conventional fiberglass sloops is on Moho Caye. In general, yacht rentals are hard to find, but they do exist. Chartering locally made fishing sloops skippered by their sometimes salty Creole owners is an interesting possibility for the truly adventuresome (see "Caye Caulker" in the Belize District chapter for details).

There are a few fully outfitted motor vessel rentals available. Contact *Frog*, P.O. Box 332, Belize City, Belize, C.A. (phone 02-33187; fax 02-31975); *Lady Valerie* (forty-one feet), 16 New Home Area, Haulover Road, Belize City, Belize, C.A. (phone 02-31690); *M/V Piper* (thirty-eight feet), 128 Esperanza Village, Cayo District, Belize, C.A. (phone 092-2792).

For sailboat rentals, contact Associated Mystic Yacht Charters, 9 Navyaug Road, Mystic, CT 06355 (phone 1-800-873-2692); Belize Marine Enterprises, Moho Caye, P.O. Box 997, Belize City, Belize, C.A. (phone 02-45798/31063); Caye Caulker Sailboats, c/o Reef Hotel, Caye Caulker, Belize, C.A. (phone 022-2196); Cottage Colony, St. George's Caye, c/o Bellevue Hotel, Belize City, Belize, C.A. (phone 02-77051/77052; fax 02-73253); Frenchie's Diving Service, Caye Caulker,

Belize, C.A. (phone 022-2234); Sun Breeze Hotel, Ambergris Caye, Belize, C.A. (phone 026-2347/2391). Most of the large hotels on Ambergris Caye have windsurfers, Sunfish, and possibly small catamarans to rent to their guests. Try Ramon's Village, Sun Breeze, and Journey's End Caribbean Club. For more comprehensive information on the types of light sailing craft available on Ambergris Caye, contact Amigo Travel, San Pedro, Ambergris Caye, Belize, C.A. (phone 026-2180) or the San Pedro Tourist Center (phone 026-2434). See "Caye Caulker" in the Belize District chapter for more information on renting locally owned and chartered fishing sloops. Farther south, Placencia's beautiful and immense Inner Lagoon is suitable for sailing as well as for sea kayaking.

Sea kayaking is centered around Placencia because of its immense Inner Lagoon, which has calm, aqua blue waters with small cayes that serve as rest and camping stops. Several businesses offer guided sea kayak adventures. Turtle Inn (phone 06-22069) and Rum Point Inn (phone 06-22017) are among the best contacts for this activity in Placencia.

Canoeing is an activity that takes place mostly in Belize's interior. The mountain lodges in the Cayo District offer canoeing on the Mopan and Macal rivers. You can also rent your own canoe in San Ignacio, the district's main town. Contact Float Belize, P.O. Box 48, San Ignacio, Cayo District, Belize, C.A. (phone 092-2188). (For more details on canoeing and rafting see the Cayo District chapter.) There are also canoe hires in Burrell Boom that allow you to paddle along the Belize River through the Bermudian Landing Community Baboon Sanctuary from the Belize River. The Belize Audubon Society headquarters at the sanctuary can also arrange for a canoe.

If you're up for a derring-do kind of canoeing, there are trips through riverine caves in the Gales Point area in large, traditional dugouts powered by outboard motors. These trips are true adventures and suitable only for people who want an authentic challenge.

Lastly, there is inner-tubing, a form of water travel that makes good sense on river systems in the tropics, where keeping cool can become a pastime in itself. There are cave floats in the Belize District and floats of many hours' duration in the wilds of the Cockscomb Basin Wildlife Sanctuary in the Stann Creek District.

Fishing: Belize is a top destination for recreational fishermen from around the world. The variety of fish and techniques employed to catch them means a range of activities for the novice and hard-core fishing enthusiast. Fly-fishing in shallow water for tarpon and bonefish is a favorite. Deep-sea fishing for marlin and tuna is also popular. Generally, oceanic species such as blue marlin, yellowfin and blackfin tuna, jackfish, mackerel, bonito, and wahoo are caught year-round. Bonefish are caught in shallows from November through March and tarpon from June through August in mangrove areas and from February through August in rivers. Reef fishing is good year-round for barracuda, jackfish, mackerel, grouper, and snapper. You are expected to eat what you catch, but in the case of bonefish and tarpon, release is the norm in most instances. Spear fishing is not permitted in Belizean waters.

Key contacts: *Ambergris Caye*—Bill Leslie (phone 026-2128), Roberto Bradley (phone 026-2116), Coral Beach Club (phone 026-2001); *Belize City*—Blackline Marina (phone 02-44155; fax 02-31975); *St. George's Caye*—Bellevue Hotel (phone 02-77051; fax 02-73253); *Caye Caulker*—Frenchie's Diving Service (phone 022-2234), Melvin Badillo, Jr. (phone 022-2111), Pegasus Boat Service (phone 022-2122), Sylvano Canto (phone 022-2215); *Placencia*—Kingfisher Sport (phone 06-23125), Pow Cabral Fly Fishing (phone 06-23132), Rum Point Inn (Brian Young) (phone 06-22017); *Dangriga*—Nolan Jackson, Tobacco Caye, P.O. Box 21, Dangriga (contact through Rio Mar Inn, phone 05-22201), Blue Marlin Lodge (South Water Caye) (phone 05-22243), Pelican Beach Resort (phone 05-22044; fax 05-22570).

Visiting Mayan Ruins: Belize was a stronghold of the ancient Mayan civilization, which endured for about 3000 years from roughly 1500 B.C. to A.D. 1200. In fact, northern Belize, particularly Lamanai, was one of the few places the Mayans still lived in concentrated numbers in a society based on traditional religion when the Spanish arrived. Judging by the size and extent of the ruins found throughout the country, the ancient Mayan population in Belize is thought to have exceeded 400,000. Today a few thousand Mayans live in traditional villages mostly in the south.

Some of the most interesting temple complexes require extra planning to visit and are on dirt roads that can become impassable during the wet season. The dry season, which runs most often from August through October, is the best time to visit the remote ruins. The most significant ruins are described in this book and include Tikal in Guatemala, which is commonly visited in one- or two-day trips by air or road from Belize. All of the sites, with the exception of Santa Rita and Cuello, are located in natural settings that integrate wildlife viewing with visits to the ruins. In most cases Mayan caretakers, who are well versed about their particular sites, are on duty from 8:00 A.M. to 5:00 P.M. daily, except holidays. The caretakers are sometimes shy, but initiating a conversation about the ruins is usually rewarding.

I visited the sites described in the text and found all of them, with the exception of Santa Rita, well worth my efforts. If you're short on time, visit Altun Ha, which is the ruin nearest to Belize City. Reached by boat and located in the Orange Walk District, Lamanai possesses the best ambience and is the most thought-provoking ruin relatively near Belize City. Caracol, which once ruled Tikal, is an immense complex in the Cayo District that offers a glimpse of an ongoing major excavation in a deep rain forest. Xunantunich, which has a spectacular temple-top vista, is right off the Western Highway in the Cayo District near Benque Viejo del Carmen. Nim Li Punit, Lubaantun, and Uxbenka are in the Toledo District, which requires an extra effort to reach. But these are beautiful ruins, each different from the other, in lush green settings shared by today's Mayans, who live in small, thatched-roof villages similar to those of their ancestors. The solitude, variety, wildlife, and settings of these ruins leave a strong impression. Finally, no assessment of Mayan civilization is complete without a trip to Tikal. It will astound you.

Mundo Maya (Mayan World) and Ruta Maya (Mayan Route) are two terms you may hear bantered about during your visit to Belize. They refer to the same program. Mundo Maya is a program for tourists visiting ruins under joint development by Belize, Mexico, Guatemala, El Salvador, and Honduras. These countries encompass what was once the Mayan world. The program is supposed to coordinate preservation efforts, launch activities to highlight the Mayan world to outsiders, and work to preserve today's Mayan culture and its environment. The idea is to give visitors an overview of the ancient Mayan world that encourages crossing borders to learn more about the complete history of the Mayans. This is supposed to include informational literature describing Mayan civilization in its entirety, without regard to national borders. To encourage travel from one country to the next, the five sponsoring countries hope to relax travel requirements. The five nations have also agreed in principle to expand access to Mayan lands in ways that do not upset

the lives of today's Mayans or the sensitive environments they occupy. Guatemala and Mexico took major steps in this program by
declaring lands occupied by Mayan villagers as biosphere reserves.
The areas involved total nearly 5 million acres.

The Mundo Maya program faces many challenges. Among them
is overcoming the destruction of the rain forest by Mayans practicing traditional slash-and-burn agriculture, which will require building trust in government intentions among Guatemalan Mayans, who
have been the victims of brutal human rights abuses. Other challenges include getting all the countries involved to agree on parity
in entry requirements for visitors. So far, concrete benefits to the
traveler are still a ways off, but inquiring about the status of Mundo
Maya may produce benefits later. For information about Mundo
Maya or archaeological sites anywhere in Belize, contact the Department of Archaeology in Belmopan, the Belize Tourist Board in New
York, or the private travel businesses listed under "Sources of Tourist
Information."

Getting to Belize

International Air Carriers from North America: There are four international carriers serving Belize from North America: TACA,
SAHSA, American, and Continental. Providing fares are equal (which
often is not the case), each airline has a different appeal depending
on where you live in North America or what time of the day you
want to travel.

The round-trip fare between Belize and North America fluctu-
ates as much as U.S. $200 during the course of a year depending
on the season, day of the week, and state of competition among
airlines. It definitely pays to shop. For example, in a check of coach
class fares on June 12, 1993, TACA charged U.S. $697 plus $17 tax
for a round-trip ticket between San Francisco and Belize, while
American and Continental both quoted a price of U.S. $821 plus
$28 tax.

TACA, a Salvadorian airline and one of oldest airlines in the
Americas, operates a fleet of 737s and wide-body 767s with more

direct gateway connections in the United States and Canada than any other international carrier serving Belize. You can book a flight from Houston, Los Angeles, Miami, New Orleans, New York, San Francisco, and Washington, D.C. TACA coordinates flight arrangements with airlines serving Canada.

A TACA flight has a definite Latin American flavor. Usually many of the passengers are Salvadorian and Guatemalan citizens because many TACA flights include stops in the capitals of San Salvador and Guatemala City on the way to Belize. Even though the predominant language on board may be Spanish, flight attendants are conversant in English. Departures from Los Angeles sometimes include late additions to a flight in the form of a half-dozen luckless deportees who are marched onto the plane handcuffed together by a U.S. law enforcement officer. Not to fear—as disconcerting as this may appear, these passengers aren't dangerous criminals, but merely undocumented workers being returned to their country of origin. Food, wine, and other drinks are free and plentiful on TACA flights. In the United States phone 1-800-535-8780. In Canada phone (Quebec) 1-800-263-4063; (Ontario) 1-800-263-4039; (other provinces) 1-800-387-6209. In Belize phone 02-77185.

Continental flies to Belize direct from Houston and continues the flight to Honduras before returning to the United States. Continental usually assigns 727s to the route. The flight between Houston and Belize takes just two hours and twenty-three minutes. However, layovers between connecting flights from some West Coast cities can be up to five hours. Frequent-flier miles accrued by the ticket buyer can be used on this route. In the United States and Canada, phone 1-800-525-0280; in Belize, 02-78309.

Presently, American routes all its flights to and from Belize through Miami. This is convenient for people living on the East Coast but less convenient for West Coast residents. American flies nonstop to Belize City daily and returns daily. The flight takes two hours and twelve minutes. For the past two years flights have departed in late-morning hours, which should allow you a good night's sleep the night before if your connecting flight originated on the East Coast. American assigns 1543 miles for the trip as part of its frequent-flier Advantage Program. If you want to trade frequent-flier mileage you've accrued in this program to visit Belize, you need 30,000 miles to cover a round-trip ticket for one person flying coach, 45,000 miles for business class, or 60,000 for first class. Frequent-flier tickets must be requested twenty-one days before departure and are not granted during black-out periods around major holidays. American occasionally offers specials designed to undercut the competition. In the United States phone 1-800-624-6262; in Canada, 1-800-433-7300; in Belize, 02-32522.

Honduran SAHSA Airline departs Houston, Miami, and New Orleans for Belize. In North America phone 1-800-327-1225; in Belize, 02-77080.

Other International Air Carriers: You also can enter Belize by commercial airplane via Flores (near Tikal) in Guatemala and Mexico. Carriers from Guatemala are Aerovias, 305-885-1775 (United States and Canada) and 02-75445 (Belize); Tropic Air, 1-800-422-3435 (United States and Canada) and 02-45671 (Belize); and Aviateca, 1-800-327-9832 (United States and Canada). Aviateca also offers service to Belize from Cancun, Mexico.

By Bus: You can enter Belize on its northern border by bus from Chetumal or by ferry and bus from Cancun, Mexico. The only other vehicular route into Belize is on the western border, which is shared with Guatemala. Guatemalan bus services drop passengers at the border town of Melchor de Mencos, and Novelo's Bus Service in Benque Viejo del Carmen on the Belizean side leaves hourly for Belize City. For connections from Cancun, phone the Belize Transfer Service (415-641-0145 in Mexico). (See also "Crossing the Mexican Border" in the Corozal District chapter and "Benque Viejo del Carmen" in the Cayo District chapter.)

By Car: Belize is often reached from North America via Mexico. From Texas the drive takes from three to six days. Add two or three days if you're starting in California. The border at Chetumal, Mexico, is the usual entry point. It is advisable to purchase maps before leaving home since quality maps are sometimes difficult to find while traveling. Make sure your vehicle is in excellent mechanical condition since car parts may not be readily available for many models. To enter Belize driving a vehicle you must have a current driver's license and registration papers proving that you own the vehicle. To avoid a stiff customs duty you must acquire a temporary entry permit at the border that is to be surrendered when you depart Belize. You must also buy insurance, which costs about U.S. $12 per day. If you stay longer than three months you must obtain a Belize driver's license, which requires a medical exam and a fee of U.S. $20.

By Private Boat and Ferry: No permits are required to enter Belizean waters in a private boat, but upon making landfall you are required to report to the nearest immigration office or the local police. You must show a ship's log with an entry of your last port of call, possess proof of ownership of the vessel, and produce four copies of a list of crew and passengers. A ferry runs between Punta Gorda in southernmost Belize and Puerto Barrios, Guatemala. This service is available a couple of times a week and is the most common way of entering Belize from the south (see "Punta Gorda" in the Toledo District chapter).

By Private Aircraft: This has become an increasingly popular way for wealthy North Americans to visit Belize. All private planes must enter Belize through Phillip Goldson International Airport near Belize City. No advance notice is required unless you are flying in from Colombia. Private pilots are required to file flight plans and receive a briefing on local weather when flying within Belize or leaving the country. Landing fees vary depending on the weight of the aircraft, but compared to the fees at most international airports they are minimal.

Getting Around Belize

Commercial Air Service: A wide range of small aircraft are used by Belize's internal commercial airlines. Most of the local carriers coordinate their flight schedules with the international carriers using Phillip Goldson International Airport. If you're scheduled for a connecting flight, chances are you'll find yourself climbing aboard anything from a single-engine Cessna to a twin-engine Otter within minutes after clearing customs. In general, domestic flights are relatively inexpensive. Prices range from U.S. $25 to U.S. $200 depending on the destination. Contacts: Island Air, phone 02-31140 (Belize City) or 026-2180 (San Pedro)—service to Belize City, Ambergris Caye,

Caye Caulker, Caye Chapel; Maya Airways, phone 1-800-552-3419 (United States and Canada), 02-7215 (Belize City), or 026-2611 (San Pedro)—service to the cayes, Belize City, Dangriga, Big Creek (Placencia), and Punta Gorda; Sky Bird, phone 02-32596 or 02-52045, ext. 515 (Belize City)—service to Belize City and Caye Caulker; Tropic Air, phone 1-800-422-3435 (United States and Canada), 02-45671 (Belize City), or 026-2012 (San Pedro)—service to Ambergris Caye, Caye Caulker, Northern Caye, Caye Chapel, Belize City, and Flores (Tikal) in Guatemala.

Charter Air Service: Javier's Flying Service, Municipal Airport, Belize City, phone 02-45332, fax 02-32731; Caribee Air Service, Municipal Airport, Belize City, phone 02-44253.

Bus Service: Most major towns in Belize are connected to the outside world by bus service. By and large, buses in Belize are former U.S. school buses. Bus service between Belize City and the major towns to the north and west runs hourly. Service to the south is daily but at less frequent intervals. Fares are inexpensive and affordable to the average Belizean. Besides the four best-known carriers listed below, there are a number of small bus operations that run between less frequently visited destinations. These small companies are listed in the text in the regions they serve. For complete schedule and fare information for the large carriers, contact Batty Brothers Bus Service, 15 Mosul Street, Belize City (phone 02-72025); Novelo's Bus Service, 54 East Collet Canal, Belize City (phone 02-77372); Venus Bus Lines, Magazine Road, Belize City (phone 02-73354), Z-Line Bus Service, Magazine Road, Belize City (phone 02-73937, or 06-22211 in Placencia).

Taxi Service: In Belize taxis are distinguishable from private vehicles solely by their green license plates. Cabs don't have meters but charge standard fares on common routes, such as between Belize City and Phillip Goldson International airport. My experience with taxis in Belize was without a single questionable incident. Fares are relatively expensive; for example, expect to pay U.S. $20 to U.S. $25 one way between Belize City and the international airport, a distance of about ten miles. Always inquire about the fare before you're under way. In Belize City, cabs are commonly found at the international airport, municipal airport, major hotels, Central Park on Regent

Street, and Cinderella Plaza. Hoteliers can help procure a cab and advise you about rates. For lengthy cab rides contact Gilbert Andrews at the Chateau Caribbean (phone 02-30800). He has very reasonable prices.

Boat Service: Most of the regularly scheduled boat services running between the mainland and the cayes connect Belize City to Ambergris Caye and Caye Caulker. The run between Belize City and Ambergris Caye (San Pedro) usually takes one hour and fifteen minutes. It usually takes forty-five minutes between Caye Caulker and Belize City. (See "Belize City," "Ambergris Caye," and "Caye Caulker" in the Belize District chapter for details on fares, pickup points, and specific boats.)

Nonscheduled boat and water taxi services on a per-hire basis also operate from Ambergris Caye, Caye Caulker, Dangriga, Punta Gorda, Corozal Town, Orange Walk Town, Placencia, Big Creek, and other locations. (See individual chapters for details.)

Car Rentals: Renting a car in Belize can be an expensive proposition. Daily rental prices often run $90 if you aren't careful. There are about a dozen car rental companies in and around Belize City and very few places to rent a vehicle anywhere else in Belize. Most of the car rental businesses do a good job, but be careful when dealing with rental companies with vehicles well past their prime. A price of about U.S. $30 a day may seem appealing, but the risks may not be worth it. Breaking down on a remote road in the hinterlands is not fun and may take a day or longer to extricate yourself from.

Among the car rental companies with "newish" cars the best deal I found was with Budget Rent A Car. Proprietor Alan Auil stocks his fleet with Suzuki two-wheel-drive Swifts and four-wheel-drive Samurais and Sidekicks. While these vehicles are not designed for high-speed driving nor to Ralph Nader's liking because of their short wheel base and high center of gravity, the two 4WDs have all the essentials for negotiating the challenges Belizean roads have to offer. The Swift (the least expensive new car I could find) is suitable for paved and improved dirt roads but not for muddy or unimproved dirt surfaces. The Sidekick is more stable and bigger than the Samurai and rents for about ten dollars a day more. Auil's vehicles are air-conditioned, well maintained, and clean.

Budget Rent A Car has two offices, one in the international airport and the other directly across from the Belize Biltmore Plaza on the Northern Highway north of Belize City. Vehicles can be picked up and dropped off at either office, which means you can avoid Belize City entirely if you choose. If you're booked at the Belize Biltmore Plaza and arrive in Belize at midday, you can simply take a cab to the Biltmore, get your bearings in a comfortable atmosphere, and then pick up a rental car across the street the next day before heading off to the areas that most interest you. This strategy allows you to catch up on your sleep, eat a couple of good meals, and save on rental car costs by not picking up a car until you're ready to roll.

Auil offers several incentives to clients. Travelers who book in advance receive reduced rates, and those who rent a car for a week get one day free. Based on 1994 rates supplied by Auil, the cheapest vehicle, the Suzuki Swift, starts at U.S. $49 per day, the Samurai rents for U.S. $65 per day, and the Sidekick rents for U.S. $75 per day. These rates include unlimited mileage. Auil will reduce rates when business is slow. His contracts are similar to those of his competitors in that damage responsibility with the mandatory insurance still leaves the customer liable for $750 in damages. Contact Budget Rent A Car, Phillip Goldson International Airport or 771 Bella Vista, Belize City. Phone 02-32435/33986 or fax 02-30237 for direct reservations, or make reservations through the Budget Reservation Center by phoning 1-800-527-0700 in the United States and Canada.

Other car rental agencies I tried and liked were Pancho's, 5747 Lizarraga Avenue, Belize City (phone 02-45554); Avis Rent A Car, Radisson Fort George Hotel, Belize City (phone 02-78367); National Car Rental, Phillip Goldson International Airport (phone 02-31586); and Melmish Mayan Rentals, Phillip Goldson International Airport (phone 02-45221). I suggest shopping among all the car rental companies listed. Though I consistently received excellent service from Budget, comparing prices in transportation-related businesses is usually worth the investment in a couple of extra phone calls.

Highways, Roads, and Maps: Belize has three mostly paved highways. (The term *highway* means two-lane road.) The Western Highway, which connects Belize City, Belmopan, San Ignacio, and the Guatemalan border, is 83 miles long. The Northern Highway, connecting Belize City to Orange Walk Town, Corozal Town, and Chetamul, Mexico, is 116 miles long. The Hummingbird Highway intersects the Western Highway at about the 50-mile mark. It connects Belmopan to Dangriga, a distance of 50 miles, and used to be the only road into the southern districts from Belmopan and Belize City. The Hummingbird is notorious for its tire-popping potholes.

The important dirt highways are the Southern Highway and New Road (also called the Manatee or Coast Road), which runs from near the Belize Zoo on the Western Highway to within seven miles of Dangriga on the Hummingbird Highway. The New Road saves about an hour's driving time between Belize City and Dangriga and can be found only on updated road maps. The Southern Highway runs between Dangriga and Punta Gorda. Roughly a hundred miles in length, it is graded dirt and a challenge in inclement weather. There are many secondary roads and two-rut tracks in Belize, all of them dirt.

The "Traveller's Reference Map of Belize" is the best road map I could find of Belize. This is a general-purpose travel map showing relief and offshore destinations. It is published by International Travel Map Productions, P.O. Box 2290, Vancouver, British Columbia, Canada V6B 3W5. The map is sold in the Belize Biltmore Plaza's gift shop but was not stocked widely throughout Belize. The Belize Biltmore Plaza is on the Northern Highway about five miles south of Phillip Goldson International Airport (four miles before Belize City) and across from Budget Rent A Car. Car rental agencies also have maps, but I found some of them outdated and sorely lacking in detail.

Driving Cautions: In general, the highways should be viewed as potentially hazardous, requiring extra vigilance. It's a good policy to drive slower in Belize than you would at home on a section of road that "looks" safe. High-speed driving is deceptively dangerous on the paved surfaces in Belize, particularly on the best-paved Western Highway, where the road is banked oddly on its few curves and the surface is screened with a material that becomes very slick during rains. I saw one fatal accident on the Western Highway, was told of others, and slid off the road myself when the vehicle I was driving slowly drifted sideways (as if on ice) during a rainstorm. A speed of between forty-five and fifty miles per hour maximum, under ideal conditions, ought to be okay. This is especially true if you're driving a Samurai (a popular rental vehicle), which has a short wheel base.

For an extensive look at Belize by car, dirt is the most common driving medium. Driving on dirt requires alertness and greatly reduced speed. Keep in mind that dirt turns to mud during rain. The longer the rain, the greater the potential that a dirt road will become impassable. If you're traveling in a two-wheel-drive vehicle on dirt and it begins to rain, especially in a low-lying area, it may be wise to retreat to a paved road before "bogs" develop or inclines become too slick to sustain traction. When in doubt, tap local knowledge about road conditions.

If someone tells you to watch for a "sleeping policeman" in the road, he or she is talking about speed bumps. All of the paved roads have them. Usually there is a speed bump at each end of a village. They're normally marked with white paint or a sign, but not always. The "sleeping policeman" is designed to protect pedestrians by slowing traffic in areas where villages are near highways.

Basic Travel Information

Climate: Belize has a subtropical climate with a definite wet and dry season. The dry season usually falls between late January and May. The wet season normally runs from June through September, with lighter rains in the north from October through January. Rainfall varies from about 50 inches in the north to 170 inches in the south. The mean annual temperature throughout the country is 80° F with summer highs of about 95° F and winter lows of 50° F. Trade winds cool the cayes and coastal areas, usually making them comfortable year-round. The highest temperatures usually occur from March to September, with the month of August, known as "the mauger," typified by generally unbearable conditions in which the humidity exceeds 90 percent and temperatures exceed 90° F in lowland areas in the interior. Humidity throughout Belize usually hovers around 80 percent most of the time.

Hurricanes can occur in the region between June and November but are most likely in August and September. Belize gets hit with a "big one" about every fifteen years. The most recent was in 1979. Hurricane Hattie, which flattened Belize City and many coastal villages in 1961, was the most destructive hurricane in recent times. Belize now has hurricane shelters in many communities and an excellent warning system.

Note: If you plan to scuba dive or snorkel, consideration should be given to avoiding visiting Belize during prolonged rainy periods. Rivers become torrents and spew silt far out to sea, affecting underwater visibility along the coast and the inner reef. The atolls, which are farther out, are less affected. Prolonged rains also can create havoc with the country's small, hand-cranked cable ferries and dirt roads, limiting access to some of the best parks and wilderness areas in Belize.

Clothes: Informal dress is the norm. Besides your bathing suit and shorts, take along a lightweight raincoat, long pants and long-sleeved shirts to protect you against bugs and sun. In Belize City, dress *not* to look like a tourist—meaning forgo loud vacation-type clothes and hats as well as expensive-looking outfits and jewelry. Also, a plain hat, and two pairs of casual walking or hiking shoes are recommended.

Entry and Visa Requirements: North Americans and Europeans need a valid passport, but no visa, to enter Belize. If you stay for longer than thirty days you must visit the immigration office (115 Barrack Road, Belize City) and pay a nominal fee. You also may be asked to prove you have enough money to cover your stay. Citizens of China, Colombia, Cuba, India, Pakistan, Peru, South Africa, and Taiwan must obtain a visitor's permit from the Immigration and Naturalization Office in Belmopan prior to visiting.

Sources of Tourist Information: Information about Belize can be obtained from three types of sources: Belizean government agencies, private travel-related businesses, and conservation groups. The best general source with free information is the Belize Tourist Board, 415 Seventh Avenue, New York, NY 10001 (phone 1-800-624-0686/ 212-268-8798). For more specific inquiries, contact the Belize Embassy, 2535 Massachusetts Avenue NW, Washington, DC 20008 (phone 202-332-9636; fax 202-332-6741). In Canada, the diplomatic contact is the Belize High Commission to Canada, 112 Kent Street, Suite 2005, Place de Ville, Tower B, Ottawa, Ontario, Canada KIP 5P2 (phone 613-232-7389; fax 613-232-5804).

From my experience with the private sector, three North American travel outfits are especially well qualified and willing to share information. The first is International Expeditions, 1 Environs Park, Helena, AL 35080 (phone 1-800-633-4734). Many of Belize's most knowledgeable naturalists lead groups organized by International Expeditions. Ask for Martin Meadows to be your leader. Another company with a great deal of experience in Belize is Tropical Travel, 5 Grogans Park, Suite 102, The Woodlands, TX 77380 (phone 1-800-451-8017 or 713-362-3386; fax 713-298-2335). Head honcho Tommy Thompson is viewed by many Belizeans as the U.S. pioneer in adventure travel to Belize. Now a thirteen-year veteran of organizing trips, Thompson has developed relationships with leading Belizean dive professionals. His packages are tailored to scuba diving, snorkeling, natural history, and archaeology destinations. Itineraries can be set up for destinations in Guatemala, Honduras, and Costa Rica. Far Horizons, P.O. Box 91900, Albuquerque, NM 87199 (phone 800-552-4575), also has a lot of expertise and knowledge about Belize. I hooked up with several of their groups by chance and was impressed with the knowledge and enthusiasm of their leaders. They are particularly strong on archaeology.

Last, but not least, are the conservation groups. They rely on donations in order to operate, so expect to pay for material from them. The most important to the visitor is the Belize Audubon Society, 29 Regent Street, P.O. Box 1001, Belize City, Belize, C.A. (phone 02-77369). Belize Audubon coordinates contacts between visitors and Belize's remote national parks, which it played a part in creating and now helps manage. Belize Audubon has developed a number of informative brochures. "A Guide to the Country and Its Wildlife" provides a quick and accurate overview of Belize's ecosystems. Other contacts are the Belize Department of Archaeology in Belmopan (phone 08-22106) (see "Belmopan" in the Cayo District chapter); the Belize Center for Environmental Studies, 55 Eve Street, P.O. Box 666, Belize City, Belize, C.A. (phone 02-45545) (see "Belize City" in the Belize District chapter); and the Programme for Belize, 1 King Street, Belize City, Belize, C.A. (phone 02-75616) (see "Rio Bravo Conservation and Management Area" in the Orange Walk District chapter). The Belize Zoo and Tropical Education Center also has a great deal of information about conservation issues facing Belize (see "Belize Zoo and Tropical Education Center" in the Belize District chapter).

Currency Exchange and Credit Cards: The Belizean dollar is assigned half the value of the U.S. dollar. This fixed rate is not anticipated to change. In my experience U.S. cash was accepted throughout the country. Most hotels, car rental agencies, and airlines accept traveler's checks and major credit cards. However, outside the hub areas of Belize City, Ambergris Caye, and Dangriga, many businesses do not accept credit cards and in many cases traveler's checks aren't accepted. In a surprising number of places only cash is accepted. Generally, gasoline is paid for in cash. To prevent a sticky situation, always ask first when in doubt about what constitutes an acceptable form of payment.

Taxes and Tips: All visitors departing the country at Belize City's international airport are charged a U.S. $10 departure tax, plus a U.S. $1.25 security tax. Only cash is accepted for these taxes. Hotels charge a 5 percent service tax. Tipping waiters, baggage handlers, cabbies, etc., at 10 percent is appreciated, but done only if the service warrants it.

Telephone and Fax: You can dial direct between Belize and North America. Dial 011 (international line), followed by 501 (Belize's country code), and then the local number, dropping the zero from the prefix. For example, Pelican Beach Resort's local number is 05-22044. From North America you would dial 011-501-5-22044. Sending a fax works in the same manner. (A ringing phone in Belize sounds more like a repetitive buzz than the ring of most North American phones, so when you hear a constant sound on the other end after the ringing ceases, push the "send" button.) Within Belize, dial 113 for directory assistance and 90 for emergencies requiring medical aid, police, or fire-fighters. Phones are common in homes and businesses in Belize City and the largest towns in the districts; however, a community telephone is the only telephonic link to the rest of Belize for many small communities, particularly in the southern half of the country. In the *Belize Telephone Directory*, on the page preceding Belize City numbers, there is a list of community telephone numbers.

Language: English is the official and primary language, which allows North Americans to converse easily with people of the many cultures found in Belize. This is the only place in the world where Mayan villagers speak English and the only place in the American tropics where the national language is English. Most Belizeans are bilingual and speak the language of their culture — Creole, Garifuna, Spanish, Mayan, or, in the case of the Mennonites, a dialect of archaic German. In recent years solely Spanish-speaking immigrants from neighboring countries have created pockets of people who do not speak English. Following are a few words and phrases from some of Belize's colorful languages.

Creole: Viewed as either nonstandard English or a separate language, Creole is spoken widely in Belize. Often a Belizean communicating in standard English will lace his or her sentences with Creole words, expressions, and pronunciations. To a standard English speaker, Creole is understandable at times. Creole proverbs are entertaining and to the point—for example, on keeping bad company: "You lie wit' daag, you catch dem flea." When it comes to wildlife, there's a whole new vocabulary: mountain cow (tapir), baboon (black howler monkey), quash (coatimundi), agouti (rabbit), and tiger (jaguar).

Yucatec Mayan: Tene quimako uxamalen (I'm proud to be a Mayan); *Bix a bel?* (How are you?); *Bix a kaba?* (What is your name?); *Quimac in wo* (I'm happy); *chakmool* (jaguar); *u tzimin gax* (tapir); and *ha* (water).

Garifuna (also called Garinagu or Black Carib): Dundeiwahama wasanigu lidoun Garifunaduau (Let's teach the children the way of the Garifunas); *Ida biahgi* (How are you?); *Kagi biri* (What is your name?); *Bieti teriuhoun* (She's beautiful); *giegous* (jaguar); and *dandei* (tapir).

Business Hours and Holidays: Businesses are generally open Monday through Friday from 8:00 A.M. to 5:00 P.M. Many tourist-oriented businesses are open on Saturdays and a few on Sundays. Most gas stations are open only during daylight hours. Banks open at 8:00 A.M. and close at 1:00 P.M. on Monday through Friday. On Fridays banks reopen between 3:00 P.M. and 6:00 P.M. Banks and most businesses are closed on national holidays, which are: New Year's Day, January 1; Baron Bliss Day, March 9; Good Friday; Easter Sunday and Monday; Labor Day, May 1; Commonwealth Day, May 24; St. George's Caye Day, September 10; Independence Day, September 21; Columbus Day, October 12; Garifuna Settlement Day, November 19; Christmas Day, December 25; and Boxing Day, December 26.

Shopping: Belize is not a shopping mecca. Black coral jewelry, wood carvings of wildlife, and Mayan stone (slate) carvings are the primary products created by locals for tourists. These commercially produced art objects range greatly in value and quality. There are also nature-related T-shirt businesses on Ambergris Caye and in Belize City. The Garcia sisters (Yucatec Mayans) of the Cayo District produce a wide range of stone carvings. Mayans in the southern Stann Creek District and Toledo District produce stone carvings and good-quality woven products. (*Note:* Purchasing Mayan antiquities or attempting to take them out of Belize is a criminal offense.)

Restaurants: Belize has a number of good restaurants located in Belize City and in other towns and villages. Many hotels have their own restaurants. Restaurants listed in this book have been categorized as falling within one of three price ranges: budget (B), U.S. $2.50 or less; moderate (M), U.S. $2.50 to U.S. $6; and expensive (E), U.S. $6 or more. There are restaurants that charge in excess of U.S. $25 per meal, so always check menu prices before ordering. Most Belizean dishes include rice, beans, and a meat or seafood dish, which is usually chicken, fish, or lobster. Conch soup is also a popular local dish. Besides Belizean food, North American, Chinese, and Mexican cuisines are especially well represented in eateries.

Accommodations: This book provides listings of places to stay throughout Belize. Each accommodation has been categorized as falling within one of three price ranges: budget (B), U.S. $5 to U.S. $25; moderate (M), U.S. $26 to U.S. $50; and expensive (E), U.S. $51 or more. Prices change, however; so always inquire at the time you are making reservations. In general, hotels in the expensive and moderate ranges run a tad high for service comparable to similarly priced North American hotels, but there are some exceptions, which are identified in the text. In resort areas you're paying a bit extra for the ambience and location. Often the key to the good deals is figuring out where the Belizean business traveler stays, which is usually at the budget or moderately priced accommodations.

Camping: Camping is permitted in designated areas and should not be undertaken on a casual basis on either private or public land for both legal and safety reasons. If you plan an expedition-type camping trip in Belize independent of an adventure travel company, contact the Ministry of Natural Resources, Belmopan (phone 08-22037/22232).

Drinking the Water, Inoculations, and Other Health Concerns: Water is generally drinkable throughout Belize. For peace of mind you may want to use water purification tablets, but I found no record of health problems related to drinking the water. I experienced no ill effects from food or water consumed throughout the country.

No inoculations are required to enter Belize. Along the coasts, there are no disease risks that don't occur in North America. In the interior and southernmost Toledo District, antimalaria pills are recommended. Updates on inoculation requirements and health risks are issued to U.S. physicians by the Centers for Disease Control in Atlanta, so check with your doctor before your trip.

Most health concerns fall into the self-induced category. Dehydration, sunburn, mosquito bites, and motion sickness are all real possibilities on a trip to Belize. If you're exerting yourself outdoors (including scuba diving and snorkeling), drink at least an extra quart of nonalcoholic liquid each morning and afternoon. For sunburn, wear long-sleeved shirts and a hat that protects your face and neck. Use strong sunblock on exposed skin. Remember, this is the tropics. Fifteen minutes of exposure of a previously unexposed body part can result in a burn. Include bug repellent in your travel kit. Along the coast the constant breeze usually keeps the bugs (mosquitoes and sand flies) away, but when the breeze stops and/or after the rainy season, look out, especially in swampy and rain forest settings. In the interior, the mountain areas of the Cayo District are often remarkably free of bugs for much of the year. If you're prone to motion sickness figure out a strategy for dealing with it. This can become very important if you're a scuba diver. On two occasions I saw scuba divers get sick to their stomachs far below the surface due to motion sickness that had developed on the boat ride to the dive site. The ramifications could have been life-threatening, but weren't.

Both the reef and the rain forest have organisms whose survival strategies include defenses that can cause you discomfort or worse. As a rule, don't touch plants and animals. Stinging corals are common in Belizean waters, along with stingrays in shallow water and a number of other potentially pain-evoking creatures. Open-water sharks are very rare around inner reefs and are not often sighted elsewhere. Many rain forest plants can cause you harm, particularly the give-and-take palm (which has a thorn that breaks off under your skin, causing pain) and poisonwood (which causes irritation similar to that of poison oak and ivy).

The most talked-about poisonous snake of Belize is the fer-de-lance, also known as the yellow-jaw or by various other names. It is a large-fanged, short-fused reptile that is active night and day in pursuit of rodents and birds. Young fer-de-lances climb trees, and those of any age take to water like ducks. After miles of hiking in rain forests I saw just one five-footer, and it went the other way. It was marked somewhat like a rattlesnake, but with yellow on its lower jaw and no rattle. One of the fer-de-lance's Spanish names translates as "ten steps," which is the distance a victim supposedly gets before succumbing to a bite. Tropical rattlesnakes occur in Belize but are not seen often. The coral snake, which also lives in Belize (and in the United States), has the most toxic venom of all, but it's more retiring than the fer-de-lance and less capable of inflicting a fatal bite. In general, regardless of the continent or the kind of snake, most fatal snake bites occur when a person stands, sits, or inadvertently touches a snake. When bush-walking keep your eyes peeled and don't venture off trails.

Medical Emergencies: Emergency medical aid or a doctor's services can be found throughout Belize, but assume that you'll have to reach a hospital or doctor on your own. Belizean authorities are working to improve emergency responses, but financial realities limit what can be done. An all-purpose emergency phone number has now been established. In an emergency, dial 90, which will connect you to an ambulance service, police, or fire department.

Embassies and consuls supply the names of doctors to their citizens visiting Belize. Each district in Belize has at least one medical clinic or hospital. Key contacts: Belize District, in Belize City, Belize City Hospital (phone 02-77251) and Medical Associates (phone 02-30303); Stann Creek District, in Dangriga, Doctor's Quarters (phone 05-22085); Toledo District, in Punta Gorda, Punta Gorda Hospital (phone 07-22026); Cayo District, in San Ignacio, San Ignacio Hospital (phone 092-2066), and in Belmopan, Public Hospital (phone 08-22263); Orange Walk District, in Orange Walk Town, Orange Walk Hospital (phone 03-22143); Corozal District, in Santa Rita Hill, Corozal Hospital (phone 04-22076).

For scuba divers in need of a recompression chamber, the only one in the country is located on Ambergris Caye at the north end of the island's airstrip (see "Ambergris Caye" in the Belize District chapter for details).

Basic Facts about Belize

Geography: Belize is a tiny nation. It occupies about 8866 square miles, which is about the size of Israel or the state of New Hampshire. Located on the Caribbean Sea directly below the Yucatán and next to Guatemala, Belize is roughly rectangular in shape with a north-south orientation and measures 174 miles long and an average of 68 miles wide. The country's offshore natural wealth is in a class by itself. Just offshore lies its 180-mile-long Barrier Reef. This is the longest reef in the Western Hemisphere, though much smaller than the Great Barrier Reef in Australia and several other South Pacific reef systems. Besides the well-known Barrier Reef there are three huge atolls farther out in the Caribbean and hundreds of cayes. Most of the cayes are uninhabited, partially submerged mangrove islands, but some are palm-studded islands with sandy beaches and sparkling blue waters. The coast is mostly low and swampy with large stands of mangroves and fresh and saltwater swamps. Belize's few coastal beaches, at places such as Hopkins and Placencia, are much appreciated. Inland there is arable land where sugar cane, citrus fruits, bananas, vegetables, and livestock are raised. In the lower half of the country's interior the natural fortress known as the Maya Mountains dominates, creating a large wilderness. Its highest recorded point, Victoria Peak (3675 feet), lies just outside the Cockscomb Basin Wildlife Sanctuary in the Stann Creek District. The Maya Mountains are typified by plunging valleys, rushing rivers, and miles of tropical rain forest with the highest areas covered by pine trees. The northwest portion of the country consists of huge tracts of uninterrupted lowland rain forest. Intersecting all of Belize is a matrix of river systems.

Economy: Compared to its neighbors in Central America, Belize is better off. All children receive a compulsory basic education, and health care is available to all citizens. The standard of living has improved, but the average annual income hovers around U.S. $1500 a year. Many Belizeans rely on garden plots, fish, home-grown poultry, town-square produce markets, and bartering for food. For transportation most Belizeans take buses or ride bicycles.

The Belizean economy is fragile and dependent on foreign aid in order to function. The United States is Belize's chief trading partner. Largely because of the need for gasoline and finished goods, Belize imports about 50 percent more than it exports. The Belizean economy is further hampered by able-bodied workers moving abroad — particularly to the United States — to earn a living. It is estimated that one-third of Belizeans able to work are living abroad. However, many Belizeans living outside their country send money home to their families.

Belize's leading export and top moneymaker is agriculture, with sugar cane the leading crop, followed by citrus. Sugar cane is a volatile market subject to price swings controlled by other nations and impacted by unexpected disease and weather-related problems. Tourism is the second-largest source of income and is closing in fast on agriculture. Approximately U.S. $45 million is spent by approximately 140,000 people visiting Belize annually. The number of people visiting Belize, primarily as eco-tourists, is projected to increase. There is hotel space enough to accommodate 220,000 people annually. The transport of illegal drugs from Belize to the United States is thought to be a major income source to a small number of Belizeans and a stimulus to local investment in legitimate businesses. The creation of fish cooperatives in coastal communities has allowed Belize to export lobster, shrimp, and other fish to the United States, but this resource may be operating at or over capacity. The worldwide economic malaise of the 1980s and 1990s is blamed for the slowdown in economic growth in Belize. Still, Belize has reason for optimism. The government is stable. Workers are literate and trainable. The growth of eco-tourism has been rapid and promises to increase as more areas are made accessible. There is unused agricultural land, and foreign investment is encouraged.

Government and Law Enforcement: When it comes to government and internal stability, Belize is an anomaly for Central America. It is a true democracy, operating under the English-style parliamentary system. Belize remains a member of the British Commonwealth. The country has an excellent civil rights record. Pick up any Belizean newspaper and you'll see that freedom of speech is practiced without inhibition. Belize is not without its problems, but you'll find no insurrection in the jungle here.

For protection Belize has a small defense force and an ongoing agreement with Great Britain, which keeps a garrison in Belize and a few Harrier jets. Over the years this force has repelled occasional forays across the border by Guatemala, which takes to bullying Belize from time to time. For internal security Belize has about 300 civil police who rarely carry weapons.

Laws are created by elected representatives. During the period of self-government, which began in the 1950s, and after Belize became a nation in 1981, the People's United Party, led by George Price, has dominated Belizean politics. However, the United Democratic Party, led by Manuel Esquivel, has held the majority of seats on two occasions. Transfer of power from one political party to another has occurred without incident. Both political parties have endorsed the development of Belize as an eco-tourism destination by passing laws that are protective of the environment.

In terms of laws involving your own conduct and crimes in general, Belize is much like North America. A small number of tourists find themselves in trouble when they mistakenly interpret the casual atmosphere in Belize as lax toward drug laws. Buying or using marijuana or other drugs is against the law and can be quite risky. Belize law enforcement authorities are under pressure to curb the flow of drugs to the United States that sometimes passes through Belize from Colombia or was grown locally and shipped abroad. The U.S. Drug Enforcement Agency (DEA) opened an office in Belize in 1992. An easy way for Belizean police to show they are doing their part to stem the tide is to arrest a few "street dumb" North Americans and other foreigners who solicit drugs.

As for criminal behavior that may affect tourists, see "Caution" in the coverage of Belize City and Guancaste and Blue Hole national parks.

National Symbols: The national flag symbolizes Belize's history. The flag's center depicts two woodcutters of black and white racial backgrounds, reflecting the mixed ethnic makeup of Belize and the former colony's beginnings as a source of logwood and mahogany. Behind the two figures is a mahogany tree, the tree that was harvested most intensely in the late 1800s and early 1900s. The two horizontal red stripes bordering the top and bottom of the flag symbolize the two-party political system that has dominated Belize since the period of self-government that began in 1950.

The mahogany tree is the national tree. It is massive, with immense buttresses and a large, dense crown. In the country's coat-of-arms is the slogan *Sub Umbra Floreo,* which means "Under the shade [of the mahogany tree] I flourish." The tree was the foundation of the British colonial economy in Belize for more than a hundred years.

The black orchid is the national flower. This fairly common beauty grows on the sides of rain forest trees. The flower occurs in clusters and is not dramatic from a distance. Close up it is stunning, with light green outer petals and a deep purple, black, or brown "lip" with ligher purple veins.

The tapir, dubbed "mountain cow" in the Creole dialect, is the national mammal. The tapir found in Belize is the Baird's tapir, one of four species that exist in the world. All species are endangered. The tapirs in Belize are among the last reproductively viable populations, and it is against the law to hunt them. There is no mistaking a tapir, with its large, donkey-size brown body, short legs, and long, flexible snout vaguely similar to an elephant's trunk. Related distantly to both the horse and rhinoceros, the tapir is shy and prefers the deep forest.

The keel-billed toucan is Belize's national bird. Unmistakable because of its large, multicolored, banana-shaped bill, the keel-billed toucan possesses the most outrageous-looking bill in the bird world. It is one of three kinds of toucans living in Belize. The keel-billed is the largest, measuring twenty inches. Its body is mostly black with yellow on its cheeks and a red rump. Instead of singing it makes a croaking sound like a frog. Keel-billed toucans are fairly common in Belize. If you spend time in the interior there's a good chance you'll see one.

Beliken beer is the undeclared national drink of Belize. This gentle brew was perfected by Belizean entrepreneur Barry Bowen, who years ago hired German brew masters to develop it. Beliken is bottled in Belize and can be purchased throughout the country. When someone asks if you want a Beliken, he or she is asking if you want a beer. In Belize, Beliken and beer are synonymous.

TWO
BELIZE DISTRICT

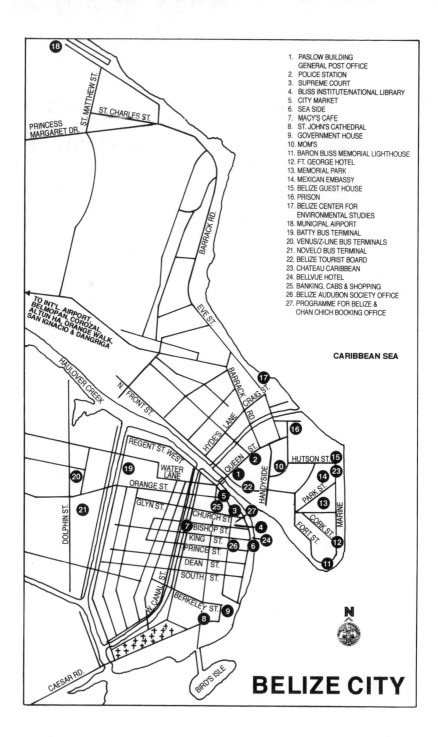

1. PASLOW BUILDING
   GENERAL POST OFFICE
2. POLICE STATION
3. SUPREME COURT
4. BLISS INSTITUTE/NATIONAL LIBRARY
5. CITY MARKET
6. SEA SIDE
7. MACY'S CAFE
8. ST. JOHN'S CATHEDRAL
9. GOVERNMENT HOUSE
10. MOM'S
11. BARON BLISS MEMORIAL LIGHTHOUSE
12. FT. GEORGE HOTEL
13. MEMORIAL PARK
14. MEXICAN EMBASSY
15. BELIZE GUEST HOUSE
16. PRISON
17. BELIZE CENTER FOR
    ENVIRONMENTAL STUDIES
18. MUNICIPAL AIRPORT
19. BATTY BUS TERMINAL
20. VENUS/Z-LINE BUS TERMINALS
21. NOVELO BUS TERMINAL
22. BELIZE TOURIST BOARD
23. CHATEAU CARIBBEAN
24. BELLVUE HOTEL
25. BANKING, CABS & SHOPPING
26. BELIZE AUDUBON SOCIETY OFFICE
27. PROGRAMME FOR BELIZE &
    CHAN CHICH BOOKING OFFICE

CARIBBEAN SEA

TO INT'L. AIRPORT,
BELMOPAN, COROZAL,
ALTUN HA, ORANGE WALK,
SAN IGNACIO & DANGRIGA

BELIZE CITY

Overview

The Belize District is the heart of the country and the starting place for most people visiting Belize. The district measures 1633 square miles. The Cayo, Orange Walk, and Toledo districts are larger in size, but when it comes to islands, the Belize District possesses the lion's share, claiming most of Belize's more than 200 cayes within its boundaries.

The Belize District includes the country's two travelers' hubs: Belize City (including Phillip Goldson International Airport) and Ambergris Caye (including the town of San Pedro), which is located fifteen minutes offshore by light aircraft. Most visitors begin and end their trips at these places. Belize's three major highways start just outside Belize City. The Western Highway arrives at Guatemala after 82 miles. The Northern Highway stretches 116 miles and ends just short of Chetumal, Mexico, the exit and entry point to the north. The Southern Highway (which is dirt) ends at Punta Gorda 210 miles to the south. Visitors reach Guatemala from Punta Gorda via ferry boat.

The Belize District has plenty of worthwhile destinations. Belize City is home to one-third of the country's population. In many ways, being in the city is like stepping back into the last century. Working sailing craft anchor in the heart of the city in the Haulover Creek river mouth each evening. Every morning and evening the antiquated Swing Bridge creaks open, stopping vehicular traffic. With the channel that divides the city open, wind fills the sails of the old wooden boats as they glide past the bridge to and from the sea. Belize City has its charm and earthiness. I like the city, but it isn't for everyone. You can avoid it entirely and stay in places such as the Belize Biltmore Plaza hotel near the airport on the Northern Highway. Across from the Biltmore is Budget Rent A Car and its well-maintained fleet of small four-wheel-drive vehicles. I launched many a foray into the wilds of Belize from the convenience of these two businesses.

From your hotel room, wherever it is, you can easily spend a week day-tripping to the district's numerous sanctuaries and points of interest. Some of the top spots are the Belize Zoo, where the wild animals of Belize are displayed in their natural habitats; the Bermudian Landing Community Baboon Sanctuary, where local subsistence farmers have banned together to create a sanctuary for the endangered black howler monkey; Crooked Tree Wildlife Sanctuary, a vast wetlands and world-class birding area; and Mayan ruins such as Altun Ha. To the south there is the emerging eco-tourist destination around Gales Point, an area known for watercourses that run through caves, large populations of manatees, and sea turtle nesting sites.

The district's islands, atolls, and reefs are a world unto themselves: aqua blue water, palms swaying in the constant breezes, and some of the best scuba diving, snorkeling, and fishing in the world. As a result, this chapter includes a great deal of specific information about snorkel and scuba diving sites that are visited from the major and more obscure islands and atolls. Ambergris Caye, Caye Caulker, Caye Chapel, St. George's Caye, Half Moon Caye, Northern Caye, and the atolls at Turneffe Islands, Lighthouse Reef, Glover's Reef and other offshore destinations have been assessed firsthand in terms of accommodations, each island's unique ecology, and the dive sites with something special to offer.

You could spend most of your Belize vacation on the islands in the Belize District and spend another vacation visiting the district's mainland destinations. Many people do it on one trip, splitting their time between the cayes and the mainland—sampling the best of both worlds. If you spend enough time in Belize, you'll realize that the Belize District is a microcosm of Belize itself.

Belize City

Belize City sits approximately at the midway point on the Belizean coastline. The city straddles the mouth of river-size Haulover Creek, which discharges its sluggish brown water into the Caribbean Sea. Carved out of mangrove country centuries ago, the city's site has been home to Mayan fishermen, English pirates, colonial loggers known as Baymen, and the loggers' African slaves, whose descendants are now represented in the city's predominantly Creole population. Today, Belize City covers about ten square miles and is mostly single-story urban sprawl. It is home to 65,000 people, which is one out of three Belizeans. Though it has had different names in different centuries and has suffered greatly from periodic hurricanes, Belize City survives as the commercial and social hub of the country.

Belize City has no beaches or rain forests and possesses little in the way of natural beauty that attracts foreigners to the region, yet it has the earthy charm of a laid-back port city reminiscent of a setting for a Joseph Conrad novel.

Belize City is usually most appealing to the self-reliant seasoned world traveler and less attractive to the tourist whose curiosity about other cultures is overshadowed by insecurity and ethnocentricity. Regardless of where you place yourself between these extremes, you may experience some culture shock during your first few days in Belize City. This is urban life in what is commonly called the Third World. Most visitors find initial solace in English as a common language and a generally friendly citizenry. The flavor is more Jamaican-like than Latin American.

In Belize City you'll see open canals that double as sewers and rusty, metal-roofed, clapboard houses and businesses tilting this way and that. Most structures are in need of paint and repair. More than one tourist publication has bad-mouthed Belize City because of its run-down look and its panhandlers, who prey most aggressively on tourists toting expensive cameras and conspicuously dressed foreigners. There is no getting around these negative truths, but for the adventuresome visitor there is another Belize City — one that is beguiling, romantic, and affordable. The sagging porches, faded paint, rusting metal roofs, old sailing craft bobbing at anchor in the river mouth, and grand old colonial structures are authentic survivors of a bygone era.

In Belize City's Central Square you'll find an antiquated fleet of taxis awaiting your call, neatly dressed Creole business owners and office workers going about their chores, and old folks sitting around swapping stories on park benches. You'll see a few drifty-eyed, sullen Rastafarian types, whose body language makes it clear that allowing them as much sidewalk as they want is a smart policy. You'll see children dressed in tidy uniforms walking arm and arm on their way to and from school. While standing in line in the bank you may encounter sober-faced Mennonites whose dress suggests Midwestern farmers circa 1930. And, on street corners, it's not uncommon to be serenaded by a dozen shiny-faced North American "missionizers" singing religious hymns to passers-by, who largely ignore them. This is Belize City, accepting and diverse to the extreme. Racial and social tolerance is the norm. The average citizen is outgoing, helpful, literate, and tolerant. If a ghost pirate ship from the seventeenth century dropped anchor in the river mouth and its crew rowed ashore, they'd fit in here with barely a raised eyebrow. Belize City is unlike anywhere I've ever been.

Perhaps Belize City's unique charm is best symbolized by the Swing Bridge at the center of town that it has spanned Haulover Creek (really a river) since 1932. Haulover Creek divides the city into two districts, known as the North Side and the South Side. Twice a day the bridge is spun manually on its axis to allow the flotilla of old, wooden, sand-hauling schooners and sloop-rigged fishing boats in and out of the city. Most of these wide-bodied sailboats have no auxiliary power and rely entirely on the wind to get around. While the Swing Bridge rotates open, the boats designed in the last century hoist their sails and glide down the channel to or from the sea. All crosstown traffic comes to a standstill, seemingly in honor of the maritime past that brought the first Europeans. The bridge is then swung back across Haulover Creek, reuniting the two sides of the city and once again allowing traffic and commerce to resume. The Swing Bridge performs this feat between 5:30 A.M. and 6:00 A.M. and 5:30 P.M. and 6:00 P.M. every day.

Once you adjust to Belize City's ramshackle look you'll find a wide variety of quality restaurants, accommodations, and sights worth exploring. There are sections of town with stately colonial structures, funky night spots, large marketplaces, luxury hotels, and romantic seaside guesthouses. Relish the fact that unlike North America, Europe, parts of Asia, and Australia, you'll never see a Kentucky Fried Chicken, Denny's, or K-Mart. Belize City provides a glimpse of an urban world that hasn't been made over, sanitized, franchised, and zoned into numbing conformity. However, signs of change are apparent in Belize. With a world focus on Belize's natural beauty and international hotels gaining footholds outside the city, it is a matter of conjecture on how long present-day Belize City can maintain its traditional charm.

North Side of Belize City

The North Side is the part of Belize City most people see first because the Northern Highway, which connects Belize City to the Phillip Goldson International Airport (nine-and-a-half miles north of town), enters the north end of Belize City. As you head south on the Northern Highway, the city begins just past the statue of five life-size, copper-colored human figures (referred to by locals as the "five blind mice") in the median. Past the intersection just south of the statues, the Northern Highway becomes Haulover Road. It later changes to Freetown Road. If you're headed for Fort Point, where most of the expensive hotels are located, you'll continue on Barrack Road, Green Street, and Handyside Street and onto Fort Street.

Car Rentals: Most car rentals are located on the Northern Highway between Belize City and the international airport or on the North Side of Belize City. Many car rental companies operate in some capacity with the Phillip Goldson International Airport, which means you can pick up a rental car when you arrive at the airport. Car rentals in Belize fall into two categories: reliable and unreliable. Reliable means clean, regularly maintained, "newish" vehicles and a sincere effort to ensure that each vehicle is in top mechanical condition prior to being rented to a tourist, who will be negotiating the demanding roads that crisscross Belize. Unreliable, which I experienced, means cars that break down, have faulty gas gauges, vibrate unmercifully, lack a spare tire, have defective windshield wipers, can't be locked, have nonworking air-conditioning, and have bald tires. Renting an unreliable vehicle is a sure way to ruin a vacation, especially in a country with limited towing services and no way of replacing a vehicle should one break down outside Belize City.

Budget Rent A Car, 771 Bella Vista, Belize City (phone 02-32435/33986; fax 02-30237), across the street from the Belize Biltmore Plaza at mile 3 on the Northern Highway, had the best deals for reliable vehicles during my many trips to Belize. Proprietor Alan Auil buys new Suzuki four-wheel-drives (4WDs), rents them for a year, and sells them. If you plan on slogging around on Belize's many dirt roads, these mini 4WDs are the most suitable vehicles at an affordable price. Alan is somewhat flexible in long-term rentals. For example, he usually gives customers a day for free if they rent for a week. Still, expect to pay about U.S. $50 a day, with adjustments made for seasonal differences and length of time you plan to use the vehicle. (Caution: Suzuki's have a short wheel base and must be driven more conservatively than most conventional vehicles for safety reasons.) Other car rentals that were problem-free for me: Melmish Mayan Rentals (phone 02-45221; fax 02-77681); National Car Rental (phone

02-31586); and Pancho's (phone 02-45554). When talking to car rental companies, be specific about air-conditioning, maintenance, make of car, and other factors that are important to you. Keep in mind that, other than the Northern Highway, Western Highway, and Hummingbird Highway, Belize's roads are mostly dirt and may require four-wheel-drive after prolonged rains.

Embassies and Consuls: As you enter the city you'll pass through neighborhoods of time-weary clapboard houses and businesses, including Belize Hospital, before reaching Fort Point, the best-known hotel district. (See "Accommodations" for details on North Side hotels and guesthouses.) Embassies and consuls are scattered throughout the North Side. The U.S. Embassy is located at 29 Gabourel Lane, (phone 02-77161) and the Canadian Consulate at 87 North Front Street (phone 02-31060). For the addresses of any of the other eighteen foreign governments with representation in Belize (most in Belize City, but some in Belmopan, the capital), see "Diplomatic Listings" in the green section of the Belize telephone directory. Diplomatic missions can keep you apprised about travel advisories, assist in locating a doctor, and give you a list of lawyers should you run afoul of the law.

Municipal Airport: The Belize City Municipal Airport, which receives visitors from the cayes and Phillip Goldson International Airport, is also on the North Side. It is located in the northern suburbs and is too far out for you to walk to Fort Point or the South Side, where banking and other essential businesses are found. If you arrive at the municipal airport, either have a rental car waiting or be prepared to take a cab to your city destinations. Barracks Road is the normal access road to the Fort Point area from this airport.

Belize Tourist Board: The Belize Tourist Board, under the direction of Joy Vernon, has done a commendable job of organizing tourist information about Belize. Located at 83 North Front Street (phone 02-77213/73255), the Belize Tourist Board has information on hotels, restaurants, and national parks, and the office staff is knowledgeable about the transportation and accommodations infrastructure of Belize. *Belize, the Adventure Coast, Travel Industry Sales Planner* is the most comprehensive publication on basic travel information in print and is updated annually by the Belize Tourist Board (BTB). The BTB is the government-run organization, not to be confused with the Belize Tourism Industry Association (BTIA) office at 99 Albert Street (phone 02-75717/78709) on the South Side. The BTIA is also a good source of information, though it is not as comprehensive as that offered by the Belize Tourist Board.

North Side Travel and Tour Connections: S and L Tours and Rentals, 91 North Front Street (phone 02-77593; fax 02-77594), is one of the most respected, reliable, and longest-operating domestic tour companies in Belize. Owners Sarita and Lascelle Tillet are flexible and usually personally involved in bookings, accompanying larger groups to destinations such as Ambergris Caye, Altun Ha ruins, Crooked Tree Wildlife Sanctuary, Bermudian Landing Community Baboon Sanctuary, and the Belize Zoo. Universal Travel, 13 Handyside Street (phone 02-44667/30964), handles ticketing for domestic and international travel needs. Nearby Mom's Triangle Inn, 11 Handyside Street (02-45523), is well connected with tour operators throughout Belize, especially those going to national parks and conservation-related destinations. The boat operators that leave from the Shell Station on North Front Street often eat here. For a complete listing of travel and tour companies, visit the Belize Tourist Board or the Belize Tourism Industry Association.

Diving, Snorkeling, and Fishing Operations: Most of the scuba diving and snorkeling commences on the cayes. Blackline Marine, located two miles up the Northern Highway (phone 02-44155), is the notable exception to the many quality offerings on the cayes. Blackline is a boat works, full service and sales dive shop, and charter dive and fishing operation. It also offers boat tours to the Southern Lagoon to visit with the manatees. (See "Gales Point" for more about visiting manatees.)

Entertainment: There are nightclubs throughout Belize City, many of them in hotels. The two drawing the biggest crowds are the Hard Rock Cafe at the corner of Queen Street and Handyside (phone 02-32401) and the Big Apple Disco at 67 North Front Street (phone 02-44758). Expect Bob Marley–type music, punta rock (a mix of traditional Garifuna and reggae music), and other Caribbean sounds. The Hard Rock Cafe is the tamer of the two, but this is a relative term. Check with your hotel about getting to and from these clubs safely after dark. A chaperone-type arrangement with a local accompany-ing tourists is advisable. Check with your hotel for advice.

Belize Center for Environmental Studies: On the North Side you'll also find the Belize Center for Environmental Studies at 55 Eve Street (phone 02-45545). Run by longtime North American transplant Lou Nicolait, this nonprofit organization is both a watchdog and an un-censored information-disseminating source on all natural resource questions facing Belize. The organization often works with USAID and other international organizations in conducting environmental assessment studies in sensitive areas in Belize. The center also has a technical library with a tremendous amount of information about environmental issues facing Belize's most extraordinary scenic areas. Much of the organization's miniscule budget is derived from donations.

Other Essential Services and Sights: On North Front Street near Hyde's Lane you'll find a Shell Station, where you can take boats to the cayes. The post office, in the impressive old Paslow Building, is located on the corner of Queen Street and North Front Street. Up-stairs in this building is the Department of Natural Resources, where you can buy special-edition stamps commemorating Belizean wildlife. Just north of the post office, in the first block of Queen Street, you'll find the police station (phone 02-44646 for emergencies) and the Angelus Press (10 Queen Street; phone 02-45777), a good source for books, postcards, maps, and other printed material on Belize, plus stationery, office supplies, and computer-related materials (the lat-ter is limited). Other common destinations and points of interest on the North Side include the Belize Hospital (phone 02-77251; for emergencies, phone 90) on Mortuary Road (!) and, in the Fort Point area, the city prison, on Gaol Lane. The old, high-walled prison was built of timber and mortar in 1857 and is operating at double its carrying capacity. A few Americans are serving time there on drug charges. Along the Marine Parade (a nice walk) you'll find the Mexi-can Embassy, which occupies one of the prettiest old buildings in the city, the Belize Guest House, Chateau Caribbean, Memorial Park, Raddison Fort George Hotel, the Fort George Pier, plus the Baron Bliss Tomb.

Baron Bliss, Belize's Benefactor: The name Bliss is a reoccurring place name in Belize, for good reason. Baron Henry Edward Everest

Victor Bliss, who was an English adventurer and yachtsman, took ill and died on his yacht, the *Sea King,* in Belize City harbor in 1926. Before Bliss slipped away, he bequeathed his personal fortune to Belize (then British Honduras), making Bliss a national hero and Belize's number one individual benefactor. Bliss's place in Belizean history is celebrated on March 9, a national holiday featuring a sailing regatta with native dugouts and the large, sloop-rigged sailboats you see anchored at the mouth of the river. Betting is heavy on the March 9 race, and much of the city involves itself in the regatta, even if it's only to listen to radio coverage.

Crossing to the South Side: If you're on foot, merely walk across the Swing Bridge. If you're in a car headed to the South Side across the Swing Bridge, you'll need to find your way to North Front Street, which is one-way leading onto the bridge from the south. Though most maps don't show it, you can't turn left — only right — from North Front Street onto the Swing Bridge. If you find yourself headed south on North Front Street (on the stretch north of the bridge) hoping to get across the Swing Bridge, turn right on Queen Street, go one block, turn left on New Road, and in one more block turn left on Hyde's Lane (very narrow, one-way lane), which intersects North Front Street (one way) south of the bridge. Turn left onto North Front Street and in about a block you'll be in a position to turn right over the Swing Bridge. Crossing the Swing Bridge from the South Side is a straight shot. Head down Queen Street one block, turn left on New Road, and in a short while you'll be on the northern outskirts of the city.

South Side of Belize City

On the South Side, Albert and Regent streets make up the principal business district of Belize City. The city was first settled along the southern foreshore. You'll see old colonial structures with brick used for the first floor and wood used for the rest of the house. During the early 1800s, slaves were kept in chains in escape-proof brick basements, quite literally under the feet of their masters.

Belize City Market: Where Regent Street meets the Swing Bridge you'll find the Belize City Market housed in a new three-story structure on the South Side of the Swing Bridge. The market was formerly held in the open air, but moving it indoors has not changed its offerings. You can buy everything from bush medicines and seafood to Mennonite furniture, portable radios, and inexpensive meals.

Banking: You'll find banks across the street from Central Square on Albert Street. The Bank of Novia Scotia, Bank of Belize, and Barclays Bank are within a stone's throw of one another and Central Square.

Media Connection: At nearby 7 Church Street is the office of the *Belize Review*, Belize's only environmentally oriented magazine, which is published monthly. You can buy current and back copies of the magazine, and you'll find no more knowledgeable person on the political aspects of conservation in Belize than editor Meb Cutlack.

Provisions: At the intersection of Albert and Regent streets you can stock up on provisions at Brodie, which carries everything from groceries to mosquito repellents and clothes. Also the Belize City Market, which is most impressive on Saturdays, has terrific buys on fresh fruit and still wriggling seafood.

Gifts and T-shirts: For Belizean T-shirts with humorous nature themes, stop at Go-Graphics at 23 Regent Street. American expatriate Isabel Goldberg owns the shop and prides herself on her original designs. A diversion to 53 King Street will include a visit to John Vasquez's Gift Shop, featuring black coral jewelry, ziricote wood carvings, and T-shirts. Along the same lines there's Elvis Samuel's Black Coral Jewelry at 6 Water Lane.

Central Square and Supreme Court Building: Central Square is across the street from the banks on Albert Street. The square is a taxi stand (any car with a green license plate), a former horse-watering area, and today a place to congregate and catch up on gossip. Walk toward the foreshore from Regent Street and you'll pass by some attractive large colonial buildings. The central-most white building with the attractive clock tower, embellished with iron latticework and an overall look that is decidedly British colonial, is the Supreme Court Building, located on the corner of Regent and Church streets.

If you walk down Church Street and continue east on Southern Fore-shore away from the river mouth, you'll come to the Bliss Institute (see below) and the Bellevue Hotel (see "Accommodations"), which has the best hotel restaurant and bar on the South Side.

Bliss Institute: On the Southern Foreshore (also called the Bliss Promenade) behind the Supreme Court Building you'll come to the Bliss Institute (1 Bliss Promenade), a cultural and art center that features high-quality Mayan stelae and altars excavated from the interior of Belize. The inscriptions on these impressive antiquities are translated into English. The institute also houses a research library with rare texts and displays on subjects ranging from mangrove conservation to Garifuna music. From the Southern Foreshore there are excellent photographic opportunities of the waterfront and the mouth of Haulover Creek, which is the anchorage for traditional working sailing craft. However, watch your backside here, as panhandlers sometimes congregate in this area.

Emory King and Basic Information: The Admiral Barnaby Art Gallery and Coffee Shop (9 Regent Street) is the abode and business of well-known gadfly Emory King, who refused to leave Belize when he ran the sailboat *Vagabond* aground on an offshore reef in 1953. Emory, who spent time as a journalist in the United States, was sailing around the Caribbean with two friends from Florida at the time. Always adorned in a straw hat, the cigar-smoking King is a colorful, engaging character who will charm you with stories about Belize. Try to catch him in the morning hours; he often naps in the afternoon. The coffee is fine and the art gallery marginal. King's greatest value to visitors are his publications *A Tour of Belize City South Side* and *A Tour of Belize City North Side,* which contain excellent city maps directing you to fifty-nine historic sites. *Emory King's 1990 Driver's Guide to Beautiful Belize* is the only publication approximating a detailed road guide in the entire country.

National Park and Conservation Connections: The headquarters of the Belize Audubon Society, the most influential conservation organization in Belize, is located in a small, two-story building down a driveway at 29 Regent Street (phone 02-77369). The group assists travelers by alerting park wardens via radio that visitors are coming to a park. The staff maintains radio contact with the following remote parks and monuments: Half Moon Caye Natural Monument, Hol Chan Marine Preserve, Cockscomb Basin Wildlife Sanctuary, Bermudian Landing Community Baboon Sanctuary, Guancaste National Park, and Blue Hole National Park (the one near Belmopan). The office staff is sometimes overwhelmed, so you may have to be patient. Belize Audubon can help arrange for park personnel to meet you at your desired destination, especially when your visit involves a group. They also can tell you about any special conditions involving an intended destination. You can purchase posters and literature about the parks, sanctuaries, and preserves at the Audubon office.

Programme for Belize and Chan Chich Lodge Booking Office: Located at 1 King Street are the offices of the Programme for Belize, which manages La Milpa Mayan ruins and the Rio Bravo Conservation and Management Project, encompassing 200,000 acres of rain forest. You can schedule a visit to the region here. Sharing the same floor is Chan Chich Lodge's booking office. Located in 150,000 acres of virgin jungle, Chan Chich Lodge is perhaps the most prestigious birders' lodge in Central America. Belize's leading entrepreneur, fifth-generation Belizean Barry Bowen created the lodge. Bowen works upstairs in the same building running his Coca-Cola and Beliken Beer enterprises and numerous other businesses.

St. John's Anglican Cathedral and Government House: At 71 Regent Street is St. John's Anglican Cathedral. It was built in 1812 by slaves using ballast bricks from windjammers. This holy place saw the crowning of two Mosquito Coast Indian kings — reputed to be the only kingly coronations ever to occur in an Anglican Church outside England. The kings were from local Indian groups, with the last coronation taking place in 1815. Across the street from the cathedral on well-kept, palm-studded grounds is the Government House, also built in 1812 during the colonial period. Today, the Prime Minister occasionally makes use of office space here, and high-ranking foreign officials on state business bunk here.

South Side Bus Terminals: Batty Brothers Bus Service, 15 Mosul Street (phone 02-72025), has routes that take in the Western and Northern highways to the Guatemalan and Mexican borders. Novelo's Bus Service, 54 East Collet Canal (phone 02-77372), offers many of the same routes. Venus Bus Lines on Magazine Road (phone 02-73354) travels to Dangriga and other points south. Z-Line Bus Service (phone 02-73937) also serves the south and shares the terminal with Venus.

Where to Eat in Belize City

The idea of a travel writer claiming to be an expert on where to dine in a city in which he has spent only a couple of weeks has always bothered me. Superficial coverage, influenced by the restaurant owners who latch on to the writer, is the product of such writings. Instead of being part of this problem, I asked Australian-born Meb Cutlack, a longtime resident of Belize City and a self-professed expert on local restaurants, to lend his assessment of local eateries to this book. Cutlack is editor of the *Belize Review* and is well known throughout Belize for stating things exactly as he sees them.

Meb's advice on where to eat in Belize City: "The problem with the answer is that it usually invites a listing of all the obvious places — the upscale hotels and restaurants — and listing their best-known dishes. Try the stuffed grouper at Four Fort Street (E) (4 Fort Street), the giant crab claws or the stuffed steak at the Raddison Fort George (E) (2 Marine Parade), the shrimp at the Chateau Caribbean (E) (6 Marine Parade), and the stuffed steak at The Grill (E) (164 Newtown Barracks).

"But wait. There's more to eating out in Belize City than the obvious places or the obvious dishes. The patio restaurant at G.G.'s (M) at 2B King Street serves a delicious broiled fish, a mouth-watering fried chicken, good inexpensive wine, and a homemade hot sauce that aficionados cross the continent to reach. For good Mexican food there's a tiny place on the corner of King Street and East Canal called the Mexican Corner (B) that produces fresh fruit juices, tamales, tacos, a spiced 'Kiki' chicken dish, good escabeche, and a fine black chicken chimole. Macy's Cafe (B), a corner away on Bishop Street [and which Harrison Ford described as his favorite restaurant in the world], serves delicious Belizean food, including game meat such as gibnut and an exceptional chicken curry (usually on Friday night). For the adventurous, trying missing breakfast at your Belize City hotel and head for the Belize City Market (B). You'll find small food stalls offering plates with johnnycakes, fried beans and eggs, Mexican tacos, scrambled eggs and lobster, or a variety of dishes and hot coffee, and all for a couple of dollars. Another small favorite of mine is Gon's (B) on the corner of Hyde's Lane and Barracks Road. It looks like no more than a lean-to but has the best garnaches, tacos, and tamales of any place in town.

"Out of the way, down toward the bottom of Regent Street, is Orchida House (M), a guesthouse and small restaurant that is different but good, and if you don't mind a short drive out of town, there's Mohammed's (B), at about the four-mile mark on the Western Highway, where there's always good chicken, rice, and beans, and cold, cold beer. In contrast, on the other side of town and about three miles out is the Belize Biltmore Plaza hotel restaurant (E), which is very elegant indeed. When it really comes down to it, two of my other favorite eating places in Belize (but not in Belize City), are Elvie's Restaurant (M) in San Pedro on Ambergris Caye and, on the truly economical side, Eva's (M) in San Ignacio. Of course, in San Ignacio, the San Ignacio Hotel (M) now serves fine food, and Chaa Creek Cottages (E) out toward the Guatemalan border is worth the detour— try the avocado mousse!"

I have three additions to Meb's list. Earl's Cafe (M) (formerly the Sunnyside Restaurant), located on North Front Street just north of the Swing Bridge, overlooks picturesque Haulover Creek, which is filled with old sailing boats. Proprietor Robert Argue is the former chef at the Raddison Fort George restaurant. The seafood and lasagne are terrific. The Katie House (B, M), opened in 1993 by longtime master cook Cajeo Flowers and located in the Belize City Market on the South Side of the Swing Bridge, offers a tasty assortment of short-order dishes. Mom's Triangle Inn (B, M), 11 Handyside Street, serves up tasty meals.

Accommodations

There is no shortage of hotel space in and around Belize City. In fact, long-established hoteliers in Belize City and San Pedro confided that a building boom to create new hotel space far exceeded the demand and that the U.S. economic recession had slowed tourism below expectations. The result has been competitive prices among hoteliers. This is the good news. The bad news is that unfortunately most of the newly constructed space is aimed at the high end of the market; and though there are places with budget prices as low as U.S. $14, expect spartan conditions, as well as possibly minimal security and shared bathroom facilities. Ferreting out the good-quality, moderately priced places became the challenge for me. I found striking differences among comparably priced hotels in terms of location, view, cleanliness, dining, connections with the conservation community and recreational businesses, and security.

Expect to pay an extra 15 percent to 20 percent above the listed hotel price once you factor in a service charge, tip, and up to a 3 percent handling charge if you use a credit card. Major credit cards are accepted in all but a few of Belize City's hotels.

Budget: The Seaside Guest House (B), 3 Prince Street (phone 02-78339), may be the best deal in town in this price range. The rooms are small, clean, and cooled by sea breezes. There is no hot water and the bathroom is shared. German-born proprietor Mary Jo Prost is helpful in arranging for sightseeing and is knowledgeable about transportation. The guesthouse is located near downtown and bus terminals. Other budget hotels that appear well run are the North Front Street Guest House (B), 124 North Front Street (phone 02-77595), and the Mira Rio Hotel (B), 59 North Front Street (phone 02-44970).

Moderate: The Fort Street Guesthouse (M, E) is a beautiful old colonial run by former Coloradan Rachel Emmer. Accommodations are upstairs above the Four Fort Street restaurant in large rooms with wooden shutters and slow-moving ceiling fans. The restaurant is one of the best and most popular in town. Rachel has close ties with conservationists throughout Belize and is knowledgeable about inland tours and cayes. You can obtain quality advice to help fine-tune your travel plans here. Contact the Fort Street Guesthouse, 4 Fort Street, P.O. Box 3, Belize City, Belize, C.A. (phone 02-30116; in the United States and Canada, 1-800-538-6802; fax in Belize, 02-78808).

The Belize Guest House is another colonial jewel (more attractive on the inside than the outside) in the moderate price range. It is located on the North Side and is right on the water. Proprietor Charles Hope, a former justice of the peace, lives here and has created an atmosphere that is more like a shared residence than a hotel. There's a small library and sitting room. The rooms for rent collect wonderful sea breezes, and some are spacious. Kitchen facilities

Typical colonial architecture: Four Fort Street, a hotel and restaurant in Belize City. *Photo by Eric Hoffman.*

are available for guests. There is also a detached bungalow right on the water that would be hard to beat for romance or quiet contemplation. Charles Hope is a warm and gentlemanly host and helpful in procuring a car at a good price. Rooms rent from U.S. $33 to U.S. $44. Contact the Belize Guest House, 2 Hutson Street (and Marine Parade), Belize City, Belize, C.A. (phone 02-77569).

Also on the foreshore down Marine Parade past Memorial Park is the Chateau Caribbean, a well-kept colonial structure facing the Caribbean. It is owned by Vera Lo, whose grandfather was among the first Chinese immigrants to the region. Most travel guides list the Chateau Caribbean with the upscale hotels, but with rooms starting at U.S. $50 and U.S. $80 (the latter for luxury), it can also be considered in the moderate price range. I ate excellent lobster at the restaurant here, but my most memorable experience was taxi driver Gilbert Andrews, who claims the Chateau Caribbean as his turf. For U.S. $10 he drove me all over the city for four hours, showing me the sights most important to him. Our first stop was Prime Minister George Price's modest residence. "I can go talk to the Prime Minister when I got a problem," declared Gilbert. "Once a week any citizen can come here and discuss matters. Only Belize has this." Gilbert is an elderly, Jamaican-born Belizean with twenty-eight children to his credit. He also had four wives " . . . Two moved away and two died." Gilbert has a strong sense of civic pride. He received a Citation for Valiance for jumping from his cab and stopping a mugging of a tourist. A news account of the incident explained that the rescued tourist was taken to his destination free of charge by Gilbert. "It wouldn't have been right to charge the man for his troubles, because the man had not asked for a lift. I was extending my hand to a man who needed help," explained Gilbert. If he's still in front of the Chateau Caribbean, have him take you around town. Contact the Chateau Caribbean, 6 Marine Parade, Belize City, Belize, C.A. (phone 02-30800; fax 02-30900).

Mom's Triangle Inn, near the Swing Bridge on the North Side, is also popular with conservation-minded travelers. Proprietor Sue Williams has strong ties with the Belize Zoo and Tropical Education Center. The inn is a homey place with rooms from U.S. $20 to U.S. $35 with and without air-conditioning. (Sue's brother, Jim Black, owns Blackline Marine two miles north of town. Blackline handles trips to see manatees in the Southern Lagoon and has the only full-service dive supply in Belize City, plus dive and fishing charters.) However, if you're allergic to cats or dogs, stay away from Mom's. Sue provides a homey atmosphere, which includes getting to know her three cats and one small dog. Mom's only drawbacks are that there is no ocean view and it lacks the trade winds common in many other accommodations to cool the rooms. Contact Mom's Triangle Inn, 11 Handyside Street (phone 02-45523).

On the South Side, both the Mopan Hotel, 55 Regent Street (phone 02-77351), and the Orchida House, 56 Regent Street (phone 02-74266/74642), are well-run, clean, full-service accommodations.

Expensive: For in-city, my favorite is the Bellevue Hotel, located on the South Side near the Bliss Institute. It's easy to forget you're in Belize City while staying in the Bellevue. From the hotel to its dock is only a few steps, and from there it's a pleasant thirty-minute boat ride to St. George's Caye, to the Cottage Colony—two rows of tidy cottages with a restaurant/bar and a snorkeling, diving, sail charter operation—which is also owned by Bellevue co-owner Roger Dinger's family. Dinger is an unforgettable character whose fish stories ought not to be believed. The cottages and diving operation are favorites of U.S. Embassy personnel. At the Bellevue's restaurant, the wines are European, but not pricey, and the seafood menu has excellent selections. The ambience in the dining area is casual but tasteful. The Bellevue's bar has an excellent view of the harbor and is an attractive and popular meeting place for business types and tourists alike. Rooms are spacious. There's a swimming pool and dancing some nights. The Bellevue also has an in-house tour operation for day trips to ruins, the Belize Zoo, and other destinations. Considering the ambience and convenience, the rates are reasonable at about U.S. $80 for a single or double. Contact the Bellevue Hotel, 5 Foreshore, P.O. Box 428, Belize City, Belize, C.A. (phone 02-77051; fax 02-73253).

Another top-of-the-line in-city hotel is the Raddison Fort George. Besides rooms in the motel section, the Fort George has luxury suites with sea views that are comparable to deluxe rooms anywhere in the world. The hotel has comfortable bars and a swimming pool. The hotel's manager, Paul Hunt, an English hotelier, has run the Fort George for twenty years and has developed keen insights into and contacts with Belize's domestic travel industry. The gift shop offers the most complete selection of publications about Belize of all the city's hotels and a nice variety of wood carvings and clothing, though most of it is a little overpriced. If you're serious about exploring Belize's islands, buy the *Cruising Guide to Belize and Mexico's Caribbean Coast,* by Freya Rauscher, which is sold here. This is mostly a sailing guide, but the detail is impressive and usable for snorkeling, diving, and island-hopping as well. I found the Fort George pricey, but impressively run, especially for a tiny country such as Belize. Rooms range from U.S. $100 to U.S. $165 a night. Contact the Raddison Fort George, 2 Marine Parade, Box 321, Belize City, Belize, C.A. (phone 02-77400; fax 02-73820). In 1993 the Raddison Fort George purchased the adjacent Holiday Inn Villa Belize, which was on par with the Fort George in every way. This merger puts 108 rooms under the control of a single company well known for its cuisine and quality room service.

Last but not least of the upscale hotels I can recommend from firsthand experience is the Belize Biltmore Plaza, located three miles out of town on the Northern Highway. In operation since 1990, the Biltmore's primary advantage over the competition is its location out of town, making it the nearest quality hotel to the international airport and a place to stay for visitors who do not want to visit Belize City proper. With Budget Rent A Car directly across the road, visitors can stay at the Biltmore, rent a car, and visit the parks, Mayan ruins, and wildlife areas and never set foot in Belize City. The rooms and service are comparable to Travel Lodge chains in the United States. Manager Paul Mills, an Englishman with decades of hotel management in Guatemala under his belt, is a caring person who will go out of his way to help visitors make key contacts. He has especially strong ties with Mountain Equestrian Trails, one of the top mountain lodges in the Cayo District that regularly takes visitors to the Mayan ruins at Caracol. Mills's interpersonal skills no doubt account for the friendliness of his staff, the most responsive I met in Belize. The Biltmore is the preferred hotel of international business travelers. The restaurant's reasonably priced meals range in quality from adequate to excellent; the fish and chicken dishes were my favorites. The bar scene here is a mixed bag of English military officers, expatriates of various origins, and Belizean business types; there aren't many tourists. Rooms range from U.S. $50 to U.S. $75. Contact the Belize Biltmore Plaza, Mile 3 Northern Highway, Belize, C.A. (phone 02-32302; in the United States and Canada, 1-800-327-3573; fax in Belize, 02-30132).

Getting Around Belize City

By Cab: There are cabs waiting at Phillip Goldson International Airport and the Belize City Municipal Airport. Expect to pay between U.S. $15 and U.S. $20 for the ride into town from the international airport and about U.S. $7 from the municipal airport. A cab can be distinguished from a private vehicle only by its green license plate. Contacts: Albert Street Stand (South Side business district), phone 02-72888; Cinderella Plaza taxi stand (North Side, near buses), phone 02-45240.

By Car: Driving in Belize City is a challenge, but the small size of the city makes it hard to stay lost for long. The twisting, narrow, one-way streets—which become gridlocked at 5:00 P.M. quitting time each day—are as frustrating as they are quaint. Before making a turn, always look carefully for an arrow indicating the traffic direction and look for a red circle with a line through it, meaning no entry. Some streets change from two-way to one-way and are signposted with a no-entry sign. It is easy to become completely lost in Belize City without a road map. Even with a road map you'll be challenged to find your way with the many one-way roads and the sometimes nonexistent street signs. Just when you identify the street you're looking for, you'll notice it is one-way, the wrong way. As frustration begins to mount, keep in mind that for every one-way street going the wrong way, just one block away a street will be going the opposite way — usually. Any car rental agency will have a map of Belize City. I've found it helpful to use a felt-tipped marker to trace my route on a map prior to getting under way. A quick glance while driving allows me to find my place on the map.

By Bus: All of Belize's bus lines — Batty Brothers (phone 02-72025); Novelo's (phone 02-77372); Venus (phone 02-77354); and Z-Line (phone 02-73937) — deposit incoming passengers on the South Side of town. It is usually a fairly substantial distance from the respective bus depots to most hotels. Lugging suitcases through the back streets of Belize City isn't recommended for comfort and safety reasons. You can take a cab to the hotel of your choice for a few dollars. Usually there are cabs close at hand.

By Boat: *Miss Belize,* which docks behind the Supreme Court Building, and *Andera,* which docks at the Bellevue Hotel pier, run regularly between Belize City and San Pedro on Ambergris Caye. (See "Ambergris Caye" for details.) *Pegasus, Soledad,* and other boats run regularly from Caye Caulker and dock at the Shell Station on North Front Street. (See "Caye Caulker" for details.)

Caution: Aggressive Panhandling

For many visitors to Belize City the panhandler hassle factor is the biggest detraction. This usually occurs in the form of a pushy character who requests (or demands) money or that you purchase some dope. Giving to the downtrodden is, of course, a personal decision. Belize City has its soup kitchen, and its government officials boast that nobody goes wanting for food. The beggars causing the trouble are clearly able-bodied.

Compared to panhandlers in the United States, those in Belize City are often surprisingly articulate, aggressive, at times affable, and sometimes verbally abusive, especially to women. Put in perspective,

Belize City's crime problems don't come close to the level of violence or callousness in American cities with a similar-size population. A substantial effort by police, with positive results, is under way in Belize City, though more progress needs to be made. Badgering, not the use of weapons, is the preferred panhandler technique in Belize City. And, Belizean citizens will usually come to the aid of a person being harassed, if they are aware of it. Still, the U.S. State Department's travel advisory on Belize specifically states that "Visitors are advised not to walk alone on city streets, especially at night." The State Department also notes that "Thousands of tourists and business travelers visit Belize each year and the vast majority experience no problems during their stay."

Some victims set themselves up and learn a lesson. In talking with U.S. Embassy personnel, it appeared that some mugging victims may have been shopping for illegal drugs in the worst part of the city after dark.

Belize's panhandlers prey on people who appear vulnerable. They watch for people who appear lost or dress in a way that distinguishes them as foreigners. The nerdier-looking and smaller in stature the potential victim, the bolder and more intimidating the panhandler. If you wear jewelry and tote expensive camera gear, expect to be hassled. Your show of wealth acts as a lure.

Avoiding hassles is usually a matter of blending in. When I was in Belize City I dressed in casual long pants, conventional shoes, and a long-sleeved dress shirt, and I carried a spiral notebook. I deliberately did not look like a tourist. A panhandler couldn't tell if I was an evangelical Christian on a mission or a businessman, both less attractive marks than a tourist. It's also worth mentioning that after I became a semifamiliar face on the streets of Belize City, I was entirely ignored by those who'd approached me earlier. It was then that I truly began to appreciate Belize City and its many fine citizens.

What should you do if confronted? Don't linger long. Whatever is said between you and a panhandler should be said without your breaking stride. The encounter is a test of wills that is best dealt with by behaving calmly but with a response that takes the panhandler out of his game. Stopping or appearing intimidated or flustered is what the panhandler wants. To the demand for money I sometimes hand over a dozen coins tightly wadded up in a small amount of paper money. I carry this "donation" in my hand. If approached, I hand over the money rapidly without breaking stride, as if I'm dropping it into a Salvation Army cup. The recipient stops to unravel what I've handed him, giving me ample time to move on. In other cases I've said, "Sorry, I just gave my money to a guy on the last block. Maybe some other time," or "I gave you money last week. Find a new person." To demands to buy dope, I say, "I don't use dope. Sorry," or, to the aggressive pusher, "Wait here. I'll be back in half an hour. I have to get my partner." As the guy ponders what this means, I move on. The next day the same guy will wave and smile, acknowledging me in a warm manner. He doesn't approach, knowing it won't get him anything.

Finally, as a general rule, always ask hotel staff about the relative safety of where you intend to go in Belize City, and don't walk the streets at night.

Crooked Tree Wildlife Sanctuary

Created in 1984 and located thirty-three miles north of Belize City, Crooked Tree Wildlife Sanctuary is a maze of connected lagoons that is habitat for hundreds of species of birds. Most visitors hire a guide with a small boat to tour the wetlands, which is the best way to sample the magnitude of the bird life that congregates here. You can also take walks along the shoreline and through the classic rural Creole community of Crooked Tree. A day or two here is well worth it, especially from February through May, the time of greatest bird concentrations as many species collect en masse before migrating north.

There are 520 species of birds in Belize; 370 of them are permanent residents. The remainder are migratory birds that come and go from North America, so don't be surprised if you see a warbler that looks like the bird you last saw sitting on your backyard fence at home. Many of the birds in Crooked Tree are exotic-looking tropicals unfamiliar to most North Americans and Europeans.

The people of Crooked Tree are generally friendly and usually belong to large, tightly knit extended families. It seems like half the village's last name is Tillet. The casually laid out village affords a glimpse of traditional rural Creole life. Founded in the early 1800s as a logging village, Crooked Tree is one of the oldest rural villages in Belize and until recently was reached only by boat via the Belize River and Black Creek. Though the sanctuary status of the area is changing the local economy and has put the village's inhabitants in constant contact with the outside world, the pace and ambience has changed little in the last twenty years. You'll see Creole "plantations" (actually small farms) and a rural lifestyle not readily experienced by most short-term visitors to Belize. And, unlike my experience at Bermudian Landing, I wasn't hustled for a few extra dollars. The temperament and attitude of the citizens of Crooked Tree was refreshingly noncommercial and warm.

Besides tourism as a new income source, villagers continue to reap the riches from a healthy fishery in the nearby lagoons, pick mangoes and cashews from the impressive 100-year-old trees, and manage their farms and livestock. The ambience is casual, slow-paced, and friendly. The staff at the small Crooked Tree Wildlife Sanctuary Visitors' Centre at the sanctuary office (just off the road to the right as you leave the causeway and enter the village) was the friendliest and most cooperative I dealt with during my travels in Belize. The Visitors' Centre has well-designed interpretative displays that quiz you on your knowledge of habitats and identification of native species.

Plentiful Bird Life: Crooked Tree Sanctuary is a wetlands with many distinct habitats, which partly accounts for the wide variety of birds. Four kinds of kingfishers nest here. The largest is the ringed kingfisher, a sixteen-inch gray-blue bird with a rust-colored chest and distinctive crest. The rest of this family is progressively smaller in stature. The Amazon, green, and pygmy kingfishers have green backs with varying degrees of rust on their chests. They all hunt fish in a similar fashion, by diving headlong into the water, often after hovering for an instant. The white ibis and roseate spoonbill are two of the more exotic-looking large birds here. The ibis pokes its long beak into soft mud to extract a meal, and the spoonbill sifts delicately through shallow water for small invertebrates. Northern jacanas, with their oversized feet for creeping about on lily pads and bright yellow underwings that flash when the bird flies, are especially plentiful. Practically every heron in the Americas is represented here. On a one-day outing I saw bare-throated tiger herons, boat-billed herons, yellow-crowned night herons, green-backed herons, little blue herons, and great blue herons, along with great egrets, snowy egrets, and cattle egrets. During the wet season the wading birds are particularly plentiful along the causeway that connects Crooked Tree to the Northern Highway. Belize's two native ducks—the black-bellied whistling duck and the Muscovy duck—nest in trees near the lagoons. Both duck species are large. The male Muscovy has a bare, red, knobby face, which distinguishes it from a distance. On the woodland fringing the lagoons and in large trees along the banks of creeks and in the village I noticed quite a few forest species: parrots, toucans, and warblers.

Specialized raptors are also plentiful. The snail kite is the most specialized. It dips into the water and retrieves apple snails, its primary diet. Ospreys and black-collared hawks are more exciting to watch as they snatch fish that dare swim along the surface. But the biggest treat is the peregrine falcon. During a visit in the wet season (June through August), which is the poorest birding period, I saw one of these amazing birds hunt. Capable of speeds of 175 miles per hour, a peregrine in a hunting mode is an unforgettable sight. My guide first saw the peregrine fluttering along the shore in short, choppy wing strokes. He cut our boat's motor and we silently witnessed the bird as it began a shallow dive with long, powerful strokes until it became a blur due to its incredible speed. It streaked across the sky in the direction of a flock of coots and northern jacanas on the surface of the lagoon. The jacanas knew what to do. They all dived under the water. The coots flew. Then—*wham*—the peregrine smashed into a coot and it dropped like a rock from the sky. Before it hit the water the peregrine dived and grabbed it. Flapping its wings vigorously to stay airborne, the peregrine carried its meal toward the forest from which it had come.

The endangered jabiru stork, which stands five feet tall with an incredible ten-foot wingspan, also lives in the sanctuary. It is thought that the largest nesting population of jabirus in Central America resides in Belize. Still, this only amounts to about thirty birds. They nest in lowland pine savanna areas. Two, possibly three, pairs are known to nest in the sanctuary. The birds arrive each November and disperse themselves throughout Belize; then they congregate in April and May at Crooked Tree and wetlands in southern Mexico. With the onset of the rainy season they fly to North America. This large white stork can be confused with the smaller wood stork, which also has a white-plumed body. Seen side by side, the jabiru is clearly much bigger. The wood stork has black on its wings and tail; the jabiru's wings and tail are only white. The wood stork also has a straight beak and gray head, while the jabiru has a beak that curves slightly up and a black head with a distinctive red collar separating its head from its white body. Consider yourself lucky to see a wood stork and doubly lucky to see a jabiru.

Black Creek: If you take extra time to investigate Black Creek, which connects the lagoons to the Belize River, there's a chance you'll see iguanas, Morlet's crocodiles, hikatees (endangered large turtles), black howler monkeys, and coatimundis. The large trees along Black Creek also harbor jungle bird species. You may see toucans and several species of parrots. Some of the lagoons and connecting waterways worth a visit are Crooked Tree Lagoon (also called Northern Lagoon), which is the starting place for most visitors; Spanish Creek (including Sapodilla Lagoon); Western Lagoon; Revenge Lagoon; and Calabash Lagoon. Guides will know what each area has to offer. The route I took from the sanctuary headquarters to the upper end of Black Creek, Southern Lagoon, and Spanish Creek took the better part of a day, but it was well worth it. This is a commonly visited route because it takes in much of the rich diversity Crooked Tree has to offer. All of the waterways are explored in aluminum boats with small outboard motors.

Walking Trails: There are also several short hiking trails in the village. The Limpkin Trail is suitable only in April and May. According to Donald Tillet, the warden at the time of my visit, the Trogon Trail is excellent in the morning and evening for birders wanting to see forest and wetland species. The Jacana Loop Trail, which starts at the Visitors' Centre, is also highly recommended. Much of this trail travels along the lagoon. For details on the trails, talk with the warden.

Mayan Ruins: Chau Hiix (pronounced Chow Heech), which means "jaguarundi" (one of Belize's five kinds of wild cat) in Mayan, is the name of small, but interesting, unexcavated Mayan ruins in the Spanish Creek area. A lodge with the same name (see "Accommodations") is nearby these ruins and has posted a guard to prevent looting. There is a special feeling to the place, perhaps because we arrived by boat through endless lily pads and hiked a short distance through jungle. The ruins are comprised of middle-size pyramids long ago reclaimed by jungle. Some partial clearing and archaeological activities have removed enough undergrowth to enable visitors to see the outlines of the larger structures. Judging by the pottery shards and stone fragments strewn around, this sight has not had many visitors.

Hiring a Guide: The only way to fully appreciate Crooked Tree is by small boat. You can probably rent a boat on your own (motorized, rowboat, or canoe), but the complex waterways connecting the maze of lagoons would undoubtedly result in wasted time and possibly getting lost. The guides on call from the sanctuary headquarters are generally knowledgeable about bird life and know the sanctuary extremely well. For this reason I recommend hiring a guide and a boat, not just a boat. Generally, guides with an aluminum boat equipped with an outboard motor hire by the half-day for a set price no matter how many are in the party (six is the capacity of most boats). Expect a half-day to run between U.S. $50 and U.S. $100 per boat. Don't be shy about asking the guide to cut the motor when you want silence.

The Belize Audubon Society (phone 02-77369) can contact the sanctuary's Visitors' Centre and arrange for a boat and guide. If this can't be done, you can call 02-44101, the number of Crooked Tree's public phone. A call to the public phone requires that the person taking the call relay your request to the warden, who will do his best to procure a villager with a boat. But don't expect a return call as confirmation since the warden would have to pay for it. If you arrive at the sanctuary unannounced, as most people do, and the warden is not in, ask for assistance at Jax Shop, which is fifty yards past the Visitors' Centre.

Be Prepared: Expect a warm tropical day, but also prepare for rain. Protection from the sun is essential. Keep in mind that weather conditions can change rapidly and you may find yourself in a small boat for two to five hours. If you're prone to motion sickness, take the appropriate medication. Carry a good pair of binoculars and, before leaving for Belize, purchase a copy of *Mexican Birds*, a 298-page Peterson Field Guide by Roger Tory Peterson and Edward L. Chalif. This is the best bird book I found for birds of this region. It retails for about $20. The book can't be purchased in Belize, but the guides at Crooked Tree are familiar with it and also highly recommend it.

Accommodations: There are a number of interesting places to stay in and around Crooked Tree, and most of them fall into the budget category of less than U.S. $26 per night. Since there are no street numbers and only a public phone at Crooked Tree, review the map of Crooked Tree to find your way. All accommodations, except for Chau Hiix Lodge, can be reached on foot from the Visitors' Centre. Always inquire about acceptable forms of payment because some places only accept cash.

Chau Hiix Lodge (E) is the most exotic place to stay in the area and also the most expensive. Located by water about forty-five minutes and nine miles south of the sanctuary's Visitors' Centre on Spanish Creek, Chau Hiix Lodge is definitely isolated and unique. New manager Steve Sanders, a West Virginian, has refurbished the lodge, which is made of a colorful assortment of native woods. The main lodge has a spacious dining room and library, and the separate sleeping areas are solid mahogany duplexes outfitted for four people. All units have private baths, maid service, and meals. The lodge will not cater to more than fourteen guests at a time, which guarantees the solitude and quality of your interaction with nature. A favorite activity for many guests is canoeing through the wetlands. The lodge's property includes 4000 acres of jungle populated with a plethora of Belizean wildlife. The lodge sits on the water's edge facing the swollen part of Spanish Creek known as Sapodilla Lagoon. The nearby Mayan ruins of Chau Hiix, the lodge's namesake, is another excursion. My visit did not include meals or the daily routine, but if appearances, location, and setting matter, this place appears hard to beat. Naturally, the combination of a civilized lodge and such a remote setting costs. A three-night, four-day individual package exclusive of airfare runs U.S. $525. A four-night, five-day package costs U.S. $635, and a seven-night, eight-day stay costs U.S. $935. For more information, contact Steve Sanders, Chau Hiix Lodge, P.O. Box 185, Flatwoods, WV 26621. An additional contact in the United States and Canada is P.O. Box 1072, Sanford, FL 3277 (phone 1-800-765-2611).

There are other offerings at Crooked Tree. O and Maggie Rahburn call their place the Local Guest House (B), though there is no name as such identifying it. The Rahburns' accommodation has four spacious rooms, each for U.S. $15 per night; three meals a day for U.S. $10; and a shared toilet facility. Cuisine is Spanish and Creole. Phone 02-44101 (the public phone). Crooked Tree Hotel and Cabanas (M, E) has five thatched-roof cabanas, all with running water and fans but no air-conditioning. Prices range from U.S. $50 for a single-bed cabana to U.S. $60 for a double. Rudolph Crawford, one of the two owners, claims his Belizean dishes are the best part of his menu. Rudolph can take bookings in the United States at 718-498-6019. Across from the post office is Steve Tillet and Sons Enterprises (B), which rents rooms for economy travelers. Steve seemed to be a solid citizen and is a member of the village council. Rooms rent for U.S. $10 per person and U.S. $3 per meal. During my visit the women of the Tillet clan were cooking a wonderful meal. Meals vary but are strictly Belizean. I had fried fish, Creole bread, beans, rice, chicken, and a Beliken beer. Steve says he can take people to the jabiru nests, which makes sense since his nephew is a sanctuary warden. The Crooked Tree Resort (E) has a series of cozy, thatched-roof cabanas with a lagoon view. The resort has a dining area and comes with optional activities of horseback riding, boat rentals, and guided sightseeing. Phone 02-77745. The Maruba Resort and Jungle Spa (E) is a true luxury resort with a hedonistic flair that is competitive with any international standard. It is forty-five minutes away from Crooked Tree in nearby Maskall. Phone 03-22199; in the United States and Canada, 1-800-627-8227.

Access: Crooked Tree is thirty-three miles north of Belize City on the Northern Highway. The village is two miles west of the Northern Highway on a dirt road that travels along the top of the new causeway that links it to outside motor vehicle traffic. Check with Batty Brothers (phone 02-72025) and Venus (phone 02-73354) bus lines, which run between Belize City and Crooked Tree. Also, the Belize Audubon Society, 29 Regent Street, Belize City (phone 02-77369), can coordinate group visits with the sanctuary office.

Bermudian Landing Community Baboon Sanctuary

The Bermudian Landing Community Baboon Sanctuary, which protects black howler monkeys (called baboons by local Creole people), is one of the most innovative low-budget conservation programs in

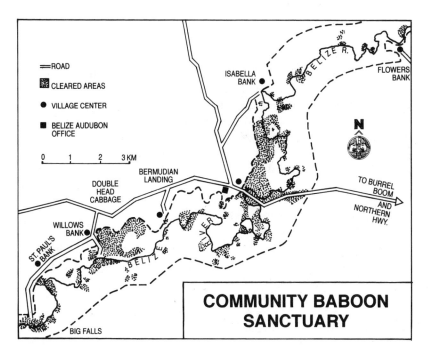

**COMMUNITY BABOON
SANCTUARY**

Map legend:
- ROAD
- CLEARED AREAS
- VILLAGE CENTER
- BELIZE AUDUBON OFFICE

0 1 2 3 KM

ISABELLA BANK
FLOWERS BANK
BELIZE R.
BERMUDIAN LANDING
DOUBLE HEAD CABBAGE
WILLOWS BANK
ST. PAUL'S BANK
BELIZE RIVER
BIG FALLS
N
TO BURREL BOOM AND NORTHERN HWY.

the world. Around Bermudian Landing the protection afforded black howlers and their habitat is provided by local Creole subsistence farmers on a voluntary basis. Black howler monkeys are one of two species of monkeys living in Belize, the other being the spider monkey. Both species are listed as endangered by CITES (Convention on International Trade in Endangered Species).

A trip to Bermudian Landing guarantees sighting the usually sleepy, but sometimes active and noisy, howlers in the low treetops along the Belize River, where they live in proximity to many other kinds of creatures also protected by this unique program.

Other Life Forms and the Creole Dialect: Besides visiting with monkeys, Bermudian Landing offers a glimpse of rural life on Creole "plantations," the word Creoles use for small farms. The villagers you meet may speak English and Belizean Creole plus blends of both. To North Americans who visit Bermudian Landing most of what the villagers say is generally understandable, except for the names used to identify many of the kinds of wild creatures in the sanctuary. In the interest of understanding your Creole hosts in Bermuda Landing and adjoining villages, here are some English-to-Creole translations: coatimundi (quash), agouti (rabbit), kinkajou (honey bear), armadillo (harmadillo), gibnut (paca), brown jay (piam piam), and spiny-tailed iguana (wish-willy). Also living in the area, but more difficult to find, are the jaguar (tiger), ocelot (also tiger), manatee (sea cow), hikatee (jicotea), Morlet's crocodile (alligator), and the red-eyed tree frog. The green iguana (bamboo chicken) is common, as are dozens of bird species. More than 200 bird species have been sighted in the area. Montezuma oropendulas are among the most interesting, with their woven nests hanging from treetops. There are also warblers, at least a dozen species of blackbirds, kingfishers, raptors, parrots, and wading birds.

The Black Howler Program: The program to protect black howlers was the brainchild of Dr. Robert Horwich, a U.S. biologist who visited the low, riverine forest while studying primates in 1984. The black howler is one of six species of howlers, all living in Central and South America. The black howler (*Alouatta pigra*) prefers lowland river environments in diverse broadleaf secondary-growth forests such as those found along the Belize River and its tributaries. Throughout much of its range, which includes parts of Mexico and Guatemala, hunting and habitat destruction had eliminated black howlers. In much of Belize, but particularly in Bermudian Landing and nearby communities, the villagers and monkeys had been living side by side for generations. Molesting the monkeys had been a long-standing taboo, but howlers were still vulnerable to loss of habitat from farmers who cleared the jungle for crops and pasture.

"Dr. Rob," as the villagers call him, met with the community council and pointed out the importance of preserving the trees essential to the howlers' well-being. He also proposed that individual farmers create a sanctuary by dedicating portions of their land to the monkeys. This was no easy decision for subsistence farmers whose cultivated land provides their livelihood. Key to Dr. Rob's plan was maintaining the trees along the riverbanks in corridors about twenty-five yards wide and preserving trees in areas away from the river that are sources of food or aerial pathways used by the monkeys to get from one place to another. In the beginning, eleven farmers joined the plan, which protected about 150 monkeys. Three years later, more than a hundred farmers had joined the plan, protecting more than 1000 monkeys and involving several communities with the novel names of Double Head Cabbage, Big Falls, Flowers Bank, Isabella Bank, Saint Paul's Bank, Scotland Half Moon, and Willows Bank.

The Belizean Audubon Society, in conjunction with the World Wildlife Fund and other organizations, funded a manager's position for the sanctuary and materials to build a natural history museum. The villagers donated their labor and constructed a metal-roofed structure that contains exhibits devoted to the black howler monkey. Villagers have hacked trails in the dense forest where they take visitors to view howlers. A guide from the turquoise-colored natural history museum and headquarters guides visitors. From the sanctuary office/museum the short walk to and from the howlers, plus camera time, takes about an hour or two. The nominal fee, about U.S. $10, for this service goes toward salaries plus maintaining the museum and trails.

In one area, where a group of howlers known as the Fig Tree Troop cross the road to reach their favorite fig tree, a suspension ladder was constructed so that the monkeys can avoid traffic and hostile dogs from the villages. This group, which is on the southwest side of the Belize River near the bridge in Bermudian Landing, is often easy to photograph. To locate the Fig Tree Troop, stop your car near the suspension ladder — signposted "Caution: Baboon Bridge" and for monkeys only — crossing the road and look in the large fig trees south of the road. The School Troop, which lives in the center of the village near the school, is also easily approachable.

About the Black Howler: A male howler's roar can be mistaken for that of a jaguar. It's that loud. The deafening noise is a territorial vocalization of immense proportion for a mere fifteen-pound monkey. As a male howler matures, a resonating chamber in his throat develops and acts as a bellows to amplify his roar, which is audible for a mile or more. The roaring usually takes place at dawn and dusk, when males bellow their presence to the next nearest territorial male, which often bellows in return. Females also roar, but less often and in higher-pitched tones. This dawn and dusk roaring allows troops to keep well apart and avoid fighting. Two troops that suddenly come upon each other can provide a truly memorable sight. The troops will bluff (much neck rubbing, body posturing, and short charges) and roar until the troop that has crossed into the other's territory retreats. Troops are usually most active at dawn and dusk, when it's cooler.

Local Creoles will tell you that howlers roar more often when it rains. In their research, Dr. Robert Horwich and Jonathan Lyon found that there is some truth to this, but they also found that howlers will begin roaring at other steady sounds — such as those of a car engine, wood chopping, or a barking dog — as well as at the pitter-patter of rain.

Each troop is made up of a dominant male and two to ten females and their babies. The troop lives in a specific territory ranging in size from two to twenty-five acres. Though the monkeys are rather sluggish during the hottest period of the day, you may still see entertaining behavior. Monkey business includes grooming one another and flirtation, which is manifested when howlers of the opposite sex stick out their tongues at each other or stare for a prolonged time into each other's eyes. This may precede copulating, which is done safely aloft with the help of each animal's tail, which serves to anchor the howler to a branch. Watch for baby monkeys clinging to the undersides of their mothers or riding on their backs. Baby howlers are incredibly cute, mischievous, and curious. If you are very still and lucky, a young monkey's curiosity may compel it to descend within feet of you to investigate the odd-looking, clothed primate in their midst. Youngsters living on the Belize River have been known to yank on the tail of a basking iguana and watch it launch itself into the river.

Nature Walks: There are two nature trails. The first and most used trail starts at the sanctuary office and heads past the school into the low trees, a distance of less than a half-mile. However, perhaps the best nature viewing in the sanctuary is on the self-guided Nature Trail near the Belize River. There are twenty-five numbered posts on this trail. Each numbered post is meant to draw your attention to a unique plant or creature. The trail takes about an hour to complete and is longer in distance than the usual tour that commences at the sanctuary's office. The self-guided walk takes in the cohune palm and riverine flora environments while skirting the Belize River. Besides being clued in on the flora, you'll see monkeys, green iguanas, and the spiny-tailed iguana (wish-willy), plus a variety of tropical birds.

If the above seems too strenuous or adventuresome for you, the vantage point from the nearby bridge over the Belize River also

affords excellent wildlife viewing. Often, monkeys can be seen forag-
ing in branches overhanging the river. Among the monkeys you'll
see mature green iguanas, whose scientific name is *Iguana iguana,* the
same iguana sold in pet stores in the United States. In the sanctuary
it is protected, but throughout much of Belize it is used for food
and known as bamboo chicken. The lizard's dietary value to local
people has severely impacted its distribution in much of Central
America. Often seen as a caricature of a living dinosaur, the reddish-
colored male "green" iguanas at Bermudian Landing are among the
largest and healthiest I've seen. Males can measure six feet, including the tail. The females are shiny green and blend much more readily with the foliage. If you come within about thirty feet of these
iguanas, they'll drop from a sunning spot into the river and swim
off. The spiny-tailed iguana (*Ctenosauria similis*), or wish-willy, measure up to three feet in length and is more apt to be sighted on the
ground. This grayish lizard eats insects and plants and is a swift run-
ner. In the area of Mussel Creek you may find manatees, Morlet's
crocodiles, and hikatees (large endangered turtles).

Possibly the most memorable way to appreciate the sanctuary is
from the Belize River, which flows through it. Canoe rentals are advertised in the nearby village of Burrell Boom. Inquire at the Belize
Audubon Society in Belize City or at the sanctuary office about canoes.
The sanctuary office will arrange for canoes if notified in advance.

Be Prepared: A raincoat, bug repellent, long pants, hat, and camera
are essential. Trails can be muddy and overgrown. Water-resistant
boots make for a more comfortable outing. Mosquitoes are often
present.

Beware of Fake Guides: When you arrive at the sanctuary you may
find yourself eagerly approached by a smiling villager who offers to
take you to the "baboons." The eagerness to show the way is accompanied with a request for U.S. $10 or more. In my case this "guide"
walked with me about a quarter-mile to the edge of some low forest
before suddenly excusing himself from my presence. Nearby, I found
the official guide with a group of camera-toting European tourists.
It turned out that my "guide" was not authorized to guide visitors nor
was he particularly knowledgeable. Beware of this kind of "pounce
and fleece" around the sanctuary; it can mar an otherwise pleasant
outing. Keep in mind that even if an unauthorized guide is knowl-

edgeable, the money you give him goes into his pocket instead of the sanctuary's meager treasury. During my days in Belize I talked to several foreigners who had hired fake guides, some of them knowledgeable and personable. To avoid giving money to the wrong person, locate someone with an official-looking khaki shirt, usually with a Belize Audubon emblem on the shoulder. On most days someone is in the office all day, but if nobody's around, wait until a guide returns. Regardless of who you end up hiring, Belize Audubon recommends that all visitors ask for a signed receipt for any money paid to the sanctuary or its guides. A Belize Audubon notice posted on the museum's wall states, "All receipts should be carbon-copied and signed by both the person making the payment and the person receiving it. Absolutely no payments should be made without the issuance of a receipt."

Schedule Your Visit: Scheduling your visit in advance works in your favor. On busy days a guide may take as many as ten groups to the howlers. If you're a drop-in on such a day, be patient and wait; a guide will return. Better yet, let the sanctuary manager know you're coming by contacting the Belize Audubon Society (phone 02-77369) in Belize City. Belize Audubon has a radio hook-up with sanctuary headquarters and will alert the manager that you are coming. The only other telephonic communication with Bermudian Landing is via the community's one public telephone (02-44405), which won't necessarily put you in contact with anyone in an official capacity with the sanctuary. However, whoever answers can tell you about bus schedules and weather conditions.

Donations: Donations to the sanctuary's tax-deductible fund can be made out to Howlers Forever and sent to Dr. Robert Horwich, R.D. 1, Box 96, Gays Mills, WI 54631 (phone 608-735-4717). A donation of U.S. $50 or more entitles you to a quarterly newsletter updating you on the activities at the sanctuary, plus an attractive, stylized poster of howler monkeys. The World Wildlife Fund, Lincoln Park Zoological Park in Chicago, the Zoological Society of Milwaukee, and the Inter-American Foundation have donated money to the sanctuary. You may wish to donate through these organizations, but first check to see if they're still involved with the program.

Other Publications: Dr. Robert Horwich and Jonathan Lyon have published *A Belizean Rain Forest: The Community Baboon Sanctuary*, a

420-page book that talks about the flora and fauna of the area in great detail and discusses conservation issues relevant to the sanctuary's welfare. The book is an easy read and full of information that is useful in other parts of Belize. Send U.S. $14 to Dr. Robert Horwich at the address noted above. The price includes postage. You'll also find attractive posters and brochures for sale in the sanctuary office.

Accommodations: Villagers are installing flush toilets and offering the extra room in their modest houses to international travelers who come to see their "baboons." The two conversions I checked out appeared very spartan and overpriced. Room prices should run about U.S. $5 for a single and U.S. $8 for a double per night and U.S. $3 for a meal. Since a visit to the sanctuary is usually a half-day activity, you may be better off returning to comfortable lodgings you have located in or around Belize City or elsewhere in the area. The changing status of accommodations can be accurately assessed by contacting the Belize Audubon Society's main office in Belize City at 29 Regent Street (phone 02-77369). There is a strong push to develop good-quality, budget-priced B&Bs in the area to help the local economy.

Access: Bermudian Landing is about twenty-six miles northwest of Belize City and seven miles west of Burrell Boom. Most visitors reach the sanctuary by traveling north from Belize City on the Northern Highway (paved) fifteen miles and turning west onto a dirt road to Burrell Boom, which is about four miles off the highway. You can also reach the sanctuary from the Western Highway by taking a nine-mile dirt road commencing northeast of Hattieville. If you're starting from Belize City, the Northern Highway approach is fastest. Most tour companies offer excursions to the sanctuary, though traveling in a rental car allows you to enjoy the area at your own pace and with more solitude.

There is bus service to Bermudian Landing from Belize City and back, run by private individuals owning secondhand U.S. school buses. Young's Bus Service is one of the operators with this route. The fare is U.S. $3.50 one way, and Belize City departures are usually in the afternoon or evening, with a return at 6:00 A.M. each day. The ride takes about ninety minutes. There are other operators that may offer different schedules. These buses travel one way each day, requiring that you overnight in or around the sanctuary. They usually don't travel on holidays and Sundays. There are rooms in houses for rent, but there are no guarantees that you'll like the rooms or that one will be available. To learn more about buses going to Bermudian Landing, contact the Belize Audubon Society's headquarters in Belize City at 29 Regent Street (phone 02-77369).

Altun Ha ("Rockstone Water") Ruins

Altun Ha is the nearest major Mayan ruins to Belize City. The original Mayan name for the site is not known. Today's name, Altun Ha, means "Rockstone Water," which is a rough Mayan translation for today's nearby village named Rockstone Pond. Altun Ha is a relatively small site compared to the better-known ruins in the Mayan world, but well worth the visit, especially if your time is limited and you will not be going to Caracol, Lamanai, the ruins in the Toledo District, or Tikal in Guatemala.

Altun Ha consists of about a dozen major structures grouped around two plazas. Two of these are classic large temples. The Temple of the Sun God and the Temple of Masonry Altars rise about seventy feet above their respective plazas. The summit of the southernmost large temple affords an excellent view of the ruins and low jungle that stretches to the coast seven miles away. There are eleven other structures encompassing the plazas, and an ancient Mayan reservoir nearby that contributes to the abundant bird life that is most active in the morning. Small parrots, trogons, keel-billed and aracari toucans, roadside hawks, and raucous brown jays are common sights. You may want to carry along a bird book. During my visit, two small brocket deer trotted through the ruins.

Altun Ha makes an excellent morning outing with a picnic lunch. In the stillness of early daylight, sitting atop the tallest pyramid with a jungle view for miles, your imagination will allow you to step into the ancient world of the Mayans.

The site had permanent, organized settlement from 200 B.C. until A.D. 900, which is an unusually long occupation. It is thought that Altun Ha began as a ceremonial center that shifted in emphasis to become a trade link between the coast and larger centers in the

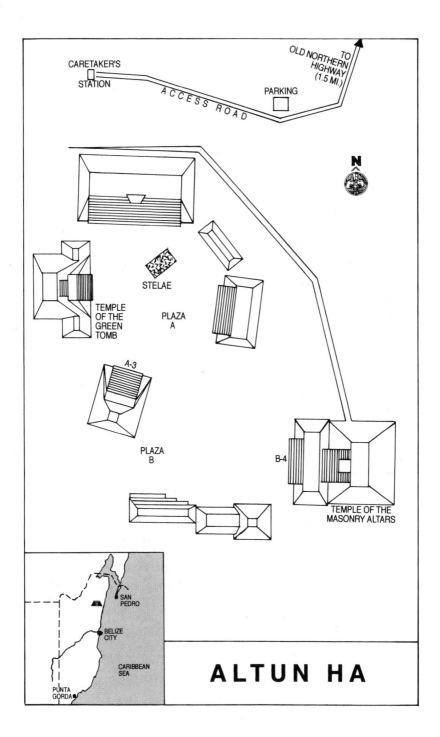

CARETAKER'S STATION

TO OLD NORTHERN HIGHWAY (1.5 MI.)

ACCESS ROAD

PARKING

N

STELAE

TEMPLE OF THE GREEN TOMB

PLAZA A

A-3

PLAZA B

B-4

TEMPLE OF THE MASONRY ALTARS

SAN PEDRO

BELIZE CITY

CARIBBEAN SEA

PUNTA GORDA

ALTUN HA

interior during its prime in the Classic Period (A.D. 250–900). Stone implements and other goods from Teotihuacan, outside Mexico City, have been unearthed at Altun Ha, proving that trade routes from faraway places were well established during the Classic Period.

Noted Canadian archaeologist Dr. David Pendergast excavated Altun Ha from 1964 to 1970. He established the role Altun Ha played as a trade center and made several significant discoveries here. In a burial tomb in the Temple of the Sun God (labeled structure B-4 in Plaza B on maps of the site), Pendergast found a unique, painstakingly sculpted jade head of Kinich Ahau, the Mayan sun god. Weighing nearly ten pounds and measuring six inches across, it is the largest carved piece of jade from the Mayan world, and today its image appears on all Belizean paper money. Pendergast unearthed the Temple of the Green Tomb, a particularly rich burial tomb with human remains and a wide assortment of jade figures and jewelry. He also concluded that the one-square-mile central ceremonial site was densely populated during Altun Ha's heyday. He believes that about 3000 people lived in the central square and as many as 10,000 lived nearby. In all, 500 structures and mounds have been identified, though only about a dozen structures in the two plazas kept open for visitors attract the curiosity of the average tourist.

Each individual temple is more than the single structure it appears to be. It is actually composed of several structures spanning centuries of occupation. Typically, over centuries, a temple grows taller and wider as successive structures are added to already existing structures. These different phases can be identified by different construction techniques. The temples you see at Altun Ha were also much more ornate than they appear today. Colorful stuccoes, colonnades, and impressive altars embellished the pyramids, which were used for ceremonial purposes and as burial chambers for important people. As with most Mayan sites still operating around A.D. 900, this one appears to have ceased functioning about the same time as the collapse of the rest of the Mayan world. Pendergast found evidence that a violent uprising of the Mayan lower classes may have been the cause of Altun Ha's demise. Occupation of the site by small numbers of Mayans continued into the fourteenth century, but without the grandeur of the past.

Accommodations: For most visitors, Altun Ha is a day or half-day trip from Belize City, not requiring an overnight stay. However, there are budget accommodations in nearby Maskall (eight miles north); expensive top-flight accommodations two miles farther north at Maruba Resort and Jungle Spa (E) (phone 03-22199); and several hotels (B, M, E) in the town of Orange Walk, about thirty-five miles north of the ruins.

Access: Most tour companies based in Belize City include Altun Ha in their list of offerings. Altun Ha is thirty-one miles (an hour) north of Belize City on the Old Northern Highway (the original Panamanian Highway) past Cowhead Creek. There is no public transportation to Altun Ha. From Belize City head north for about twenty miles on the Northern Highway. Just past Sandhill look for a turnoff to the right onto the Old Northern Highway. This section of the Old Northern Highway is scenic, narrow, but paved, with a few potholes that require your alertness. Continue on the Old Northern Highway about nine miles in the direction of Santana and Maskall. You'll see a sign to Altun Ha and Rockstone Pond village at the tiny village of Lucky Strike. The dirt road, which is about a mile in length, is bumpy but well compacted. There is a caretaker/interpreter at the site and a place to buy soft drinks.

Note: The northern end of the Old Northern Highway past the ruins has a few rough spots, requiring 4WD during prolonged rains. If you're headed north during the rainy season, you may want to inquire about the condition of the road.

Belize Zoo and Tropical Education Center

The Belize Zoo is one of the most celebrated places in Belize. Known formally as the Belize Zoo and Tropical Education Center, it is a beacon of conservation that has influenced Belizean society. The zoo conservation program reaches 20,000 children a year. For the tourist, the zoo is the best place in Belize, and possibly all of Central America, to photograph the jungle animals that live in Central America. The animals are housed in natural settings. You'll meet April, the tapir (the captive representative of the national animal of Belize); Rambo, the toucan; Rex, the king vulture; Pete, the jaguar; Sarge, the Morlet's crocodile; and scores of other residents, including the miniature-looking gray foxes that prefer climbing trees to sitting on the ground, and my favorite for cutest tropical creature, the eight-inch-long, arboreal silky anteater. You'll also see the wolverine-like tayra, Belize's two species of monkeys, and lesser known felines such as the jaguarundi, ocelot, and margay. You may even meet the zoo's founder and director, Sharon Matola.

In large part due to Matola's efforts, Belizeans have traded their indifference toward the natural environment for pride in their wildlife. The Belize Zoo is a special place not only because of its impressive collection of native animals, but because it has served as a catalyst for the conservation ethic that is so much a part of today's Belizean character. When you visit, carry plenty of film. The animals are most active at dusk. You'll get photographs that appear to have been shot in the wild.

Today's Belize Zoo moved to its present site at mile 32 on the Western Highway in December 1991. This site is about a half-mile from where the original managerie was housed in a shantytown of rusty cages. The new Belize Zoo has thirty-five exhibits featuring 125 creatures in enclosures built around existing trees and bushes in the animals' natural habitat. At the entrance stands the Gerald Durrell Visitors' Centre, whose namesake helped build it. A 1700-acre deciduous forest nearby, a gift of the Belizean government, will be the site of the zoo's new field station. What makes all this remarkable is that this state-of-the-art zoo and education center was created by a woman who arrived in Belize with only a few hundred dollars to her name and in a country where the per-capita income only recently climbed to $1500 a year.

In 1982, Matola, a Baltimore native, was hired by a small film company to clean up after native animals used in the movie *Selva Verde*. When the filming was over, Matola's boss left town for six months and put her in charge. The problem was that all the money was gone. "Most of the animals had always lived in captivity and would never have made it in the wild," Matola recalls. "In good conscience, I couldn't release them. I also couldn't afford to feed them."

The irony of her dilemma helped solidify her commitment to wildlife. As Matola puts it, "Here was a group of unwanted animals that were used in a film to create greater appreciation and understanding of their kind in the United Kingdom and United States, while in Belize—where the animals actually live—efforts to educate and develop appreciation for them were nonexistent. It occurred to me that a zoo featuring native species could be the first step in educating Belizeans about their animals."

So in January 1983, on a tropical savanna dotted with palmettos, white-trunked crabos, and Caribbean pines, the Belize Zoo—then just a collection of animals in small, saggy-wired cages—was born. With no income and facing the likelihood that her menagerie would be forced to leave when the filmmaker who owned the land returned, Matola devised a survival plan. "I figured that with the support of the schools and government I might make it socially difficult to evict me," she says.

She started a newsletter, *Balboa Rides Again,* which covered activities at the zoo, visits to schools, and various conservation issues. To support herself, she led tours for International Expeditions and raised chickens, which she sold to restaurants and resorts on the coast. Twice a month for two years, Matola climbed on her Kawasaki 650 wearing a backpack stuffed with eighty pounds of fresh chicken meat and drove for hours over bumpy dirt roads.

The motorcyle and backpack also came in handy for her school outreach programs. "I'd put Balboa [her favorite boa constrictor] in my backpack and drive to the primary schools. For many kids," she said, "Balboa was the first snake they'd seen that wasn't chopped in half." She visited about 600 kids that first year. Now, ten years later— with the help of an education director and two full-time instructors— more than 20,000 youngsters receive Matola's conservation message, which stresses human threats to animals and the importance of maintaining habitats. Most of the zoo's residents were victims of humans' activities (orphaned, gunshot victims, discarded pets, etc.) and offer poignant examples of humans' insensitivity to animals.

Not long after Matola launched her newsletter she began a multimedia blitz. She wrote articles for Belizean magazines on subjects ranging from zoo matters to discoveries on jungle expeditions. She took to the airwaves, creating a children's radio program with such characters as Bardi the Baboon, a talking howler monkey. Matola also wrote *Hoodwink the Owl,* a children's book published in 1988. The book delivers a strong conservation message and is part of every school's curriculum.

Still, these efforts didn't pay all the bills. Matola's annual fundraising forays into the United States were almost always fruitful. A trip in 1986 netted the zoo's current assistant curator, Amy Bodwell, former assistant curator of education at Zoo Atlanta. Matola has also garnered financial support from groups such as the World Wildlife Fund, the Inter-American Foundation, Conservation International, and Wildlife Preservation Trust International, which has contributed more than $300,000. Private citizens and businesses in Belize and throughout the world also donate to the Belize Zoo.

Once seen as a place run by a crazy lady living with a bunch of discarded animals, Matola's menagerie has evolved into a full-fledged zoo, which educators throughout Belize recognize as an important source of conservation information. Matola still rides a motorcycle, but rather than go it alone she now has staff meetings and a budget; professional keepers, educators, and a curator; and scores of volunteers. "It's been a very rewarding experience," says Matola. "We've helping wildlife by changing the way people think. And," she adds, "we couldn't do it without the financial support of a few dollars from schoolchildren to twenty-five dollars to thousands of dollars from ordinary people who want to help."

Donations: There is a nominal fee to enter the zoo. Additional donations can be made at the zoo itself or mailed to the Belize Zoo and Tropical Education Center, P.O. Box 474, Belize City, Belize, C.A.

Be Prepared: It may be hot at the zoo, with intense sunshine. Dress protectively, use sunscreen, and carry bug repellent.

Access: The Belize Zoo is thirty-one miles west of Belize City on the Western Highway, or fourteen miles east of Belmopan. On the Western Highway, look for a sign for the zoo on the north side of the road. The entrance is about a half-mile down a dirt road from the highway. Two bus lines—Venus (phone 02-73354) and Batty Brothers (phone 02-72025)—run up and down the Western Highway daily from Belize City to points west and back again. If you take the bus, make sure you don't miss the last bus of the day on the return or you may find yourself sitting in the scrub swatting bugs all night until bus service commences the next morning. You can also arrange for a taxi to take you to the zoo, but the cost will be about U.S. $30. Hitchhiking is not recommended.

Caution: The Western Highway is paved, but deceptively dangerous, especially in the rain. Twice in the last twenty-five years while driving I have slid from the roadway against my will, both times on the Western Highway between Belize City and the Belize Zoo. The surface is as slick as ice when wet, and the few corners on this road are banked incorrectly. Both of my departures (at about fifty-five miles per hour) began with a slow slide. I obviously survived, but I also witnessed a fatal accident when a car I was following slid off the road in a similar fashion and rolled over on top of the driver, who had been thrown from the vehicle. Drive about fifteen miles per hour slower than you would in the United States and you should be fine.

Monkey Bay Wildlife Sanctuary

Monkey Bay Wildlife Sanctuary is located at mile 31 on the Western Highway, across the road and a couple of miles west of the Belize Zoo. Owned by North Americans, this privately run reserve of 1070 acres is situated between the Sibun River and the Western Highway. According to manager Matthew Miller there are six plant zones in the sanctuary: pine, small palm savanna, broken ridge (thicket), cohune palm, broadleaf tropical forest, bamboo and cane stands, and gallery forests with riverine figs. Miller is well versed in all aspects of local plant and animal life. He is a graduate of the environmental studies department of the University of California at Santa Cruz and has been in Belize for an extended time. The sanctuary's many habitats have contributed to the sanctuary's bird list of more than 250 species, including 2 species of falcons, toucans, oropendulas, parrots, herons, and egrets. Tropical mammalian life is also well represented.

Visitors are welcome, and meals, guides, and side trips can be provided at a price negotiated with Matthew. One popular trip is riding through an extensive riverine cave system on inner tubes. Accommodations are novel and spartan. Guests sleep in a safari-style tent and bake their bread in a steel drum heated by fire. If the weather turns bad, guests can retreat to nearby Belmopan for conventional accommodations. There is talk of building some rooms for guests beneath the stilt house occupied by Matthew. Bathing is done in the river.

For more information and to make reservations, contact Monkey Bay Wildlife Sanctuary, P.O. Box 187, Belmopan, Belize, C.A. (phone 08-22915), or Monkey Bay Wildlife Sanctuary, c/o Kellog, 11928 Nyanza Road S.W., Tacoma, WA 98499 (phone 206-584-7725).

Access: Monkey Bay Wildlife Sanctuary is located at mile 31 on the Western Highway, practically across the road from the Belize Zoo.

Gales Point
(Manatee Lagoons)

The Gales Point region is arguably the most intriguing and diverse coastal environment in Belize. The region's most accessible features — the Northern Lagoon and Southern Lagoon — harbor the highest concentrations of manatees in Central America. Located about fifteen miles south of Belize City by water and about forty-five miles by land, the area has been largely bypassed by tourism-related businesses, except for sport fishing and boat tours from Belize City to see the manatees. However, change is close at hand for Gales Point, a village of about 300 people that sits on a narrow peninsula poking into the Southern Lagoon. Both Glenn Godfrey, former Minister of Tourism and the Environment, and Dr. Robert Horwich, the organizer of the Bermudian Landing Community Baboon Sanctuary, have led the way with ideas to develop Gales Point in ways that help the local economy, protect critical habitat for the area's many rare and endangered species, and make the area's vastly different ecosystems accessible to tourists.

When I met with former Minister Godfrey at his office in Belmopan to be briefed on the uniqueness of Gales Point and the Southern and Northern lagoons, Godfrey was visibly exuberant. He unrolled a map, spread it over the piles of paperwork on his desk, and began by pointing at the reef offshore from the lagoons.

"The diversity and richness of the area are amazing," Godfrey said. "In the space of five miles there are five distinctly different eco-systems. The reef system sits just off the coast, followed by pristine beach, where you'll find one of the few known nesting sites of the hawksbill turtle. Next come the lagoons, with manatees, tarpon, and fish with names such as billam, draw me long, and yellow gal." God-frey's finger wandered to a small island in the Northern Lagoon. "Here's a bird sanctuary where you'll find white ibises and egrets in great numbers during nesting season." His hand swept inland. "Far-ther west we get into more lagoons, wetlands, rivers, and cave systems with crocodiles and Mayan artifacts. Here you find karst mountains and low rain forest and, farther, the pine ridge area. This entire area is intersected with several river systems, some of them emerging from caves. Jaguars, ocelots, peccaries, otters, and many other creatures live in the region."

Godfrey took a breath, switched gears, and described the area's unique human history. "The extensive caves were refuge to escaped slaves during the sixteenth and seventeenth centuries. [Robert] Hor-wich has found artifacts from Africa in the caves, which probably means that some of the slaves brought to Belize were quick to run away. Such runaways would be apt to maintain parts of their origi-nal culture. To this day the village of Gales Point, where the descen-dants of the escaped slaves settled, is probably the most African village in Belize. The village is a very friendly place but has a separate cultural identity. In their village meetings, which I sometimes attend, they conduct themselves differently. Often they all talk at once and in this way reach consensus," recalled Godfrey, who was intrumen-tal in having Gales Point designated a "special development area."

Land Use Proposals: Dr. Robert Horwich, with help from other North Americans and the villagers at Gales Point, wasted little time in sub-mitting a plan to the Belizean government for the use and develop-ment of the entire region. Working with Horwich were some annual visitors to the region: Massachusetts artist Christian Augustus, Peace Corps worker Christian Rich, and Barbara Boardman, a Fulbright scholar from Harvard with expertise in rural zoning. The compre-hensive plan given to the government will go through a multiyear review and modification process that will take into account protect-ing critical wildlife habitat, developing some areas of citrus farm-ing, selective logging, building bed-and-breakfast accommodations, developing a rotation system for boatmen taking visitors to the lagoons and on longer trips, conservation-oriented fishing practices, and designing expeditionlike outings for more adventuresome visitors who want to travel by native dugout up rivers.

"The government has to approve the concepts, which we think they will during the years to come," says Horwich. "But all the planning in the world won't amount to much unless the locals benefit economically. The idea is to protect critical habitat and designate less essential habitat for agricultural use. The key is developing a comprehensive plan that makes sense for the environment while integrating the needs of the locals into the plan, rather than allowing a piecemeal approach that may have short-term economic benefits at the expense of important resources and habitats."

Wildlife Viewing and Wild River Adventuring: Without a doubt, Gales Point is going to embrace change. But, for the present, many of the best nature experiences remain difficult to access for the casual visitor. With the exceptions of viewing the manatees in the Southern Lagoon (where they're most easily found) and the bird life at Bird Caye Bird Sanctuary in the Northern Lagoon, visiting the hinterlands by river requires an expedition-like commitment. Christian Augustus, who has traveled inland on most of the major watercourses, described wondrous environments with crocodiles, peccaries, and riverine caves. He also described treacherous and strenuous boating experiences in which he was entirely reliant on guides from the village to return safely. According to Augustus, the guides know these remote areas intimately. The going can be quite challenging. Augustus recounted negotiating difficult passages through riverine caves with two-story-high logjams. The Manatee River trip received good recommendations from both Barbara Boardman and Augustus as being among the least difficult and richest in terms of scenery and wildlife. Augustus discovered a previously unknown large population of spider monkeys (an endangered species) in this area. This river has a 1.5-mile-long cave with a 450-foot-high ceiling.

Heavy, but durable, native dugouts are the traditional way to visit the rivers. If lightweight canoes or other transportable watercraft should become available in Gales Point, accessing these river systems from the bridges across New Road (also called the Coast Road or Manatee Road), which runs inland and parallel to the coast, can cut as much as a day of travel time off reaching the river caves. For more on adventure river travel in the area, contact boatmen in Gales Point.

Manatee Viewing and Bird Watching: The common experience for a visitor to the region is to cruise through the two main lagoons, stopping in the Southern Lagoon to see manatees, continuing through the narrow waterway connecting the two lagoons, and boating around Bird Caye Bird Sanctuary, where you can take spectacular photographs of nesting colonies of white ibises, egrets, and possibly roseate spoonbills. Nesting activities occur from April through June, but birds are plentiful here year-round. Access to these areas can be achieved by motorized dugout from Gales Point, by modern motor launch from Belize City, or by a combination of car and boat from Dangriga (see below).

About Manatees: The manatees in the lagoons (and other Belizean waters) are West Indian manatees (*Trichecus manatus*), which are found throughout the Caribbean, including Florida, various island nations, and the coastal waters of northern South America. Separate manatee species are found in the Amazon, West Africa, and Australia (where they are called dugongs). The adult West Indian manatee weighs more than 2000 pounds and measures twelve feet in length. Its diet consists of gargantuan amounts of plant life—about 200 pounds daily. The manatee is the only living marine mammal that is strictly a vegetarian. Manatees have been protected in Belizean waters since 1935. The population in Belize is believed to be about 600 animals, which is about 10 percent of the manatees living in the Caribbean. Belize, particularly the Southern Lagoon, is a manatee stronghold that is on par with any other Caribbean nation in terms of being home to a viable reproductive population. In Belize the manatee population is growing, though in recent years a few poaching incidents have been reported. Manatees are entirely defenseless, relying on their thick-skinned bulk and the inaccessibility of their swampy, brackish-water homes for protection. Humans have been their only predator. The Mayans hunted them with spears for their highly valued tender meat and thick hides. They were likewise exploited by Europeans, especially the early Spanish, who classified them incorrectly as fish so that they could eat them on Fridays. For more details about manatees in Belize, purchase *A Belizean Rain Forest: The Community Baboon Sanctuary,* by Robert Horwich and Jonathan Lyon. The book can be found in bookstores and hotel lobbies throughout Belize or purchased directly from Dr. Robert Horwich, Howlers Forever, R.D. 1, Box 96, Gays Mills, WI 54631 (phone 608-735-4717). The book costs U.S. $14, postage included.

Access by Local Dugout from Gales Point: I visited the manatees and bird sanctuary in a native dugout that was about twenty feet long and powered by an outboard motor. Efren, the elderly boatman assigned to me in the village's guide rotation system, was friendly and gracious. Indeed, just spending the afternoon with Efren, his craft, and Samuel (Efren's elderly friend from childhood who came along for the ride and to help with the anchor) was well worth the trip, even if we had not sighted a manatee. Both men were eager to help me maximize my experience and were extremely knowledgeable about the area and its wildlife. However, communication between us was difficult at times because Efren's brand of Creole/English was difficult for me to understand, especially with the belching of his outboard motor in the background.

Manatees live throughout the lagoons but are found most easily at the southern end of the Southern Lagoon in an area reached in ten minutes by dugout (at ten knots flat out) from the piers at Gales Point. The water is supposedly a few degrees warmer in this area, causing them to congregate. On the day of my visit, manatees were plentiful. In part, our success in seeing them was due to the clever motorless, downwind-drift approach and anchoring technique used by Efren, making us appear to the manatees more like a wind-driven log than a boat. Groups of animals, including babies, surfaced at a single time near our boat. However, because of the lack of water clarity, viewing the manatees mostly amounted to seeing body parts: a rounded tail flipper, a bulbous back, the pink, stubble-free muzzle of a baby, and the grizzled and stubbled muzzle of an adult. Occasionally an entire animal was silhouetted on the surface. Photographic opportunities are not particularly good above or below water because of the water's cloudiness. According to Efren, attempts to swim with the manatees haven't been too fruitful. "German folks takes off de' clothe and jumps in da' water with da' sea cows [the local name for manatees]. Da' cows t'ink 'em crazy and swim away," explained Efren. Set aside an hour if you want to visit the manatees only and not travel to the Northern Lagoon.

If you're headed for the bird sanctuary in the Northern Lagoon by dugout from Gales Point, after first visiting the manatees, count on at least two-and-a-half hours of boat time. The large dugouts are quite seaworthy, but you'll get splashed by wind-driven foam while crossing the open areas of the lagoons. At Bird Caye Bird Sanctuary the opportunity to photograph ibises, egrets, and assorted other wetland species is excellent year-round. The tiny island is only about thirty yards across, but heavily vegetated and safe from predators. When we approached the island Efren cut his motor. He and Samuel slowly poled the dugout around the island, taking great care to talk in whispers so as not to disturb the birds. Occasionally they'd point to a bird half hidden in the vegetation that they thought I might not have seen.

Like Efren, most boatmen operate from the west side of the village. They have developed a rotation system for guiding people and abide by it for community harmony. The full two-and-a-half-hour trip cost me U.S. $80.

Access by Boat from Belize City: You can also visit the bird sanctuary and the manatees in the Southern Lagoon from Belize City in comfortable, modern launches that leave Blackline Marine on a regular schedule. Blackline Marine is two miles up the Northern Highway, or south one mile from the Belize Biltmore Plaza and Budget Rent A Car. Blackline Marine owner Jim Black moved to Belize from the United States twenty-five years ago. He also runs a sport fishing service and has the most complete scuba shop in Belize City. The trip to the lagoons is a pleasant ride in a fast-moving, enclosed boat that travels through canals and natural waterways before reaching the lagoons. Bird life can be plentiful. The entire trip takes about two hours but may vary depending on extra excursions and how long passengers want to spend viewing the manatees and birds. Besides the standard round trip, Blackline Marine also offers a one-way ride to see the manatees and bird sanctuary that ends in Gales Point. If you're heading south to Dangriga or Punta Gorda this makes sense. Traveling by boat is definitely a more pleasant way to travel than by bus to Dangriga. The catch is that there's no public transportation connecting Gales Point to Dangriga, a distance of twenty-four miles. You must make arrangements to be picked up and taken to Dangriga by a Dangriga hotel offering the service. For the one-way or round-trip boat ride from Belize City, contact Blackline Marina, Mile 2, Northern Highway (phone 02-44155).

Access by Land: If you arrange to get off the Blackline Marine launch in Gales Point, the Pelican Beach Resort, which is in nearby Dangriga, can arrange a ride from Gales Point to the resort hotel. This works only if you contact Pelican Beach in advance (phone 05-22044).

From Dangriga, Pelican Beach (and possibly other hotels in Dangriga) offers day trips to and from Gales Point. There is no public transportation to Gales Point. If you're traveling in a rental car, the trip from Belize City to Gales Point via the New Road (also called Manatee Road or the Coast Road) takes about two hours. From Dangriga, the twenty-four miles to Gales Point is on mostly dirt road and usually takes forty-five minutes.

Gales Point Sailing Regatta: If you're in Gales Point during Easter Week you'll see a unique regatta. Lightweight, very fast, hand-crafted sailboats are raced at breakneck speeds on the eastern side of the Gales Point peninsula. The races are local competitions or warm-ups for the Bliss Regatta, held in Belize City each year on March 9. The races are held near shore to maximize spectator "speculation." Walter Goff, head of the village council; Sir George Brown, Belize's High Court chief justice; and Leonard Myers, four-time winner of the Bliss Regatta, often have fierce competitions. The villagers also race in "pit-pans," which are locally made, shallow-draft boats that are paddled furiously by crews of ten. The contest pitches old against young men. In a lighthearted rite of passage a father may be competing against his son. The "young" pit-pans are usually victorious.

Accommodations: There were community efforts to develop modest guesthouse (B) accommodations in Gales Point in 1992. As you enter the village by car you'll see a "Guest Houses" sign on the left side of the road. Stop here and ask to talk with Hortense Welch, who coordinates guesthouse activities. If she's not around, ask for Ione Samuels. Accommodations are very basic, but friendly. There is also a more upscale accommodation at the fishing lodge on the tip of the peninsula. However, it was closed during my visit. Only cash is accepted for payment at Gales Point accommodations. The village has a tiny store that carries basic staples, soft drinks, and candy. Camping is allowed, and it is recommended that visitors contribute small donations to the community's development by giving them to a village councilman. The community is attempting to collect enough funds to build a police station. If the offerings at Gales Point are too spartan for you, Dangriga offers Pelican Beach Resort and other fully outfitted accommodations.

Offshore

From the hub that includes Phillip Goldson International Airport and Belize City (nine-and-a-half miles between them), most of the northern and central island and reef destinations are easily accessible. In many instances, connecting flights in light aircraft await international arrivals. Within minutes of clearing customs you may find yourself climbing aboard a single- or twin-engine aircraft and in fifteen to thirty minutes be standing in a hotel at your island destination.

Ambergris Caye

Ambergris Caye (pronounced "key") is Belize's most popular island destination. The island's name comes from the ambergris extracted from whales that were once hunted here. Whaling ceased long ago, and now even spear hunting of fish is banned. Ambergris Caye is a very flat, twenty-five-mile-long ribbon of limestone with substantial stands of mangrove on its western shore and narrow beaches and palms along its eastern shore. The island serves as the gateway to the spectacular scuba diving, snorkeling, fishing, sailing, and other water-related recreational activities on Belize's Barrier Reef and atolls.

For many foreign tourists, staying on Ambergris Caye is the full extent of their visit to Belize. They only see the mainland when passing through the international airport. Operating from their island hotel, they take day trips around Ambergris Caye or to other islands, where they snorkel, scuba dive, fish, sail, and sunbathe. At night they dine out, visit a pub, or stroll the streets of San Pedro browsing at gift and T-shirt ships.

History: Only a narrow channel separates Ambergris Caye from Mexico's Yucatán Peninsula. It is thought that this original channel separating the island from Mexico was dug by Mayan Indians to help facilitate their trade long before Columbus arrived. Today, the Mayan presence is appreciated on the island's southern terminus at the Marco Gonzalez archaeological site, which is considered a significant ruin because of what has been learned here about Mayan trade routes. It is not as impressive visually as the many Mayan temples on the mainland.

San Pedro: Probably 90 percent of the human activity on Ambergris Caye occurs in the town of San Pedro. San Pedronians, as they call themselves, number about 1200 permanent residents, and there are as many foreigners on the island. More than the rest of Belize, San Pedronians trace their ancestry to immigrants from the Caste Wars (1847–1863) in Mexico. To this day, most families speak English and Spanish. Traditionally, San Pedronians made their livelihoods from fishing, but for the last decade the emphasis has changed from fishing to tourism.

San Pedro is a laid-back, friendly place, nearly free of crime and bugs (the dastardly duo in the tropics). The town is four blocks wide, six blocks long, and hemmed in on two sides by water. The streets are white sand and lined with rusty-roofed, sun-bleached houses and colorfully painted colonial hotels and businesses made of clapboard. Strolling, bicycling, golf carts, and the rare taxi are the ways of getting around. Regardless of the mode of transportation, the pace is always slow. Along the eastern shore, where most of the hotels line Barrier Reef Drive (formerly Front Street), a constant onshore breeze usually keeps bugs grounded, allowing you to sunbathe and wear skimpy clothing without being victimized by mosquitoes. San Pedro's isolation from the mainland keeps out the panhandlers that plague Belize City.

The action is on the town's waterfront. There are a dozen light piers poking out into the azure sea. On most piers you'll find a dive shop and a line-up of locally constructed, seagoing, plywood speedboats (called launches or skiffs) awaiting their next group of divers and snorkelers. Characteristically these boats are well maintained and brightly painted with such brassy names as *Hustler* and *Sun God.* They are powered with twin high-horsepower outboard motors, have canvas tops to keep the sun off, and carry about eight snorkelers or divers. They are designed to cover great distances rapidly for divers and snorkelers wanting to visit offshore destinations. They cruise at about forty-five knots on calm water.

Overhead along the piers you'll see magnificent pterodactyl-looking frigate birds glide or "stand" into the wind on their fragile-looking six-foot wings. These highly acrobatic birds are tremendously

DOWNTOWN SAN PEDRO

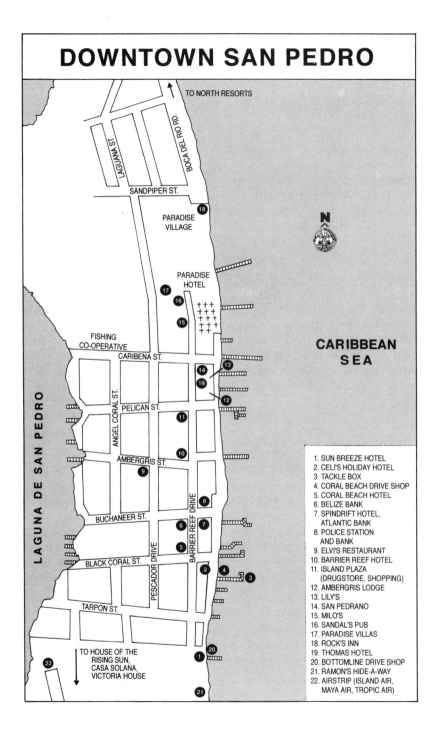

TO NORTH RESORTS

LAGUANA ST.

BOCA DEL RIO RD.

SANDPIPER ST.

PARADISE VILLAGE

PARADISE HOTEL

FISHING CO-OPERATIVE

CARIBENA ST.

ANGEL CORAL ST.

PELICAN ST.

AMBERGRIS ST.

BUCHANEER ST.

BARRIER REEF DRIVE

PESCADOR DRIVE

BLACK CORAL ST.

TARPON ST.

TO HOUSE OF THE RISING SUN, CASA SOLANA, VICTORIA HOUSE

LAGUNA DE SAN PEDRO

CARIBBEAN SEA

N

1. SUN BREEZE HOTEL
2. CELI'S HOLIDAY HOTEL
3. TACKLE BOX
4. CORAL BEACH DRIVE SHOP
5. CORAL BEACH HOTEL
6. BELIZE BANK
7. SPINDRIFT HOTEL, ATLANTIC BANK
8. POLICE STATION AND BANK
9. ELVI'S RESTAURANT
10. BARRIER REEF HOTEL
11. ISLAND PLAZA (DRUGSTORE, SHOPPING)
12. AMBERGRIS LODGE
13. LILY'S
14. SAN PEDRANO
15. MILO'S
16. SANDAL'S PUB
17. PARADISE VILLAS
18. ROCK'S INN
19. THOMAS HOTEL
20. BOTTOMLINE DRIVE SHOP
21. RAMON'S HIDE-A-WAY
22. AIRSTRIP (ISLAND AIR, MAYA AIR, TROPIC AIR)

entertaining to watch as they pluck fish from the sea or from the bill of another seabird. There's no doubt that San Pedro possesses a seductive charm, but it's also a place with a few ominous clouds on the horizon.

Overdevelopment Worries: At last count, there were forty-five moderate- to small-size hotels offering about 600 beds on Ambergris Caye. Most of them are in San Pedro. The ability to accommodate this volume of visitors assures that Ambergris Caye will maintain its role as gateway to the northern third of the 170-mile Barrier Reef and atolls that have made Belize so well known.

The island's rapid hotel growth and real estate speculation since the mid-1980s have also created serious concern within both the conservation community and longtime Belizean hoteliers about the possible pitfalls of overdeveloping Ambergris Caye as an "eco-tourism" destination. When the subject of Ambergris Caye is broached with Belizeans, from those occupying high government positions to vendors selling coral jewelry on street corners in San Pedro, the island's growth rate and changing ambience are inevitably their concerns. "How much change will it take to kill the goose that laid the golden eggs?" is a question Belizeans ask themselves, according to one longtime hotelier. Most everyone agrees that the present state of development is either too much or enough. The water and sewage works are hard pressed to keep up with growth. New hotels abound; some of them, such as the swank Belize Yacht Club with its fully equipped gym and a North American condo-complex appearance, look like transplants from Lido Isle in Los Angeles. This kind of development is in striking contrast to the classic, colorfully decorated, Belizean colonial structures overlooking the water on Barrier Reef Drive, where the main drag is soft, white sand.

Still, for the time being and for many reasons, spending a vacation on Ambergris Caye makes good sense. This is a friendly, low-key place with unsurpassed water-related recreational activities. San Pedro's hoteliers have fine-tuned and polished their packages — which often include a guaranteed number of dive or snorkel trips or visits to ruins — and have strong ties with travel companies in the United States. You can choose a package deal that has been time-tested by a volume of travelers. The adventure here is underwater. What happens on the island is as predictable and as relaxed as at any resort in the United States or Europe. The diving and snorkeling sites are endless (see "Changa Paz's Top Dive and Snorkel Sites" below and the dive and snorkel sites listed with each atoll and island), but get-ting to them requires paying for boat travel. Prepaying in the United States as part of a package deal is often less expensive.

Where to Eat: There is no shortage of good-quality eateries on Am-bergris Caye. Many of them are in the hotels. My favorites are as follows. Elvi's Kitchen (M) on Pescador Drive (formerly Middle Street), across from Martha's Hotel, had the best seafood dishes for the price. Holiday Hotel (M) offers a menu that rivals anything in San Pedro. You can elect to eat outside under the stars there. Mary Ellen's Little Italy restaurant (M) at the Spindrift Hotel bested most Italian food I've had in the United States. Proprietor Mary Ellen Greer, a former lawyer from the States, has even developed a fledg-ling wine list. The Sun Breeze (M) (linen tablecloths, informal dress, but no bathing suits), near the airstrip, has good chicken and fish dishes. The Hut (M, E), located near the soccer field, has tasty conch soup and shrimp dishes for moderate prices. The restaurants at Ra-mon's Village Resort (E) (outside dining) and Victoria House (M, E) also have excellent dishes and attractive Caribbean-style settings.

Travel and Rental Connections: In many instances these services can be handled at the front desk of your hotel. For everything from snor-keling, diving, and sailing to airline tickets and trips to Tikal, contact Amigo Travel on Barrier Reef Drive (phone 026-2180). Proprietors Gach and Dali Guerrero also handle long-term accommodation ren-tals and can procure a moped, bicycle, windsurfer, or glass-bottom-boat ride for you. Universal Travel, which has offices at the San Pedro Airport and on Barrier Reef Drive, offers many of the same services (phone 026-2031/2137).

Books and Printed Material: For books and maps, some of them by Belizean writers, try the Book Center on Barrier Reef Drive across from the Holiday Hotel. If you need a good paperback novel, buy *The Sinners' Bossanova*, written by Glenn Godfrey, Belize's former Minister of Tourism and the Environment. Besides a law degree, God-frey earned a master's degree in creative writing from Stanford University. You can buy literature about the Barrier Reef at the Hol Chan Marine Preserve office halfway down Barrier Reef Drive.

Gifts, Banking, and Shopping: Belize isn't what you'd call a shop-per's paradise. Toucan Too, on Barrier Reef Drive, sells good-quality black coral jewelry and a wide assortment of original T-shirts with nature themes. Also try the Emerald House for jewelry, carvings, and T-shirts. Most hotels accept major credit cards and will cash traveler's checks. On Barrier Reef Drive you'll find a Belize Bank and an Atlantic Bank. For food, Rock's Shopping Center is a mom-and-pop operation with the basics. At the Coop, on the northwest end of Caribbean Street, you can buy fresh fish, which helps local fishermen.

Pubs: The Tackle Box, located on a pier about halfway down Barrier Reef Drive, is the most novel pub in town, and a candidate for the most novel you'll find anywhere. It has a sand floor, and out the back door is an aquarium of sorts holding sea creatures: "pet" six-foot-long sharks, sea turtles, rays, and other large fish. There's no doubt that the animals are well fed, but the enclosure could stand some enlarging to benefit its captives. Ramon's, Holiday Hotel, Victoria House, Barrier Reef Hotel, and Barefoot Bar and Grill also offer relaxed social scenes. All are lively and distinct from one another. You'll find the crowd you feel comfortable with in one of them.

Special Events and Holidays: The oddest weekly events are the Chicken Drop (Wednesday nights) and the Crab Races (Monday nights), held at the Spindrift Hotel. The Chicken Drop is unique. People bet on the square of a large grid on which they think a chicken will relieve itself. The bettors on the square that gets the chicken shit win. This is a serious event to heavy bettors. You see some of San Pedro's most colorful characters in action here. If you arrive on March 1 through 3, you'll think San Pedronians are particularly weird. They dance in the streets and paint themselves or anyone else they can catch. This is Carnival, which is only celebrated here. San Pedronians observe all Belizean national holidays as well.

Day Trips to the Mainland: Day trips from San Pedro to mainland destinations are growing in popularity, as well they should. Belize's best wildlife-viewing areas and Mayan ruins are on the mainland. My favorite day trip is streaking across Chetumal Bay in a high-powered marine speedboat and up the New River to explore Lamanai ruins, which are extensive and surrounded by jungle with troops of monkeys and other tropical wildlife. The *Hustler,* which works in conjunction with the Barrier Reef Hotel, takes people to Altun Ha, a slightly less impressive ruin, in a similar manner. From the San Pedro

Airport, visitors can catch day flights (approximately U.S. $200 round-trip) to spectacular Tikal in Guatemala or other points of interest in Belize. For the adventuresome, there is canoeing for wildlife viewing through the mangrove channels on the leeward side of the island. You may see crocodiles, perhaps a manatee, and a wide assortment of birdlife, especially at Little Guana Caye Bird Sanctuary, where sighting spoonbills, a half-dozen species of herons, pelicans, and plovers is expected. Hawksbill turtles sometimes nest on remote parts of the island.

Changa Paz's Top Dive and Snorkel Sites: "What are the top dive sites that can be visited from Ambergris Caye in one day?" is the question I put to Changa Paz, a well-known, much-in-demand dive master and instructor with sixteen years of full-time experience on Ambergris Caye. Changa's diving area normally extends north of San Pedro to the Mexican border and south to include Caye Caulker, Chapel Caye, St. George's Caye, and two of Belize's three atolls—the Turneffe Islands and Lighthouse Reef. If you try to locate the sites named by Changa, keep in mind that these are commonly used names for dive and snorkel sites that may be known by other names as well. Also, Changa's top sites are not ranked in any particular order. The idea is to match your tastes, skill, and budget with the appropriate places. Barring adverse conditions, none of them will disappoint you. The boat time listed for each site is calculated from San Pedro.

Changa's top diving spots are:

1. Hol Chan Marine Preserve: five minutes to site; 0- to 20-foot depth; great numbers and diversity of approachable fish; convenient and safest quality night dive in region.

2. Half Moon Caye Wall: three hours to site on Lighthouse Reef; 40- to 60-foot depth; large, yellow tube sponges; favorite cruising grounds for spotted eagle rays, roof and open-water fish galore, garden eels, tunnels, spectacularly dramatic coral buttresses, and pronounced narrow spur and groove formations.

3. Blue Hole: three hours to site on Lighthouse Reef; 150-foot depth; eerie dive, unlike all others, and sharks (lemon, bull, and black-tip) are sighted about 70 percent of the time.

4. Victoria Tunnel: ten minutes to site; 95-foot depth; deep canyons, tunnels, nurse sharks, and great variety of fish and coral.

5. Sandburg Canyon: fifteen minutes to site, halfway to Caye Caulker; 40-foot depth; large nurse and black-tip sharks.

6. Northwest of Rendezvous Point, also called Dory's Channel: forty-five minutes to site at Turneffe; 45- to 60-foot depth; very colorful yellow-tip barrel sponges, black sponges, gorgonian trees, pelagic fish, spotted eagle rays, and turtles.

7. Cockroach Wall: forty-five minutes to site at Turneffe; 80- to 90-foot east-facing wall, large sponges, fans, coral patches, and reef and open-water fish.

8. Long Caye: three hours to site; 25- to 80-foot depth; many world-class dives in small area; black corals, gorgonians, colorful sponges, inspiring coral towers, short tunnels, large groupers, and plethora of fish life.

9. Inside reef dives at Mexican Rocks and Coral Gardens: ten minutes to site; 10- to 30-foot depth; good for warming up; excellent variety of fish amid sandy bottom and coral heads; and protected from wind and current.

Changa's top snorkel sites are Hol Chan Marine Preserve, Mexican Rocks, and Coral Gardens (all described above). Each is protected, shallow, and populated with colorful fish.

Larry Parker, the NAUI representative for Central and South America with a longtime dive business (Reef Divers Ltd.) in Belize, has a few favorite places of his own. Some are the same as Changa's, but he added these dive sites: (1) Outside Mexican Rocks — five minutes from Journey's End resort; 65- to 100-foot depth; not heavily dived; large jewfish, glassy sleepers, and horse-eyed jacks; M and M Caverns (a set of three caverns from 35 to 40 feet in length; great diversity in a single dive). (2) Pescador Caverns — ten minutes from San Pedro, directly in front of Pescador Hotel; 70- to 80-foot depth; dive consists of a long swim through sandy bottom cavern, with a vent 20 feet across most of the way. (3) Sandy Point — just north of Journey's End; 55- to 80-foot depth; spur and groove topography with ridges and many deep drops to sandy bottoms; barrel sponges three to four feet across, large sea fans, plentiful nurse sharks, and reef and open-water fish. Parker adds one additional snorkeling site: The Barge — near Journey's End, about ten minutes north of San Pedro; 4- to 17-foot depth; a barge sunk twelve years ago is now home to a great variety of small reef fish, including damsels, juvenile tangs, spotted drums, puffers, and trunkfish.

For more on diving and snorkeling sites, see the individual atolls and the "Offshore" sections of the Stann Creek District and Toledo District chapters.

Dive and Snorkel Connections: There are numerous dive operations on Ambergris Caye. Asking dive masters and instructors for proof of certification is advisable. Dive masters often move from one operation to the next during the course of a year. I've always thought the dive master is more important than the business he may own or work for. Following are three dive master/instructors who impressed me: Changa Paz, Amigos del Mar, San Pedro, Ambergris Caye, Belize, C.A. (phone 026-2706; fax 026-2648); Elbert Greer, Barrier Reef Drive, San Pedro, Ambergris Caye, Belize, C.A. (phone 026-2437/2293; radio frequency VHF-FM 14.772.5); and Larry Parker, c/o Journey's End Reef Divers, P.O. Box 13, San Pedro, Ambergris Caye, Belize, C.A. (phone 026-2173; fax 026-2028). Also recommended by dive masters was Out Island Divers, P.O. Box 3455, Estes Park, CO 80517 (phone 1-800-BLUE-HOLE), or P.O. Box 7, San Pedro, Ambergris Caye, Belize, C.A. (phone 026-2151; fax 026-2151). For the most up-to-date information, contact the Belize Tourist Board, 83 North Front Street, P.O. Box 325, Belize City, Belize, C.A. (phone 02-77213/73255). Try to get a copy of *Belize, the Adventure Coast, Travel Industry Sales Planner,* which is updated annually.

Life-saving Dive Chamber: San Pedro has a privately owned double-lock recompression chamber at the north end of the San Pedro Airport for emergency situations that used to be handled by airlifting divers (at great expense) to Miami. It's the only recompression chamber in Belize. The chamber stands by on radio frequency VHF 14.4600 twenty-four hours a day with a hyerbaric medical technologist on call. The chamber operates from donations of one dollar per cylinder of air sold by local dive shops and does not accept insurance. You might check to see if your dive master or dive shop participates in this life-saving program. Divers are welcome to inspect the chamber.

Cautions: Divers are schooled in safety and should follow the rules. Occasionally I've been on dives (and snorkels) where the ability level of the participants varied a great deal, causing impatience for some and struggle for others. Don't let peer pressure compromise your personal safety. If you feel you are about to be part of a dive or snorkel that is too rigorous for you, stay on the boat. For scuba divers, stay close to your dive master.

Be Prepared: Snorkelers should wear T-shirts. Sunscreen, medication for seasickness (if you're prone to it), a hat, an extra change of clothes, a light windbreaker, and plenty of nonalcoholic liquids should be taken along.

Sailing: The Barrier Reef is a few hundred yards to a half-mile offshore. It acts as a breakwater, creating a calm waterway between the island and the reef that is ideal for sea kayaking, windsurfing, and sailing. These activities are underdeveloped and are only now catching on as alternative forms of recreation to the underwater variety. Possibilities include *Me Too,* a catamaran owned by Ramon's Village Resort. For windsurfing and day sailer instruction or rental, try the Sea Breeze Hotel and Journey's End resort. For a comprehensive review of sailing activities on Ambergris Caye, drop by Amigo Travel or Universal Travel on Barrier Reef Drive.

Fishing: Ambergris Caye is well known for its tarpon (February–August), wahoo (February–August), bonefish (November–April), and year-round barracuda, jackfish, mackerel, grouper, snapper, and blue marlin. Charter fishing operators include Melanie Paz (phone 026-2437), Billy Leslie (026-2128), Luz Guerrero (026-2034), Coral Beach Club (026-2001), and Roberto Bradley, Jr. (026-2116). Most, but not all, operators accept major credit cards.

Accommodations: As with Belize City, think in terms of adding upward of 15 percent to advertised rates due to hotel service charges, tips, and credit card handling fees. Also, find out what kinds of extras come with your stay. For example, some package deals include gratis snorkel or dive trips, which may include free refills for scuba tanks. Other hotels may offer scuba lessons, windsurfers, small sailboats, and excursions to Mayan ruins with their package. When it comes to accommodations, the budget category is least represented, and much of the moderately priced space is basic compared to North American places. In part, you're paying extra for location, ambience, and availability of activities. Most places accept major credit cards, but always inquire in advance to be sure.

Thomas's Hotel (B, M) (phone 026-2061) may have the best low-to-moderate cost, centrally located rooms on the island. This tiny hotel is three-quarters of the way to the north end of Barrier Reef

Drive. It is run by Thomas Paz, a longtime fisherman, whose four sons are well-known dive masters on the island. The rooms are tidy with no frills.

For a traditional, first-rate Belizean colonial experience at its best, try Celi McCorkle's San Pedro Holiday Hotel (M) (phone 026-2014/2013). Located on Barrier Reef Drive near the Sun Breeze Hotel and across from the elementary school, the Holiday Hotel is an attractive, multilevel, original structure that you'll also see on postcards in shops. Celi is a pioneer hotelier on San Pedro with twenty-six years' experience. She represents a dwindling number of Belizeans who have survived the onslaught of corporate and foreign buy-outs of the island's hotels. The Holiday Hotel faces the water and has its own dive shop, barbecue pit, and manicured sunning area among palms. Celi's seafood dishes are her own personalized concoctions in which she takes pride for the simple reason that they taste so good. Her "secret sauces," sautéed lobster, and shrimp Dejonghe and creole are superb. Many of the patrons I met were North Americans who had been coming to Celi's place for years. The hotel has the feel of an enlarged private home. The emphasis is on service, and the staff are refreshingly casual and egalitarian toward guests. They work with guests to tailor snorkeling, diving, and fishing activities, which can be included in package stays.

The Paradise Resort Hotel (M) (phone 026-2021), located at the south end of Barrier Reef Drive, is also a good value for its price, including its offering of recreational activities.

If you want to rent an apartment and prepare your own food, try House of the Rising Sun (M) (phone 026-2336/2505), located on the water to the south of town.

The Sun Breeze Hotel (E) (phone 026-2347/2191) is hard to miss. Walk east about twenty-five yards after getting off the small plane that takes you to the island and you'll bump right into it. The motif is Spanish. Rooms are spartan, but large and entirely private. All rooms open onto a large courtyard that faces east, collecting the constant sea breeze from the Caribbean. There is a private dock and a place set aside for sunbathing. The restaurant staff are friendly and the service is fast. The hotel's Bottom Time Diveshop is a few steps from the hotel. Windsurfers are also available. Rates are at the low end of the expensive category.

Ramon's Village Resort (E) (phone 026-0271/2213; in the United States, 601-649-1990) is immediately south of the Sun Breeze Hotel.

It has sixty rooms in meticulously constructed, palm-thatched cabanas, most of which have sea views. Ramon's has an excellent restaurant and is a popular night spot for both Belizeans and foreigners. Ramon's provides daily dive trips, dive and snorkel charters, sail trips on the catamaran *Me Too,* and glass-bottom-boat rides.

Journey's End (E) (phone 026-2173) is four-and-a-half miles north of San Pedro and reached from the island's airport by a combination of van and boat. The ride is pleasant, but the resort is isolated from town. Being self-contained, Journey's End has something for everyone: well-lit tennis courts, a large pool, a wide selection of small sailing crafts, captive jungle animals, a top-flight restaurant, and perhaps the best-equipped dive shop and expertise in Belize. There are also two private homes, one that has been rented by former President Jimmy Carter on a couple of occasions. This is the only resort I visited that provides an area for nude sunbathing. The crowd here varies but often includes high rollers who arrive in Belize via private planes and a few more Europeans than I'd seen elsewhere. Larry Parker carries the title of Water Sports Activity Director at Journey's End. His company, Reef Divers Ltd., is an independent business that operates in conjunction with Journey's End.

Finally, the Coral Beach Hotel (B) (phone 026-2001), Lily's Caribbean Lodge (B) (phone 026-2059), and Rubie's Hotel (B) (phone 026-2063/2434) cover the basics, including private bathrooms.

Access: It takes fifteen minutes by air to reach San Pedro from Phillip Goldson International Airport in Belize City. One way usually costs less than U.S. $30. Tropic, Island, and Maya (Belize's small airlines) make many flights daily. The Belize City Municipal Airport also connects with the island on regularly scheduled flights.

You can also arrive via boat from Belize City. The *Andrea* operates from Belize City to San Pedro, departing the Bellevue Hotel (phone 02-77051/77052) dock at 4:00 P.M. on Monday through Friday and 1:00 P.M. on Saturday. You're out of luck on Sunday. *Miss Belize* makes daily runs and departs from the docks behind the Supreme Court Building. Tickets can be purchased from Universal Travel, 13 Handyside Street, Belize City (phone 02-44667/30964). The *Thunderbolt* and *Hustler* also run between Belize City and San Pedro daily. Schedules are subject to change. The trip takes an hour and fifteen minutes.

Hol Chan Marine Preserve

This much-celebrated preserve takes its name from the Mayan word for a channel in a reef. Located four-and-a-half miles north of San Pedro, the preserve was created in 1987 due largely to the spearheading efforts of Belizean marine biologist Janet Gibson with the encouragement of Dr. Jacque Carter and Archie Carr III and the support of Wildlife Conservation International, the Belize Audubon Society, and other groups. The reef portion of the preserve occupies an area known as the "cut." It has fabulous snorkeling and scuba diving with a maximum depth of about twenty-five feet. For good reason, Hol Chan is the most visited underwater destination in Belize.

Within the boundaries of Hol Chan are approximately 250 acres of coral reef, 750 acres of associated sea grass beds, and 250 acres of mangroves, amounting to five square miles of reserve. The three areas are the essential life zones of the reef community. Boca Ciega Blue Hole, one of dozens of underwater cave systems, also is within the boundaries of the reserve, and not far from the mangrove section is the Marco Gonzalez archaeological site.

The creation of Hol Chan Marine Preserve set an important precedent for the future protection of other sensitive sections of the Barrier Reef. When proponents of Hol Chan persuaded the government to include the less glamorous sea grass and mangrove communities in the reserve, the Belizean government acknowledged the importance of the ecosystems that contribute to the reef. It is expected that when the government moves to protect other sensitive areas of the Barrier Reef it will consider the ecological zones that contribute to the reef's overall health.

The coral reef section of the preserve is formally known as Zone A. This is where you'll find human visitors ogling the amazing plethora of sea life that congregates around the currents that pull and push through the "cut." On most days several boats are anchored at Hol Chan while their human cargo snorkels or scuba dives. Some of the hotels also provide glass-bottom-boat visits. The currents are manageable for an average swimmer but must be taken into account by those entering the water. Ask the person in charge about the immediate tidal currents.

Underwater, along the sides of the cut, you'll see extensive areas of elkhorn, leaf, and finger coral. You'll also see giant, boulderlike brain corals, sea fans, and good-size basket sponges. Unwittingly, some snorkelers will stop swimming and stand on coral heads near the surface. This is forbidden and damaging to the reef. Remember the sign you'll see in front of the San Pedro police station: "Take only photographs, leave only bubbles."

The fish life is unusually unafraid due to years of living unmolested in a sanctuary. Along the walls of the cut, in the areas of the swim-through caves, green morays are often seen. These creatures are semitame. Though it shouldn't be done, I've seen dive masters feed the eels from their hands. You'll also see fairy basslets with purple heads and shiny orange bodies, several species of parrotfish, gray angelfish, squirrelfish, filefish, triggerfish, porkfish, four-eye butterflyfish, sergeant majors, trunkfish, and dozens of other species. There's a good chance that groupers will be staring back at you from only a few feet away as soon as you roll into the water and focus through your mask. They want a handout, which is forbidden. The practice of feeding the fish no doubt continues, judging by the solicitous behavior of some of the fish.

The largest zone in the preserve is the lagoon, or Zone B. It features sea grass, a rather monotonous looking sea bottom to most visitors. This area between the reef and mangroves is the largest of the three life zones and supports a wide range of sea creatures, including young fish not adept enough to survive in the deeper waters around the reef. You'll also see conch, lobsters, mature parrotfish, and other schooling fish eating here. With a little luck you'll see one of Belize's three species of sea turtle or a manatee. The lagoon is shallow, usually clear with 100 feet or more of visibility, and protected from surface turbulence by the reef. Usually it is very bright, which makes taking underwater photos here easier than in the deeper, more varied terrain of the reef, providing you can find a willing subject. The lagoon also has Boca Ciega Blue Hole, created when a section of the area's karst surface collapsed, creating a sinkhole. This sinkhole opens into a large cavern that is known to be home to large groupers and jewfish. Entering this blue hole (or any underwater cave) is dangerous and can be done only by scuba divers under the supervision of a local dive master and with permission from the reserve manager.

The mangrove section, or Zone C, consists of seven small mangrove cayes at the southern terminus of Ambergris Caye. Red, white, and black mangroves, the three species found in Belize, are found here. The prolific root systems of the red mangroves offer refuge for the widest variety of fry and juvenile fish. It is possible to snorkel between the mangrove channels, where you'll see the small fish darting out of your way and young barracudas eating them. You'll also be surprised to see white grunts, gray snappers, butterflyfish, and angelfish, which you'd think belong with their kin in deeper water by the reef. If you try this, take care to avoid kicking up the light sediment that will quickly cloud the water, erasing all visibility for the person snorkeling along behind you.

Night Diving: Hol Chan is also the primary night diving site on Ambergris Caye. Snorkeling with lights may be permitted, but I found nobody offering the service. Night diving at Hol Chan is an extremely enriching experience. Night brings on a whole new cast of characters, and you can witness marvelous defensive strategies. After drifting to the bottom, I remember swinging my light upward and spotlighting a reef squid hovering above us. Poof! In an instant it was gone. Green morays were prowling the walls. Multitudes of luminescent shrimp passed by, flashing in green bursts of light that confuse predators. Many of the daytime's most active fish were still as stone, hiding deep in the coral and in cracks between rocks. Parrotfish could be seen motionless in their mucus cocoons, which they weave each night as protection against predators. As we swam deeper into the cut, our beams of light converged on a school of large tiger groupers that had entered the cut from deeper water to capture a meal. They seemed entirely unimpressed by our presence as we swam within a few yards of them. Two middle-size barracudas seen swaggering along a wall were not so nonchalant. Our lights picked them out of the darkness and they sped off. Since this dive is shallow, a tankful of air lasts longer; one hour of water time is the norm. Both in winter and summer the water is warm enough to dispense with a wetsuit.

Caye Caulker

Located ten miles south of Ambergris Caye and twenty miles north of Belize City, Caye Caulker ("Corker" on some maps) is a low-key, low-budget contrast to the bustle of Ambergris Caye. Caye Caulker is like the Ambergris Caye of yesteryear, before the international travel industry changed it. Above all else, it's cheap to stay in Caulker, and in terms of natural phenomena, Caulker has what Ambergris has.

History: There's a romantic, out-of-reach-from-society aspect to Caulker that may have originated with the pirates who supposedly named the island. According to some islanders, "Caulker" came from English pirates who bastardized the word *coco* by mispronouncing it as "corker." This, somehow, became Caulker. Apparently, the wild coco plum, which grew in profusion here, enticed seasonal visits from English sea dogs, who took time out from plundering Spanish galleons to quench their taste for coco plums. The other story told by some of the same islanders is that the name is derived from the words *cayo jiaco*, which is Spanish for "coconut island." The island's first permanent settlers came from Mexico after the Caste Wars and began cultivating coconut plantations here in the late 1800s. *Cayo Jiaco* supposedly became twisted by pirates to Caye Caulker. Since written records are nonexistent, oral histories provide these differing accounts of the origins of the island's name. Probably most telling is today's islanders' insistence that pirates figure into all versions (even the one of Mexican settlement, which postdates pirate activities by a century) without evidence that pirates had anything to do with the name. Mysteries and inconsistencies aside, more than any island in Belize, Caye Caulker attracts young, low-budget travelers from around the world who like stories about pirates. Today, many of the descendants of these original Hispanic settlers have remained on Caulker.

Physical Description: The island is about a fraction of the size of Ambergris Caye and nearly identical in terms of geological and floral composition—limestone, mangroves, patches of dry land supporting coconut palms, and a few narrow beaches. Caulker has the same french-fry shape as Ambergris and sits on the same north-south orientation directly south of Ambergris. However, unlike Ambergris, Caulker is actually two islands. In 1961 it was sliced in half by Hurricane Hattie, which blew a narrow channel, called the "cut," through the island. The cut has become a great convenience to Caulker's residents. Mostly mangrove swamp lies north of the cut, and the village, which is also called the "cut," lies directly south of it, making reaching three sides of the village by boat much easier than when the northern mangroves were still attached to the northern half of the island. The cut also serves as a nice swimming area, though the current can be strong.

   Homes and businesses are spread out along sandy tracks that make up the village grid. From most approaches the island first appears uninhabited. As your boat glides along a mangrove shoreline you'll know you've reached the area of human habitation when you see a few shallow-water piers (called "bridges" by locals) poking out into water. The "streets" aren't signposted, but their arrangement is simple to figure out. Front (east side) and Back (west side) streets run parallel in a north-south direction. These sandy lanes are connected by four or five sandy tracks that run east to west. The entire village is found in this area, except for the portion of Front Street that extends along the east shore for a half-mile north of the grid to the cut. Because homes and businesses are not generally clustered, you'll sometimes wonder if the track you're walking along is leading anywhere. Rest assured, if it's a sandy track wide enough for a vehicle, it's a thoroughfare. The mode of transportation on the island's sandy tracks is walking, since there are fewer than a half-dozen vehicles, and everything on the island related to commerce is never farther than a mile away. Goods and suitcases are often moved by wheelbarrow.

Instead of bright lights, native dance and drum troupes, and corporate-owned resorts, Caye Caulker features quiet moonlit nights, uninterrupted siestas in hammocks, a half-dozen low-budget hotels, and tiny restaurants that double as homes or mom-and-pop groceries owned by the islanders themselves. The accent is on casual. The police station is opened intermittently. There are no booking agents. Dive operations tend to be single-boat, single-dive-master affairs. There are sail charters on traditional wooden, gaff-rigged fishing sloops run by the owners or friends of the owners. The island has a diverse population, which includes artists, fishermen, Rastafarians, professional photographers, and young Europeans who have moved in with locals temporarily or permanently, ending their world travels here. After a couple of days and a couple of walks down the island's sandy tracks, you'll know practically everyone who wants to be known. To find your way around, just ask. There are about 800 permanent inhabitants. The population doubles during the peak of tourism, around Christmas.

Cultural Diversity: Over time the island has accumulated more ethnic and cultural diversity than mainland Belize, which is quite a feat. On Caye Caulker these disparate groups don't segregate themselves along cultural and ethnic lines. Origins and skin color don't seem to matter. The prevailing social atmosphere is a slow-paced, live-and-let-live ambience that absorbs arrivals from everywhere. One of the first people I met was Emma Gill, a trim, middle-aged, Creole woman with a beautiful smile and strong Caribbean accent. She was busily painting personalized T-shirts of Belizean ocean scenes under the shade of a coconut palm overlooking the beach. Emma holds a master's degree in art from UCLA, owns a couple of classic wooden sailing boats (see "Sailing" below), and lives in a tiny cottage on the beach. She retreated from Los Angeles "many years ago. I wanted to live closer to my roots." There's Frenchie, a tall, handsome man with Mayan features whose real name is Etrain Novelos. He and his Austrian-born wife, Gertraud, run Frenchie's Diving Service, one of the most popular dive outfits on the island. I met a disabled U.S. Vietnam veteran with hair to the middle of his back who looked like he'd stepped out of a 1960s time capsule. He had not felt comfortable in the United States after being released from a hospital in 1972 and has been a commercial fisherman living on Caye Caulker for the last ten years. While I was snorkeling offshore, three Germans from Hamburg, wearing only scuba tanks and sporting golden, full-body tans, pulled their boat near me to enthusiastically describe the beautiful diving they had been experiencing. They rolled from their boat and swam off underneath me to deeper water, where they hoped to find an underwater cave. The Belizean who owned the boat stayed topside with his fishing pole and book.

Eccentrics, wanderers, adventurers, and those wanting a little extra space collect on Caulker. However, the island's laid-back atmosphere is undergoing culture shock. After much debate, and minor sabotage, an airstrip connecting the island with the outside world was completed in 1992. Prior to the airstrip, isolation was guaranteed, since the only way to reach Caulker was by boat. But change is inevitable. How fast it will come, and in what form, is what's left to debate. Foremost on many islanders' minds are retaining land ownership and local control, which hasn't been the case on Ambergris Caye.

Legal and Social Considerations: The owners of a local business told me that villagers are concerned about European attitudes regarding nudity and that I should explain to my readers that longtime Caye Caulker residents are offended by nudity around the village. Residents are also intolerant of substance abusers and petty thieves, who sometimes come here only to be rounded up and taken away to the ancient prison in Belize City. Respecting drug laws, which are comparable to those in the United States, and a little discretion in covering up around town are expected of visitors. These concerns aside, during my time on Caulker the only transgression I witnessed in sight of the village was a magnificent frigate bird stealing fish from the back of a fisherman's boat.

Where to Eat and Other Basics: The Northern Fishermen's Cooperative that operates on Caulker keeps island residents and restaurants stocked with fresh lobster and fish, which are usually served for very reasonable prices, most often with the Belizean staples of rice and beans. The exception to Belizean cuisine is the Aberdeen Restaurant (B, M) which serves Chinese food. The Tropical Paradise (B, M), near the water in the southwest corner of the village across from the church, serves excellent fish and lobster dishes. Owner Ramon Reyes also makes homemade ice cream. A number of local women serve meals from their homes. You need to make reservations at "home restaurants" by dropping by early on the day you plan to come for a meal. Celie's, Riva's, and Ms. Evelyn's are recommended by locals. The Martinez Restaurant, on the west side near the soccer field, may be the only place serving three meals a day. For groceries, the J&L Grocery, on the next street west from the Aberdeen Restaurant, has the most complete offerings. You can buy freshly baked bread at Dalmi's, near the grocery, or pastries and bread at Glenda's Snacks, located northeast of the post office (which is in the south-central village area). The post office is also Celie's Mini Mart and Restaurant. There is a public telephone across from the soccer field near the Martinez Restaurant. Its hours most days are 8:00 A.M. to 12:00 noon and 3:00 P.M. to 6:00 P.M.. The phone is closed Sundays and some holidays.

Artists: Island artists include underwater photographer James Beveridge (see below); Ellen McRae, a California marine biologist and wildlife photographer; Emma Gill, a seascape and T-shirt artist; and Phillip Lewis, a.k.a. "Karate," a T-shirt artist, producer of a popular street map of the island, and codesigner of Belizean paper money. Ellen McRae's shop, Galeria Hicaco, has samples of her extensive underwater and terrestrial photographs plus art from all of Belize's cultures: Mayan, Garifuna, Hispanic, and Creole. Ellen also offers educational seminars and inexpensive snorkel trips (see below).

Dive and Snorkel Services: Frenchie leads dives directly offshore to the Swash, Sponge Avenue, and South Cut sites, as well as to Hol Chan, Turneffe, and Lighthouse Reef, including the Blue Hole. His is the only Caulker dive operation ranging this far afield. Contact Frenchie's Diving Service, Caye Caulker, Belize, C.A. (phone 022-2234). Professional underwater photographer James Beveridge offers guided underwater photography excursions. He's been operating in Belize since 1972 and has the most complete collection of nature transparencies in the country. Often his wife, Dorothy, acts as an underwater guide. His company, Seaing is Belizing, is well respected in the conservation community throughout Belize. Besides leading photographic outings, Beveridge offers slide shows on reef ecology and the rain forest. Sierra Club groups have used his services. The Beveridges are usually busy, so make arrangements with them well before showing up on Caulker. The Beveridges' island studio is open to visitors wishing to buy quality images of Belize or obtain literature on environmental issues in Belize. Contact Seaing is Belizing, P.O. Box 374, Belize City, Belize, C.A. (phone 022-2189). Marine biologist and photographer Ellen McRae offers educational seminars and budget snorkel excursions to the reef. Contact Ellen McRae, Caye Caulker, Belize, C.A. (phone 022-2178). The Belize Diving Service also operates on Caye Caulker, offering PADI certification classes and often leading dives on the nearby reef and in the extensive cave system just offshore. If you have your own equipment, you can get tank refills upon proof of certification and buy or fix equipment here. For snorkelers, the Belize Diving Service rents a mask, fins, and snorkel for U.S. $5 per day. The shop is located directly west of the soccer field. Contact Fred Bounting, Belize Diving Service, P.O. Box 667, Belize City, Belize, C.A. (phone 02-2134).

Dive and Snorkel Sites: The Barrier Reef is about a mile offshore, necessitating hiring a boat or joining a party headed somewhere you want to snorkel or dive. Besides the dive services listed above, many islanders will take you out to the reef for a small sum. The North Cut, Swash, and Sponge Avenue sites are good to excellent snorkel/dive sites. These are located directly east of the island. Boats from Caye Caulker also travel to Hol Chan at the southern end of Ambergris Caye for snorkeling. George's Rock and Mackerel Hole, near the South Cut, are highly recommended dive sites. The best-known dive at Caulker is the extensive cave system that commences in shallow water off the west side of the island. The first feature is a 320-foot-long passage that is so narrow that only one diver can pass down it at a time; turning around is not possible until the tunnel ends at a depth of 90 feet. This tunnel opens into a large cavern with massive stalagmites and stalactites. The cavern, which is directly beneath the island, rises to within 30 feet of the surface. This dive carries considerable risks and is not for the inexperienced, claustrophobic, or, in my opinion, the fully sane. If you are realistically confident about your skill and equipment and like narrow passages, you will probably enjoy it. However, keep in mind that several divers have lost their lives in this cave system. If you decide on this cave dive, it should be done only with an experienced dive master. Fred Bounting of the Belize Diving Service has led this dive many, many times.

Caution: For scuba divers there's always a risk, but if you plan on cave diving, take note of the description of the cave system above. Don't do the dive if you have reservations, or because divers you are with urge you to do it despite your doubts. The cut has a strong current, which must be respected when venturing into the water in this favorite swimming area.

Fishing: Tarpon (from February through August), snapper, grouper, snook, shark, and barracuda are some of the fish caught in the waters around Caye Caulker. Fishing charters include Frenchie's (phone 022-2234), Pegasus Boat Service (022-2122), Sylvano Canto (022-2215), and Melvin Badillo, Jr. (022-2111).

Sailing: Upon request, James and Dorothy Beveridge will organize and guide snorkeling or diving trips by sailboat. Between November and April, Emma Gill also offers sail charters through her business, I and Jah International Outrigger Sailing Club. Emma owns a few traditional forty-foot, wooden, gaff-rigged sailboats, known as "lighters," the staple craft of traders and fishermen in Belizean waters. These are working boats with no frills. When I visited, Emma's crewmen were a weathered group of young, free-spirited Jamaicans and Belizeans who in appearance could pass for pirates of yesteryear. If a client's pocket is deep enough, Emma's boats will explore the entire coast. Depending on the trip, they stop at San Pedro on Ambergris Caye, Caye Chapel, St. George's Caye, Goff's Caye, Tobacco Caye, South Water Caye, Sandfly Caye, Hopkins Caye, Dangriga,

Placencia, Laughing Bird Caye, and Raguana Caye. "We do coastal cruising, stopping whenever dockage is possible or when there is interest to take a look around. We'll go as far south as Guatemala, sleeping aboard or camping. Meals are included. All customers who sail with us for three days or more get a complimentary painted T-shirt of a Belize sea scene. It will be very beautiful and make you happy after you go home," explains Emma. Contact Emma Gill, Caye Caulker, Belize, C.A. (no phone). Her shop is next door to the Aberdeen Restaurant. Also try the *Gamusa*, owned by the Reef Hotel. Contact the Reef Hotel, Caye Caulker, Belize, C.A. (phone 022-2196).

Caution: Indigenous sail hires can be found in isolated places along the Belize coast. This kind of sailing is a cultural experience with a few considerations and risks not normally associated with bareboat (without a crew) or charter (with a crew) sailing. Don't expect radio gear, marine insurance, or safety-inspected boats. You're signing on for a once-in-a-lifetime experience that relies on your crew's skill and local knowledge of the area. The quality of the experience is contingent upon your good judgment as to the temperament of the crew and your ability to remain flexible and get along with people who probably come from an entirely different background from your own. For the harmony of everyone involved, make sure that the price and method of payment (cash, in most cases) are understood, as well as who is responsible for what, including what will be eaten, imbibed, and smoked, and in what amounts, before you leave the dock.

Be Prepared: From June to November, mosquitoes and sand flies have their way with islanders. During this season, inland breezes are less reliable in driving the pesky bugs away from the dry open areas and beaches, where people live and recreate. The bugs are always at the ready and can swarm in from nearby strongholds in the mangroves when the wind dies. Also take care to avoid sunburn. Sunscreen, bug repellent, and a hat are mandatory on land, and always wear a T-shirt while snorkeling.

Accommodations: In general, places you can rent are cheap, basic but clean, and effective for keeping out rain and bugs. Very few hotels serve meals. Most rooms have fans, but for the most part, air-conditioning, phones, and payment by credit card haven't made it here yet. There is limited camping. I met a couple from France who had been staying in hammocks for a week. Accommodations on the eastern shore get the benefit of a constant sea breeze during peak season, from December to May. Most accommodations are in the budget range; even the places that fall into the moderate range only barely do so. I had difficulty finding a room for more than U.S. $30.

To satisfy creature comforts most easily, try the Rainbow Hotel (B, M) (phone 022-2127) on the east shore. It has private baths and hot water, two rarities on Caulker. Also, this plain-looking stucco hotel is conveniently located at the end of a pier, which makes transferring luggage a workable situation. There are no cabs or shuttles. Unless you've made arrangements, you can end up lugging your heavy suitcase or pack around the island as you ferret out a place to stay, not a fun activity in the midday tropical sun. The Rainbow Hotel is also close to the Aberdeen Restaurant. The Rainbow is one of the few businesses that accept Visa and traveler's checks. If budgeting your money is an overriding concern, stay at Mira Mar (B) on the east shore near the Rainbow Hotel. Small rooms, which share a common bathroom, rent for U.S. $5 for a single and U.S. $8 for a double — cash only. The Aberdeen Restaurant-Bar-Hotel (phone 022-2127) is a meeting place of sorts for islanders because it has a couple of pool tables. The restaurant's daily menu is posted on a chalkboard; on the day of my visit the chalkboard read "Lobster or Fish Dinners, The Choice Is Yours." The Aberdeen also has a bar and eight rooms for rent. The room rate is U.S. $8 a day. Proprieters Alan and Wai-lan Chan are descendants of Chinese immigrants who arrived in Belize as laborers at the turn of the century. Vegas' Far Inn (B, M) (phone 022-2142), operated by descendants of one of the original settler families, covers the spectrum of accommodations offered on Caulker. In a two-story clapboard structure, the Vegas have rooms with private baths and rooms with shared baths. They also offer camping sites, but loud partying isn't tolerated for long. Reservations are necessary during peak season; contact Maria Vega. The Split Beach Resort (B) near the cut and Tom's Hotel (B) are meeting places for the young diver and snorkeler crowd.

Access: Until 1992 the only way to reach Caulker was by boat from either Belize City or Ambergris Caye. With the island's airstrip completed, there is now air service from Phillip Goldson International Airport and the Belize City Municipal Airport. Inquire at the Tropic, Island, or Maya ticket counters in either airport. Usually flights are arranged to coordinate with incoming international flights. From the international airport the flight takes about fifteen minutes and costs U.S. $25 one way.

Boats to Caye Caulker from Belize City leave from the Shell Station on North Center Street. The boats are seagoing speedboats (called skiffs or launches) that are fast, fun, and bouncy in rough weather. If you're prone to seasickness, medication may be in order. The *Soledad* (phone 022-2151), skippered by popular Caye Caulker resident Chocolate, makes the run several times daily, as does *Pegasus* (phone 022-2122). For further information, stop by Mom's Triangle Inn, at 11 Handyside in Belize City. Chocolate often eats here, but if he's not around, you can find out his schedule. Departing Caulker, the *Soledad* usually leaves from the pier across from the gift shop on Front Street. From Belize City, the first boat usually leaves at 6:30 A.M. From Caulker to Belize City, service starts at 7:30 A.M. If you arrived from North America on a morning flight and are headed for Caulker, you'll find that a boat usually leaves the Belize City Shell Station at 11:00 A.M. Take a cab to the North Center Street Shell Station to catch the boat to Caulker. There is also the *Andrea,* which leaves at 4:00 P.M. from the Bellevue Hotel dock in Belize City six days a week and returns, stopping at Cayes Chapel and Caulker, in the afternoon.

From Ambergris Caye to Caye Caulker, regularly scheduled boat runs don't have tremendous life spans. The *Andrea* is one boat that has been making this run for quite a while. It runs from the Bellevue Hotel in Belize City to Ambergris Caye six days a week and will make stops at Cayes Chapel and Caulker. On its return to Belize City, it starts at the Barrier Reef Hotel on Ambergris Caye. Check with the hotel for departure times. Private boat hire is another, more adventuresome method of reaching Caulker from Ambergris. Locals on Ambergris will take you to Caulker for an afternoon. The trick is finding someone who will do it for a reasonable price. Most people with boats on Ambergris are attuned to luxury rates associated with scuba divers. Tony (U.S. $20 per half-day), who owns a small aluminum boat and hangs out at the Tackle Box (a pub on a pier about halfway down Barrier Reef Drive) proved to be reliable and an excellent guide. He seems to know just about everyone on Caulker and likes to catch up on gossip, which is spoken mostly in Creole and translated, censored, and embellished by Tony. Please don't let Tony's speech impediment lead you to feel shy about hiring him. He's had a pronounced stutter his entire life. After five minutes you'll find he has a sharp sense of humor and an able intellect.

On Caye Caulker, besides the regularly scheduled runs of *Soledad, Pegasus,* and *Andrea* to and from Belize City, Gerald Pacheco operates a water taxi from a pier on the west side (phone 022-2114).

Caye Chapel

Caye Chapel is about a mile south of Caye Caulker and measures three miles long, perhaps a mile wide, and is made of the same limestone as Caulker and Ambergris. The social atmosphere is entirely different from Caulker. Caye Chapel is synonymous with Pyramid Island Resort, the only resort on the island. Pyramid Island Resort is a large (by Belizean standards), thirty-two-room, single-story, stucco structure on the windward side of the island. Over the years the island has been made over: denuded in areas, beaches widened, an airstrip cut across its center, and the undergrowth and many palms removed around the resort. The emphasis is on water sports: scuba diving, snorkeling, sailing, fishing, and sunbathing. The island also has a full-service marina for the international sailing set.

There is a good-quality beach directly in front of the resort and a mangrove lagoon at the south end of the island that has a diverse population of shorebirds, including several species of herons and egrets, roseate spoonbills, and pelicans; ospreys may also be seen. At the island's north end are secluded beaches that are normally reached via the resort's motorized three-wheelers.

The resort has a fleet of boats to meet all needs. There is the fifty-foot *Offshore Express,* used on overnight dive trips to the Turneffe Islands and Lighthouse Reef. A thirty-seven-foot Ensign is used for diving and fishing, and high-powered, open-water speedboats capable of speeds of sixty miles per hour are used to access faraway destinations such as Turneffe, the Blue Hole, and other dive spots on Lighthouse Reef. For those who want to view the reef without getting wet, the resort uses a glass-bottom boat along the inside of the reef. There are also boats outfitted for tarpon, bonefish, and grouper fishing and a conventional runabout for water-skiing.

Dive and Snorkel Sites: For snorkelers, the water immediately off-shore is mostly sea grass beds that support some tropical fish. Most snorkeling is done from boats after about a ten-minute ride to selected sites. Short-distance diving outside the Barrier Reef offers the same spur and groove underwater topography as found around Ambergris. The resort's boats also go to the Turneffe Islands and Lighthouse Reef and stop at many of the sites recommended by dive master Changa Paz (see his top dive and snorkel sites in the "Ambergris Caye" section).

Accommodations: Pyramid Island Resort (M, E) is your only choice, and there is no camping. The resort has a range of room types and a restaurant, bar, and gift shop. Contact Pyramid Island Resort, Caye Chapel, P.O. Box 192, Belize City, C.A. (phone 02-44409; fax 02-32405). Book in advance during peak season, November through May.

Access: Most people arrive on the island via light aircraft from Phillip Goldson International Airport (ten minutes) or Belize City Municipal Airport. Airfare costs less than U.S. $30. Boats from Belize City, Caye Caulker, and Ambergris Caye also call here. Try the *Andrea,* which runs back and forth from the Barrier Reef Hotel dock on Ambergris Caye and the Bellevue Hotel dock in Belize City.

St. George's Caye

St. George's Caye is a small sand island about ten miles from Belize City and is the island of choice for many established, successful Belizean families, who have private homes here. The island figures prominently in Belizean history. It was the unofficial capital of the unofficial British colony from about 1660 to 1784 and the site of the single biggest event in Belizean history. From St. George's Caye in 1798 a ragtag contingent of English colonials, squatters, former pirates, and their slaves defeated a much larger Spanish force that arrived in a fleet from Mexico. The Spanish had come to drive the English colonial loggers, called Baymen, from their toehold in Central America. Everyone, including the English, expected the Spanish to succeed. Surprise! With more than a dozen warships overcrowded with hundreds of foot soldiers poised to go ashore, and with more than twenty times the firepower, the Spanish were routed by a single English schooner, a few well-placed cannonballs from a battery on St. George's Caye, and the Baymen's greater willingness to fight.

The Battle of St. George's Caye put an end to the Spanish claim to the area and set into motion the creation of an English colony that officially became British Honduras in 1862. St. George's Caye Day is celebrated throughout Belize as a national holiday every September 10.

Today, St. George's Caye is a destination for affluent Belizeans with summer cottages on the island and for snorkelers, divers, sailors, fishermen, and people just wanting to get away from the city. The island has two resorts: Cottage Colony and St. George's Island Cottages. Compared to those on other islands, the houses and buildings on St. George's are tidy, well kept, and architecturally consistent, and the island seems to be set in its appearance, in contrast to the frantic construction under way on Ambergris Caye. The diving and snorkeling are surprisingly good for being so close to Belize City. Judging by the number of foreign embassy personnel I met here, St. George's Caye appears to be a favorite island for the diplomatic corps serving in Belize. The island has its colorful characters too. One local woman walks the beach daily with a parrot on her shoulder. Harry, the tame brown pelican and five-year resident of the Cottage Colony dock, will follow you around like a dog and gulp down fish thrown to him. The Barrier Reef is only one mile away, so in terms of convenience from Belize City and the short amount of boat time to dive and snorkel sites, St. George's Caye will always be appealing.

Snorkel and Dive Sites: There is good snorkeling right off the Cottage Colony pier. Juvenile fish of many species reside around the pier in an artificial setting created by the strategic placement of piles of cinder blocks. Young puffers and cowfish are particularly plentiful. Most of the dive sites are within ten minutes of the island. Much of the underwater landscape is spur and groove, with larger concentrations of fish than most dives and snorkels I experienced in Belize. Some of the more popular dives are Alladins, featuring spur and groove; Ice Cream Cone, with large gorgonians; Little Finger, known for large groupers; Eel Gardens, with large concentrations of moray eels in water fifteen feet to twenty feet deep; and Bruce's Column, a strange, singular, massive outcrop with large elephant ear sponges and Nassau groupers that don't mind being touched. Cottage Colony often takes divers to a twenty-five-feet, swim-through cave that starts at a depth of eighty feet.

Day Trips: Twelve miles south of St. George's Caye is a favorite day-trip destination: Goff's Caye, an idyllic, five-palm island with excellent snorkeling about 200 yards from shore. Gallows Point Reef is also nearby for scuba divers. Other diversions from St. George's include diving on the southern end of the Turneffe Islands, particularly at Rendezvous Wall, known for its 200-pound jewfish. Nonunderwater excursions include all kinds of fishing, as well as bird and manatee watching in the mangroves of nearby Drowned Caye.

Sailing: Wright Saylor, the dive master and instructor for Cottage Colony, operates *Ddraig*, a Freedom 40, double-ender ketch from Cottage Colony. Saylor is a PADI-certified scuba instructor and conducts sailing/scuba or snorkel trips for two-, three-, and four-day outings. For details, contact Captain Wright Saylor, Cottage Colony, St. George's Caye, P.O. Box 428, Belize City, Belize, C.A. (phone 02-77051; fax 02-73253).

Accommodations: There are two resorts on the island: Cottage Colony (E) and St. George's Island Cottages (E). Both accept credit cards and feature aesthetically pleasing architecture, excellent cuisine, and high-quality diving/snorkeling and fishing operations. St. George's Island Cottages has a lodge with an impressive cathedral ceiling made of large beams of native Santa Maria and beautifully crafted furniture and a bar of native rosewood. Owner Fred Good moved here in the 1970s after years of running a dive shop in California. Contact St. George's Island Cottages, P.O. Box 625, Belize City, Belize, C.A. (phone 02-44190; in the United States and Canada, 1-800-678-6871; fax 02-30461). Cottage Colony is owned by the Bellevue Hotel, among my favorite Belize City hotels. Janet (Dinger) Finlayson runs Cottage Colony and has put together an impressive European and Creole menu, based, in part, on her ten years of living in Europe. Her brother, Roger Dinger, master storyteller of the fish that got away, splits his time between the Bellevue and Cottage Colony. Accommodations are in fifteen cottages built in an attractive colonial apartment style. The cottages open onto a manicured hard-sand courtyard. Each cottage has a phone. The bar and dining area overlook the dock where guests snorkel and fish. The atmosphere is homey, and most of the guests during my visit were embassy personnel from several nations. Contact Cottage Colony, St. George's Caye, P.O. Box 428, Belize City, Belize, C.A. (phone 02-77051; fax 02-73253).

Access: St. George's Caye can be reached only by boat. From Belize City the ride is about thirty minutes. Along the way you pass Drowned Caye, a home to marine birds and manatees. The boat to Cottage Colony leaves the Bellevue Hotel dock on the southern foreshore of Belize City daily. For travel to St. George's Island Cottages, make arrangements by contacting the resort.

Other Cayes

Located about two miles northwest of Belize City, Moho Caye was the home of Sail Belize. Though this sail charter business went under in 1992, the island was made into a full-scale marina. If you're interested in sailing, inquire at the Belize Tourist Board, 83 North Front Street, Belize City, Belize, C.A. (phone 02-77213/73255) about the status of this island. It is likely that another sail charter outfit will take it over. For coverage of additional Barrier Reef cayes — particularly the superb diving and snorkeling at South Water Caye near Dangriga and the Sapodillas near Punta Gorda — see the "Offshore" sections of the Stann Creek District and Toledo District chapters. For descriptions of the hundreds of Belizean cayes, refer to *Cruising Guide to Belize and Mexico's Caribbean Coast,* by Freya Rauscher (contact Wescott Publishing Company, P.O. Box 130, Stamford, CT 06904).

The Atolls

Belize's three immense atolls — the Turneffe Islands, Lighthouse Reef, and Glover's Reef — lie east of the Barrier Reef and offer some of the best diving and snorkeling in the Caribbean. Together they cover more than 400 square miles, with a total perimeter of 140 miles of reef with hundreds of patch reefs in the inner lagoons of the reefs. The atolls comprise as much reef surface as the Barrier Reef itself. Only a small percentage of the atolls' potential snorkel and dive sites are used on a regular basis.

Unlike Pacific Ocean atolls built on volcanoes, the Belizean atolls sit atop two parallel north-south-oriented submarine ridges close enough to the surface to allow the formation of massive coral and sponge growths. Though fishery activities have impacted some species, the three reefs are largely undisturbed habitats, quite literally bursting with as colorful a matrix of diverse marine life as you'll find anywhere in the Western Hemisphere.

Turneffe Islands

Located about twenty-five miles southeast of Ambergris Caye and fifteen miles due east of Belize City, the Turneffe Islands are part of the largest atoll in Belizean waters. Covering 210 square miles and measuring approximately thirty-five miles long and about five-and-a-half miles wide, Turneffe is five miles east of the Barrier Reef, making it the closest atoll to the Barrier Reef and the mainland.

Turneffe is different from Lighthouse Reef and Glover's Reef in that it has more channels through its reef rim—twenty-three cuts, most of them less than fifty yards wide. Some of these offer excellent snorkeling and diving. For the most part, Turneffe's central lagoon is shallow sea grass beds, encircled with rich green mangrove cayes. Some of the islands have small fishing camps used by native fishermen, who often overnight on the islands because of their many safe anchorages. It is thought that Lighthouse Reef (to the east) has provided Turneffe protection from wind-driven wave action, allowing extensive mangrove islands to form this far from the coast.

Hurricane Damage: More than any other atoll, Turneffe suffered severe damage through its central-most section from Hurricane Hattie in 1961. Hurricanes can severely alter a reef's ecology. In Turneffe's case, Hattie blew away nearly all the mangroves and destroyed most coral formations in a twenty-mile swath. Regeneration of mangroves was rapid, but reef regeneration is expected to take between thirty and seventy-five years. Because of the hurricane's effects, the principal dive and snorkel sites are at the northern and southern ends of the Turneffe Islands.

About the American Crocodile: The Turneffe Islands are the stronghold of the American crocodile (*Crocodylus acutus*), called the "saltwater crocodile" in Belize. Studies by Judith Perkins, working for the New York Zoological Society and the Yale School of Forestry and Environment, singled out Turneffe as the most populous American crocodile area of ten survey points along the Belizean coast. You'll have to make an effort to see one, however, due to their learned response of avoiding humans. An endangered species, and thus protected by international law from the hide trade, American crocodiles appear to be making a slow recovery, though poaching still occurs.

Besides populations living in Belize and in isolated areas throughout the Caribbean, perhaps 400 live along the southeastern coast of the United States, where they are not nearly as plentiful as alligators. Crocodiles can be distinguished from alligators by the way they show their teeth. With its mouth closed, only an alligator's top teeth protrude from its upper jaw, whereas with crocodiles, both top and bottom teeth show outside the jaw, giving them a more fearsome look. Generally, American crocodiles are less aggressive than alligators, though the saltwater crocodile living in Australia and New Guinea is extremely aggressive toward humans.

Distinguishing the American crocodile from Belize's other native croc, the Morlet's crocodile (*Crocodylus morletti*), can be difficult. American crocodiles can grow to twenty feet, as opposed to a mere seven feet for the Morlet's, and American crocodiles have narrower snouts and are found in marine environments such as Turneffe. Along the coast the two species overlap, but only the American crocodile is found far from the mainland because it has well-developed glands that filter excess salt from its body.

The surest way to see crocodiles is at night with a powerful light. In the breeding season male crocs can be heard bellowing in search of mates — a truly unique experience awaiting an adventure traveler on the Turneffe Islands.

Bird Watching: There is a great deal of bird life in the Turneffe Islands. Blue herons, magnificent frigate birds, brown pelicans, terns, and egrets are commonly sighted.

Dive and Snorkel Sites on Northern Turneffe: Most of the dive sites regularly visited from Ambergris Caye are at the northern end of Turneffe (see "Changa Paz's Top Dive and Snorkel Sites" under "Ambergris Caye"). Dory's Channel (fifty-foot depth) is particularly memorable for its colorful, yellow-tip barrel sponges, giant tube sponges, and numerous gorgonians as large as a person. After a thirty-minute dive my fish list included rock beauties, banded and spotlight parrotfish, squirrelfish, hogfish, queen angelfish, yellow-tail snapper, four-eye butterflyfish, yellow-tail damsel, rock hind, sergeant majors, banded butterflyfish, fairy basslets, southern stingray, blue tang, great barracuda, nurse shark, and spotted eagle ray. Cockroach Wall (ninety-foot depth) was impressive with its giant tube sponges and varied topography, including a sandy area with garden eels. On the day of my dive, fish were less plentiful here than in Dory's Channel. The wall near Crawl Caye (seventy-foot depth) is also very dramatic and home to sea fans, large barrel sponges, tube sponges, and open-water and reef fish.

Changa Paz and other dive masters from Ambergris Caye often lead two morning dives to these areas of northern Turneffe. Changa usually breaks for a barbecue fish lunch on Mauger Caye, where there is a funky old lighthouse. He then leads one more dive after lunch before heading back to Ambergris Caye.

Snorkel sites are numerous. Much of the inner lagoon of Turneffe is quite shallow and covered with sea grass. The trick for snorkelers is finding a boat that will cater to both snorkelers and divers because many of the preferred dives are in deep water.

Dive and Snorkel Sites on Southern Turneffe: At the southern end of Turneffe, radiating out from Caye Bokel, there are a number of excellent snorkel and dive sites. The Elbow is probably the best known, though due to currents, exposure to the open ocean, and depth, it is best suited for advanced divers. It is noted for concentrations of large, pelagic fish and eagle rays, which congregate here to feed. Often dozens of eagle rays cruise the area in a single, graceful formation. Hollywood, on the leeward side of the Turneffe Islands, offers a protected, shallow dive site that is suitable for snorklers and for divers needing a refresher. Corals and sponges are diverse and prolific, plus plentiful fish life, featuring more damsels than in other places. Blue Creek, a cut, is also a good spot for divers and snorkelers. Night dives take place here too. Good snorkeling also can be found in the waters near Blackbird Caye Resort.

Fishing: The flats around Turneffe are renowned to light-tackle fly fishermen and deep-water trollers. Barracuda and, in the months of March to June, tarpon are numerous. The many channels cutting through the Turneffe Islands are good fishing grounds for bonito, marlin, sailfish, tuna, grouper, and wahoo. Fishing contacts in San Pedro on Ambergris: Billy Leslie (phone 026-2234), Melanie Paz (026-2437), Luz Guerrero (026-2034), and the Coral Beach Club (026-2001). Fishing contacts on Caulker: Frenchie's (022-2234), Melvin Badillo, Jr. (022-2111), Pegasus Boat Service (022-2122), and Sylvano Canto (022-2215).

Accommodations: There are several primitive fishing camps on the Turneffe Islands used by local fishermen, as well as small resorts catering to sport fishermen, serious divers, snorkelers, and the occasional birder. Of these, Blackbird Caye Resort (M, E) deserves the most mention. Belizeans backed by North American benefactors have worked hard to develop a resort that is oriented to foreign guests, Belizean and foreign students, and scientists interested in reef studies. The entirely private, 4000-acre island's research center is being used by the Biosphere and Oceanic Society. Services include diving, snorkeling, and fishing. The resort does not accept major credit cards or traveler's checks. When North American diver and educator Dr. Roger Luckenbach visited the resort in late 1992, he rated the diving as excellent and reported, "This was an excellent location for a number of reef experiences ranging from deep wall dives to exploring pristine mangrove channels. Porpoises were plentiful, which ought to provide a great deal of behavioral information and entertainment to visitors." Contact Blackbird Caye Resort, 81 West Canal Street, Belize City, Belize, C.A. (phone 027-7670; in the United States, 713-658-1142; fax 027-3092).

Accommodations are also found at the southern end of the atoll at Caye Bokel. One resort there is the Turneffe Diving Lodge (B), which caters to snorkelers and fishermen besides its primary focus on scuba diving. Cash only for drop-ins. Contact the Turneffe Diving Lodge, P.O. Box 480, Belize City, Belize, C.A. (phone in the United States and Canada, 1-800-338-8149; fax in the United States, 904-641-5285). Turneffe Flats (B) is a small resort that covers the basics. It offers six rooms and caters to fishermen and divers. Cash only. Contact Turneffe Flats, 56 Eve Street, Belize City, Belize, C.A. (phone 02-45634).

Access: The northern end of Turneffe is visited most often by boats from Ambergris and Caulker cayes. Passage over calm seas takes about forty-five minutes. Southern Turneffe is visited by live-aboard dive boats and dive operations from St. George's Caye, Belize City, and the island resorts mentioned in "Accommodations" above.

Lighthouse Reef

Lighthouse Reef is an immense reef system covering roughly ninety square miles and measuring twenty-three miles long and four miles wide. It is the easternmost atoll in Belizean waters and lies in a north-south orientation directly east of the Barrier Reef and the Turneffe Islands atoll. Half Moon Caye Natural Monument is the most visited natural feature of Lighthouse Reef, followed by the Blue Hole. Half Moon Caye is often visited by scuba divers, but it is also worth the effort for the non–scuba diver because of its idyllic setting and rare bird life. The area has excellent snorkeling and is surrounded by the kind of aqua blue water seen on postcards of the Caribbean. The entire reef system is known worldwide in scuba diving circles for its spectacular diving. The Blue Hole, made famous by Jacques Cousteau in his 1970 visit and subsequent television special, is probably the most famous dive site, but to me, even more stunning are the wall dives here and the overall undisturbed diversity and magnitude of the reef system itself. Lighthouse Reef easily rivals anywhere in the Caribbean as representative of a healthy, undisturbed reef environment.

Lighthouse Reef Resort, located on Northern Caye (Northern Two Caye on some maps) at the far northern end of the reef, is the only resort on the reef and a little-known destination. It has been perhaps the best-kept secret among quality diving resort destinations in Belizean waters. The question is what lies ahead for this island. In 1989, the resort was purchased by a North American group whose development plans were not entirely clear during the short time I talked with them.

Half Moon Caye Natural Monument: Declared a national monument in 1981 due to efforts of the then fledgling Belize Audubon Society, Half Moon Caye is located in the southeast corner of Lighthouse Reef. It is an idyllic, forty-five-acre island and primary bird rookery for the red-footed booby, a large, graceful seabird with, as its name implies, colorful feet. The red-footed booby is the main reason the sanctuary was declared: the white plumage on these particular boobies is extremely rare and is found in only one other nesting colony, near Tobago. Usually, red-footed boobies are tan in color.

About 4000 boobies nest here in low trees, along with magnificent frigate birds, which sometimes torment the boobies by stealing their eggs. The birds start nesting in December, and if all goes well, plump fuzzball chicks will be demanding food nonstop in March and April. The frigate birds are unmistakable in contrast. The males sport a bright red throat sack, which they puff up when courting. They are dark-colored birds whose fragile-looking, six-foot wingspan and distinct wing profile are easy to identify. Both birds nest in the heavily wooded section at the west end of the island. There is a bird-viewing platform in the middle of the nesting area that can be reached on a trail that begins on the north side of the island and meanders along the shore before cutting inland. Watch for large hermit crabs on the trail. The impenetrable vegetation at the western end consists of fig trees (white trunks and large leaves), gumbo-limbo trees (reddish bark), and ziricotes (with orange-red flowers). The vibrant, healthy quality of the plant life is due to the bird droppings, or guano, fertilizing the area. Besides these large seabirds, ninety-eight species of birds have been recorded on the island, but the majority of them are migratory. Ospreys regularly use the island and can be seen hunting at all times of the day. White-crowned pigeons, egrets, and mangrove warblers are also common.

Rarely seen reptilian species are found on the island. Loggerhead and hawksbill turtles pull out on the southern beaches and deposit their eggs in the sand there. The hawksbill is distinguished by a hooked beak and a colorful shell of overlapping plates in shades of orange, gold, and dark brown. It usually weighs about 125 pounds. The larger loggerhead sometimes weighs in at 300 pounds. It has a proportionately larger and rounder head than a hawksbill, and its shell is heart-shaped and a less colorful brownish red. Both species are endangered and still hunted throughout the Caribbean despite their status. If you spot a possible nesting site—an area of sand around which you see fresh turtle tracks—stay clear of it. Disturbing nests and inadvertently destroying eggs is one of the many reasons these turtles are endangered.

There are three harmless lizard species on the island. The iguana (*Iguana iguana rhinolopha*), more often reddish black in color than the standard iguana green, is found here. It can reach five feet, including its tail. The three- to four-foot, spiny-tailed iguana (*Ctennosaura similis*), or wish-willy, is yellowish with black stripes on its back. A smaller gray lizard (*Anolis allisoni*), which occurs only on Caribbean islands, also lives here.

The island's eastern half features coconut palms standing tall over the undergrowth-free sandy interior and beaches along the northern and southern shores. Visitors come ashore at a small pier on the leeward northern side. The prettiest beach is on the southern shore directly across the island from the northern pier. During my first visit to Half Moon Caye, I found a half-dozen British soldiers snoozing here in hammocks stretched between the palms. Their trusty helicopter was sitting on a mound of coral rubble near the lighthouse. They said they were on reconnaissance. I later met up with them diving at Lighthouse Reef Wall with cameras at the ready, still completing their reconnaissance.

At the island's eastern tip you'll find a weather-worn lighthouse that was built in 1931. This relic replaced a succession of lighthouses, the first one dating back to 1821. The lighthouse is unmanned and solar-powered today. By climbing its rickety staircase you'll get a magnificent view of the island and the surrounding reef and water, as well as a few far-off traditional working sailing craft. You'll see evidence for the necessity of maintaining a lighthouse in the form of the rusting hulk of a Caribbean steamer sitting high on a reef northeast of the island. The sanctuary's warden/lighthouse keeper, who lives in the two small houses near the lighthouse, will present a visitor's book to you to sign.

Sanctuary Regulations: You can camp overnight on Half Moon Caye and are required to remove all trash. You must carry along your own water supply and food. Collecting any plants or animals or their by-products is forbidden. Venturing from the trails at the west end of the island or from the bird-viewing platform (even for photographs!) is forbidden. Much of the underwater area around this natural monument is included in its boundaries. Take only pictures and leave only bubbles—that's the law. Cooking fires are restricted to the designated firepits.

Dive and Snorkel Sites: Three of Changa Paz's top dive sites for the region are on Lighthouse Reef: Half Moon Caye Wall, Long Caye, and the Blue Hole. The dives around Long Caye could easily be expanded into five more spectacular dives. Having dived all of these with Changa, I agree with him on the first two. The combination of a mixed topography of swim-throughs, sandy bottoms, and immense coral buttresses and pillarlike formations decorated and interspersed with black corals, gorgonians, whips, fans, and large sponges and a diversity of reef and open-water fish guarantees that these are hard to beat. The Blue Hole (see below) was definitely stimulating because of its notoriety and depth, but I found it somewhat overrated, unless you like diving in a void.

Snorkel sites are everywhere on Lighthouse Reef. Just swim to an outcrop near your anchorage. The buttressed coral formations just southwest of Half Moon Caye are spectacular. Snorkelers can look down fifty feet or more to sandy bottoms, coral outcrops decorated with huge sponges, and fish everywhere. There also is excellent snorkeling off the north side in the direction of the wreck. The reef surrounding the Blue Hole is very shallow and teeming with fish. If your boat captain is worth his salt, he ought to be able to find a point of entry that is excellent for both snorkelers and divers.

The Blue Hole: This is the much-celebrated dive site seen on postcards and discussed among divers worldwide. From the air it is a perfect circle, about 1000 feet across, of cobalt blue water surrounded by shallow reef. There are two entry points for boats: the north and east entrances. This unusual-looking geological feature is representative of many such "blue holes" in Belizean waters. This one is deeper than the rest of them and more dramatic on the surface because of its perfect symmetry and pronounced color difference compared to the light blue water of the shallow reef surrounding it. The Blue Hole was created by the collapse of the roof of a karst-eroded cave system that formed between 8700 and 18,000 years ago.

The Blue Hole is 415 feet deep, and scuba diving into it should not be taken lightly. To see the stalagmites and stalactites, you must dive to a depth of 120 to 155 feet, which is a dive requiring decompression. The dive is particularly eerie and forbidding because after about 60 feet, the hole's cylindrical wall begins to widen slightly. As you move down the wall, it looms over you and your bubbles bounce along its stony face on their way upward. From this point on, there is a void of sea life. The coral formations slope toward the hole and stop at about 60 feet. From there you go through a thermocline of about an eight-degree temperature drop at about 90 feet. You'll see feather-duster worms and algae on the wall in this area.

Between 120 feet and 155 feet you'll find stalactites and stalagmites (stalagmites are most prevalent) twice as big around as a person and 14 feet long. This is where people pause for photographs before beginning their ascent. During my dive, two four-foot sharks glided past us at about 70 feet as we followed our bubbles upward. Changa Paz says on most dives in the Blue Hole he sees few fish, but when fish appear they are usually in the form of mature sharks or groupers of various types. He was once greeted by more than twenty sharks. The reef around the hole offers excellent shallow-water snorkeling and diving.

The Blue Hole is about midway between Half Moon Caye and Northern Caye. By boat, either island is about fifteen minutes away. Changa Paz, in his wooden, canvas-canopy *Island Princess* with a high-powered outboard, often makes a Blue Hole dive part of a day trip from Ambergris Caye—a two-hour, forty-five-minute journey in calm seas. The trip includes a second dive (or snorkel) on Lighthouse Reef and a barbecue at Half Moon Caye, with enough time for a swim and bird watching. On the return trip, Changa stops (upon request) at the Turneffe Islands for a refreshing swim. Day trips also originate from Caye Caulker, Belize City, and Northern Caye. Caye Caulker and Belize City are about two hours away. Lighthouse Reef Resort is fifteen to twenty minutes from the Blue Hole. Live-aboard dive boats visit the Blue Hole; from Ambergris Caye, with nine divers, the fee is U.S. $125 per person.

Northern Caye (or Northern Two Caye): Northern Caye is a 1100-acre mangrove and sand island with an inner lagoon located at the northern end of Lighthouse Reef. Lighthouse Reef Resort on the island's northern shore is farthest from the mainland of any resort in Belize. It is also entirely isolated, except for some light use of Sandbore Caye, a smaller caye immediately to the north. On Northern Caye and nearby reefs there will be no crowds and no visibility problems such as those associated with winter rains along the coast. The waters around Northern Caye rival anywhere I snorkeled in Belize or Australia. The variety and volume of fish life were astounding. During my visit a young porpoise had befriended the resort's dive master and had become a regular attraction for visitors. The backwaters of the island have American crocodiles up to six feet long and plentiful bird life.

To glimpse the marine life, I entered the water in the channel directly across from Sanbore Caye. This is a shallow area covered with sea grass. About 150 yards from shore, in about five feet to fifteen feet of water, an unforgettable panorama unfolded. There were great numbers of fish, often in schools too numerous even to begin to count or estimate. There were yellow-tail snappers numbering in the thousands, smaller schools of large angelfish of several species, black durgeons, blue tangs, spotted eagle rays gliding past just out of reach, countless numbers of sergeant majors, queen triggerfish, schools of redband parrotfish, rock beauties, black groupers, tiger groupers, southern stingrays, scrawled tigerfish, Atlantic spadefish, squirrelfish, yellow jacks, four-eye butterflyfish, blue-striped grunts, and large barracudas. There were little fairy basslets and damsels too. It was a virtual kaleidoscope of moving color. Of all the places I visited in Belize, only the east side of South Water Caye near Dangriga rivaled this location in terms of the richness of its fish life. Corals and sponges were not as impressive as the fish life; elkhorn coral, common sea fans, and brain corals seemed to dominate. However, in water this shallow, which is constantly buffeted by wind-driven wave action, you can't expect much in the way of coral gardens.

A final incident illustrates the marvelous wild quality of this place. As I snorkeled toward shore over shallow sea grass beds and small coral outcrops, I watched a houndfish cruise near the surface a few yards ahead of me. Suddenly, in a startling splash, it disappeared. I looked skyward as an osprey made off with the fish. "Maybe it was my lucky day," I thought. It is hard to imagine a greater display of marine life than I had witnessed in one hour on Northern Caye.

Spectacular wall dives are the norm here. Many of the walls front an open ocean, allowing divers to see reef species as well as large predatory fish. Dolphins are also common. To the northwest of the caye is a large and beautiful gorgonian forest on a flat surface at about forty feet, near the drop-off of a wall that plummets a thousand feet or more. In all, the staff at Lighthouse Reef Resort on Northern Caye has identified forty dive sites on Lighthouse Reef. Twenty-seven of the sites are in the northern portion of the reef within a short boat ride of Northern Caye. Simply put, Northern Caye will be hard to beat. The only thing left to consider is affordability.

Accommodations: Lighthouse Reef Resort (E) was bought by a group of wealthy North Americans in 1989. The group goes under the name of Lighthouse Reef Development Co. Ltd. They have upgraded the facility a great deal since purchasing it and have built a few ornately embellished beach houses complete with full kitchens, wainscoting, and matching furniture. These are the nicest rental units I visited on an island. There are only five such structures created for people wanting beach houses with their dive packages. The facilities rented by divers are tidy cabanas that are much more spartan. Most visitors stay a week in a prepaid dive package (about U.S. $1200) that includes two or three dives, meals, and accommodations. For the luxury beach houses with the same dive package, it is $1325 per week. Credit cards are accepted for bookings. *Reef Roamer,* one of the liveaboard dive boats operating in Belizean waters, has made Northern Caye its port and picks up its customers on the Northern Caye airstrip. Contact Lighthouse Reef Resort, P.O. Box 1435, Dundee, FL 33838 (in the United States and Canada, phone 1-800-423-3114; in Belize, 02-31205).

Access: The island has a slightly hair-raising, 2000-foot-long sand airstrip that is long enough for Tropic Air's Twin Otter to put down. The plane comes and goes every Saturday, taking out one group and delivering another. Charter air services from San Pedro and Phillip Goldson International Airport also make the trip. It isn't unusual for carriers and schedules to change, which won't matter to you since visitors come here on prepaid dive/snorkel packages from their home countries.

Glover's Reef

The Belize Audubon Society's top marine biologist, Janet Gibson, winner of the prestigious international Goldman Environmental Award for her success in helping create Hol Chan Marine Preserve, rates Glover's Reef as the richest, most diverse marine ecosystem in Belize. It is also the most remote. Besides scientists like Gibson, only the most adventuresome recreational divers — willing to pay the price and invest the time to get to it — experience Glover's Reef. Most of Glover's Reef remains unexplored.

Located seventy miles southeast of Belize City and directly east of Dangriga, Glover's Reef is a roughly north-south-oriented coral formation spread over ninety square miles. The reef is named for pirate John Glover, who operated from one of the tiny islands two centuries ago as a plunderer of Spanish galleons in the Bay of Honduras with the unofficial blessing of the British Crown. The reef is usually reached by water, but there is a tiny private airstrip on one island. Live-aboard dive boats visit only occasionally, and there are two lodges catering exclusively to hard-core divers.

Glover's Reef is clearly defined from the air, with the perimeter of the reef at sea level and only three channels cutting through it in its southern section. This perimeter supports six sandy cayes, four of them named: Northeast Caye, Long Caye, Middle Caye, and Southwest Caye. Middle Caye, recently purchased by Wildlife Conservation International, is used as a base to conduct marine studies that may ultimately help the area be declared a biosphere reserve. The purchase also headed off developers with heavy impact plans from buying the caye in what is arguably the most pristine and sensitive atoll ecosystem in the Caribbean. Belize Audubon Society officials feel that Glover's Reef should eventually become a protected part of the reserve and park system that already controls approximately 30 percent of Belizean territory.

Yale University researcher Judith Perkins, in conducting a 1971 assessment of Glover's Reef for the New York Zoological Society, noted that "approximately 700 patch reefs speckle the inner lagoon, which is significantly deeper (max. 43 m; average 27–37 m) than those of the other atolls." With each patch reef as a potential snorkel or dive site there is more than a lifetime of prime snorkeling and diving here.

Dive and Snorkel Sites: Glover's Reef should be viewed as largely unexplored. This is a place for the adventure diver. Finding dive masters who are even somewhat knowledgeable about the reef is difficult. Even the live-aboard dive boats usually visit the reef only under special charter and not as part of their regular routines. Favorite dive and snorkel sites include Emerald Forest Reef (fifteen to fifty feet deep) on the reef's west side. Impressive elkhorn coral with ten-inch bases and spreads of ten feet dominate the middle depths. These coral growths harbor many small species of tropical fish and crustaceans. Trunkfish, groupers, and middle-size reef fish live in the corals as well. Split Reef is also an excellent area for both snorkelers and divers. There are two reef habitats there: a shallow reef, rarely exceeding thirty-five feet deep, and a deeper reef. The shallow one is known for its great diversity. There are large stands of cactus and elkhorn coral mixed with sea whips, a variety of sea fans, and vibrant sponges. This kaleidoscope of form and color is constantly dashed with schools of small, colorful tropicals, including fairy wrasses, blue chromis, blue tangs, and porkfish. The deeper reef starts at about sixty feet. Other well-documented dive (and possibly snorkel) sites, containing virtually all known reef organisms in colorful profusion, are Long Caye Wall, with stunning coral buttresses forming columns of coral archways with sand corridors, and Shark Point, known for its variety of sharks. For more details on Glover's Reef dive sites, consult *Diving and Snorkeling Guide to Belize*, by Franz O. Meyer. This small book is strictly about diving and has a strong emphasis on Belize's three atolls.

Accommodations: There are two places to stay on the atoll. Glover's Reef Resort (E), located on twelve-acre Northeast Caye, is best described as spartan. Visitors stay in one of eight cabanas and eat in the small restaurant. At last check there were no flush toilets or hot water, but those staying here forsake such conveniences for the excellent diving and fishing. The resort has a compressor for tank refills and guarantees introducing divers to areas that have never seen a diver. Contact Glover's Reef Resort, Long Caye, P.O. Box 563, Belize City, Belize, C.A. (phone 08-23505). Advance bookings only. On Southwest Caye, another twelve-acre sand island with coconut trees, is Manta Reef Resort (E), which caters to both fishermen and divers. The resort has a small fleet of open boats to move clients around the atoll. Contact the Manta Reef Resort, Glover's Reef, 3 Eyre Street, Belize City, Belize, C.A. (phone 02-31895). Advance bookings only.

Access: Expect to pay at least U.S. $150 round trip to visit Glover's Reef by small boat. You may be able to charter boats for the trip from Punta Gorda, Placencia, or Dangriga. There is a tiny airstrip on Southwest Caye that can be used when permission is granted by the owners of the Manta Reef Resort. Make arrangements to reach the atoll with the island lodges, or visit the reef on a live-aboard dive boat.

THREE

STANN CREEK DISTRICT

Overview

The Stann Creek District is Belize's second-smallest district, measuring 986 square miles. What it doesn't have in size it more than makes up for in variety in terms of superb tropical jungle wildlife habitats, a truly unique culture, and island paradises surrounded by some of the world's best diving and snorkeling sites. Dangriga, the northernmost town in the Stann Creek District, is twenty minutes to the south from Belize City by light airplane, one-and-a-half hours (via the Coast Road) by car, or two-and-a-half hours or longer by bus.

The Stann Creek District is the heart of Garifuna (also known as Garinagu or Black Carib) culture, which evolved more than 350 years ago from an isolated mix of Carib/Arawak Indian and escaped African slaves (see "History and Cultures" in the Overview chapter). The district possesses the Cockscomb Basin Wildlife Sanctuary, originally known for being the first sanctuary set aside for jaguars, but now recognized as a premier rain forest wildlife sanctuary (complete with hiking trails) for hundreds of tropical species, many of them threatened elsewhere. The rugged Maya Mountains, including Belize's highest point, Victoria Peak (3675 feet), are the backdrop to the eastern portion of the district. Much of the fertile lowlands has given way to large citrus and banana holdings, begun by Europeans in the 1920s and 1930s. Many of the agricultural properties are owned by the descendants of the original pioneer families that settled here.

The Stann Creek District is also the gateway to the largely undisturbed central and southern sections of the Barrier Reef, which include thirty-five cayes. Most of the cayes are regularly accessed from the towns of Dangriga and Placencia. Among the better-known cayes are South Water (also listed as Water on many maps), Tobacco, Carrie Bow, Man-of-War (bird sanctuary), Wee Wee, Colson, and Laughing Bird (national park) cayes. Glover's Reef (see the Belize District chapter), with Long, Middle, and Southern cayes, is due east from Dangriga, about ten miles past the Barrier Reef. For the adventure traveler, it is important to know that many of the islands and reefs offshore from the Stann Creek District are visited less often than better-known Ambergris Caye, Caye Caulker, and St. George's Caye, and that they compare favorably to the more highly promoted islands to the north.

The district's principal towns — Dangriga, Hopkins, and Placencia — are located on the coast. Each has a different personality, and only in the last few years have they been touched by modernization. Hopkins, for example, was without electricity until 1992. These towns are laid-back places whose generally friendly inhabitants are predominantly from the Garifuna and Creole cultures. Mayan villages dot the district's interior, though these villages (with the exception of Maya Center) aren't as accessible and prepared for visitors as are Mayan villages in the Toledo District to the south.

Dangriga

Dangriga is the closest thing to a citified hub in the Stann Creek District. The town is visually unimpressive but provides basic necessities. Banks, groceries, fuel, and accommodations all can be found on the main drag, Commerce Street (which is named St. Vincent Street and Havana Street south of the North Stann Creek bridge), or within walking distance of it. The town is small and uncomplicated. If you're driving, you'll enter the town on Stann Creek Valley Road. At the gas station, turn left on Havana Street, which becomes St. Vincent Street in a couple of blocks at Havana Creek. In six more blocks, St. Vincent Street becomes Commerce Street at the North Stann Creek bridge. When in doubt, ask. Just about everyone knows where everything is. For groceries, stop at Omar's Store at 111 Commerce Street. Both Barclays Bank and the Bank of Nova Scotia can be found on Commerce Street. The police station (phone 05-22028) is on Commerce Street three blocks north of the bridge over North Stann Creek. The Dangriga Hospital (phone 05-22078) is located on Court House Road (a right turn from Commerce Street after crossing the bridge) near the beach. The gas station (corner of Stann Creek Valley Road and Havana Street) and the post office (on Mahogany Street near the beach) are the only basic services found south of the North Stann Creek bridge.

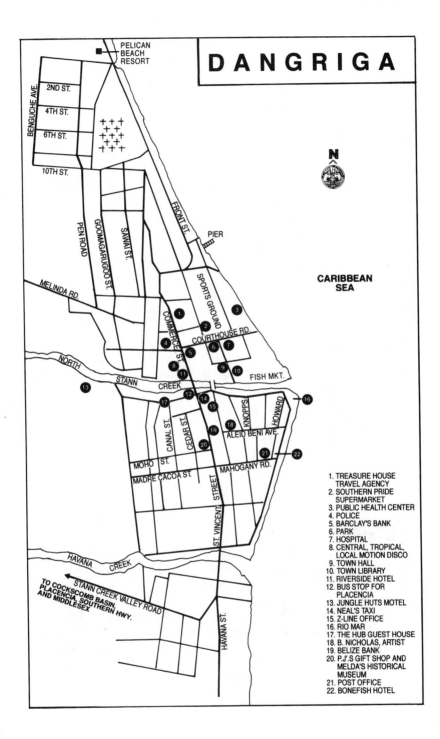

DANGRIGA

N

CARIBBEAN SEA

PELICAN BEACH RESORT

BENGUCHE AVE.
2ND ST.
4TH ST.
6TH ST.
10TH ST.

FRONT ST.
PIER

PEN ROAD
GOOMAGARUGOO ST.
SAWAI ST.

MELINDA RD.

COMMERCE ST.
SPORTS GROUND
COURTHOUSE RD.

NORTH STANN CREEK

FISH MKT.

CANAL ST.
CEDAR ST.
KNOPPS
HOWARD

MOHO ST.
MADRE CACOA ST.
ALEID BENI AVE.
MAHOGANY RD.

ST. VINCENT STREET

HAVANA CREEK

TO COCKSCOMB BASIN,
PLACENCIA, SOUTHERN HWY.
AND MIDDLESEX

STANN CREEK VALLEY ROAD

HAVANA ST.

1. TREASURE HOUSE
   TRAVEL AGENCY
2. SOUTHERN PRIDE
   SUPERMARKET
3. PUBLIC HEALTH CENTER
4. POLICE
5. BARCLAY'S BANK
6. PARK
7. HOSPITAL
8. CENTRAL, TROPICAL,
   LOCAL MOTION DISCO
9. TOWN HALL
10. TOWN LIBRARY
11. RIVERSIDE HOTEL
12. BUS STOP FOR
    PLACENCIA
13. JUNGLE HUTS MOTEL
14. NEAL'S TAXI
15. Z-LINE OFFICE
16. RIO MAR
17. THE HUB GUEST HOUSE
18. B. NICHOLAS, ARTIST
19. BELIZE BANK
20. P.J.'S GIFT SHOP AND
    MELDA'S HISTORICAL
    MUSEUM
21. POST OFFICE
22. BONEFISH HOTEL

History: Dangriga's potholed main street with a single-lane bridge at the halfway point is lined with paint-needy clapboard houses and modest storefronts that belie the town's unique history and culture. Settled by Garifunas in 1832, Dangriga is the hub of Garifuna culture in Belize. In the early 1800s the town was called Carib Town by missionaries baffled by the area's inhabitants, whose physical features and skin color were African, but whose belief system included elements of Island Carib, Arawak Indian, and West African tribes. For most of the twentieth century the town has been called Stann Creek, but the name was changed to Dangriga in 1975, when the town's people decided on a name from the Garifuna language, which is spoken, along with English, by most of the city's 8100 inhabitants. The word *dangriga* means "standing water" in Garifuna, and the town's name refers to the water left standing in large pools when the Stann Creek overflows its banks and then recedes after the rainy season. North Stann Creek flows through town to the sea.

Pelican Beach Resort: To many visitors, Dangriga is Pelican Beach Resort and not much more. For the tourist or adventurer, Pelican Beach Resort serves as a comfortable, self-contained staging area for one- to three-day journeys to the district's many natural wonders. The resort offers a variety of high-quality eco-tourism packages that can be purchased as part of your stay. Proprietors Tony and Therese Rath are dedicated conservationists involved in all aspects of conservation in Belize. You won't find greater expertise about the region. (For details, see "Restaurants," "Tour and Charter Operations," and "Accommodations" below and the "South Water Cave" section.)

Garifuna Artists: Dangriga has a half-dozen artists whose work has received international recognition for its depiction of Garifuna culture, including Garifuna history, customs, and domestic rural life when cassava cultivation was dominant. The artwork displayed in the lobby and recreation room at Pelican Beach is representative of the best of this form, which is called primitive realism. Typically it is distinguished by flat, one-dimensional perspective, bright colors, and stylized figures placed in natural settings. Pen Cayetano and Benjamin Nicholas are among the best known of this group. Cayetano now lives in Germany with his family, but he sells some of his work through a Dangriga outlet. Contacts with artists in Dangriga are usually best accomplished with the help of a third party, such as

Therese Rath at Pelican Beach Resort. With Cayetano living in Europe, the most sought-after local artist is Benjamin Nicholas. You can try to make contact on your own, but there's no guarantee you'll successfully meet with him on short notice. For direct contact regarding Pen Cayetano's work, visit the Dangriga Art Center at 74A St. Vincent Street. The Art Center also sells baskets, drums, Garifuna music cassettes, and Mayan embroidery. To contact Benjamin Nicholas, try 27 Oak Street, or ask around. Because of back orders, prepaid commissioned paintings sometimes take a while for Benjamin Nicholas to complete. For a fee, Pelican Beach Resort will check on such work in progress and assist in shipping.

For slightly less ambitious artistic acquisitions, try P.J.'s Gift Shop on St. Vincent Street. This is a good place to get souvenirs. Owner Janice Lambert likes to share her knowledge and show visitors around her modest Garifuna museum. Janice is also an excellent source on local information, especially pertaining to Garifuna culture.

And, if you need a few superb pictures of nature subjects that you didn't quite capture with your own lens, Tony Rath sells dupes of his professional-quality nature slides of endangered birds, jaguars, jaguarundis, Mayan villages, and more. His outstanding images have been showcased in a nature video used by eco-tourism businesses throughout Belize and the United States. You can purchase the video by mailing a check or money order for U.S. $25 to Naturalight Photography USA, Box 410, Bruno, MN 55712. If you are visiting Pelican Beach Resort, the video will be shown to you there.

Culture in Transition: "We just want the respect all men and women deserve. We want our young people to know of our ways. But today most young people say they are going to the city to be a policeman, teacher, or office worker. Not so many say they'd like to farm and do a little fishing," explained the gentlemanly Pablo Lambey. A lifetime resident of Dangriga, Lambey is chairman of the Garifuna Council. In our March 1992 meeting in his home on Oak Street, he lamented the rapid changes confronting Garifuna culture in the last decade. However, though Lambey fears his culture may disappear, he also sees some reason for hope. "Today's young people are saying good-bye to living our traditional ways. They want more. They are being 'Americanized.' Many have gone to the United States and not returned. At the same time, what some people call 'revitalization' is happening. Many people value the old ways and want to learn more about them," explained Lambey. Putting the worry of the community's elder statesman in perspective, I would guess the two days of cultural celebration I saw on Settlement Day would put a smile on Pablo Lambey's face. If Settlement Day is a litmus test of Lambey's efforts to maintain a cultural identity, he has plenty of supporters.

Settlement Day: Settlement Day is a national holiday throughout Belize. It commemorates the coming ashore of 200 Garifunas on November 19, 1832, under the leadership of Alejo Beni, who was leading his people from persecution in Honduras. These immigrants settled with Garifunas already living in the vicinity of North Stann Creek.

Settlement Day is celebrated every November 19, and though it is observed elsewhere in Belize, it is celebrated in Dangriga like nowhere else. It attracts tourists and Garifunas from throughout Belize and from as far away as Guatemala, Nicaragua, New York, and Los Angeles.

Settlement Day festivities start at dawn with a reenactment of the 1832 Garifuna migration by boat to Stann Creek. Modern-day Garifunas paddle dories ashore. The boats' occupants adorn their heads in leafy green crowns. Once on shore the reenactors make offerings of cassava, coconuts, plantains, live chickens, possibly fish and shrimp, and other traditional foods. These offerings are in thanks for the safety and productive crops provided by their new home. Next there is a drum-led procession to the town's Catholic church (Sacred Heart Parish at 1 Church Street), where mass is said in Garifuna by the Roman Catholic bishop of Belize, who is a Garifuna.

This formal religious ceremony will be different from anything you've seen. Besides being conducted in Garifuna, the mass has elements of West African, South American Carib, Arawak Indian, and European cultures, all of which played a part in the formation of Garifuna beliefs. As in all the churches, a collection plate is passed. It is bad form for those in attendance not to give.

In the afternoon, would-be and high-ranking politicians take turns at speechmaking on subjects ranging from the significance of Settlement Day to what ails the present-day Belizean government. Some of the oratory is self-serving, some of it heartfelt, and most of it articulately expressed. Still, to most attendees, Settlement Day amounts to a grand celebration with music and dance that commences on the night of November 18, or earlier, and continues all of the next day and into the night before slowly winding down as exhaustion takes hold of the nonstop dancers and music makers.

Garifuna musicians celebrate Settlement Day in Dangriga. *Photo by Eric Hoffman.*

Several Settlement Day recollections stand out for me. On the night of November 18, all of Dangriga came alive with the rhythmic drumbeats of dozens of bands pounding powerfully in the warm night air. The bands had been practicing all week, I was told. That night I found the Garifunas extremely polite, even young people who were consuming alcohol. The style of dancing emphasized rapid pelvic motion—a certain weight reducer if practiced earnestly. I wandered around from band to band until 2:00 A.M. and was often the only white person in sight. "Hey, you like our music?" was the most common question, followed by "Where you from?"

The next day (Settlement Day) a huge, sixteen-wheel, flatbed truck with a band on its bed gave new meaning to the word *parade*. The big truck crawled around town while throngs of dancers gyrated along behind, chanting and singing tirelessly. Two professors from Colorado State University with whom I was sharing a few beers thought the whole event looked more West African than South American. Driving a car down St. Vincent Street during Settlement Day isn't advisable. If you try it, there's a strong likelihood a shoeless reveler will dance across your hood or roof.

Caution: If you have been conditioned to fear congregations of people of a different race, leave this kind of conditioning at home

151

in your country of origin. In Dangriga, on this most celebrated of days, racial differences do not evoke the kind of hostilities that can be found in some U.S. cities. Still, as with any event in which young people arc heavily represented and alcohol is being consumed, take care not to offend the locals (use your camera politely) or appear vulnerable. Participating as a member of a small group rather than solo is probably the best approach to maximize your experience and your own safety.

Punta Music: Settlement Day participants dance and sing to the music of traditional Garifuna instruments: drums made of cedar and stretched leather and sea turtle shells (despite the shells' original inhabitants' endangered or rare status). Gourd rattles, two sticks, and an occasional blast from a conch shell may also figure into an ensemble. The music is repetitive, fast-paced, inspiring, and a little eerie late at night when emanating from a beach with musicians silhouetted against a glistening sea. This traditional music is known as punta. Modernized versions of punta in which the traditional drums, rattles, and shells are supplemented with vocalists, electronic amplification, and elements of reggae and other Caribbean sounds is called punta rock. In the United States, punta rock has its aficionados, who may not know that the sound originates from Dangriga.

Traditional Garifuna Beliefs and Practices: Central to Garifuna practices is a belief in the mystical *obeah,* whose revered practitioners can reputedly contact the spirits of dead relatives and deal with good and bad spirits through trancelike dances and seances. Belief in *obeah* can be traced to West Africa. Practitioners of *obeah* often combine bush medicines with symbols such as feather-filled amulets to combat evil spirits or enhance good spirits. Some particularly potent amulets placed near a person's house are thought to cause the recipient harm and even death. "Our belief is that there is a constant struggle between good and evil," explains Pablo Lambey. "We believe in a supreme being that is responsible. For example, Wenani is a strong evil force. He is like the devil. We do certain rituals to make sure that fella keeps his distance." Symbolic acts ranging from the placement of an amulet to animal (usually a chicken) sacrifice may play a part in these rituals.

The all-important healing rite is *dugu,* a practice of marshaling good spirits that culminates in a curing ritual often designed to placate long-dead relatives (*amaliha*). The curing can be broad in scope, including not only physical ailments but mental and economic troubles as well. *Dugu* can take as long as a week to prepare for and days to perform. The ritual takes place in a private home or cult house (*dabuyaba*). Usually communication is established with ancestor spirits through trancelike experiences by relatives participating in a *dugu*. Through the spirit person, or *buyai*, ailments are understood and courses for cures are explained. Often a *buyai* distinguishes an affliction that occurs naturally from an illness sent by an ancestor spirit. The latter usually involves more complex curative strategies. A *buyai* can be either a man or a woman. Dangriga's current *buyai* is a man.

A *dugu* usually starts in song. Symbolically, ancestors are welcomed by dory (from St. Vincent Island, where the Garifuna culture originated in 1635, when two Spanish slave ships went aground, disgorging their captives into a population of Arawak and Carib Indians) or through the ground (ancestors who are buried locally). Dancers perform in a trance. A *buyai* interprets events for those for whom the *dugu* is being performed. Essential to a *dugu* is the *lanigui garaun*, or "heart drum," the central and most important drum of the three that are used in most Garifuna ceremonies. The drums are usually beaten in harmony with the *buyai*'s gourd rattles while a person possessed (in a trance) dances.

Much of the understanding of *dugu* expressed here comes from the work of anthropologist Dr. Byron Foster, once a resident of Dangriga and author of the book *Heart Drum* (which can be purchased in many places throughout Belize). Foster chose "heart drum" for the book's title because this drum is central to Garifuna music, and its physical presence and beat are symbolic of the heart and life of the culture.

Because of their beliefs, the Garifunas were often ostracized in Belize and treated suspiciously. They were banned from the main market in Belize City after sunset as late as the 1950s. Today, much of the traditional belief system still remains, but it is often mixed with secular and Christian beliefs. As much as any group in Belize, Garifunas have committed themselves to the benefits of public education. Many of the young people Pablo Lambey laments as having left their cultural roots behind can now be found in the ranks of schoolteachers, public servants, hotel workers, and policemen throughout Belize.

Garifuna Cuisine: The Garifunas are private and somewhat shy by nature. Besides their public activities on Settlement Day and the John Canoe Dance during the Christmas season, chances are you won't witness any of their ceremonies. However, Dangriga is a good place to sample Garifuna cuisine. Central to the food is cassava bread (more like a large biscuit), which comes in two primary varieties: "king" cassava, which is about a half-inch thick, and common cassava, which is about a quarter-inch thick. Pablo Lambey has an open hearth oven behind his Petty Shop (B) at 35 Oak Street, where you can purchase the freshly baked bread. There is a great deal of technique involved in preparing the fleshy roots of cassava for the oven. Pablo also rates *serre la sus,* a dish of fish simmered in coconut milk, as "nice as can be." This dish is often served with a mixture of boiled ripe and green plantains that have been pounded in a *mata.* A *mata* works much like the mortar and pestle used by indigenous people throughout the Americas. The *mata* is made from a two-foot-high log stood on end with its top half hollowed in the shape of a rough-hewn bowl. The bottom half of the log is its base. The plantains are beaten unmercifully with a four-foot stick that has been rounded on the ends. You may see *matas* in use while walking the side streets of Dangriga.

There are four Garifuna alcoholic brews: *hiu,* or cassava beer, which is tasty but used mostly for rituals; cashew wine; *kususa,* a brew of sugar cane, ginger, and yeast; and a fourth drink that is a mixture of coconut water (not milk) and rum.

Restaurants: Pelican Beach Resort (M, E) (phone 05-22044), near the airstrip, serves three meals daily, each cooked in the resort's spacious kitchen. The quality ranges from good to excellent. You don't have to be a guest to dine at Pelican Beach. Look for traditional Belizean dishes with chicken, fish, or shrimp as the main course. Service is prompt and responsive. In town there is the Sea Flame Restaurant and Bar (M) at 42 Commerce Street (phone 05-22250). Owner James Wesby has put together a tasty seafood menu with modest prices. Patrons are a cross section of Belize: Garifuna fishermen, citrus growers, owners of local businesses, and an occasional tourist. There are several Chinese restaurants on Commerce Street. The Sunrise (M) and Starlight (M) are two of the best. Ritchie's Dinette (B, M), 84 Commerce Street (phone 05-22112), has excellent Creole and Spanish food.

Tour and Charter Operations: Pelican Beach Resort is tops in the Dangriga area. The resort organizes trips to the Cockscomb Basin Wildlife Sanctuary, Gales Point, South Water Caye, and lesser-known destinations. Land trips are in a new eight-seat Toyota Landcruiser. Proprietors Alice Bowman and Therese and Tony Rath are rarities in the hotel business, providing much more than lip-service eco-tourism. At the tender age of twenty-nine, Therese was elected president of the Belize Audubon Society, the strongest environmental lobbying group in Belize. Tony is a marine biologist who came to Belize to manage the Smithsonian Institution's research station on Carrie Bow Caye. He married Therese and now works on conservation programs throughout Belize. Together, they possess an intimate knowledge of the natural wonders of the Stann Creek District and are committed to high-quality, low-impact eco-tourism. Among their many accomplishments, they played a major role in creating the Cockscomb Basin Wildlife Sanctuary.

Pelican Beach Resort's offerings include: hiking in the Cockscomb Basin Wildlife Sanctuary with Mayan guides; accommodations on South Water Caye, perhaps the best snorkeling and scuba diving area in Belize; manatee watching in the Southern Lagoon (one of the largest manatee populations in the Caribbean); a Sittee River tour, including a visit to an abandoned sugar mill and a cruise on the Sittee River, viewing iguanas, birds, and bamboo forests; a tour of modern citrus factories; reef tours that include a stop at Man-of-War Caye (nesting site of magnificent frigate birds and brown boobies) and snorkeling and lunch at South Water Caye; fishing trips for barracuda, tarpon, grouper, and more; and advice on photographic safaris, fishing trips, bird watching, and other personalized activities.

Rosado's Tours, 35 Lemon Street (phone 05-22119/22020), has been in operation for three years and is relied on by several hotels. Jorge Rosado offers car and van service to any attractions in the Stann Creek District and charter boat tours to snorkeling, scuba diving, and fishing sites on the reef.

Taxi and Van Services: Tino's Taxi Service, 127 Commerce Street, offers in-town taxi service as well as drives to the Stann Creek District's attractions. Contact Celestino Tzul (phone 05-22438). Other cabs and vans include Henry Requena (05-22467), Rodney's Taxi (05-22513), and Charles Neal (05-23309).

Accommodations: First and foremost is Pelican Beach Resort (M, E), my home away from home while in southern Belize. This small hotel is a family heirloom of sorts, dating back four generations to Henry Bowman, Sr., a well known agricultural pioneer in the nearby Stann Creek Valley. Today Alice Bowman, her daughter, Therese Rath, and Therese's husband, Tony, run the place. The Casablanca-like ambience of the place and the hospitality and competence of the staff were much appreciated. The resort is large enough to maintain a steady flow of world travelers, yet small enough for personalized service. This includes optional excursions throughout the Stann Creek District that are designed by the Raths. The airstrip is about seventy-five yards away, which makes getting to Pelican Beach easy.

Usually kids greet arriving flights and offer (for a negotiated price that shouldn't exceed U.S. $1 per bag) to carry your luggage to the resort. Since the resort is so close, but not readily visible, you'll know your baggage carrier is on the right track if he heads in a southeasterly direction. If you arrive by car, turn north onto Pen Road as you enter town and drive to the end of the road. If you reach St. Vincent Street without seeing Pen Road, you've missed it and need to backtrack a few blocks.

Situated on the beach at the north end of town, Pelican Beach Resort is a converted dance hall with twenty self-contained rooms, each with a ceiling fan. Ask for a room facing the sea. You'll get the benefit of a balcony with a seascape and extra cooling from the nightly inland breezes wafting through your room. Each room has a private bath.

Guests are served three meals a day, and lunches can be ordered for day trips. The resort has its own pier, windsurfers, a recreation room featuring Ping-Pong, samples of the best of Garifuna primitive realism art, and a souvenir shop. Guests often spend sunset hours under the resort's spacious veranda sipping a concoction from the well-stocked bar and getting to know other guests from around the world. Pelican Beach's South Water Caye accommodations feature Osprey's Nest (M, E) and Frangipani House (M, E), also possibilities for snorkelers and divers.

Pelican Beach offers rates in both European and American plans. The American plan includes meals, tax, and service charge; the European plan does not. The American plan runs about U.S. $140 per day for two during peak season, from November to May. The European plan runs about U.S. $75 per day. Off-season rates are about

20 percent less. Major credit cards are accepted. Contact Pelican Beach Resort, P.O. Box 14, Dangriga, Belize, C.A. (phone 05-22044; fax 05-22570).

Bonefish Hotel (M, E), located near the water on Mahogany Road, is a well-run, clean establishment that caters to snorkelers, fishermen, and people headed for the cayes. It was recently purchased by the Zabaneh family, who also run Blue Marlin Lodge on South Water Caye. The hotel can arrange dive tours through local Earl David and can arrange for inland tours by Jorge Rosado, who transports tourists to the Cockscomb Basin Wildlife Sanctuary and other destinations. Rates range from U.S. $25 to U.S. $100 for a room. The hotel boasts cable TV, and major credit cards are accepted. Contact Bonefish Hotel, 15 Mahogany Road, Dangriga, Belize, C.A. (phone 05-22165/22447).

The Hub Guest House and Restaurant (B) is a cinder-block structure located on Stann Creek. It is funky, but clean, and has an ocean view. The Hub is appropriately named because it is only fifty yards off St. Vincent Street, which puts it near a bank, groceries, and the bus. Rooms rent for U.S. $25 to U.S. $40 per night, plus tax. Cash only; no credit cards. Contact Hub Guest House and Restaurant, 573A South Riverside, Dangriga, Belize, C.A. (phone 05-22397; fax 05-22813).

Rio Mar Inn (B), located where Stann Creek meets the Caribbean Sea, is a good place to stay the night before Settlement Day because the coming-ashore reenactment paddles up the creek at dawn. There is a restaurant, and each room has a private bath. Rooms are spartan but clean and tidy. The staff can arrange trips to inland attractions and to cayes for diving, snorkeling, scuba diving, and fishing. The Rio Mar has contacts with local fishermen who frequent Tobacco Caye, one of the more attractive cayes offshore. These fishermen cater to backpackers and lower-income travelers wishing to experience an offshore island with excellent snorkeling. Mark Bradley and Nolan Jackson are among the most reliable and experienced fishermen catering to travelers. Cash only; no credit cards. Contact Rio Mar Inn, 977 Southern Foreshore Street, Dangriga, Belize, C.A. (phone 05-22201).

Pal's Guest House (B) has clean rooms at reasonable rates facing the Caribbean. Cash only; no credit cards. Contact proprietors Austin and Sally Flores, 868 Magoon Street, Dangriga, Belize, C.A. (phone 05-22095).

Located in town on North Stann Creek, Jungle Hut (B, M) was completed in 1992. It consists of four cabanas that range in price from U.S. $23 to U.S. $160 per cabana, depending on the season and number of people. Cash only; no credit cards. Contact Jungle Hut, Ecumenical Drive, P.O. Box 10, Dangriga, Belize, C.A. (phone 05-22142).

Access: Dangriga, the Stann Creek District's northernmost town, can be reached from Belize City on the Coast Road (also called Manatee Road or New Road) in about one-and-a-half hours (seventy-five miles) during dry weather. Opened in 1992, the Coast Road designation is a bit misleading since the road never comes closer than a few miles to the coast. The key to finding the Coast Road is to look carefully at about mile twenty-nine on the Western Highway from Belize City. The road is dirt and can be a challenge after prolonged rains.

Traveling to Dangriga from Belize City via Belmopan and the Hummingbird Highway takes two-and-a-half hours (105 miles). From Belmopan to Dangriga is fifty-five miles.

Note: There are no car rental agencies in Dangriga. When I last visited, Budget, near Phillip Goldson International Airport, offered the best deal for reliable, small, 4WD vehicles suitable for wet or dry roads.

By boat, it is only thirty-six miles along the coast from Belize City to Dangriga, or you can travel south on waterways to the Northern and Southern lagoons, where you can visit the Bird Caye Bird Sanctuary (mostly ibises, egrets, and herons) and spot manatees in the Southern Lagoon before going ashore at Gales Point. From there it's about twenty miles to Dangriga. Since there's no scheduled transportation, you'll have to arrange to be picked up (a service offered by some hotels) or "bum" a ride.

By air from Belize City takes about twenty minutes. Maya Airlines flies daily in single-engine four-seaters or twin-engine ten-seaters. Check with your travel agent before leaving home to make sure you've booked a seat for the Belize City to Dangriga leg. To avoid an unwanted delay, book straight through or reserve a seat. Buying over the counter is usually not a problem, but one large party can take up an entire flight, which can mean a few hours' to a whole day's wait for the next flight. Check with Tropic and Island airlines to see if they are flying to Dangriga. Maya (phone 02-72312/44032) has been the most consistent carrier on this route and throughout southern Belize. Expect to pay about U.S. $50 for a round-trip ticket.

Z-Line bus service (phone 02-73937) also connects Dangriga and Belize City three or four times daily from near St. Vincent Street and North Stann Creek. As with most bus lines in Belize, the fleet is made up of retired U.S. school buses. The buses are slow but safe. The one-way fare is U.S. $5.

Offshore

South Water Caye

South Water Caye offers one of the most thoroughly exciting and high-quality scuba and snorkel experiences you'll find in Belize, if not the Caribbean. Located off the southern Belize coast about ten miles southeast of Dangriga, South Water Caye should be a high-priority destination for anyone interested in reef environments. (On many maps South Water Caye is named Water Caye, resulting in two such named cayes in Belize. If you become confused, this (South) Water Caye is the one immediately north of Carrie Bow Caye.)

South Water Caye is a half-mile-long sand atoll sitting directly on top of the Barrier Reef on the reef's easternmost extremity. Fifty to seventy-five yards from the island's eastern side, the reef drops off sharply into open ocean. To the south and north are deep cuts through the reef that have some of the best wall dives in the Caribbean. For the scuba diver or snorkeler, South Water Caye is arguably the best readily accessible island from Dangriga that has accommodations and is set up to comfortably see the best of Belize's underwater world. With no other island dive operations in the region, you won't see other divers or their telltale signs. And, to the north sits Tobacco Caye, a privately owned island, with accommodations and camping. Nearby Man-of-War Caye is a primary nesting sight for magnificent frigate birds, known for the male of the species' inflated brilliant-red throat displays. South of South Water is Carrie Bow Caye, with an oversize, colonial-like building that occupies much of the tiny island. Carrie Bow is owned by the Bowman family (owner of Pelican

Carrie Bow Caye, offshore from Dangriga. *Photo by Tony Rath.*

Beach Resort in Dangriga) but is leased to the Smithsonian Institution, which conducts long- and short-term tropical marine biological studies here.

Scenic Boat Journey: The usual approach to South Water Caye is memorable. In an open boat with a powerful outboard it takes about fifty minutes from Dangriga. On the way you pass through low, mangrove-laden Coco Plum Caye and see several other cayes off in the distance. If it's stormy, fishing sloops often take refuge from northerlies in the cut in this caye. To the west the rugged Maya Mountains cut a jagged silhouette of dark green along the horizon. The lonely sail of a traditional wooden-hulled fishing sloop is usually visible somewhere on the horizon. If the sea has kicked up a bit, you'll see flying fish suddenly pop into the air and glide fifty feet or more before being swallowed by the sea from which they came. The overwhelming feeling is of solitary adventure, not of the hustle and bustle sometimes felt around Ambergris Caye and other better-known island areas to the north. South Water Caye is first visible because of its tall palms. It appears as a shimmering mirage, idyllic and isolated, seemingly afloat in an azure sea.

Snorkeling: The best snorkel site I visited was on the northeastern side of the island directly behind Blue Marlin Lodge. The entry point is near the pier.

The site is memorable for its abundance and diversity of sea life. The area is somewhat unique in that the shallow reef extends only a few hundred feet and then drops off into deep water of 600 feet or more. The isolation of South Water Caye and the quality of the reef and its closeness to deep water make a potent environment, giving a snorkeler a glimpse of a world usually reserved for only hardcore scuba divers. In a word, the site was exhilarating. I snorkeled with a friend who has experienced most of the top-ranked diving areas throughout the world, and he judged the site first-rate.

In forty-five minutes we were able to identify an incredible variety of fish — and this was on a day when the sea was choppy and visibility limited to about fifty feet. In many instances we saw both juvenile and mature members of the same species. Fish included yellowtail damselfish (the juveniles don't have the yellow tail but are distinguished by iridescent blue spots), blue-striped grunt, four-eye butterflyfish, spotfin butterflyfish, blue chromi, blue tang (and yellow juveniles), redband parrotfish, spotlight parrotfish, squirrelfish, creole wrasse, rock beauty, queen angelfish, gray angelfish, fairy basslet, blue hamlet, barred hamlet, porkfish, small-mouth grunt, sergeant major, spotted drum, black durgeon, yellowtail snapper, trunkfish, scrawled filefish, Spanish hogfish, queen triggerfish, banded butterfly, spadefish, honeycomb cowfish, harlequin bass, neon goby, graysby, bigeye, grouper (either Nassau or tiger), and great barracuda. Corals and sponges were no less impressive: knobby brain coral, elkhorn coral, staghorn coral, sheet coral, fire coral, lobed star coral, leaf coral, elliptical coral, mountainous star coral, common sea fan (numerous and large), Venus (or green) sea fan, sea whips, and vase sponges. There were also plenty of organisms we could not identify.

Caution: As you enter the water, beware of sea urchins, which can easily penetrate a rubber booty. We also saw fire coral, which can cause a painful sting. Looking, not touching, is always the best policy. Also, be respectful of swells that can lift you onto coral heads. The island is unprotected, and winds often come from the east.

Dive Sites: Expect spectacular wall dives. I made three, descending to a depth of eighty to ninety feet and slowly working my way up to a wall's shallow point at about thirty feet. The dives I experienced were south of Carrie Bow Caye. With nondescript names such as Cut 5 and Cut 7, the sites proved to be much more spectacular than most of my dives to the north, especially in the variety and numbers of schooling fish. My well-traveled diving companion rated the wall that had been dubbed Cut 7 "as good as anything I've seen in the Caribbean." This particular wall dive was a vertical cut through the reef from the open ocean. We descended to ninety feet and worked our way up. The abundance of life was astounding. Large barracudas measuring four feet and middle-size barracudas cruised out from the wall, as did yellow jacks. In fact, one curious three-foot barracuda accompanied me for about half of the dive. We spotted a half-dozen lobsters, a few of which were collected by members of our group. Practically all of the reef fish mentioned in the "Snorkeling" section were here too, but there were more schooling fish, particularly grunts, snappers, porkfish, and varieties of parrotfish. In cracks along the wall we found graysbys, Nassau groupers, and even one very robust jewfish half hidden under a ledge. The wall's covering was an exploding smorgasbord of reef life, featuring sea whips, sea fans, and a variety of corals, with an occasional huge barrel sponge and giant tube sponges. There seemed to be more orange and red wall sponges than in other places we'd dived. The time spent on this dive and others ranged from forty to seventy minutes, depending on the individual's air consumption rate.

Seasonal consideration: Diving in the wet season (which can extend from June through November) can result in reduced visibility. The section of coast in this region averages between 100 and 130 inches of rain a year. Our dives were in November, the end of the wet season. Even though we were well offshore (ten miles), the lack of visibility (optimum is 80 to 150 feet) was blamed on the discharge of coastal rivers. On some dives our visibility was about 50 feet.

Accommodations: Blue Marlin Lodge (E), owned by Belizeans Rosella and Michael Zabaneh, is the high-profile place to stay on South Water Caye. It is a scuba diving operation that caters mostly to dedicated North American scuba divers. Most people using the lodge are mainstream divers with many dives under their weight belt. During my stay, a scuba club from Seattle, Washington, had rented the place for the week. I did not hear a single complaint from a guest about accommodations, meals, dive sites, equipment, or resort staff. For me, it was the best-run dive resort I visited in Belize. Blue Marlin Lodge's cabanas, dining hall, and dock are on the northern end of the island. The lodge shares the island with several Belizean families, whose vacation houses and property make much of the island off-limits.

The domed cabanas at Blue Marlin Lodge are comfortable. There are ten bedrooms in two buildings and three private dome-shaped cabanas with double and triple bed configurations. There is no air-conditioning. The rooms are cooled by fans and sea breezes, or people take to the plentiful hammocks strung between coconut trees. Meals were excellent, with seafood dishes making up the menu. We had lobster, conch soup, shrimp, and snapper with large salads. The thatched-roof dining hall and veranda open to the leeward (west) side of the island and sit over the water. The setting offers excellent sunsets and a super ambience.

Scuba divers, often in groups, plan trips directly with Blue Marlin Lodge, most often for week-long stays. Package deals can be purchased from the United States, including air transfer and returns from Belize City's Phillip Goldson International Airport to Dangriga, water transfers to and from the island, dives, and accommodations.

Blue Marlin offers three different packages. There is a five-day, four-night dive package (about U.S. $900) and an eight-day, seven-night (about U.S. $1200) offering. These include three meals a day, two dives (plus a night dive), tanks, unlimited air, and weights. Regulators, fins, buoyancy control devices (BVDs), and other gear can be rented. All dive packages start on Saturdays. You will be asked to show your PADI or NAUI certification card before you are allowed to dive. A third package is a vacation special that does not include scuba diving. Inquire for details. The lodge is open from November through July. Contact Blue Marlin Lodge, South Water Caye, P.O. Box 21, Dangriga, Belize, C.A. (phone 05-22243; in the United States and Canada, 1-800-798-1588; fax 05-22296).

Osprey's Nest (M, E), Frangipani House (M, E), and Pelican University (M, E) are owned and run by Pelican Beach Resort in Dangriga. These three large, vacation-style houses offer a more rustic and less expensive stay. The largest building was dubbed Pelican University because it can accommodate twenty-two people in its five bedrooms. It caters primarily to groups of North American university and high school students interested in reef, rain forest, and cultural experiences. Most of the student groups include a few nights at the Cockscomb Basin Wildlife Sanctuary and a few nights on South Water Caye in the structures mentioned above. Usually island stays include a Garifuna culture lecture, dance performances, and nature slide shows. The smaller Osprey's Nest and Frangipani House are classic Belizean coastal homes that each sleep six comfortably. Each converted vacation home has a kitchen. All three are furnished with linen, a cooking stove, utensils, kerosene lighting, and a fifty-pound block of ice for refrigeration. A bed ranges from U.S. $50 to U.S. $95 per day. Pelican Beach also can provide a cook (at a price). Snorkel gear rents for U.S. $10 per day. Boats can be arranged for fishing and snorkeling while on the island. The Pelican Beach accommodations attract marine scientists, adventurers, and solo travelers as well as students and divers.

If you're a scuba diver, you may want to stay at Osprey's Nest or Frangipani House and pay for dives at Blue Marlin. This is more economical than a week's stay at Blue Marlin, which is the usual dive package. Definitely for the visitor wanting to complete one dive or multiple-day snorkels, accessing the island through Pelican Beach is more economical than competing deals, plus you get a private beach to yourself. Pelican Beach also offers a one-day excursion that includes snorkeling at South Water Caye, a visit to Man-of-War Caye (frigate and booby nesting), and occasional visits to ongoing Smithsonian studies at Carrie Bow Caye. Because of the Bowman family's long-standing lease arrangement with the Smithsonian Institution, they are able to take groups to Carrie Bow when a particularly interesting study is under way. (For more details, see information on Pelican Beach Resort in the "Dangriga" section.) Contact Pelican Beach Resort, P.O. Box 14, Dangriga, Belize, C.A. (phone 05-22044; fax 05-22570).

International Zoological Expeditions (IZE), a third commercial entity on the island, also has accommodations at the center of the island. IZE often reserves its space for U.S.-based students studying marine biology in winter and spring. Contact International Zoological Expeditions, 210 Washington Street, Sherborn, MA 01770 (phone 508-655-1461).

Access: You reach South Water Caye from Dangriga in an outboard-powered fiberglass dory. The usual departure point is the dock owned by the Blue Marlin's Rosella and Michael Zabaneh at the southern end of town. The ride takes about fifty minutes. Maya Airlines flies to Dangriga many times daily from Belize City, or you can reach Dangriga by Z-Line bus.

Tobacco Caye

Tobacco Caye is located about four miles north of South Water Caye and is normally reached via boat connections in Dangriga. Tobacco Caye is an attractive, quarter-mile-long, palm-covered island with excellent beaches and is surrounded by dazzling, light-blue waters due to the shallow reef along the island's eastern and southern shores. The island has rustic resorts owned by fishermen, some vacation houses, and a few permanent residences. Its modest development is a step back to a time before Belize was known as a tourist destination. Indoor plumbing is a rarity. The social atmosphere is laid-back and relaxed. Camping is allowed. The southern end of the caye has a beautiful beach that wraps around about one-third of the island. There are sea grass beds off the western side, with the best snorkeling found off the southern and western shores. Tobacco Caye is an exceptional find for both low- and high-budget travelers. The question is, How long will it stay this way?

Accommodations: Try Fairweather and Noble Rose (B), Tobacco Caye, P.O. Box 240, Belize City, C.A. (phone 05-22201), and Reef End Lodge (B), P.O. Box 10, Dangriga, Belize, C.A. For camping, contact Island Camps (B), Tobacco Caye, 51 Regent Street, Belize City, C.A. (phone 02-72109 and 05-22201).

Access: Contact Nolan Jackson or Mark Bradley through Rio Mar Inn, 977 Southern Foreshore Street, Dangriga, Belize, C.A. (phone 05-22201). Both are fishermen who sometimes supplement their income by taking adventurers to Tobacco Caye.

Garifuna Villages

Garifuna villages once dotted the shore of the Caribbean from Honduras to central Belize. Dangriga is the hub of Garifuna cultur' in Belize. Besides Dangriga (8100 pop.), only Hopkins (800 pop.), Seine Bight (450 pop.), Georgetown (450 pop.), Punta Gorda (1100 pop.), and Barranco (200 pop.) are identified as predominantly Garifuna communities in Belize today. Of these towns and villages, Hopkins, a twenty-mile drive south of Dangriga, is probably most representative of the traditional Garifuna villages. Only the villages in the Stann Creek District—Hopkins, Seine Bight, and Georgetown—are discussed here. Punta Gorda and Barranco are covered in the Toledo District chapter. (For details on Garifuna culture, see "History and Cultures" in the Overview chapter.)

Hopkins

Hopkins is the most celebrated of the Garifuna communities because of its simple appearance, absence of modern conveniences, and location on an idyllic beach lined with coconut palms. At sunrise the village lends itself to postcard imagery. Hopkins' easy access (only thirty minutes from Dangriga by car) allows a glimpse of a purer form of the traditional Garifuna lifestyle than what you'll find in Dangriga. The village's clapboard houses on stilts overlook an often glass-smooth bay. Locally made fishing dories and dugouts carved from tree trunks are hauled out along the beach. Garden plots are situated near the village. Chickens plus a few too many dogs wander through the village. Naked children splash in the shallow water along the beach under the watchful eyes of a mom or older sibling. Indeed, most of the journalistic coverage of Hopkins conjures up a picture of paradise lost, an idyllic setting where tranquility is achieved by isolation and subsistence farming and fishing. This is only part of the picture.

A Culture in Transition: Beneath the calm surface of this traditional Garifuna village is another story. This has to do with the intensifying struggle for the village's inhabitants, who are torn between living the traditional Garifuna lifestyle and exploring opportunities that are already hard at work changing all aspects of Hopkins. As a group, Garifunas place great value on education. Unlike members of many subsistence cultures held in place by lack of education or opportunity, many Garifunas have capitalized on Belize's ability to provide a basic education for its citizens. As a result, many young Garifunas from Hopkins and other villages are teachers, civil servants, and hotel workers throughout Belize. Villagers coming of age and moving away from their traditional homes has resulted in a population of older Garifunas living in Hopkins and other villagers year-round.

When Hopkins was in the process of receiving electricity in March 1992, the village was excited about the change. The coming of television was the talk of the town, but not everyone saw it as a positive step. A young mother explained to me that she feared television would corrupt the village's children. Also at work on the village's character is the increasing influx of tourists. Expensively adorned tourists emerging from air-conditioned cars to photograph Garifuna children on the beach or fishermen repairing their dories intrude upon some of the villagers' sense of privacy and pride. It was my impression that tourism is tolerated by most residents and actually endorsed by a handful of Hopkins' more money-oriented individuals. However, when the less than subtle tourist makes insensitive comments about the absence of modern appliances and services, locals resent it.

Village History: The emergence of the Garifuna culture dates back to the wrecks of two Spanish slave galleons in the seventeenth century on St. Vincent's Island in the Caribbean. The Garifunas have lived in the Hopkins area for a century, but the village has existed in its present form only since 1961, when it was rebuilt after Hurricane Hattie demolished it. Its relative newness does not affect its authenticity or traditional appearance. The village's namesake, Frederick Hopkins, was a popular Catholic bishop who lived in the area until he drowned there in 1923.

Social Caution: Guard against projecting ethnocentricity. For me, Hopkins was interesting because I saw self-reliant people of a little-known culture living comfortably mostly from what they grow and catch. This way of living is in sharp contrast to the way of life in Europe and North America. Poking around Hopkins and contemplating the straightforward simplicity of the local economy can be thought-provoking, but visitors walk a fine line. The villagers with whom I spoke were cordial enough, but they were busy repairing nets, cleaning fish, caring for garden plots, and taking care of children. Keep in mind that you are visiting people whose daily activities revolve around extracting a livelihood from their environment. For the sake of perspective, put yourself in their place. What would you consider acceptable behavior if tourists descended on your community to photograph your home, your interactions with fellow citizens, and your work activities? Relating to the people of Hopkins on human terms, rather than as if they were props in a lifelike museum exhibit, is the approach. Ask permission to use your camera if you're directing it at people from close range. Keep in mind that the residents may be speaking Garifuna, but they also speak and understand English. Chances are the fishermen you see fixing their nets have relatives and friends in New York and Los Angeles.

Short Visit: Under most circumstances Hopkins is considered a short-stay destination. Most visitors stop here for a couple of hours on the same day they take a boat tour up the nearby Sittee River or while returning or going to Dangriga from the Cockscomb Basin Wildlife Sanctuary.

Acccommodations: Try Sandy Beach Lodge (B) (phone 05-22023), a modest accommodation at the southern end of Hopkins. It is unique because it is run by a local women's co-op. The day I visited, the women in charge were cleaning fish that had been delivered to them in laundry baskets. For slightly "upscale" accommodations, try the Tropical Paradise Hotel on the left side of the main street, about four structures after turning right from the road commonly used to enter the village. It is unmistakable with its huge satellite dish atop a two-story, green-cement building — a nonconforming move to modernity. Basic meals are served at these two accommodations; otherwise the village has no restaurants. However, meals can be negotiated with local women. Expect dishes with a main course of chicken or something from the sea, supplemented with vegetables, rice, and beans. Sittee River Village also has low-budget accommodations at Frank Andrew's Sittee River Lodge (B) four miles to the south.

Access: The traditional way to reach Hopkins is by boat — still worth the effort for its authenticity, as Garifuna commerce was historically by sea. Today most people reach the village via the Southern Highway from Dangriga, about twenty miles by car. The turnoff is 6.6 miles south of the northern beginning of the Southern Highway. From the turnoff the village is another four miles. From the south (Punta Gorda), you can reach Hopkins via the same turnoff, or turn earlier from the Southern Highway at Sittee River. Though maps don't show it, a fair-weather road exists from Sittee River Village to Hopkins that will take you past the ruins of the Sittee River Sugar Mill, along the river to Sittee River Village, through tropical wetlands, and along the coast before entering Hopkins. This approach, though it floods through the wet season, is prettiest. Inquire in either Hopkins or Sittee River Village as to the road's condition. Both approaches to Hopkins take you through excellent wetlands habitats that are well populated by many species of waterfowl as well as wading birds such as egrets, bitterns, herons, roseate spoonbills, and even the occasional endangered jabiru stork.

Seine Bight

Seine Bight lies on the narrow Placencia Peninsula just sixty-five miles south of Dangriga and five miles north of Placencia. The popular settlement story places European pirates in the area as long ago as 1629. Seine Bight was named after a French fisherman who settled here after being deported by the British from Newfoundland in the 1800s. The first Garifunas settled here in 1869, when Walpy Morreira led his extended family here from Honduras. Others followed. Located on a section of the peninsula that is only 1000 feet wide, Seine Bight is flanked to the west by Placencia Lagoon, a saltwater mangrove swamp rich in fish, and to the east by the reef-protected Caribbean.

This community was entirely destroyed by Hurricane Hattie in 1961. Miraculously no lives were lost. Until five years ago the village was isolated and reached only by boat, making Seine Bight the best example of an isolated Garifuna community in Belize that was not accessible by car. (Today only Barranca holds this distinction, but even it has a circuitous, fair-weather, 4WD track connecting it to the outside world during the dry season.)

In appearance Seine Bight is much like Hopkins, but it is only half as large and not graced with as beautiful a natural setting. Homes consist of thatch-and-tin-roofed one- and two-room stilt houses. The village's character has changed since the road was built down the peninsula to Placencia. The community is no longer isolated. Residents can go and come easily by bus, which has resulted in young people leaving to seek work and education. Since Hurricane Hattie, a health clinic and hurricane shelter have been built. There is no significant infrastructure for tourism.

Georgetown

Georgetown lies west of the Southern Highway fifteen miles north of Mango Creek. This tiny village was created after Hurricane Hattie temporarily erased Seine Bight. Enticing homesteaders with an offer of free land, the Belizean government encouraged Garifunas from Seine Bight to move inland to farm. Today, this plot-farming community is the only inland Garifuna community in Belize. Most of its members have relatives living in Seine Bight. For most travelers Georgetown amounts to a signpost at the halfway point between Red Bank and the turnoff to Placencia.

Sittee River Sugar Mill

In 1991 the Belizean government cleared away five acres of jungle and reclaimed the extensive ruins of an 1860s state-of-the-art sugar mill. The mill is on the road to Sittee River Village, which is signposted on the Southern Highway but also named Middle Sands on many maps. At one time the Regalia Sugar Estate and the Serpon Sugar Estate used this site for processing sugar cane. The latter estate was owned by Thomas Bowman, an emigrant Scotsman and great-great-grandfather of Therese Bowman Rath, who runs Pelican Beach Resort in Dangriga with her husband, mother, and family.

When I walked the site there was an impressive array of steam-powered locomotives and large machinery sitting where it had been abandoned in the late 1800s. Some of the relics have literally become one with trees that have grown through them. The size of the equipment and the overall operation are impressive considering that mules were used to cart the mill parts to the site from ships anchored offshore. The cast iron names on the equipment indicate origins in England and Richmond, Virginia. The large steam engine with "Richmond, Virginia" clearly showing in relief through its rusty veneer is a Tredgear, the only one of its kind in existence according to the Belizean government.

U.S. Civil War Settlers: The Virginia equipment connection provides an interesting historical footnote. During the U.S. Civil War, wealthy Confederates hedging on their losing cause moved to Belize, then called British Honduras. Confederate planters arrived with substantial capital and expertise in large-scale agriculture. Though none of them lasted long in Belize, the village named Alabama inland from Georgetown, the Alabama Wharf near Independence and Big Creek, as well as a settlement near Punta Gorda attest to the era.

Ironically, one of the underlying reasons the Confederate planters' efforts failed was due to a small mandatory salary that had to be paid to each worker monthly. This strictly enforced local ordinance was designed to ensure a basic standard of living for East Indian and ex-African slaves from both Belize and Jamaica, who worked as cane cutters and laborers. In an odd political alignment, Great

Britain was a Confederate ally even though the central issue of slavery, which had brought about the U.S. Civil War, had already been resolved by the British with the abolishment of slavery in all colonies in 1834–38.

History of Sugar Cane: Sugar cane cultivation came to Belize via immigrants from Mexico's bloody Caste Wars of 1847–63. These immigrants had worked on plantations in the Yucatán. Some years later sugar cane production received a boost when Confederate Americans immigrated to the Sittee River area and northern districts, though today sugar cane production is limited primarily to the northern Corozal and Orange Walk districts. Sugar accounts for approximately U.S. $30 million in exports, by far Belize's most important cash crop.

Maximizing Your Enjoyment: Set aside about an hour for the sugar mill. The length of time you stay will depend on your interest in antiquated technology. Approach the site with the frame of mind of solving a jigsaw puzzle with a few parts missing. There may be a one-page brochure available to aid you in trying to figure out how discarded steam engines, boilers, chimneys, tanks, and immense gears fit together to process sugar. You'll also see wildlife. Lowland birds species were plentiful, and carpenter ants were particularly active during my visit.

Be prepared: Mosquitoes can be a problem here depending on the season and weather conditions. Also, carry something to drink since there is no drinking water available at the site.

Access: The Sittee River Sugar Mill (also called the Serpon Sugar Mill) is located nine miles south of the northern end of the Southern Highway and three miles east of the highway on the signposted road to Sittee River Village. A short distance farther is the village and the starting point for the Sittee River tour and the boat pickup for Possum Point Biological Station.

Sittee River Tour

For good reason, the Sittee River is a fairly regular destination for tour operators based in Dangrigo. This major watercourse enters the Caribbean about fifteen miles south of Dandriga. Its headwaters are in the Maya Mountains. Customers are taken up a major river to see an assortment of wildlife and a large bamboo forest. A twenty-five-foot, shallow-draft, fiberglass dory powered with a fifty-five-horsepower outboard is the craft most often used to make the journey. This trip covers a lot of river quickly. The boat holds a dozen people, but a small group with a guide is optimum for birding, iguana spotting, negotiating a few shallow spots, and just stretching out in the sun and watching the riverbank race by. The boatmen are locals who also work for nearby Possum Point Biological Station. They are usually well versed in flora and fauna.

The river tour starts at Sittee River Village and continues upriver to stands of giant bamboo, which is the turnaround point. The elapsed time for the journey is between two and three hours, taking in about ten miles of waterway. During the course of this trip you'll see small banana plantations, dense jungle, a wide variety of bird life, and iguanas. In fact, the Bermudian Landing Community Baboon Sanctuary was the only place I saw more iguanas. The ones along the Sittee River are wary because they are still hunted (a legal activity providing they are consumed locally). When startled they drop from fifty feet or more into the river from tree limbs. The highest dives sometimes momentarily stun the animals, causing them to float on the surface before swimming off. Herons, egrets, bitterns, and king-fishers are common. On the day of my tour, I also saw snakebirds, flocks of parrots, and colorful tanagers in the trees along the riverbanks.

My visit to the Sittee River was in early March, which is during the dry season, when the river is low. The river's size was still impressive, measuring thirty yards or more across for most of the journey. The current was gentle and the river placid. Depending on how low the river is and the number of people on board, you may have to jump from the boat and help push it upstream through two short, shallow areas.

Saving the Iguana: March is when female iguanas lay their eggs along the riverbanks. This attracts hunters, who take advantage of the lizards' vulnerability when they are on the ground preoccupied with egg laying. We came across two groups of aged Belizeans hunting iguanas from dugouts with one ancient, rusty rifle. More important than the rifle was a mongrel that had been conscripted to retrieve the lizards, which it did by swimming rapidly to a stunned iguana lying on the surface from its drop into the water. The dog had captured four iguanas, which the hunters showed us with great delight. Three of them were still very much alive.

The iguana, known in Belize as "bamboo chicken," is a traditional source of protein for rural Belizeans. Unfortunately, iguanas are being killed faster than they can reproduce, which has caused these harmless vegetarians to disappear through much of Central America.

If you come across iguana hunters, notice that they usually don't kill a captured lizard on the spot because the meat might spoil before they return to their village. Instead they immobilize the lizard by tying its back legs together so that it can't run. If you're inclined to spare the life of a captured iguana in a socially acceptable way, offer to purchase ones that appear uninjured and able to return to the wild. Your boatman can help you select a release site upstream that is an unlikely place for hunters.

Giant Bamboo Forest: The boatman breaks out lunch when you've reached the giant bamboo forest at the turnaround point. The fifty-foot-high clumps have been arranged by the plant's own spacing mechanism. Each impenetrable clump measures about thirty feet across and is about forty feet from the next nearest clump. The stocks near the outside of each clump lean outward and touch stocks from the next nearest clump at a point about fifty feet above the ground. This leaning together of the clumps creates a solid canopy in the shape of gothic vaulting; thus the bamboo forest is often referred to as a "bamboo cathedral." Underneath this canopy the ground is bare except for a foot-thick cushion of dry bamboo leaves. The cathedral is a shady, peaceful, surreal place. For a refreshing drink, our guide chopped out a section of bamboo that was six inches in diameter, and we drank the cool, pure water inside.

Access: The river tour starts from a small pier slightly east of the elementary school at Sittee River Village. You must arrange for a boat and a guide in advance. In the Stann Creek District, the Pelican Beach Resort (phone 05-22044) in Dangriga and the Possum Point Biological Station (phone 05-22006) on the Sittee River are the businesses most involved in river tours and have constant contact with boatmen on the Sittee River. If you arrive in Sittee River Village without having made arrangements and want to take the river tour, ask locals to direct you to a boatman.

Possum Point Biological Station

The Possum Point Biological Station is located on the opposite bank and downstream about a half-mile from the pickup point for the Sittee River boat tour. This is an intriguing place to spend a few days or to study as part of a preplanned educational experience. Possum Point Biological Station has been in business ten years and is also known as the Northeast Marine Environmental Institution, Inc. It claims to be "the only true biological station in Belize designed solely for educational and research purposes." And, though they do most of their business with U.S. school groups who arrive to conduct biological studies, owners Paul and Mary Shave are not averse to renting a bed to unattached visitors provided they don't disrupt the program.

Possum Point, where the station is located, juts sharply into the Sittee River. As you approach the station's dock, palms dominate the skyline. The grounds around the bungalows contain an impressive collection of specimen trees, punctuating the rich green grass and giving the station a parklike appearance. Most of the forty-four-acre site is lowland jungle intersected by well-maintained trails. The trails are used for ongoing studies by college and high school groups, most commonly from the eastern United States. I talked with two high-schoolers from the East Coast who were studying the blue morpho butterfly.

Wildlife: The area is rich in wildlife. More than 100 species of birds frequent the grounds around the station. During my short visit a parrot screeched from the rooftop of the dining hall. Other commonly sighted birds include practically every wading bird in Belize, raptors, and a healthy population of chachalacas, whose squawking serves as an alarm clock each morning. Peccaries, pacas, anteaters, and coatimundis are often sighted on the trails. "Occasionally our visitors are treated to the grunt of a jaguar whose territory includes our property," says Mary Shave. The staff, made up of locals, was friendly and well versed in the language of nature studies.

Wee Wee Caye: For marine studies, the Shaves have a small marine lab on Wee Wee Caye. The lab and spartan accommodations are the only structures on the island. They serve as a good example of how to set up accommodations on a sensitive mangrove island with very little impact. Visitors to the caye are shuttled four miles down the Sittee River and nine miles due east across the sea. Transport is by a twenty-five-foot fiberglass dory powered by an fifty-five-horsepower outboard, the preferred watercraft throughout Belize.

The waters around the caye contain a succession of marine environments: mangroves, turtlegrass beds, patch reefs, and sand cones fringed with gorgonians and huge sponges. Besides a wide variety of tropical fish, spotted eagle rays and porpoises are often sighted. The area contains spur and groove plus patch reef formations that typify the Barrier Reef. Snorkeling and scuba diving are excellent. Excursions to mangrove islands for birding are optional.

Accommodations: Possum Point Biological Station (B) has six bungalows on stilts that can house about thirty people. Meals are served in a large dining hall that doubles as a classroom. The bungalows are attractively nestled among trees on spacious, grassy grounds, but none of them have electricity or plumbing. Instead, there are separate shower and toilet blocks. As attractive as the setting is, I found the midday heat and humidity oppressive during my March visit. This was during a hot spell. Cooling off was accomplished by sitting in the river or taking a midday shower (there's no hot water). Contact Paul and Mary Shave, Possum Point Biological Station, Sittee River, Stann Creek District, Belize, C.A. (phone 05-22006; fax 05-22038).

Access: The only way to reach Possum Point (and Wee Wee Caye) is by boat. Make arrangements for a visit by contacting the Shaves as noted above, or ask around Sittee River Village for a boatman.

Cockscomb Basin Wildlife Sanctuary

The Cockscomb Basin Wildlife Sanctuary is the ultimate jungle experience. It is as pristine an expanse of rain forest as you will find that is easily accessible, well managed, and relatively inexpensive to visit. "The Cockscomb," as it is commonly called, is a spectacular, immense basin of tropical rain forest hemmed in on three sides by the jagged Maya Mountains. From various vantage points the Cockscomb evokes the special awe and commands the soul-penetrating reverence one feels when contemplating Yosemite Valley, Ayers Rock, or the Serengeti. The rather modest entrance to the Cockscomb at Maya Center is twenty-one miles south of Dangriga on the Southern Highway. Under normal conditions the drive takes about forty-five minutes from Dangringa.

The Cockscomb name refers to the shape of the nearby Maya Mountains when viewed from the north or south. With a little imagination, you can see a cock's comb in the profile. The Cockscomb is incredibly rich in plant life and packed with all forms of jungle wildlife. It is one of the few places you'll find 5 species of wild felines sharing the same habitat. There are also more than 290 species of birds, among them Belize's national bird, the keel-billed toucan; the spectacular king vulture; many species of parrot, including the endangered scarlet macaw; and the endangered great curassow and agami heron.

Humidity, warm temperatures, wet weather, and rough terrain dominate the Cockscomb region. The basin is mostly subtropical wet forest, one of several types of rain forest found in Belize. The climate is characterized by a short dry season (March through May) and a predominant wet season (June through February). High humidity and about 140 inches of rain annually are the norm. Geographically the basin is somewhat isolated from the rest of Belize, with mountains rimming the Cockscomb on three sides. Adjacent to and marking the sanctuary's northern boundary is Victoria Peak, at 3675 feet the designated highest point in Belize (though there is controversy over an unnamed peak to the south being higher). The basin's interior of lowland jungle is actually divided into two basins covering 102,000 acres — for comparison, nearly one-third larger than Yosemite National Park. South Stann Creek (a major river) drains the eastern basin and the Swasey Branch drains the western. As in most rain forests, the soil is shallow — in this case granite-based — and nutritionally lacking. The basins' floors are intersected by three river systems and countless streams. Ninety-nine percent of human visitors access the eastern basin on the trails emanating from the sanctuary's headquarters at Guam Bank. The western basin can be reached by foot only on a two-day round-trip trek with the approval of the Cockscomb's director.

Human History and Impact: From time immemorial, the basin has experienced only the fleeting presence of humankind, which accounts for its pristine quality. Even during the Mayan heyday, around A.D. 70, the basin was not heavily used. Apparently the Mayans were stymied by an unusually long wet season and a scarcity of limestone, essential as a building material for their temples. Only Chucil Baalum, a relatively small ruin from the Mayan Classic Period, has been found in the entire basin, and it may not have been occupied year-round. Chucil Baalum is reached in a long day's walk from sanctuary headquarters. In recent times a small Mayan village existed where today's headquarters and campground are situated at Guam Bank, five miles inside the sanctuary's eastern boundary. In 1984 the Mayans living at Guam Bank were moved to the eastern border of the sanctuary to the new village, Maya Center, which acts as gateway to the park. Maya Center's population of about 140 people is transitioning from a milpa farming/hunting livelihood to laboring for large citrus growers, making tourist handicrafts, and working in the sanctuary as watchmen, guides, and wardens.

In 1888 the Roger Goldworthy Expedition, the first European group to climb Victoria Peak, noted that colonial loggers had entered the area to extract cedar and mahogany. Logging activities were seasonal and have been sporadic since the last century, though a few areas continued to be logged as recently as 1950. The impact of the loggers was not as severe as it could have been. Large trees were removed, affecting the upper canopy, but the region was apparently never heavily timbered with the much in demand mahogany or cedar. Today, besides the explosion of regrowth around Guam Bank, where the modern Mayans' milpas had been, the most apparent evidence of logging activities can be found on regional maps, where the names of logging camps reflect the less than cheerful assessment loggers made of the area. Go to Hell Camp and Sale Si Puede (Leave If You Can) are two place names still found on maps purchased in Belmopan.

The 1980s ushered in a critical era for the Cockscomb Basin. Arduous efforts by local and foreign conservationists within and outside government created today's Cockscomb Basin Wildlife Sanctuary. Working for Wildlife Conservation International, which is funded by the New York Zoological Society, Dr. Alan Rabinowitz completed a jaguar study in the basin in 1984. Some of the large cats in Rabinowitz's study group had fallen victim to hunting by Mayan villagers and agricultural interests that had expanded to the outer edges of the basin. Rabinowitz's discovery—that the Cockscomb had one of the densest jaguar populations recorded anywhere—initiated a dialogue between people wanting to protect jaguars and government ministers interested in the well-being of Belize's wildlife. In 1984, with funding from World Wildlife Fund U.S., the 99,000-acre Cockscomb Basin Forest Reserve was created. The reserve's "no hunting" regulation extended to all animals so that prey species important to the jaguar wouldn't be depleted by humans. However, the regulation did not protect the area from future logging and other highly invasive activities. In 1986 the 3600-acre Cockscomb Basin Jaguar Reserve was carved out of the 99,000-acre forest reserve, with protection from all types of exploitation. Even though jaguars once ranged from the United States to Argentina, an area that includes twenty nations, this was the first sanctuary ever set aside specifically for the big cat.

However, a 3600-acre reserve was too small to protect a viable population of jaguars. In fact, research showed that the territorial requirements of even one jaguar were not protected in the sanctuary. This kicked off a strong lobbying effort to expand the reserve to include the entire Cockscomb Basin. The struggle was undertaken by the Belize Audubon Society, World Wildlife Fund, Belize Zoo, and local conservationists, including Tony and Therese Rath from nearby Dangriga and Martin Meadows of San Ignacio.

Besides Rabinowitz's work with jaguars, a series of earlier studies helped nudge the area toward sanctuary status. Working independently, researchers Bruce King and James Kamstra documented the importance of the watershed and the diversity of plants and animals.

In 1988 the Cockscomb Basin Wildlife Sanctuary Expedition verified
the existence of endangered wildlife living in the basin, which added
to the ecological importance of the area. The expedition members
were locals: biologist Tony Rath, forester Martin Meadows, medicinal plant expert Rosita Arvigo, zoo director Sharon Matola, and
Ernesto Saqui, a Mopan Mayan schoolteacher at the time who would
later become the sanctuary's director. Their field work produced
sightings of rare or endangered scarlet macaws, great curassows,
agami herons, otters, tapirs, jaguar signs, and dozens of other creatures, including *Smilisca phaeota,* a frog never before recorded in Belize. The expedition found a breeding area literally hopping with
thousands of rare red-eyed tree frogs and dubbed it "Frog Town."
All of these findings figured heavily in convincing Florencio Marin,
former Deputy Minister of Natural Resources, that the area deserved
permanent sanctuary status. In 1990, former Prime Minister George
Price granted the entire basin of 102,000 acres permanent sanctuary status and its name was changed to the Cockscomb Basin Wildlife Sanctuary. Today the sanctuary is appreciated for jaguars and
a plethora of other tropical animals, as well as the high-quality habitat
that supports them.

Human and Hurricane Damage: The basin is basically pristine, but
human and natural forces have conspired to affect the upper canopy.
The aforementioned harvesting of large mahogany and cedar trees
and hurricanes have "trimmed" the upper canopy in much of the
rain forest. The result is a very dense midlevel canopy between thirty
to forty-five feet that effectively eliminates direct sunlight from reaching much of the basin floor. This allows shade-tolerant tropical plants
to flourish in profusion. In addition, the combination of hurricanes,
a yellow fever epidemic, and hunting wiped out the basin's black
howler monkeys by the mid-1960s. However, recently transplated
howlers are making a rapid comeback.

Mayan Managers: Clearly the Cockscomb is a special wild place, but
preserving it requires working the needs of the local Mayans into
the formula. Sanctuary Director Ernesto Saqui, himself a Mopan
Mayan, explains, "When I became involved, a Peace Corps worker
and an American scientist were the ones trying to run things. They
didn't know how to work with the people who had been moved from
the basin and resettled at Maya Center. How were these Mayans to

make a living? Could they adjust to a new lifestyle? The Mayans had been told that they must move and that there would be no more farming nor hunting where they had lived. Since I am a Maya I knew how they felt. I also knew what was at stake from the conservation view. It seemed like I could help. Today, six of the wardens and watchmen come from Maya Center. These men understand the ideas behind conservation. The village is now making crafts for tourists. More and more villagers are asked questions about the Cockscomb by foreigners, which reinforces the special qualities of the area."

Saqui was educated in North America in wildlife management principles and wildlands management. His dedication to the development of the sanctuary and to the needs of the Mayans at Maya Center has made him a respected figure and important resource person in Central America. Therese Bowman Rath, president of the Belize Audubon Society, says, "Ernesto is the key because he understands the values and perspectives of the cultures involved in the sanctuary. Winning the hearts and minds of the locals is essential, and so is developing economic stability for everyone involved."

The park's personnel maintain the trails, watch for poachers, guard the campground at night, lead special expeditions, and assist in scientific studies. Mayans are legendary for their knowledge of the rain forest and ability to travel through it, extracting sustenance as they go. If you engage the Mayans in conversation, keep in mind that they are often initially shy around strangers but are willing to share their knowledge and help direct you to your areas of greatest interest.

Immigration Threat: There is increased concern throughout Belize about the influx of undocumented subsistence-level immigrants from Guatemala and El Salvador. These immigrants live off the land, clearing forests for milpas and hunting for meat. The fear is that if they settle near the Cockscomb they may use it as their own private hunting preserve. "The immigrants pose a serious challenge because they haven't been part of the ongoing education effort designed to teach an appreciation of wildlife that is prevalent throughout Belize," explains Therese Rath.

Flora Galore: More than 4000 species of plants live in Belize and more than 700 of them are trees, the most visible plant forms because of their size. The majority of these trees are found in the Cockscomb. Among the trees are negrito, nargosta, bri bri, mammee apple, yemeri, Caribbean pine, quamwood, mahogany, barba jolote, yemen, strangler fig, banak and cohune and give-and-take palms, and the immense ceibas, thought to connect the underworld (through its roots) to the heavens (through its majestic branches, high in the canopy) by the Mayans. The trees provide shade or homes to more than 250 kinds of orchids, tree ferns, air plants, and vines, including varieties of philodendrons, passion fruit vine, contrebo vine, and fish vine (traditionally used for stunning fish).

Punctuating the forest floor in areas where sunlight penetrates are the brilliant heliconias in reds, oranges, and yellows. Strangely, the basin is very rich in diversity, but not well stocked with the medicinal plants that were highly valued by the ancient Mayans.

Amid the explosion of greenery there are apparent oddities, such as the buttercup tree (one large specimen overhangs the road from Maya Center to Guam Bank), which is leafless but bursting with fragrant yellow flowers from February through April. Among the many buttressed trees is the strangler fig, with its seemingly sinister survival strategy. It starts out as a seed in the upper canopy and grows to the forest floor before twining back up a nearby tree in the form of a vine. Eventually the strangler's trunk thickens and its foliage blocks the sun from its host, killing it. By the time the host decays, the fig appears as a thick-trunked tree (with a hollow interior where its host once stood), looking like so many other trees in the forest.

The give-and-take, a kind of palm, is plentiful. Its trunk is protected with nail-like thorns that break off into the flesh of any creature that brushes it. Biologist Carolyn Miller of the tiny northern rain forest village of Gallon Jug explained the origins of the palm's name: "The nasty thorns sticking in your flesh accounts for the 'give' in the palm's common name. The 'take' refers to the palm's medicinal use. A white cotton fiber found in the palm's crown is applied to wounds and is thought to cause clotting. During the years of active chicle [a sap product used in chewing gum] harvesting, it was not uncommon for the *chicleros* to fall and injure themselves while working deep in the forest, where medical aid was nonexistent. The give-and-take was reputedly used to stem the bleeding of serious injuries."

In the Cockscomb there is also poisonwood, with its harmless-looking grayish bark that causes a rash similar to poison oak or ivy. For the novice visitor to the Cockscomb, the best strategy is to look but not touch. The plant life has developed numerous strategies to protect itself.

Plentiful Wildlife: The inhospitable conditions that have always limited the presence of people act as a safeguard, allowing the jungle animals to live undisturbed. There is a great variety of wildlife, including fifty-five mammal species, which is about 75 percent of the species found in Belize. The largest mammal is the pony-sized Baird's tapir, an endangered denizen of the deep forest. Though it has a large, bulbous body and a tapered, flexible snout, giving the impression that it is related to the elephant, the tapir is more closely related to the horse. Skid marks left where this shy creature enters the water can be found on riverbanks.

There are also two species of peccaries, brocket deer, white-tailed deer, anteaters, kinkajous, oversize rodents known as gibnuts and pacas, plus armadillos and dozens of rat-size creatures, including half a dozen kinds of marsupials. And to eat these creatures there are half a dozen predators: jaguars, ocelots, jaguarundis, margays, pumas, tayras, coatimundis, and foxes.

Birds: More than 290 species of birds have been recorded in the basin, making the area a birder's dream. Avian fauna includes the king vulture, white hawk, boat-billed heron, great tinamou, keel-billed toucan, dozens of species of parrots and hummingbirds, mott-motts, trogons, and endangered species such as great curassow, crested guam, agami heron, and scarlet macaw. The macaw is found only in the western basin, which is reached in a one- or two-day hike that must be approved by the sanctuary's director.

From January to mid-April, North American visitors to the sanctuary may see birds familiar to them, including the gray catbird, wood thrush, black-and-white warbler, magnolia warbler, ovenbird, and indigo bunting.

Five Species of Wild Felines

The Cockscomb Basin is one of the few places where five species of wild cats share the same territory. The abundance of feline and other predators is seen as proof of the excellent general health of the Cockscomb's ecology. The best-known predator is, of course, the jaguar, the third-largest cat species in the world. Two other spotted species of wild cat, the ocelot and margay, live here, along with the jaguarundi and mountain lion. All cats in the basin have been studied, except the mountain lion (or puma), due to its elusiveness.

These felines are sighted less often than the basin's other active predators—tayras, kinkajous (called honey bears), and coatimundis (called quash)—since they are generally secretive, operating in heavy foliage, and rarely giving human visitors more than a glimpse of their sinuous bodies. All species of cats use hiking trails and abandoned logging tracks to travel through their territory and hunt. It is common to find the tracks of all five wild cats along them.

Why are there so many kinds of wild cats? Judging by the studies of Alan Rabinowitz, his partner Ben Nottingham, and University of Florida graduate student Michael Konecny, the answer seems to be that each species of wild cat behaves differently and utilizes a different part of the Cockscomb habitat.

Margay: Researcher Michael Konecny found that the distinctly spotted, large-eyed, tiny, ten-pound margay is almost entirely nocturnal and arboreal—that is, it lives and hunts in the trees at night and sleeps in the trees by day. Margays have legendary agility. They come equipped with double-jointed hind feet, which afford them great dexterity in climbing. Margays have the rare ability to descend a tree front first, instead of the usual backing-down descent practiced by most cats. They can also leap from one tree to another and catch themselves with a single outstretched claw and can jump vertically eight feet from the jungle floor onto a branch. Margays dine on birds, tree-dwelling mice, and rat-size mammals more than the other cats. An endangered species persecuted for decades by pet traders and skin hunters throughout most of its range, the margay appears to be the least common of the three spotted cats living in the Cockscomb.

Ocelot: The ocelot is about three times the size of a margay, weighing about thirty pounds. Unlike the margay, the ocelot has spots that often run together in a horizontal pattern, giving the coat a striped appearance from a distance. The ocelot eats creatures it catches on the jungle floor and along the fringes of the rain forest.

It hunts most actively at dawn and dusk and has a more general-ized diet than the margay. Judging by their scat, ocelots in the Cocks-comb prefer middle-size mammals, such as armadillos and opos-sums, as well as small brocket deer and peccaries. An endangered species due to the illegal activities of skin hunters and past (and pos-sibly present) activities of animal importers supplying zoos, private collectors, and the pet trade, the ocelot appears to be holding its own in the Cockscomb.

Jaguarundi: Looking somewhat uncatlike with short legs, a long body, a flat face, and small, rounded ears, the house cat–size jaguarundi is a wanderer and a daytime hunter. The jaguarundi is distinctive among the small cats because it is a solid color, usually dark brown, and not spotted. It walks great distances and usually has a territory many times larger than that of a jaguar, which is fifteen times the size of a jaguarundi. Unlike the ocelot and margay, the jaguarundi rarely retraces its steps, perhaps to avoid being a victim of the larger cats, which may pick up its scent. The jaguarundi dines on small ro-dents, amphibians, birds, and occasionally fruit, having the most varied diet of all the small cats. Jaguarundis are relatively plentiful but elusive in the basin.

Mountain Lion: The mountain lion, or puma, remains a mystery in the Cockscomb. Rabinowitz was unable to catch one and fit it with a radio collar. The reddish color variation of the mountain lions found here has given the animal the name red tiger locally. The red tiger is the same species of tawny-colored mountain lion found in North and South America, but in the tropics it rarely weighs more than 70 pounds. Mountain lions can weigh as much as 200 pounds in North America. The red tiger is known to have overlapping terri-tory with jaguars and is thought to prefer drier parts of the basin. Judging by its scat, it eats small mammals. If you see a large solid-colored cat in the Cockscomb, report it to park personnel.

Jaguar: There are probably about sixty jaguars living in the Cocks-comb Basin. Chances are you won't see a jaguar, but if you do, there's no mistaking one. The third-largest cat in the world, the jaguar is much larger than the ocelot and margay, and though they all have black spots on a yellow coat, the jaguar is much thicker proportionately through the shoulders and neck than the other two. Jaguars weigh as much as 200 pounds, measure six-and-a-half feet from tail to nose, and are powerful enough to dispatch anything in the forest, even an adult tapir weighing 600 pounds. As physically impressive as the jaguar is, its diet consists primarily of middle-size animals, with brocket deer, peccaries, armadillos, and opossums making up most of its diet. It usually hunts at dawn and dusk from ambush. A jaguar maintains a specific territory that often overlaps with those of other jaguars.

Using telemetry equipment and live bait, Rabinowitz found that healthy jaguars avoid people and their livestock unless the stock wander into the jungle. Incidents of stock killing are usually attributed to an old, injured, displaced, or inept young jaguar being unable to tackle prey in the forest. In fact, the jaguar's reputation as a stock killer resulted in some of the cats in Rabinowitz's original study being shot prior to the creation of the sanctuary. There have been no cases of jaguars attacking people in the Cockscomb, and jaguars have had ample opportunity if they were so disposed. For reasons known only to jaguars, people are not part of their menu, and most encounters with people are fleeting.

During my visit, night watchman Alphonso Ical of Maya Center recounted watching a jaguar and her cubs saunter along the trails within yards of sleeping campers on a couple of occasions. "The jaguars don't want trouble with people. They just want to do their business in the forest and know when it's best to go about unnoticed," explained Alphonso.

The jaguar is called *el tigre* in Spanish, and the Mayan word for the large cat is *baalum*. The jaguar had great religious significance for the Mayans. Once found as far north as the southwestern United States, the jaguar now lives only in the remote jungle areas of Central and South America. It is endangered, but still hunted by ranchers (sometimes merely because it is seen in the proximity of livestock) and trophy hunters in most countries in which it lives. In Belize, there is a nationwide hunting ban.

Other Animals

Tayra: Known locally as the "bush dog," the tayra is a wolverine cousin that is sighted often in the Cockscomb. It appears to be a broad-spectrum forager and is active during the day. I've seen tayras work-ing as a team on riverbanks, with one tayra scaring rodents from hiding places down the bank into the waiting jaws of its partner. The tayra is an omnivore and often frequents trees with ripening fruit. It is unmistakable in appearance. Looking like a thick-bodied weasel and about the size of a large house cat, the tayra has a white or fawn-colored head and a dark coat. It runs in a rocking-horse fashion and often pauses and looks at people entering its domain. It has a repu-tation of relying on its olfactory sense and often stops to smell the air. Mayans claim tayras can smell the ripest wild fruit in the forest and hone in on a tree from far away. They are often seen near mamey trees, which produce voluminous amounts of fruit.

Howler Monkeys: With the area protected for now, the sanctuary's director, Ernesto Saqui, a team of biologists, and government officials have undertaken the reestablishment of black howler monkeys in the Cockscomb Basin. The New York Zoological Society provided financial assistance for the project. Fourteen howlers were moved from Bermudian Landing Community Baboon Sanctuary in north-ern Belize and released in the Cockscomb in 1992. According to Dr. Robert Horwich, the transplant was entirely successful. "The origi-nal fourteen monkeys quickly multiplied, and additional transplants are planned," he says. Horwich says the goal is to release forty howlers for a new breeding nucleus.

The monkeys were released near headquarters on the trails lead-ing to South Stann Creek, and this is where you'll find them. Morn-ing and dusk are their most active times. The males usually perform their amazingly loud territorial vocalizations at dawn and dusk. (See "Bermudian Landing Community Baboon Sanctuary" in the Belize District chapter for more information on howlers.)

Reptiles: The reptilians are the quiet inhabitants of the rain forest and not as readily noticed as the birds or large mammals. The old man lizard is fairly common. This mini-dinosaur scrambles from sun-ning spots as you walk along trails. Iguanas laze high in trees along South Stann Creek, but not in the numbers found in Bermudian Landing Community Baboon Sanctuary or along the Sittee River. Iguanas are almost always found near water. The males are most no-ticeable because of the orange cast to their skin, and their surprisingly large bodies measure four feet to the tip of the tail. The more agile, emerald green females are smaller. Despite an iguana's sleepy appearance, be assured that at least one of its eyes is trained on your every move. If you come too close, it will drop into a river and swim to safety. Despite their dwindling numbers and laws that curb molesting them, iguanas are still eaten by Belizeans.

During a morning walk in the Cockscomb, some other visitors and I came upon a plump, six-foot boa constrictor slithering through the undergrowth without a sound. The nonvenomous constrictor's intent was to put distance between us and it.

The sanctuary is also home to a number of poisonous snakes. The deadly fer-de-lance (its name is French and means "arrowhead," which is the shape of the snake's head) lives in the sanctuary and is sighted occasionally. Locally it is called a Tommy Goff or Yellow-jaw. The snake has no rattle, a brown to olive cast to its skin, and diamond-shaped markings along its back similar to those of a rattlesnake. Tommy Goffs have the distinction of having the largest fangs of all poisonous snakes and possess a particularly pugnacious disposition. They strike at the slightest provocation. The young, up to about two feet long, can climb trees. The older snakes lose the ability to climb. Adults can measure five feet long and six inches thick. Rattlesnakes and coral snakes round out the sanctuary's poisonous reptiles. Generally, poisonous snakes play a lay-and-wait game with the small rodents and reptiles they eat. The world over, the best way to avoid trouble with a poisonous snake is not to stand on one, followed by getting out of one's way if it heads in your direction.

There are several kinds of turtles, toads, and frogs in the sanctuary. The red-eyed tree frogs are probably the most photogenic. These large, green frogs with bright red eyes gather around ponds during the spring for an orgy of mating activities. Around midday you can sometimes find them clinging tightly to the undersides of leaves as a way to combat dehydration.

When and How to View Wildlife

Dawn is the best time for viewing wildlife on the trails radiating from Guam Bank. The crescendo of bird calls from toucans, tinamous, parrots, herons, and songbirds ushers in the new day. Coinciding with the rise in temperature and humidity, the symphony subsides by ten o'clock, and buzzing insect sounds fill the void.

Vigilance and quiet walking are the keys to seeing wildlife in a jungle setting. Be particularly watchful around watercourses. Carry field glasses and move slowly when you see something of interest. To the casual day visitor standing on the jungle floor, the Cockscomb may look like a huge peaceful arboretum, but it is also a place of dramatic encounters between predators and prey. Stealth and quiet movements are the keys to survival for the animals living here. Seeing creatures isn't easy, but probable, if you are quiet and observant. Quality photographic opportunities are usually limited to bird life. The mammals rarely stand still for long and are usually in the poor light that typifies much of the rain forest. The best place for close-up photography of wildlife other than birds and reptiles is the Belize Zoo, with its natural settings.

As testimony to the wildlife viewing tips in the preceding paragraph, my own field notes from a two-day visit should assure you that the Cockscomb won't be disappointing: "A king vulture glides about fifty feet overhead along South Stann Creek . . . Pair of river otters surface near our lunch site on South Stann Creek. Fish are clearly visible in pools. Among them are varieties of tropicals sold in pet shops in the U.S. The feathery remains of a crested guan, picked clean by an ocelot, lay on the Antelop Trail. Crested guans are thought to pair for life. The victim's mate sits mournfully nearby, providing an excellent photographic opportunity . . . Tayra crosses the trail with a rodent writhing in its mouth. With its white head and dark body, it looks like a wolverine that has fallen head first into a bucket of white paint . . . The silence is broken by the noisy flapping of a pair of great curassows [turkey-size birds] that crash and fly through the low foliage. Mealy parrots screech at this commotion from branches of a huge, buttressed ceiba tree . . . A beautiful, bright red–breasted, slaty-tailed trogon perches silently, surveying our passing, but its bright coloration makes it impossible to miss . . . In every clearing where heliconias and other plants are in bloom, hummingbirds zip this way and that . . . Tony Rath [my guide] says sanctuary is visited or home to more than fifteen species of hummingbirds . . . Walking along South Stann Creek River, nesting pair of paraquets [parakeets] try to distract us from finding their nest . . . Keel-billed toucan calls to its mate . . . Boa constrictor glides silently past us on Wari Trail."

My last entry reads: "This is great stuff, guaranteed to stimulate the senses of anyone with the slightest curiosity about avian life forms. With luck, you'll see the odd mammal, too."

The Cockscomb Sanctuary Trail System

Park wardens working on a shoestring budget regularly maintain eleven trails encompassing thirty-five miles of access to the wilds of the Cockscomb. There is talk of expanding the trail system into the western basin. Presently all trails begin at sanctuary headquarters at Guam Bank. Maps (not to scale) can be obtained at park head-quarters. If headquarters is temporarily out of maps, there is a large, billboard-type "Cockscomb Basin Wildlife Sanctuary Trail Map" show-ing ten trails and their distances. On the billboard is a key showing campsites, picnic areas, seating areas, footbridges, stairs, watercourses, waterfalls, and latrines. There is also a new structure — built entirely by the sanctuary staff — that has a three-dimensional topographical model of the sanctuary plus colorful and informative displays that give you a sense of the topography involved on particular hikes. In addition to these trails, which do not require a guide, hikes can be arranged to the western basin, near Victoria Peak. These treks into the western basin are overnight affairs, requiring that you hire a guide from sanctuary headquarters. Participants must be in good physical condition, willing to tolerate insects, and aware of the con-stant threat of dehydration while hiking in the tropics.

The trail system is well designed for day hikes lasting from thirty minutes to half a day. Generally, early morning walks afford the most comfort, since you avoid midday heat and humidity, and offer the best chance for maximizing interaction with wildlife.

River Path, Curassow Trail, and Rubber Tree Trail: These trails make up an attractive, easy-to-complete, one-mile loop. Start on the River Path, which commences directly in front of the visitors' sleeping quarters. In a short distance the Curassow Trail forks to the left. The Curassow Trail is 400 yards and descends along a creek that emp-ties into South Stann Creek. Many trees along this walk are iden-tified with labels, and many are mature with dramatic buttressing, a feature of a lot of tropical trees unfamiliar to people from colder climates. The Curassow Trail eventually comes to the Rubber Tree

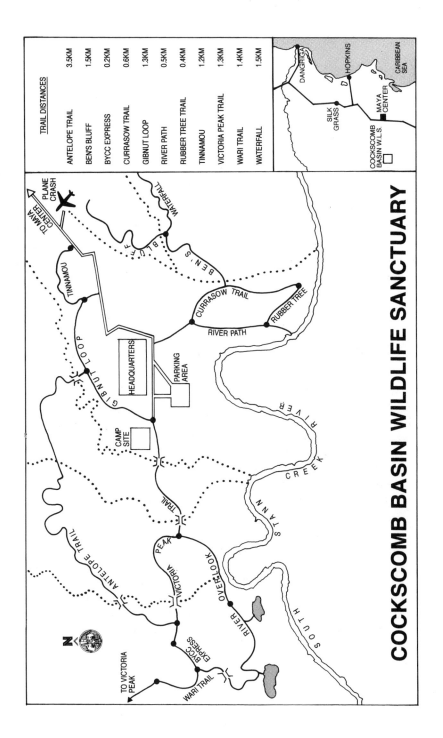

COCKSCOMB BASIN WILDLIFE SANCTUARY

TRAIL DISTANCES

ANTELOPE TRAIL	3.5KM
BEN'S BLUFF	1.5KM
BYCC EXPRESS	0.2KM
CURRASOW TRAIL	0.6KM
GIBNUT LOOP	1.3KM
RIVER PATH	0.5KM
RUBBER TREE TRAIL	0.4KM
TINNAMOU	1.2KM
VICTORIA PEAK TRAIL	1.3KM
WARI TRAIL	1.4KM
WATERFALL	1.5KM

Trail and the River Path, which takes you back to headquarters or (by heading south) to a grassy bank overlooking South Stann Creek. The intersecting trails are signposted.

This loop is a beautiful walk that captures the essence of the Cockscomb. It is commonly a guided walk for organized tours and the odd school group from Dangriga. Along the Curassow Trail you'll see an immense, buttressed ceiba tree. During my visit I joined a group of schoolchildren who were being guided by Ernesto Saqui. His stories offered a cultural and religious explanation of the Mayan view of the forest as well as an opportunity to learn to identify a variety of plants. Check with headquarters to see if Saqui or one of his assistants has time to guide you down this trail, or join a group that has prearranged a guided walk of the loop.

The River Path's riverbank terminus is perhaps the best picnic area in the sanctuary and offers excellent swimming. However, swimming is at your own risk, and caution must be exercised. The water is clear and enticing, but the current is swift just a few yards from the bank. Be aware of the strength of the current, which changes rapidly during the rainy season. You'll see mollies, swordtails, and pet store varieties of cichlids in the pools and eddies.

One group of howler monkeys was released on this loop. Look for dark forms sleeping at midday in the branches above you. The males may sound off with deep, guttural roars at any time, but they usually reserve this strenuous activity for dawn and dusk—or during the night, which will awaken you.

Antelop Trail: That's right, it's spelled without an "e." This is the longest of the day hikes, but the terrain is gentle. It is named after the small brocket deer, which is called antelop(e) by locals. The walk takes three to four hours to complete and is best enjoyed with an early start.

The Antelop Trail is a 2.5-mile loop, but walking to the starting point from headquarters and back to headquarters from the end point adds another 1.4 miles. The loop is reached by first walking west past headquarters on the Victoria Peak Trail and turning north on the Gibnut Loop Trail. Proceed on Gibnut Loop about a half-mile and look for a fork to the left. This left fork, which almost immediately crosses a creek, is the start of the Antelop Trail, which continues 2.6 miles before intersecting the Victoria Peak Trail farther west. At the western end of the trail, turn east (or left) and walk a little over a mile back to headquarters. You'll pass the designated campground along the way.

The Antelop Trail meanders along jungle streams and cuts through slope forests with a dense canopy that includes some large buttressed trees, fifteen-foot-high tree ferns, mature cohune palms, ceiba trees, and a wide assortment of vines, air plants, and orchids. The second creek crossing is the most beautiful and a convenient place for a snack or break. Even during the dry season some streams have enough water in pools for a full body soak. I walked the trail silently and saw numerous birds, including endangered great curassows. I also saw a boa constrictor, a tayra, keel-billed and aracani toucans, and numerous species of hummingbirds. I began the hike at dawn amidst nonstop bird calls of every description. By the time I returned to headquarters, the day had grown muggy and my clothes sticky. The bird calls had ceased, and creatures of all kinds seemed to be on siesta, awaiting the next period of daylight activity in the tropics — dusk.

Waterfall and Ben's Bluff Trail: Set aside at least four hours. These walks are well worth it. Both destinations are at the ends of a Y and share a common trail starting at headquarters. Take the River Path and the Curassow Trail; then cross the creek to get onto the trail to the waterfall and Ben's Bluff. The trail begins to climb through relatively dense jungle. Eventually you will come to a Y fork. The right fork climbs before descending to the waterfall. The descent requires grasping onto roots and sure-footedness. The reward is hydrotherapy in a pristine setting. The pool underneath the twenty-foot falls is ideal for a refreshing swim. You can actually paddle behind the falls and cool off with a solid wall of water in front of you. There are also numerous sunny spots around the falls to warm your body before reentering the cooling waters. This is the perfect place to spend a few hours — usually with total privacy. If you plan to visit both Ben's Bluff and the waterfall on a single outing, save the waterfall for last.

The Ben's Bluff Trail, which begins at the left fork of the Y in the trail, is strenuous but affords an astounding view of the entire Cockscomb Basin. To me, the most memorable view of the sanctuary is found at the terminus of the Ben's Bluff Trail. Once you regain your breath you'll be struck by an immense vista of the basin outlined by jagged ridges. The entire view is swathed in a patchwork of green treetops, often coated in mist, while clouds swirl around faraway Victoria Peak. The Ben's Bluff Trail is a place for quiet appreciation and contemplation, accentuated with bird and monkey calls.

Visiting Ben's Bluff and returning, with or without a detour to the waterfall, is a half-day event, and it's not easy. The trail climbs dramatically through steep jungle. There are a few strategically placed benches for resting. At times the trail all but disappears, but keep a watchful eye and you'll find it again. Because of the steepness and strenuous exertion guaranteed to produce a full body sweat, you'll swear you've traveled much farther than the 1.1 miles (each way) designated as the trail's length at headquarters. The steep climbing and heat may conspire to make you stop before reaching your goal. But you'll know you've made it when the trail breaks from the jungle onto an open slope covered in bracken ferns and thin Caribbean pines. The trail becomes extremely steep at this point, but pushing upward will afford you a west-facing view that takes in the entire Cockscomb Basin. In all, I counted thirteen ridges, each swathed in rain forest. This is a particularly beautiful view at dawn and dusk, when sunlight casts its glow on the uneven verdant ridges.

River Overlook/Wari Trail: This trail is a loop that starts at the River Overlook and ends at the Wari Trail. The trail skirts along South Stann Creek and meanders through some magical stands of large, buttressed kaway trees that support an inordinate number of flowering air plants. The kaways are pronounced examples of buttressing. I counted fourteen buttresses supporting a single kaway trunk. These outstanding trees are along oxbows of South Stann Creek. Depending on the season and the amount of rainfall, the groves may be partially submerged. The waters around these trees are teeming with tadpoles. The trail takes about an hour to complete.

To reach the River Overlook/Wari Trail, head west on the Victoria Peak Trail from headquarters. Before the forest thickens, you'll walk past the camping area through open areas of "dumb cane." This four-foot-high cane grass reputedly makes your mouth numb if you chew it. The River Overlook/Wari Trail branches off to the left (or south) and should be signposted. After about 100 yards the trail reaches the bank of South Stann Creek. Researchers and other visitors to the sanctuary sometimes float in inner tubes from this spot to the River Path picnic area, about three-quarters of a mile away.

From the point of the overlook on the South Fork of Stann Creek the trail becomes the Wari Trail and swings west along the river. In the trees along the river I sighted nesting pairs of boat-billed herons, kingfishers, black-collared hawks, and a king vulture overhead. In this stretch of river, otters are often sighted. Jaguars have sauntered across this trail directly in front of hikers on more than one occasion. To maximize your chances of seeing creatures, walk softly and talk as little as possible.

Tinamou Trail: Named after a partridge-size, ground-dwelling forest bird that is often sighted here, the Tinamou Trail is a three-quarter-mile walk that usually takes forty-five minutes to complete. The trail starts from the access road to headquarters or from Gibnut Loop, which intersects it. It meanders up and down over small streams through secondary-growth forests with a few older ironwoods, yemen, and negrito trees. There are also large cohune palms, bromeliads clinging to tree trunks, ferns, and colorful heliconias. Ernesto Saqui, who walks this trail often, says, "The trail is frequented by white-lipped peccaries, white-tailed deer, and tayras due to the abundance of wild fruit in this area of the forest. The trail is also known for its butterflies, particularly the brilliant blue morpho and owl butterfly." Bushy-tailed squirrels are often seen bounding through the canopy, and stunning, slaty-tailed trogons are fairly common. The whistling, snapping sound you may hear is the red-capped manikin, which aggressively warns other birds off its territory. The Tinamou Trail is in a low-lying area and is usually muddy and slippery.

Other Activities

Airplane in the Canopy: This is a novelty attraction. Just south of the access road into the sanctuary and east of headquarters, across from the eastern terminus of the Tinamou Trail, is a single-engine airplane suspended in the jungle canopy. Famed jaguar researcher Dr. Alan Rabinowitz experienced the thrill of a lifetime as a passenger in this small plane. The plane's pilot came in a little low and landed on the jungle canopy instead of the landing strip. The pilot, a passenger, and Rabinowitz survived with a few bumps and scratches plus a story that has become part of local folklore and Rabinowitz's

Harrison Ford image. The amazing thing is that, at the time of the crash in 1983, the jungle landing strip they were approaching was devoid of vegetation. Today the strip has been entirely reclaimed by the forest and is difficult for most travelers to locate. See if you can find the old airstrip.

Victoria Peak Expeditions: Only a handful of people have ever made it to the summit of Victoria Peak. Tony Rath, one of the few to have climbed the peak, describes the ascent as extremely dangerous due to the fractured quartzite near the summit and the two-day journey needed to get help if something should go wrong. The trek to the base of the peak takes two days with Mayan guides leading the way. Rath describes the outing as "like twenty Ben's Bluff hikes, each way." Climbing Victoria Peak is not recommended, but if you can't resist it, contact Tony Rath at Pelican Beach Resort in Dangriga or sanctuary Director Ernesto Saqui.

River Rafting: River rafting is an option for the Cockscomb that is neither organized nor talked about, but it is done on South Stann Creek. As mentioned earlier, locals using inner tubes sometimes put in at the river overlook on the Wari Trail and float to the picnic area at the end of the River Path. A longer, more ambitious float commences at either the river overlook or the River Path picnic area. From there, South Stann Creek cuts through rugged terrain covered in rain forest that gives way to farmland. The float can take up to six hours and ends where South Stann Creek passes under the Southern Highway, about 7.5 miles from the put-in points. From there, it's about 3.5 miles north to Maya Center on the Southern Highway (check bus schedules from Punta Gorda, or take your chances hitchhiking). For procuring an inner tube, inquire at Pelican Beach Resort. An inflatable, lightweight raft brought from home would also do nicely.

Tips and Essentials for a Cockscomb Visit

Caution: For hikers, Ernesto Saqui warns, "For God's sake, watch out for the fer-de-lance. Watch where you step. Try to walk on exposed ground, not on palm leaves, under which a snake might be lying. If you see a fer-de-lance, go the other way. Drink plenty of liquids while hiking so that you don't become dehydrated. Avoid strenuous walking in the heat of the day. Stay on the trails to avoid harmful plants, poisonous snakes, and getting lost, which can happen permanently in a rain forest once you've strayed from a trail."

Be Prepared: Mosquito repellent (and netting if you plan to camp), sunscreen, a container to carry liquid, light rain gear, long pants, a hat, and snake bite–proof hiking boots are recommended. For enhancing wildlife viewing, carry field glasses and a bird book. My favorite book is the *Peterson Field Guides, Mexican Birds*, by Roger Tory Peterson and Edward Chalif.

Special Note: The Mayans are attempting to diversify from an economy based purely on slash-and-burn agriculture, so visitors are encouraged to buy souvenirs and soft drinks at Maya Center. Since Maya Center is the entry point for the sanctuary, and you are required to stop here and sign the register (in the structure nearest the gate), your support would be appreciated.

Accommodations: In the sanctuary you'll find twenty beds in two structures and an campground for a nominal nightly fee of about U.S. $5. Water for drinking and showering is supplied via a cistern. Beds are rented on a first-come basis but can be reserved. Ask for the smaller of the two structures. It has only three beds, assuring privacy. Many visitors make the Cockscomb a one-day trip from their accommodations in Dangriga or Placencia. To do yourself and the sanctuary justice you should stay a minimum of one night. This is the only way to experience the special ambience of the night sounds and early morning walks that will become etched in your memory. Key contacts: Pelican Beach Resort, Dangriga, Belize, C.A. (phone 05-22044; fax 05-22570); Cockscomb Basin Wildlife Sanctuary, P.O. Box 90, Dangriga, Belize, C.A. (radio phone 2M FM 142.750); Belize Audubon Society, 29 Regent Street, P.O. Box 1001, Belize City, C.A. (phone 02-77369; fax 02-78562). Of these contacts, Pelican Beach Resort responds quickest.

Access: The Cockscomb is about twenty-one miles south of Dangriga on the Southern Highway. The highway's surface is dirt. Under friendly skies the journey takes about forty-five minutes. During the rainy season, swollen creeks sometimes inundate the Southern

Highway in the area of Freshwater Creek, stopping traffic for up to two days. (The U.S. Army Corps of Engineers may replace the bridge over this creek, making the road usable regardless of the weather.) If it has been raining, ask at your hotel about the condition of the Southern Highway prior to leaving for the sanctuary.

Buses from Dangriga to points south and from Punta Gorda to points north stop at Maya Center. Try Venus (phone 02-73354) or Z-Line (phone 02-73937/05-22211). It's a five-mile walk from there to the sanctuary unless you luck out and secure a ride with someone going to headquarters. Five cars a day is considered busy. Some resorts catering to eco-tourists, including Pelican Beach Resort in Dangriga and Rum Point in Placencia, will arrange for a van ride to and from the Cockscomb. Expect to pay in excess of U.S. $50 per person for the service. In your own rental car, visiting the Cockscomb is a matter of negotiating the potholes on the Southern Highway.

Most Cockscomb visitors arrive in Dangriga via Maya Airlines or a rental car from Belize City. They stay at Pelican Beach Resort, whose owners Therese and Tony Rath intimately know the Cockscomb. They have direct contact with sanctuary headquarters, which is helpful in lining up a Mayan guide, learning about weather conditions, and reserving a bed at the sanctuary for an overnight stay.

Placencia

Placencia is the prettiest coastal village in Belize and should be part of any serious attempt to appreciate Belizeans and the bountiful marine habitats of their country. Placencia's friendly atmosphere, range of casual-style accommodations, and ideal location as a stepping-off place to many of the best snorkel and dive sites near and on the Barrier Reef make it special. Other pluses for the adventure traveler are the community's isolation at the end of the Placencia Peninsula and its attractive physical location, which includes the longest stretch of sandy beach in Belize.

Development Dilemma: A resident of Placencia from birth, Brian Young sums up the dilemma facing Placencia this way: "We have the

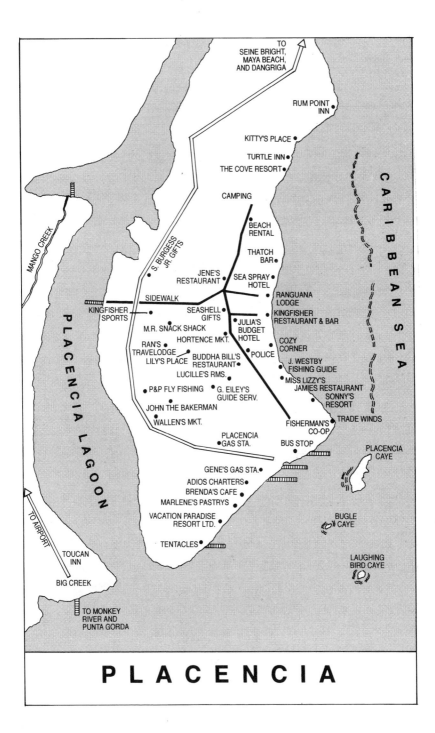

TO
SEINE BRIGHT,
MAYA BEACH,
AND DANGRIGA

CARIBBEAN SEA

RUM POINT INN

KITTY'S PLACE

TURTLE INN

THE COVE RESORT

CAMPING

BEACH RENTAL

THATCH BAR

MANGO CREEK

S. BURGESS JR. GIFTS

JENE'S RESTAURANT

SEA SPRAY HOTEL

RANGUANA LODGE

SIDEWALK

KINGFISHER SPORTS

SEASHELL GIFTS

KINGFISHER RESTAURANT & BAR

M.R. SNACK SHACK

JULIA'S BUDGET HOTEL

HORTENCE MKT.

COZY CORNER

RAN'S TRAVELODGE

POLICE

LILY'S PLACE

BUDDHA BILL'S RESTAURANT

J. WESTBY FISHING GUIDE

MISS LIZZY'S

LUCILLE'S RMS.

JAMIES RESTAURANT

P&P FLY FISHING

G. EILEY'S GUIDE SERV.

SONNY'S RESORT

JOHN THE BAKERMAN

TRADE WINDS

WALLEN'S MKT.

FISHERMAN'S CO-OP

PLACENCIA LAGOON

PLACENCIA GAS STA.

BUS STOP

PLACENCIA CAYE

GENE'S GAS STA.

ADIOS CHARTERS

BRENDA'S CAFE

MARLENE'S PASTRYS

BUGLE CAYE

VACATION PARADISE RESORT LTD.

TENTACLES

LAUGHING BIRD CAYE

TO AIRPORT

TOUCAN INN

BIG CREEK

TO MONKEY RIVER AND PUNTA GORDA

P L A C E N C I A

conveniences associated with this century, but the town feels like the last century. We know we can't expand too fast because that may ruin what's special about Placencia." Brian symbolizes the special qualities of Placencia that extend beyond the village's beautiful setting. When I met him at Rum Point Inn he was wearing shorts and a faded T-shirt, emphasizing his muscle-hard physique. He looked much like the hard-living, carefree conch and lobster fishermen I had met throughout Belize. So much for stereotypes. Brian is well versed in responsible community development, has been elected to the city council, and was a leading force in bringing refrigeration to Placencia's fishermen's cooperative so that it could compete with better situated cooperatives to the north. He also is a dive master whose expertise is greatly appreciated by Rum Point Inn, a unique, small resort just north of Placencia.

Brian talked at length about the dilemma facing Placencia and the need to move slowly when it comes to development. "For years the Producers' Cooperative [the fishermen's cooperative] was the only thing happening here that earned a dollar. In recent years Placencia has become more involved in tourism. With this hope there is danger. We need to make decisions that don't hurt our environment but allow us to make a good living." Throughout Placencia, Brian's sentiments were reiterated by expatriate Americans and Belizeans who own local businesses. How the sentiments of locals play against plans to someday "modernize and maximize" the area by developers I met in the Corozal District will be seen in the years to come.

History and Ambience: Locals will tell you that the site of today's village was used by pirates as far back as the 1600s. In this century Placencia has been a fishing village, and today's permanent population of about 400 consists mostly of Creoles but also includes North Americans, Garifunas, and Hispanics. The village has a unique social climate and charm that somehow accommodate conch fishermen, vagabond yachters, scuba divers, game fishermen, and low- and high-budget adventure travelers. There is a "live and let live" frontier quality to Placencia.

The village is made up of colorfully painted small businesses and homes sprawled haphazardly under coconut palms along a mile-long sidewalk that serves as the community's main "street." To catch the gentle onshore breeze, for safety against wood-eating insects, and for protection from hurricane-driven high tides, most of the village stands on stilts and faces the crescent-shaped beach. Offshore to the east, numerous dark-green islands poke out of a usually calm, azure blue sea. To the west is the generally shallow Placencia Lagoon, which is surrounded by miles of mangroves. On the opposite shore of the lagoon you'll find Big Creek and Mango Creek, two nondescript settlements where you can hire a skiff for the fifteen-minute ride to Placencia should you arrive by plane at Big Creek, which connects the area to Belize City via fairly regular air service.

Besides Placencia's sidewalk/main street, there is a parallel sand road down the west side of town that takes you to the end of the peninsula, where the fish co-op, gas station, and village pier are located. However, once accommodations have been procured, most people prefer barefooting it, which explains why the sidewalk was built. The sand is comfortable enough to walk on, but it is made of ground-down quartzite, which can be somewhat abrasive during a long walk — and awfully hot under the tropical sun.

People come to Placencia to relax. This takes many forms: snorkeling, sunbathing, scuba diving, hammock lounging, fishing, reading, contemplating, sailing, windsurfing, sea kayaking, photographing, birding, eating, and drinking. All these activities can be worked into a week, or a month, in a multitude of settings and at the pace you desire.

If you arrive around midday you may think the place is deserted. I remember walking the sidewalk on a particularly warm day. I passed by an empty police station, the Sea Spray Hotel, Jene's Restaurant, a tiny grocery store, Geno's gas station, and the post office and saw only two people. At the end of the sidewalk (and peninsula) I turned west past Adios Charters and Brenda's Cafe, and on the pier in front of Tentacles Restaurant I found what appeared to be most of the people in town. There they sat, quietly talking and nursing their Beliken beers and soft drinks under the shade of a fragile-looking, sun-bleached, palm-frond roof that was erected at the end of the pier. Besides the roof, this open-air configuration consisted of a few rickety benches and tables that sat on tired-looking planks with gaps large enough to view the water a few feet beneath your feet. Judging by the turnout, the airy design was much appreciated. Sitting in a pub with no walls on a pier over water was a smart way to catch the slightest breeze on a hot day. On this day, however, the sweltering heat and absolutely glass-smooth surface of Placencia Lagoon indicated that the breeze was yet to come. And it appeared that the pub's patrons were staying put in the meantime.

Basic Necessities: The village has businesses that will cover your basic needs. Hortence's Market, with basic foodstuffs, is located fifty yards north of the police station on the west side of the sidewalk. There's also Wallen's Market on the west side of the village across and north of the soccer field. For pastries and coconut breads try Lilly's Place behind Hortence's Market or Merlene's Pastries next to Vacation Paradise Resort (found by turning east on the seaside path that commences where the road and sidewalk end). There's also John the Baker Man behind Wallen's Market. Geno's gas station (including diesel), the post office, public phone, bus stop, and ice (fishermen's co-op) are at the end of the only road that skirts the east side of the village. If you can't find anyone at the post office, try the nearby snack bar. If this fails, ask anyone where you can find Janice Leslie. Janice runs the post office, public phone, and snack bar and lives just a few doors away.

Reading the Town Map: If you try to get your bearings in Placencia from the commonly distributed "Orange Peel T-Shirts" map (found in most businesses), it is generally accurate, but not all names on the map coincide with the names, or lack of names, on buildings. For example, a modest little structure with a sign "Chicken Soup on Sale Tonight" and no other identification turned out to be Karen's Fast Food. The soup was tasty. "Sometimes signs fall down; sometimes people change the names," explained the young woman who served the soup.

Snorkel Sites in the Inner Lagoon: There is no end to the possibilities of snorkeling and scuba diving destinations reached from Placencia. The cayes and shallow reefs in the area are too numerous to count. The Caribbean Sea due east to about thirteen miles from Placencia is referred to as the Inner Lagoon. Protected by the Barrier Reef, the Inner Lagoon is usually calm with exceptional underwater visibility, and sea life is as bountiful as anywhere on the reef. Your experience will depend on tailoring your interests and scuba or snorkel skills to your guide's knowledge of the area.

My one-day snorkeling survey of the Inner Lagoon took me to

five snorkeling sights, the farthest from shore being Laughing Bird Caye, which had been declared a national park in 1991, a couple of months prior to my first visit there. My trip was greatly enhanced by marine biologist Tony Rath, who led the way, and George and Corol Bevier, the owners of Rum Point Inn. In terms of natural beauty, relaxation, and variety, this one-day excursion surpassed most of my thirty or more scuba dives and countless snorkels in Belize. As you read the following site descriptions, keep in mind that underwater conditions fluctuate — visibility changes, and fish come and go — but my field notes should give you a good idea of the matrix of life here.

Our craft, a twenty-five-foot, open, fiberglass dory with a powerful outboard, was perfect for the day's outing. We started at 8:00 A.M. at Rum Point Inn's dock, which is in the mangroves on Placencia Lagoon. For ten minutes we purred through a maze of mangrove channels, watching herons, egrets, and snakebirds stand motionless or take flight as we passed. Once in Placencia Lagoon, we headed south and turned east into the Caribbean, passing the village of Placencia. From the water the sleepy village was a postcard image of expansive beach, coconut palms, a few structures, docks, and weathered yachts sitting at anchor. Aloft, frigate birds glided into the wind on their fragile, prehistoric-looking wings. Ahead lay the Inner Lagoon, an immense expanse of aqua-blue water dotted with dark-green mangrove cayes for thirteen miles to Laughing Bird Caye, our turnaround point and the last island stop to the south in the Inner Lagoon.

Colson Caye: Our first stop was the south side of Colson Caye. Under the water's surface we found a recovering reef environment with large sections of dead staghorn coral, but with healthy sponges and immense brain corals. Most of our snorkeling was in six feet of water that included sandy patches between coral outcrops. Fish were everywhere. Tony Rath coaxed a large, inflated porcupine fish, commonly called a "puffer," from its hiding place. Gray angelfish were plentiful, as were some of the largest schools of both immature and mature parrotfish I had ever seen. We spotted some fire and gorgonian corals — the gorgonians we considered a rarity at such a shallow depth.

Man-of-War Cayes: Our next snorkel was to the south of three tiny cayes known locally as Man-of-War Cayes (different from Man-of-War Caye near Dangriga). These tiny islands are nameless on most maps.

Nevertheless, this stop proved to be exhilarating. Tony had chosen the site because he thought we'd see all the habitats that make up the reef community in one snorkel in a distance of about a hundred yards. He was right. We started in about thirty feet of water above a wall that dropped off into a dark-blue abyss. We snorkeled above the drop-off and saw large numbers of mature redband and spotlight parrotfish, gray and French angelfish, squirrelfish, small-mouth grunts, and other mature reef species. All of them were staying close to coral outcrops, their refuge from predators. Out from the wall swaggered jacks and large barracudas. These open-water predators were looking for an unsuspecting meal. The tension was palpable, and for us the drama had just begun. When we turned toward the island's shallower water I glimpsed two huge, gaping mouths outlined in white coming at us from the deep. My eyes strained and my heart pounded to see the outlines of the creatures that belonged to such mouths. "Big enough to fit around a person," I noted. Instantaneously, appreciation replaced fear. A pair of curious spotted eagle rays, with their permanently open mouths, had come to investigate us. They glided within five feet of us in a display of supple and serene grace before turning sharply in perfect unison as if they'd choreographed the maneuver like two jet fighter pilots. These beautifully marked rays with seven-foot wingspans made two passes by us before disappearing.

We snorkeled toward the islands, passing over a healthy shallow reef with prominent sea fans, staghorn and brain corals, and dozens of species of reef fish. Among the more colorful fish were trunkfish, queen angelfish, gray angelfish, four-eye butterflyfish, several varieties of damsels and parrotfish, gobies, fairy basslets, squirrelfish, wrasses, hamlets, blue tangs (and yellow immatures), and the ever-present sergeant majors.

We continued past the coral into the shallows, featuring sea grass beds that are home to anemones and juvenile fish not yet big enough to tempt fate along the reef. Within forty feet of the island, houndfish appeared near the surface, and then came the sprat, millions of them. Sprat are two-inch-long, silvery fish that occupy the bottom of the food chain. With only a foot of water beneath our bodies, and our fins churning up the sand, we closed on a narrow channel that ran through one of the islands. We were totally surrounded by sprat, which glistened in great metallic clouds, swirling and flashing as the fish nearest to us reacted to our invasive presence. The sprat were so thick that we had to lift our heads above the water to get our bearings. The fish so churned the surface that it sounded as if a torrential downpour were under way. As we slipped through the mangrove channel, we glimpsed small barracudas darting into the sprat and gulping them down. And from above, frigate birds swooped and nimbly dipped their beaks into the water, extracting the sprat whose turn had come to forever depart the swirling mass. When we lifted our heads from the water to check out the island, we saw brown pelicans dive-bombing farther out and plump brown boobies perched in the branches of the mangroves, looking quite content. No doubt they were loaded down with bellies full of fish.

This snorkel site was as memorable as any I've ever experienced. In a space of about a hundred yards we had witnessed deep water, shallow reef, sea grass, and mangrove habitats and their species in colorful and sometimes deadly interactions that will remain vivid in my memory for as long as I live.

Laughing Bird Caye National Park: Laughing Bird Caye National Park was our third stop. This idyllic, palm-studded caye lies in a north/south orientation and is the southernmost island of the Inner Lagoon. The caye's name comes from laughing gulls that nested here until the island's natural beauty became so well known that the constant stream of people visiting it put an end to nesting activities. Still, this is a wonderfully stunning coral atoll, though its popularity is causing Belizean authorities problems in terms of garbage removal and sanitation. When I visited, the island was very clean. I was told that the last group of kayakers had cleaned up the island and that locals had taken it upon themselves to make sure it stayed as clean as possible. On this day the island had about fifteen people on it: scuba divers, day trippers with snorkels, and dehydrated-looking kayakers who had paddled the thirteen-mile distance from Placencia. I was told this was the usual human visitor level.

Laughing Bird Caye is about a quarter-mile in length and twenty-five to forty yards across, which doesn't give a visitor a great deal of space when sharing the island with others. Night stays are forbidden. To protect the caye, the island was made into a national park in 1991. A debate continues. The Belize Audubon Society, Placencia Tour Guide Association, and Coastal Management Unit have been lobbying the government to include the underwater areas around the island as part of the national park.

The obvious question is, Why do all dories in the Placencia area eventually head to Laughing Bird Caye? After all, there are dozens of islands and innumerable snorkel and dive sites in the Inner Lagoon. Locals say Laughing Bird Caye is unique because it has no mangroves, which breed skin-biting and sucking insects. Instead, its key features are a nice swimming beach on its western side and about thirty palms to provide shade. As you approach by boat, the island's profile suggests the perfect setting for romantic castaways. The absence of sand flies on Laughing Bird made it a popular stop for Belizean fishermen long before it came a destination for adventuresome tourists. Whatever one's business in the area, the island serves as a lunch stop for whoever is around.

When we rolled from the gunnel of our dory into the light blue sea on Laughing Bird Caye's southeast side, it was instantly apparent why the Belize Audubon Society feels so strongly about including the surrounding underwater area in the park. The east side has one of the most extensive stands of elkhorn coral I've seen. In terms of hiding places, this is a reef fish's dream. The dominant elkhorn is mixed with staghorn and brain corals. Boats anchoring here or fishermen with nets would cause harm to the coral that would take centuries to mend. We snorkeled over the coral in a northerly direction. Blue tang were the prominent schooling fish, but many other species were plentiful, including four-eye butterflyfish.

The island's eastern side is also the windward. On the day of our visit, the seas were calm. However, due to the greater exposure, there were occasional surprise swells that surged toward shore. These swells can lift and drop a swimmer onto coral heads in the shallow areas. For this reason we swam around, rather than over, coral heads near the surface. On most days the best water clarity is during the morning hours, before the combination of wind and swells works havoc on visibility. Tony Rath has scuba dived to depths of a hundred feet off the island's east side. He remembers the elkhorn giving way to plate corals and large groupers at a depth of ninety feet.

We became so absorbed in our snorkeling that we swam around the island. From the northern end of the island along the western shore, conditions and underwater scenery are entirely different. The western side is more protected, with a bottom topography of bright, sandy patches and coral outcrops. There are numerous small reef fish. Among them are damsels, butterflyfish, trunkfish, wrasses, basslets, rock beauties, parrotfish, and angelfish. But don't just look down. Near the surface you'll see houndfish, whose light color blends with the well-lighted surface. These small, torpedo-shaped predators dive-bomb the unsuspecting fish from above.

Near Mosquito Caye: On our way back to Placencia we stopped twice near small cayes in the vicinity of Mosquito Caye, which is privately owned. Though these two stops didn't have as much reef diversity as the exceptional sites described above, they were teeming with life, especially near the mangroves, where young barracudas were feeding on sprat and the juveniles of other species.

Brian Young's Top Dive Spots: In Brian's words, here's what the Placencia area has to offer: "I dive in the Inner Reef and occasionally the outer reef. I prefer not going below 100 feet. Mostly we do wall dives with shallow starts. Around Laughing Bird Caye is a popular spot. The outer reef dives have the greatest mix of really big barrel sponges and large deep-water fish, such as tuna, king mackerels, barracudas, and jacks as well as reef fish. Raguana Caye, Gladden Channel, and Buttonwood Channel have outstanding wall dives. Many of the dives aren't in dive books and have no names. Often I design dives for people's tastes. People from the north tell me my spots are as good as good can get. I also know of some sandy holes surrounded by coral that are teeming with all kinds of fish. Very large barrel and tube sponges are easy to come by. It's beautiful out there."

It takes about thirty minutes to reach the Inner Reef dive sites from Placencia, but for the outer reef, think in terms of one hour to the sites. More boat time costs more money, but not much more. Brian's rate for two dives in the Inner Reef, including a picnic, is U.S. $80 for two or U.S. $50 per person for a group of four to seven (the maximum). Brian also leads snorkeling excursions that include lunch.

Scuba Diving Operations: Kitty Fox runs the Placencia Dive Shop from Kitty's Place, and Brian Young has been running dive trips for six years, often coordinating his activities with Rum Point Inn (see below). Contact Kitty Fox, Placencia Dive Shop, Placencia, Belize, C.A. (phone 06-22027), or Brian Young, Young's Charters, Placencia, Belize, C.A. (phone 06-23166), or contact Rum Point Inn, where Brian sometimes works.

Sailing and Windsurfing: These are largely undeveloped recreational activities, especially when you consider the protection afforded boaters in the Inner Lagoon, the unspoiled natural beauty of the area, and the many anchorages. I saw two trimarans with four berths that hired for U.S. $30 per day. These boats were owned by long-term visitors but may not always be available for rental. For the status of sailboat rentals, inquire at Young's Charters (phone 06-23166), Kitty's Place (phone 06-22027), Rum Point Inn (phone 06-22017), and Turtle Inn (phone 06-22069), which also rents sailboards.

Sea Kayaking: With its magnificent underwater coral formations teeming with tropical fish, numerous islands populated with fishing birds, and the generally calm, warm conditions, the immense Inner Lagoon makes the waters around Placencia ideal for sea kayaking. The most common ambitious paddle is to Laughing Bird Caye (over-nighting on a nearby caye) and back, a total distance of twenty-six miles. There are numerous snorkel sites and stops at other islands. Unfortunately, not everyone operating a sea kayak operation in Placencia has received rave reviews. I can recommend Chris and Skip White, who own Turtle Inn (phone 06-22069). Anyone recommended by Rum Point Inn or Kitty Fox ought to be reliable also.

Fishing: The waters around Placencia are particularly rich in fish that people like to eat. Most species are caught year-round. Oceanic varieties include yellowfin tuna, blackfin tuna, bonito, wahoo (November–February), and shark. Reef fish include barracuda, jackfish, mackerel, grouper, snapper, permit, bonefish (November–April, on flats), tarpon (June–August, near mangroves). The most sought-after river fish are tarpon (February–August), snook (February–August), and snapper.

Fishing Services: Charlie Leslie, of Kingfisher Sports Ltd., has state-of-the-art equipment and has been in business for years (phone 06-23125/23104). Other time-tested services include Pow Cabral Fly Fishing (phone 06-23132); Paradise Vacations (phone 06-23179); Whiprey Caye Guiding, for fly-fishing (phone 06-23130); and Gene Redburn's (phone 06-23132).

Restaurants: Rum Point Inn (E) and Kitty's Place (M) will serve meals to nonguests who book reservations twenty-four hours in advance. Ask about prices. Both places serve excellent dishes, but to me Rum Point's offerings equaled or surpassed anything I was served in Belize.

Prepared by owner Corol Bevier, the meals often include popular local dishes: conch soup, lobster, snapper, cassava bread, and secret mixtures of spices. Corol says, "Our food is eclectic, featuring, but not confined to, tropical cuisines worldwide. For example, our soups this week were chicken rum, banana, chilled orange, tortilla, and Japanese egg drop. We also have a selection of homemade pastries, breads, and fruit sorbets. We never repeat a meal in its entirety."

Sonny's (B) and the Tentacles (B) have popular, inexpensive restaurants and bars. Turtle Inn (B, M) has a small, quiet, clean bar and restaurant right on the beach and serves moderately priced Creole and American dishes that are tasty and filling. Owners Skip and Chris White lead kayaking and snorkeling adventures and are good sources of information about the natural wonders of the area.

Accommodations: When it comes to places to stay, Placencia has plenty of choices. At the top of the heap for ambience, style, cuisine, and experience is Rum Point Inn (E), which is owned and run by George and Corol Bevier, two Stanford University graduates who opened their small resort eighteen years ago. George Bevier headed a public health project combating malaria in nearby Guatemala in the 1950s and fell in love with Placencia.

Rum Point Inn may be the best coastal resort in Belize. The resort sits on a spacious, isolated beach about two-and-a-half miles north of Placencia. Guests stay in private, attractive, large bungalows made from hurricane- and termite-proof ferroconcrete. Each bungalow is shaped differently, with sweeping curves but an overall rounded form. The white interiors of these structures have a Mediterranean Moorish look, with tile floors, plants, and large bathrooms. Each bungalow has a view of the sea and is designed to collect the sea breeze for natural air-conditioning. There are no windows. Instead, the screen-covered openings in the walls are cleverly designed to allow the person inside a view while disallowing a passer-by's view of the inside.

Guests eat their meals together at a large table in the dining hall, which is a combination of New England and eastern Mediterranean architecture. Built by a shipwright, the structure is an example of precise carpentry. Near the dining area is a small bar with a large veranda that looks out through palms across the beach and Inner Lagoon. At dusk, Creole conch and lobster fishermen are commonly seen paddling their dugouts toward Placencia.

The Beviers also have compiled an impressive library that rivals any in the country. You'll find something for all tastes, but the collection is tilted toward nature with an emphasis on Belize.

Rum Point Inn also organizes snorkeling, scuba, and fishing (spin and fly) trips; visits to the Cockscomb Basin Wildlife Sanctuary (hiking, swimming, birding, and plant and tree identification), Monkey River (swimming and viewing of howler monkeys, iguanas, and birds), and Mayan ruins (Lubaantun and others), and villages (Blue Creek); and light sailing on the Inner Lagoon on traditional open sloops and Sunfish-type day sailers. Inquire about the cost of these activities.

George Bevier says the average stay, including excursions, is four to five days. Usually a minimum of forty-five days in advance is needed to put together an itinerary; three months is preferable. High season is December to May. The summer months, which are ignored by most North Americans, have better rates, and according to George Bevier, the temperature and humidity on the sea coast are not appreciably different from conditions in Chicago or New York.

Visa, MasterCard, American Express, and Discover cards are accepted. Rates per day run from U.S. $40 for a child to U.S. $190 for a double during high season. Contact Toucan Travel, 32 Traminer Drive, Kenner, LA 70065 (phone 1-800-747-1381 or 504-465-0769; fax 504-464-0325) or contact the Beviers directly at Rum Point Inn, Placencia, Belize, C.A. (phone 06-22017).

Kitty's Place (M), about three minutes south of Rum Point Inn (or one-and-a-half miles north of Placencia) by car, is also outstanding for a moderate price range. Proprietor and former New Yorker Kitty Fox arrived here seven years ago and pieced together her own small resort, which features rooms and apartments in two handsome colonial structures—called the Belizean and the Colonial—overlooking the beach and Inner Lagoon. She also rents budget-priced one- and two-bedroom apartments in town. Just offshore, within a few yards of the beach, is a coral outcrop, which allows guests to walk to a snorkel site directly from their rooms. This is a rarity for the Placencia area. Usually a boat ride is necessary to reach a decent snorkeling site. Kitty serves meals (specializing in Italian cuisine) to her guests, has a small bar and a dive shop, and arranges activities that include sailing, snorkeling, scuba diving, windsurfing, hiking (in the Cockscomb), and bicycling.

One advantage of Kitty's Place for people wanting to stay awhile is that her apartment rental rate saves money, compared to daily rates charged elsewhere. Each of Kitty's units has a kitchen, bathroom, and veranda. For an apartment stay, the most attractive structure, the Belizean, costs U.S. $65 per day for one or two persons and U.S. $10 for each additional person. For rooms in the same structure with shared amenities, the cost is U.S. $30 to U.S. $40 per day. For the Colonial, the price range for a single room to a private apartment is U.S. $45 to U.S. $85 per day. In Placencia village, Kitty operates Ran's Villas, which are one- and two-bedroom apartments with kitchen, bathroom, dining area, sofa bed, and screened veranda; rentals here are U.S. $225 per week or U.S. $500 per month. Major credit cards are accepted. Contact Kitty's Place, Placencia, Belize, C.A. (phone 06-22027).

In the village itself there are numerous moderate and low-budget accommodations. One that is geared to the nature-oriented, young-at-heart set is Turtle Inn (M), owned by Skip and Chris White. They have six cabanas and a small restaurant specializing in Belizean cuisine with an emphasis on seafood. Much of their business is in conjunction with university programs in the United States. The cabanas are clean and face the beach. Skip leads sea and jungle adventures, and when I met him he'd just led a group of kayakers from a nearby island. Major credit cards are accepted. Contact Skip White, Tropical Learning Center, Turtle Inn, Placencia, Belize, C.A. (phone 06-22069; in the United States, 303-444-2555).

Other accommodations in town include the Paradise Vacation Hotel (B), near the Tentacles Restaurant on the path that veers right along the water past the gas station at the southern terminus of the peninsula. The rooms look tidy. Sonny's Resort (M), on the seaward side of town close to the end of the sidewalk, offers beachside accommodations with fishing or snorkeling and boat transfers to and from the airport inclusive in the daily rate for one- to eight-night stays. Daily rates start at U.S. $50 for a double. Contact Sonny's Resort, Corner of 13th and F streets, Kings Park, Belize City, Belize, C.A. (phone 06-23103). Near Sonny's is the Tradewinds (M), with five private cabanas and guided snorkel outings. Phone 06-23101/23122. Credit cards are often accepted in these hotels, but always inquire when making reservations. Camping is permitted at the north end of the sidewalk past the Thatch Bar and Beach Rental (which rents windsurfers, Sunfish, and sea kayaks).

If you end up in tiny Big Creek or Independence, across the lagoon from Placencia, stay at the Toucan Inn (M). This is an attractive lodge run by a British couple. It has a nice restaurant and clean rooms. Contact Toucan Inn, Big Creek/Independence, Belize, C.A. (phone 06-22084).

Access: If you're heading south to Placencia by car, turn east from the Southern Highway at mile 23 (or twenty-nine miles after leaving Dangriga). This turnoff is marked "Riversdale" and "Placencia." You'll reach Riversdale in ten miles, from there Placencia is twelve miles to the south at the terminus of the narrow Placencia Peninsula. The drive from Dangriga to Placencia takes about two hours. From the Cockscomb Basin Wildlife Sanctuary, also to the north, the drive is thirty-two miles and takes about an hour. All roads south of Dangriga are dirt, so in the wet season expect muddy but generally passable conditions. After prolonged heavy rains there is sometimes flooding on the Southern Highway that closes the road for a day or two.

By bus, try Z-Line from Punta Gorda, Dangriga, or Belize City. The Z-Line terminal in Belize City is located at the Venus Bus Lines terminal on Magazine Road (phone 02-73354). In Dandriga, Z-Line operates from 8 Vincent Street (phone 06-22211) and in Punta Gorda, from José Maria Nuñes Street (phone 07-2165). In Placencia, phone 06-22211 (Dandriga number) or ask for assistance from locals. The bus stops near the post office and gas station.

Maya Airlines (phone 02-72332/44027) flies eleven-seater twin props to Big Creek/Independence, which is fifteen minutes across the Placencia Lagoon from the village of Placencia. Flights can be coordinated with a skiff to take you and your luggage across the lagoon. Placencia has an airstrip near Rum Point Inn that has been nearing completion for years. You may find yourself landing here, which means you're about two-and-a-half miles out of town but within easy walking distance of Rum Point Inn and Kitty's Place.

FOUR

TOLEDO DISTRICT

Overview

The Toledo District is Belize's southernmost region. It lies south of the Stann Creek District and north of Guatemala and is an area most Belizeans have never visited. It is a land of thatched-roof Mayan villages connected to one another by footpaths and dirt roads. In the Toledo District there are entire river systems that can be visited only by boat. There are easily accessible, exquisite Mayan ruins in lush green settings and some of the prettiest island destinations in Belizean waters. Belizeans refer to Toledo as the "forgotten district" or "Belize twenty years ago." Quite often the entire district is referred to as P. G., the initials of the district's capital, Punta Gorda.

The Toledo District has a mere 17,275 people who occupy 1669 square miles, making the district Belize's third in size to the Cayo and Orange Walk districts and the least densely populated region in Belize. Punta Gorda has a polyglot population of Garifunas, Mayans, a Latin/Mayan mix called Spanish, Creoles, and a few whites. The average family lives by subsistence farming and probably does not make an income exceeding U.S. $600 annually. More than in any other part of Belize, the predominantly Mayan village population of the interior is accessible to outsiders.

Toledo is the wettest district in Belize, averaging between 130 and 160 inches annually, which can cause havoc during the wet season (June to November here) on the Southern Highway, which is dirt, and a few other dirt roads cutting inland near Punta Gorda. However, you can avoid the Southern Highway by flying to Punta Gorda and paying to be driven to the area's many points of interest.

The tourism infrastructure is fragile and somewhat limited in the Toledo District. With a frontier atmosphere and this fairly spartan infrastructure, there's no doubt that the district may not be for everyone. But for the seasoned traveler and true adventurer who is interested in spending time with the Mayans in their thatched-roof villages hidden away in verdant jungle far from electricity, motor vehicles, and other trappings of our technological age, this is the place to go. Besides the Mayan villages, the ancient Mayan ruins of Nim Li Punit and Lubaantun are nestled in stunning settings. As late as 1993, entire ruins of ancient towns abandoned more than 1000 years ago were discovered along the Monkey River in the northern Toledo District. The knowledgeable Mayan caretakers of today who show you around the ruins in the southern part of the district put the Toledo District's Mayan experience in a class by itself. And, if you're up for real adventure, you can hire a boatman and his fiberglass dory to explore the Moho, Temash, and Sarstoon rivers, or travel far offshore to the Sapodilla Cayes, perhaps Belize's most beautiful string of coral cayes. There's no doubt that you'll see wildlife in the district. To the south is Guatemala. A tiny customs station in Punta Gorda is the last contact for travelers headed by ferry to Puerto Barrios, Guatemala, which is the usual route between these two countries from this end of Belize.

The district's tiny capital, Punta Gorda, has a range of accommodations, excellent quaint restaurants, and enough cultural diversity to make a stay in the town interesting. Reached by road or airplane from Belize City, Punta Gorda is the stepping-off place to the hinterlands and the Guatemala border.

Punta Gorda

Punta Gorda reminds me of a frontier outpost from the last century. The Southern Highway, a ribbon of dust or mud that slices through pine and savanna, plantation country, jungle, and numerous creeks and rivers for more than 100 miles from Dangriga, is the principal connection to the outside world.

History and Ambience: Starting in the 1600s and up until the late 1800s, Punta Gorda was settled by Puritan traders, English pirates, Spanish soldiers, Garifunas, and expatriate American Confederates, people out of favor in their lands of origin. The name Punta Gorda was assigned during the Spanish occupation and means "big point." It refers to the well-defined promontory on which the town sits.

Punta Gorda is just five blocks long and three wide—and the blocks are small. The town's 2300 residents enjoy a charming setting

PUNTA GORDA

ARVIN'S LANDING

JOE TAYLOR CREEK

N

TO DANGRIGA &
MAYAN VILLAGES

AIRSTRIP

NORTH ST.

KING ST.

QUEEN ST.

PRINCE ST.

FAR WEST ST.

WEST ST.

BACK ST.

MAIN ST.

FRONT ST.

CHURCH ST.

GEORGE ST.

PIER

CARIBBEAN
SEA

1. NATURE'S WAY
2. CHURCH
3. HONEY COMB
4. MORNING GLORY
5. MARKET
6. CUSTOMS
7. POLICE
8. FERRY TO GUATAMALA
9. SHAIBA
10. CHARLTON INN
11. LUCILLE'S BAKERY
12. MAHUNG'S
13. FOSTERS
14. POST OFFICE
15. MIRAMAR
16. VERDES PHARMACY
17. BANK
18. GOYO'S HOTEL
19. ICE CREAM PARLOR
20. SCHOOL
21. TRAVELER'S INN
22. HOSPITAL
23. EDEN'S BAR
24. BDF BUS
25. AIR STRIP CAFE
26. ST. CHARLE'S INN
27. CEMETERY
28. VOICE OF AMERICA
29. TEXACO
30. TOWN BOARD
31. BASKETBALL

that overlooks the sparkly blue, generally calm waters of the Gulf of Honduras. Palms sway in the breeze above the rusty rooftops. Typically, a dozen watercraft ranging from dugout canoes and traditional paint-needy wooden sailing sloops to fiberglass dories and weathered yachts (clearing customs) bob at anchor offshore. The town's buildings are an assortment of brick and wood architectural designs, but nothing taller than two stories.

The pace is laid-back, though the town's politics are unusually personalized. In addition to the permanent population, you may meet transient British soldiers from a small nearby base, serious-looking American missionaries, and American personnel from the large Voice of America station south of town.

Basic Necessities: The police station and immigration office are one and the same. Take your passport here to get it stamped if you're headed for Guatemala on the ferry. The office is on the west side of Front Street across from the pier and to the right of the post office (directly across the road at the end of the pier). The public phone is between the post office and the police station. The bank is on Main Street at the northeast corner of the clock tower plaza. The hospital and bus depot are at the south end of town on Middle and Back streets, respectively. You'll find an ice cream parlor on Middle Street about fifty yards south of the clock tower. Market day (featuring everything from fresh produce to exotic fruits, dried fish, lobsters, and bakery products) is on Saturday. The market is a blue building on the sea side of Front Street, south of the Mira Mar Hotel. The Mira Mar will change your money to Guatemalan quetzales and sell you ferry tickets.

Restaurants: Nature's Way Guest House (B), at the south end of Front Street, serves good, wholesome meals to hotel guests as well as non-guests who make reservations. I had an excellent breakfast and freshly ground Costa Rican coffee here for U.S. $3, and dinners for U.S. $4.50 consisted of rice, beans, fruit, and fish in prodigious quantities. G & G's Inn (B, M), on Middle Street near the clock tower, serves dinners that are good quality and include Italian dishes, chicken stews, seafood pastas, and standard Belizean dishes. Expect to pay about U.S. $13 for a full Italian dinner. However, most Belizeans who dine here purchase inexpensive specials of meat stew, tortillas, rice, and fried beans for a couple of dollars. The Airstrip Cafe (M), near the landing strip, serves traditional meals. The Morning Glory (B), near the Mira Mar Hotel on Front Street, serves excellent breakfasts with fresh juices and freshly ground Costa Rican coffee. At the north end of town near the Texaco station is Shaiba's (B, M), which specializes in seafood. The conch soup is superb. The only drawback is the wall decorations of jaguar and ocelot skins. The Traveller's Inn (E), near the hospital, is the only upscale restaurant, complete with linen tablecloths, in town. The Mira Mar (M) serves filling dishes of local cuisine but is best known for its Chinese meals.

Accommodations: Diminutive Punta Gorda has a wide range of places to stay. Nature's Way Guest House (B), run by twenty-four-year resident Chet Schmidt, is a low-budget, clean place to stay that also serves a hearty Belizean breakfast. Staying here also makes sense because Chet Schmidt offers the greatest number of day and multiday tours in Punta Gorda. Rooms range from U.S. $12.50 for a single to U.S. $20 for a triple. The decor is funky and the clientele a mixed bag. Chet is sincere and helpful. Nature's Way Guest House is next to the church and school at the south end of Front Street. Guests have a view of the Gulf of Honduras. Cash only. Contact Chet Schmidt, Nature's Way Guest House, 65 Front Street, P.O. Box 75, Punta Gorda, Belize, C.A. (phone 07-22119).

G & G's Inn (B) is a small restaurant and hotel (nine rooms, but with plans to expand to twenty-four) that was built by owners Gregorio and Gloria Aleman over a period of ten years. Gregorio persevered to overcome poverty: "Sometimes I'd buy bricks and eat one meal a day so I wouldn't run out of money." The restaurant is frequented by locals and the rooms are rented mostly by nontourists, which makes the place interesting. Rooms have fans but no air-conditioning. Cars are parked in a protected area to ensure their safety. Rooms rent for about U.S. $15 per night. Cash only. Contact G & G's Inn, Main and Middle Street, Punta Gorda, Belize, C.A. (phone 07-22086; in the United States, try Adolf and Carmen Paiz [Gregorio's cousin] at 213-227-0665).

The Mira Mar Hotel (B), located at 95 Front Street about midway along the waterfront, caters to British soldiers, who make use of the bar, restaurant, and pool tables. There are also dances here, which ought to excite any sociologist, given the diversity of cultures and belief systems represented in Punta Gorda. The hotel has eleven small but tidy rooms, each with air-conditioning, television, and small porch. Expect to pay about U.S. $20 per night. Proprietor Alex Chee has been in business thirty-seven years. Cash only. Contact Mira Mar Hotel, P.O. Box 2, Punta Gorda, Belize, C.A. (phone 07-22033).

The Traveller's Inn (E), located above the bus depot next to the hospital and Defense Forces barracks, is an anomaly. By any measure this is an impressive place to stay. Owner Eugene Zabaneh, a member of an influential Lebanese family involved in every imaginable business in Belize, had the Traveller's Inn built to the highest standards. The motif is Arabic, featuring a very wide, tiled hallway, large bathrooms, handmade cabinets, plus dressers and closets crafted from choice hardwoods. All rooms are equipped with air-conditioning and color televisions. The roof doubles as a sundeck, complete with permanently affixed tables with electrical outlets under each table. Just whom this hotel is intended to serve is somewhat of a mystery. Placing an opulent eight-unit hotel above a bus station catering to cash-poor travelers is a unique mix of upscale accommodations and low-budget transportation. When I stayed at the inn it had been open just a month, and I was a pioneer of sorts for being the second guest ever. The eight rooms range in price from U.S. $50 to U.S. $75 per night. Cash only. Contact Traveller's Inn, José Maria Nuñez Street, Punta Gorda, Belize, C.A. (phone 07-22568).

Access: Z-Line buses connect Punta Gorda with Belize City and Dangriga. The 210-mile trip from Belize City can take six hours. The bus trip from Dangriga is 105 miles and takes most of a day. Check schedules at the Punta Gorda bus depot, located at José Maria Nuñez Street (phone 07-22165) or Z-Line offices in Belize City (phone 02-73937) or Dangriga (phone 05-22211).

Those wanting to travel to Punta Gorda by car should consider that the Southern Highway is dirt from Dangriga to Punta Gorda and, during rains, can be treacherous. Four-wheel-drive is recommended. Portions of the roadway flood during heavy rains.

By air, Maya Airlines connects Punta Gorda to the rest of Belize. There are daily flights from Belize City to Punta Gorda from Monday through Saturday, but at a different time each day. On Sunday there are two flights. Check with Maya Airlines in Belize City (phone 02-72312) or in the United States (1-800-552-3419).

Ferry to Guatemala: The ferry from Punta Gorda to Puerto Barrios, Guatemala, leaves at 2:00 P.M. Tuesday and Friday only. The fare is U.S. $5 one way. You can buy ferry tickets to Guatemala at the Mira Mar Hotel or Maya de India Tienda. You should get your passport stamped at the police station no later than 1:00 P.M. The return ferry leaves Puerto Barrios at 8:00 A.M. on Wednesday and Saturday. Passage, in *African Queen* type ferries with flat roofs and open sides, takes about four hours. Always check ferry times in advance. Schedules can change due to weather, repairs, and other variables.

Puerto Barrios consists of 23,000 people living in an end-of-the-railroad-line sort of place. Few travelers stay for long. (If you get stuck here, the Carbinea is a decent hotel near the ferry line.) You can travel by bus from here to Guatemala City. There are also boat hires to Livingston, a community with a unique character.

If you decide on a short excursion into Guatemala, head for Livingston, an isolated community of about 2500 Garifunas, Mayans, and mestizos that can be reached with a boat transfer from Puerto Barrios, your port of entry from the Punta Gorda ferry. Livingston is connected to the rest of Guatemala only by plane and boat. If you stay in Livingston, try the Tucan Dugu hotel (M). It has a thatched roof and a view of the harbor. The African Palace (E) has a tile-studded Moorish motif and serves excellent seafood. From Livingston you can take ferries up the spectacular Río Dulce, with its walls of jungle and Mayan thatched-roof houses, and onto the large lakes of El Golfete and Lake Isabel, the largest freshwater lake in Guatemala. Along the way there are hot springs, a manatee reserve, and Mayan ruins. Los Siete Altares (Seven Altars), seven waterfalls that tumble dramatically into the sea during the wet season, is also located near Livingston.

Mayan Ruins

Lubaantun ("Place of Fallen Rocks")

Lubaantun is located in one of the most serene settings of any archaeological site in Belize. The grounds are meadowlike with large, isolated trees, some of which produce colorful flowers. Birds are everywhere. Lubaantun was built in the Late Classic Period (A.D. 700–900), when other large ceremonial centers were being abandoned. There are five main plazas, eleven major structures, and numerous smaller plazas and ball courts. The ceremonial center is noted for its unusual construction, which utilizes cut stone and zipper masonry (placing each block so that it overlaps the two blocks beneath it, giving the structure greater stability) without mortar. The use of tight-fitting cut stone and brick without mortar is distinct to southern Belize. The structures are made from tens of thousands of stone blocks and bricks fashioned painstakingly from rock. It is thought that the façades and buildings on top of the pyramids were made from wood and other organic materials rather than from the plaster and masonry common in other sites. The veneers of these large structures have long since decayed, leaving only the magnificent layers of attractively laid stone bricks and blocks. In a few places the bricks have crumbled, hence the name Lubaantun, which means "Place of Fallen Rocks" in Mayan.

Once you reach Lubaantun there is a ten-minute walk from the parking place to the ruins, with a fairly substantial uphill climb that, because this is the tropics, may stress those who are older and out of shape. Dress for the weather. It is wise to wear a hat and carry a light raincoat. After parking, you'll walk downhill for about half the distance to the site before the uphill climb. At the low point in the trail there are brightly flowering heliconias and varieties of very lush broadleaf plants. I also saw keel-billed toucans as I entered the ruins. In all, it is about 300 yards to the base of the ruins. The caretaker can be found in the tiny structure at the southern end of the ruins near a ball court (with grandstands of stone still evident).

The caretaker on the day of my visit was Santiago Coc, who lives nearby. He proved to be knowledgeable about wildlife and the archaeological history of the site. Santiago says that nearly every afternoon keel-billed toucans visit the area; white-tailed deer and brocket deer (locally called antelope) also come through in the late afternoon, but less frequently than the toucans. Santiago was eager to explain the archaeological significance of the area. "This is a unique site in many regards. It's not normal for a site this large to have no stelae and no altars," he said and then related some theories on why there are no stelae or altars, which are associated with chronicling great leaders, warfare, and sacrifice. "Maybe these Mayans had grown tired of sacrifice and war."

Santiago talked about a unique discovery at Lubaantun that has had archaeologists debating one another for seventy years. "This site is known for controversy. In 1923 Thomas Gann and Mitchell Hedges found a carved crystal skull here [the piece is about the size of a child's fist], or at least that's their claim. The famous archaeologist Norman Hammond thinks the skull was not a Mayan creation. Gann and Mitchell were treasure seekers as well as archaeologists, which has caused suspicions about their motives. To this day nobody knows. The skull is in a museum in Ontario, Canada."

Santiago was an excellent guide, explaining the remnants of buildings and ball courts. Among the eleven large structures and five main plazas are a ceremonial center, market plaza, residential area, ball court, burial area, and three distinct temples. The site is also unique in that instead of leveling a hilltop for a temple, the Mayans carved slopes into vertical walls that were reinforced with retaining walls of stone block. From the highest pyramid at sixty-five feet you can see the coast twenty miles away.

No camping is permitted at the site.

Access: The drive to and from Lubaantun, once you leave the Southern Highway, is through idyllic Mayan villages tucked away on hillsides of green pastures and rolling landscape with postcard vistas of the heavily vegetated Maya Mountains. Accommodations are available in Punta Gorda, roughly twenty miles away, and in San Antonio, five miles away.

To reach Lubaantun, take the road to San Antonio off the Southern Highway about twelve miles northwest of Punta Gorda. At the 1.7-mile mark you'll see the turnoff to San Pedro Columbia and

Lubaantun. Lubaantun is located north of the Columbia River, one mile past the village of San Pedro Columbia. I found that I needed to ask for directions in San Pedro Columbia to make sure I was on the right track for the final mile, which was not signposted. There is a right turn in San Pedro Columbia next to a public water well— that is the key to not becoming lost.

Lubaantun is not accessible by public transportation, but you can get as close as San Antonio, the largest Mayan village in the region, on the Chun Bus Service, which runs from Punta Gorda on Tuesday, Thursday, and Saturday.

Uxbenka ("Ancient Place")

Uxbenka sits on a hill above the village of Santa Cruz, a classic, thatched-roof Mayan village. Uxbenka was not "discovered" until 1984. The site is attractive, as are all such ruins in southern Belize, and it is also significant from an archaeological point of view. The site has more than twenty stelae, seven of them with carvings. One of the stelae dates from the Early Classic Period (A.D. 250–550); it is the first stela from this period recorded in southern Belize and a rare find in the Mayan world. Located on a sloping ridge overlooking Santa Cruz and with the Maya Mountains as a backdrop, this is a beautiful spot.

Uxbenka means "Ancient Place," a name the site acquired from the Mayans in Santa Cruz after the discovery was made. The nearby waterfalls, on the road farther east from Santa Cruz, are suitable for swimming. It's best to visit Uxbenka during the early morning to beat the heat. Smoke twines skyward from the village's cooking fires, roosters crow, and the villagers begin their day's tasks. You'll feel you've stepped a long way back in time and marvel at the tranquility of the place.

Camping is not permitted at the site.

Access: There is no public transportation into Uxbenka. Uxbenka is located about four miles west of San Antonio on the road to Santa Cruz. San Antonio is about sixteen miles from Punta Gorda and can be reached by bus. However, most travelers visit in rental cars or as part of a tour group from Punta Gorda.

Nim Li Punit ("Big Hat")

Nim Li Punit is one of the most fascinating Mayan archaeological sites that I visited in Belize. It is twenty-five miles north of Punta Gorda off the Southern Highway and is best visited either leaving or going to Punta Gorda. Excavations at this ceremonial center indicate that it was important during the Late Classic Period (A.D. 700–900). Of the more than twenty-five stelae found at the site, at least eight are carved, one of which remains the tallest carved stela in Belize (and the second-tallest in the entire Mayan world), measuring thirty-one feet. Nim Li Punit means "Big Hat" and refers to the carving on the tallest stela of a person wearing a very large headdress.

This site is relatively small, but the stelae are outstanding, as are the hieroglyphics. And the site's natural beauty, with bright green mowed meadows, a huge ceiba tree, and a variety of other flowering trees, creates an unforgettable setting. The view to the west is stunning.

The site is not visible from the highway nor when the access road comes to an end. Signposting is minimal. The access road passes through a small Mayan settlement. In the parking area at the site, look for a trail that veers off at about a sixty-degree angle. After walking about 150 yards you'll come to an immense ceiba tree supporting philodendrons and other air plants. This is the beginning of the site. The caretaker's hut is a small, thatched structure in the flat area past the ceiba tree. Your visit will be greatly enhanced by talking with the caretaker, who is well versed in archaeological interpretations. Remember to sign the guest book. The number of guests at Nim Li Punit helps justify the need for a caretaker.

Placido Pec, who was the caretaker at the time of my visit, was very knowledgeable about the site. The tallest stela is particularly interesting. It is unusually narrow for its length. It contains a Mayan calendar and lists the exploits of past leaders, but according to Placido it also contains an error in one of the dates. Some archaeologists believe the stela was never erected in the vertical position because of this error. One wonders how this reflected on the artisan, who made an irreversible mistake on a stone weighing tons that had been brought to the site to glorify a powerful ruler.

A nearby wider, shorter stela is unique for another reason: it has a depiction of what may be a ruling family. It carries the date A.D. 732 and three figures: a man (probably a ruler), a woman (possibly his wife), and a smaller figure, who may have been the couple's son. This may also be the stela referred to as "Number 2" in writings about the site in several official publications. According to Lita Krohn in her *Writings in Belizean History,* the three figures on the stela give evidence of the ritualistic incorporation of blood-letting in Mayan rituals: " . . . the three carved figures, two standing men and a seated woman; the man and woman appear to be performing a blood-letting sacrifice. The droplets of blood (formerly thought to be grains of corn) are being collected on a rolled piece of bark which would be burnt as a sacrifice."

Also at the site are a large stela with a depiction of a jaguar throne, a stela with two opposing figures, and some underground storage areas where the Mayans kept corn and other perishables. The population at Nim Li Punit during its most active period appears to have been relatively small. Theory has it that the site may have been primarily ceremonial in nature.

Placido says Nim Li Punit is particularly beautiful from March through June: "When trees have fruit we see more birds — toucans, parrots, and songbirds." During my early March visit I saw toucans and numerous other birds. No camping is permitted at the site.

Access: Nim Li Punit is located off the Southern Highway about twenty-five miles north of Punta Gorda and is not accessible by public transportation. Buses from Belize City to Punta Gorda run three times a week past the site. When you turn off the Southern Highway to the site, the access road passes through a small Mayan community. A couple of women may approach your vehicle with the hope of selling you a good-quality woven purse for a few dollars. Most visitors reach the site in a rental car or as part of a tour group.

Monkey River Mayan Ruins and Bladen Nature Reserve

On August 4, 1993, seven ancient Mayan sites discovered on the banks of the upper Monkey River were the subject of a feature story in the *New York Times.* The sites were heralded in the archaeological community because two of them had not been looted since being abandoned 1000 years ago. This discovery proves that the jungles of Belize still hold secrets known only to the ghosts of the ancient Mayans. The discovery was made by Dr. Peter S. Dunham, an archaeologist from Cleveland State University in Ohio. Dunham was in the area on a National Geographic Society project when he made the discovery. The upper Monkey River is an extremely remote area of Belize in the northern part of the Toledo District. Though there is no infrastructure or transportation into the area for tourists, in the years to come this area promises to grow in importance for adventuresome visitors. It is located in uninhabited rain forest in a difficult-to-reach area that receives nearly 200 inches of rain annually. The area is full of wildlife and unknowns.

In the *New York Times* article, Dunham described four of the sites as "substantial Mayan centers, with sizable buildings rising from the jungle and with ancient reservoirs still containing water." He estimated the total population of the four sites at about 7000 people. The southern Maya Mountains where the sites are located were thought to have been uninhabited during Mayan times, but Dunham's find has changed that perception. Dunham theorizes that the communities revolved around the mining of minerals and harvesting of jungle plants that were traded to larger centers. On one of the four sites looters had dug pits into several areas and removed ancient caches of pyrite, a shiny mineral also known as "fool's gold." Pyrite was used by the ancient Mayans to make mirrors and decorate their teeth. Dunham also found caches of hematite, which was used to make the red color that commonly decorated Mayan tombs and temples. Working under the auspices of the National Geographic Society, Dunham plans to conduct a three-year study of the entire Monkey River area.

The sites seem to have been set up for trading. The largest area is on an island in the Monkey River and has a football-field-size plaza, several temples, and a large structure that may have been similar to a city hall. Other nearby sites have stelae commemorating high-ranking Mayan families and a ball court. The sites are most appreciated because looters have for the most part missed them, which will allow archaeologists to get a much fuller picture of how the ancient Mayans lived.

Outsiders should venture into the area only with the permission of the Department of Archaeology in Belmopan or through a tour operator who has been granted written permission to visit.

Just how rich the Monkey River area is in Mayan natural history is just beginning to be understood. The area is certain to have great potential as an eco-tourism destination.

Bladen Nature Reserve: Besides the ruins on the Monkey River, there is the nearby Bladen Nature Reserve, which encompasses 92,000 acres of watershed in the southern Maya Mountains. The Bladen, as it is commonly called, has some of Belize's best stands of old-growth rain forest. Wildlife biologists working in Belize put the Bladen on a par with the Cockscomb Basin for its untamed wildness and abundant biodiversity. The Bladen River is a tributary of the Monkey River. The Bladen has been off-limits to tourism of all kinds since it was declared a reserve in 1990. Only scientists have been granted entry. There has been talk within the Belizean government of opening the Bladen to small numbers of tourists with guides. Now, with significant Mayan ruins in the same region, the incentive for the government to allow limited tourism will increase. Undoubtedly, adventure tourism operators will lobby for access. When you visit Belize ask about the status of visiting the Bladen Nature Reserve and the Mayan ruins along the Monkey River.

Accommodations: The nearest towns with hotels are Mango Creek and Independence, which are about thirty miles north of where the Monkey River passes beneath the Southern Highway. In Independence try the Hello I Hotel (B, M) (phone 06-22011), which accepts cash only for payment. In Mango Creek try La Quinta Cabanas (B) (phone 06-22093); cash only. You may be able to stay in Monkey River Town, a small village with no hotels, but a sandy beach and a general store. When I visited the village, several residents said visitors sometimes rent rooms for a night from locals for a small amount of money. The conditions are crude.

Access: Presently there is no public access into the area of the ruins or reserve, but as control of the sites is achieved, access will undoubtedly follow. At the river's mouth is the tiny Garifuna/Creole fishing village of Monkey River Town. It can be reached by road from the Southern Highway. The road sometimes floods during the wet season. Boats can be hired in Monkey River Town, and adventure tour outfits in Placencia sometimes explore the Monkey River. Seek access only in ways approved by the Belizean government.

Visiting with Today's Maya

As much as I like visiting Mayan ruins and contemplating the many questions that these stone monuments leave unanswered, a trip to the Toledo District has something extra, not found anywhere else. Instead of ghosts from the past you can actually get to know and appreciate living Mayans. One of the great myths concerning Central America is that the Mayan culture is a thing of the past. It lives on, and in the entire Mayan world the Toledo District may be the best place to appreciate today's Mayans.

There are a number of factors that make the Toledo District Mayan experience especially enriching. For starters, most of the Mayans in Belize speak English (as a second language), which is unique in the Mayan world. Modern-day Mayans are ruled by Spanish-speaking governments, with the exception of Belize. As a result, there is no language barrier for North Americans. Second, the villages are authentic. They are not the contrivances for tourists that you find in Africa, Australia, and South America, where "natives" dress and dance for Europeans and North Americans to reenact their dead or dying cultures. These towns are the real thing. The villages in the vicinity of Punta Gorda are the same kinds of villages Mayans have lived in for centuries. Finally, there is a well-conceived plan and concerted effort (though it is politically fragile) to have small numbers of outsiders visit Mayan villages in ways that will not negatively impact the inhabitants. The emphasis is on creating an intimate cultural experience, not volume tourism.

I found my time in the Mayan villages of the Toledo District an extremely memorable experience. There are more than thirty villages in the hinterlands of the district. Some, like the village of Dolores, are accessible by river and trail. Others, like San Antonio, are reached by regular bus service from Punta Gorda. After learning about the great Mayan cities of the past, whose power and bloody rituals have been recorded in stone, the peaceful villages of the Toledo District offer contrasting qualities: tranquility, a close relationship with nature, age-old beliefs and rituals, and an inner strength that comes from strong family and community identities.

There are two groups of Mayans: Mopan and Ketchi. Though they speak different dialects and have different histories, there are few visible differences between Mopan and Ketchi villages. All of them feature single-room homes with thatched roofs made of palm fronds and walls made of local woods bound together by pliable vines. Their distinctive style is often referred to as thatch and pole. Typically, the villages are tidy and situated in areas of incredible beauty. Aside from the houses themselves, everything around a village is rich green. The houses are loosely clustered, with twenty to a hundred yards between neighbors whose common ground is green pasture that extends to the front door of each dwelling. The immediate surroundings usually include milpas (garden plots), a few horses and pigs, jungle, and the verdant and jagged Maya Mountains.

How to go about integrating tourists into Mayan village life has been a thorny issue in Toledo District politics. Balancing the needs and desires of tourists with the needs for privacy and harmony of the villagers has required sensitive planning. Tourists arriving in Punta Gorda will learn of two village tour programs: the Village Guesthouse and Ecotrail Program (contact Chet Schmidt, Nature's Way Guest House, 65 Front Street, P.O. Box 75, Punta Gorda, Belize, C.A.; phone 07-22119) and the Indigenous Experience/Host Family Network (contact Alfredo Villoria at Dem Dat's Doin' Farm, P.O. Box 73, Punta Gorda, Belize, C.A.; phone 07-22470). Both programs arrange for stays in Mayan villages. In my opinion, the Village Guesthouse and Ecotrail Program has the best interests of the Mayan participants in mind and offers visitors a broader-spectrum introduction to Mayan village life. The Village Guesthouse concept involves staying in each village's guesthouse, built specifically for visitors. Guests are treated to a range of activities: eating local cuisine with a different family for each meal, listening to music and storytelling, watching crafts being made, and guided hikes to nearby scenic areas. Paramount to this program is that each stay involves more than a dozen villagers, who share in the financial profit from your visit. In addition, participating villages have met and agreed to enter the program.

Among the Mayans themselves, I found few supporters of the competing Indigenous Experience/Host Family Network. In this program, a visitor stays in the single-room home of his or her host family, affording neither guest nor host family privacy and profiting just a single family instead of an entire village. Of the many Mayans I asked about the programs, all said the competing Village Guesthouse and Ecotrail Program was the best from their perspective. Some said the Indigenous Experience/Host Family Network program's selection of one family as the host home caused jealousy and divisiveness in their village. Because it is confusing to decipher between the programs, I suggest making sure that the one in which you're enrolled is the one with the blessing of an entire village, not just a single individual in a village.

Village Guesthouse and Ecotrail Program

As mentioned, of the competing programs to place visitors in remote Mayan villages overnight, I recommend the Village Guesthouse and Ecotrail Program. This program involves the villages of Laguna (Ketchi Mayan, pop. 225); Barranco (Garifuna, pop. 235); Santa Cruz (Mopan Mayan, pop. 300); Silver Creek (Ketchi Mayan, pop. 200); San Miguel (Ketchi Mayan, pop. 200); San Pedro Columbia (Mopan Mayan, pop. 300); and San José (Mopan Mayan, pop. 650). Some of the villages are within hiking distance of one another. There are dozens of other Mayan villages in Toledo, some quite accessible, but these communities (including the Garifuna community of Barranco) have participated in the creation of the program and have committed themselves to looking after guests in a prescribed manner. At the time of this writing, Laguna, San José, San Miguel, San Pedro Columbia, and Santa Cruz had constructed their guesthouses. Barranco had set aside land for a guesthouse and will probably have it completed in 1994. Laguna finished its guesthouse years before the others and is the most experienced in providing a half-dozen activities for guests.

Following are accounts of two memorable experiences in this enriching program. The first is my one-day experience in Laguna, which included a jungle hike to a cliff cave. The second is an excerpt from a *Belize Review* interview with two women who stayed in Laguna overnight. Both experiences were arranged by Chet Schmidt at Nature's Way Guest House in Punta Gorda. In my case, Chet arranged for me to visit Laguna, a handsome Ketchi Mayan village located about seven miles northeast of Punta Gorda, in a matter of minutes after my arrival at Nature's Way. Generally, though, villagers need a day's notice or more.

Day Visit and Guided Cave Hike: Tony Rath and I arrived at midday. The first person we saw was a young mother bathing her baby. The woman's hair was neatly piled atop her head. She was unclothed from the waist up and wore a traditional full-length skirt — fairly typical dress in villages on hot days. We asked the young woman where we could find Santos Coc, who was supposed to show us around. In perfect English she replied, "Santos was just here waiting. You must be the people he is expecting." She left to get him, and moments later Santos appeared with two curious but shy boys peering at us from behind him. Santos greeted us with a warm smile and handshake and showed us Laguna's guesthouse. Unlike the thatch and pole houses of the village, the guesthouse has a concrete floor and is partitioned into two private sleeping areas — one side for women and the other for men — with four beds on each side. The guesthouse and outhouses were clean.

Santos walked us through the village, which has no electricity or motor vehicles, and stopped to talk with villagers who were working or resting. The residents appeared genuinely interested in us and asked where we were from. In general, everyone we met seemed warm but shy. A woman preparing dinner showed us how she makes tortillas each day by mixing corn with lime water. She was also shelling cacao beans and in a short time had brewed up a fresh cacao drink. We also saw a man making a violin. Chickens and pigs wandered freely around the village, which appeared clean and tidy. Each home was a work of art, made of thatch and wood selected from the forest.

We were introduced to José Saki, who guided us to a nearby cave. The walk, which was mostly uphill, took us about thirty minutes. José explained that most visitors take as long as an hour. "Some people walk slow," he explained with a smile. José carried a machete, which he used to chop vines and plants that impeded our progress along the trail. We started our walk past a small stream and headed east on a wide track that José said led to San Felipe, the next village, eight miles away. We noticed numerous lizards scampering from our path. In a short while José turned south into what initially appeared to be impenetrable jungle. With José's chopping, and by looking closely, we could make out the trail, but it would have been difficult to follow without a guide. In places the trail narrowed through dense foliage to a tunnel about five feet high, fitting the stature of the Mayans. As an oversized six-footer, I found the tunnel-like trail a bit challenging. In an act of courtesy José chopped vigorously above his head to allow us passage without having to stoop. He also used his machete as a pointer: "Ah, see that fruit, we use it to make soap. . . . There's the bay palm. We like it because it is the best palm for making a roof for a house." As we pushed on toward the cave, José paused occasionally to explain the uses of a dozen forest plants. The trail opened into a milpa, with trees bearing a fruit that looked more like an inflated porcupine fish than any fruit I'd ever seen. The cornstalks were eight feet tall. Because trees had been cleared to make the milpa, the light reaching the ground allowed bright and beautiful heliconias to flower in profusion amid the fruits and vegetables. From the milpa we could see a cave high above us in limestone formations jutting into the sky. The final trail to the base of this escarpment was through tree ferns and large forest trees.

To reach the cave we scrambled up a twenty-foot ladder made from local wood. The cave is a home to bats, which zoomed past us as we blinked into the darkness. Nobody had a flashlight. The cave angled sharply up and branched in two directions. Each branch led to a window perhaps 400 feet above the area through which we had hiked. The left window affords a spectacular view of jungle and the Maya Mountains. José spoke of a second cave system that required a two-hour walk. "There are old drawings, but nobody knows what the drawings say," he explained nonchalantly.

We returned to the village, thanked our hosts, and were off to our next stop. We didn't have time to stay for the night's activities, which would have included music and dancing.

Overnight Stay in Laguna: In the January 1991 issue of the *Belize Review,* North Americans Janeen Wyatt and Louise Foster vividly recounted their experiences and explained the sensitivities involved.

Janeen: " . . . After [being introduced to a family] we had a little time to ourselves and then we were invited to a house where some of the villagers were playing music. There was a harp, a violin played by our old friend, and a guitar sort of instrument. After the music started, and quite spontaneously, the wife of the violin player, an elderly woman, started doing some of the traditional dances. We have done a lot of traditional dances from other parts of the world, primarily Greek and Turkish folk dances. We saw children dancing and they asked us to join in. We asked to make sure it was all right. So we danced with them for over an hour. It was great! The villagers get up very early to go to work, so by 8:30 everyone was tired—including us. We were worried about this, about disrupting village life, but they said it didn't bother them. For us the experience of being in the village and the dancing was wonderful . . . Such ceremonial dancing is getting rarer to find."

Louise on accommodations: "It was very clean, neat, and comfortable. . . . The guesthouse had a women's side and a men's side. Travelers should be prepared for that and also, in the house where the music took place, the women sat in one place and the men, along with the musicians, all sat together . . . When we ate, a little table was set for us and the women and girls . . . and the father and son sat at another table."

Louise on meals: "We ate the best tortillas we've ever put in our mouths—tortillas and eggs and fish. We don't eat meat and we were trying to explain it to them, and their answer was: 'Oh, you're vegetarians.'"

Louise on photography: "I don't like people putting a camera in my face. I suggest that visitors don't do that if they are there just for a night and day. I don't feel that it would be right because most of the settings are of the villagers' most intimate lives. Some Americans are very abrupt. These people are very quiet, gentle, and vulnerable. . . . They are excited about reviving their traditions and sharing them with outsiders. It is a fragile situation, they can so easily be exploited and hurt."

Social caution: If you see a Mayan woman doing her chores barebreasted, don't scramble for your camera and offend her and her family. And, when in doubt about customs, do as Janeen and Louise did. Ask politely and/or imitate the behavior of your gender counterparts in social situations. Women dressed in tight pants or short skirts are offensive in some Mayan communities.

Drive to Mayan Villages and Swimming Holes

The Mayan guesthouse experience described above is a special opportunity, but possibly too intense for some folks, who would rather interact more passively with the Mayan communities via a rental vehicle and cozy hotel rooms each night. There are plenty of Mayan villages and natural wonders in the Punta Gorda area that allow vehicular access. Most of these destinations are within a short drive of San Antonio, the largest Mayan community in the area and the heart of Toledo's "Mayalands." It is the only Mayan village with a small hotel (not to be confused with the Mayan guesthouses).

The road to San Antonio and other inland destinations intersects the Southern Highway about twelve miles northwest of Punta Gorda. There is a Shell gas station and small eating and snack establishment named the Four Winds Saloon at this intersection. If you're in a rental car and aren't sure how extensive your inland travels will be, make sure you top off your gas tank.

Once on the road to San Antonio you'll see the turnoff to San Pedro Columbia and Lubaantun (see "Mayan Ruins") at the 1.7-mile mark. At the 3-mile mark from the Southern Highway intersection you'll come to a fork in the road and a small grocery store, presently named Roy's Cool Spot Grocery. This is your last chance to buy snacks and soft drinks if you're headed to Blue Creek Cave. The left fork takes you to Blue Creek, a Mayan village with an exquisite nature walk in a rain forest along a beautiful stream (see "Blue Creek Cave Hike"). To the right are San Antonio, Santa Cruz, Uxbenka (see "Mayan Ruins"), San José, Santa Elena, Pueblo Viejo, other Mayan villages, and Rio Blanco Santa Elena Nature Reserve.

San Antonio: At Roy's Cool Spot Grocery, take the right fork to San Antonio. Generally this road is better than the one to Blue Creek, but because it is dirt, it will have changing conditions, depending on the season and the amount of use. From Roy's Cool Spot Grocery you'll reach San Antonio in about two miles. It is a sprawling Mopan Mayan community with a large church. You'll first see thatch and pole houses and livestock and eventually come to a large church, store, and soccer field. The stained glass windows in the church are from a St. Louis, Missouri, church. Bol's Hilltop Hotel and Grocery (no phone) are in the middle of the village. Coming from Punta Gorda, you'll find the grocery on the right side of the main road. The hotel is directly uphill behind the grocery. The community phone (07-22144) is the only phone, but more are expected in the years to come.

Accommodations: Bol's Hilltop Hotel (B) has tidy rooms with flush toilets but no electricity. The septic system was being installed during my visit. Rooms were renting from U.S. $15 per night. Owner Dioniso Bol serves his guests meals that cost a few dollars. Dioniso says he plans to have electricity and phone service in the near future. He also says he can locate modest vacant homes for visitors wanting to stay for a week or longer. This is the only hotel in the region. Cash only.

Access: If you're an economy traveler wishing to spend time in Mayan country, you can reach San Antonio via Chun Bus Service from Punta Gorda on Monday, Wednesday, and Friday for a nominal fare. The bus returns to Punta Gorda on Tuesday, Thursday, and Saturday. Also, commercial trucks, which sometimes allow riders, make the journey a couple of times a week. All other transportation in the area is by private vehicle.

The Road to Santa Cruz Village: Continuing east from San Antonio you'll pass an excellent picnic site next to two large, stream-fed, saucer-shaped pools directly off the road on the right side. The pools are within walking distance of San Antonio's soccer field. One pool is about fifteen feet higher than the other and connects to the lower pool with an attractive, perfectly symmetrical, twenty-foot-wide waterfall. There is a concrete walkway to several prime picnic spots. During my visit, Mayan children were swimming in one of the pools and waterfowl were using the other. This is a good place to cool off.

Santa Cruz: Located four miles west of San Antonio, Santa Cruz may be the most picturesque Mayan village in Belize. Its classic thatch and pole houses are spread over lush green, grassy hillsides dotted with mature cohune palms. The backdrop to the village is a jutting skyline of karst limestone formations covered in verdant jungle. Women dress traditionally in long skirts and often move about the village carrying containers balanced atop their heads. Babies are carried papoose-style. Livestock mow the grass, and chickens wander here and there. The Uxbenka ruins (see "Mayan Ruins") above the village add to the serene and timeless atmosphere. The women of the village will offer to sell you woven products, baskets, stone carvings, and pottery. You'll be helping the local economy by purchasing something.

Rio Blanco Santa Elena Nature Reserve: Three miles west of Santa Cruz is another waterfall and swimming area. This area was declared a 500-acre reserve in 1993. The site is known locally as Santa Elena

Falls, after a small village by the same name. It lies at the end of the road and requires a short walk to a waterfall overlook that is very similar to the one just outside San Antonio, but this one has bigger pools and is entirely secluded. During the dry season, which is when I visited, stream water is isolated in large rock pools above the falls. In effect, these pools become a series of naturally occurring hot tubs, suitable for a comfortable soak, and larger, cooler pools suitable for a swim, provided sharing the water with multitudes of pollywogs doesn't bother you. Above the falls are two large pools; a third, with earthen banks, is surrounded by vines and plants. I saw a dozen species of birds here and a few fat iguanas. Belizean conservationists are lobbying to increase the reserve's size to 25,000 acres.

Mayan Celebrations

Mayan villages may look like sleepy places, but a few times a year they come alive with celebrations that combine religion — past and present — with having a good time. Witnessing these activities is a rare opportunity in today's world of disappearing indigenous cultures.

The Mayans in the Toledo District are Catholic. Most of the Mayan villages are named after saints, and each village celebrates its saint's day. Also, costumed dances and ritual reenactments are performed prior to planting and harvesting crops. The celebrations have both Christian and traditional pre-Conquest Mayan significance and often include elements of both traditions. Participants wear bright, elaborate costumes, often with colorful papier-mâché or wooden masks.

These ceremonies include processions and dancing. The music making is done with a wide range of locally made instruments. Of these instruments, the flute, drum, and chirimia (a double-reed instrument made of two palm stems) are thought to predate the arrival of the Spanish. The harp, violin, and guitar are non-native instruments that have been modified and are locally made. The marimba, which is also played in many celebrations, may be of African origin. There is some scant archaeological evidence that a similar instrument existed among the ancient Mayans.

Although fun is had, these events, which occur most often during seasonal changes, are taken seriously. In essence, the villagers are asking God (or the gods) for good crops and the right amount of rain. The *alcalde,* or village leader, appoints the dancers and musicians. The musicians are always men, and only an occasional young girl participates as a dancer. Women are "chosen" to prepare tortillas for the community feed. Usually the entire village turns out as both spectators and participants. Often, the same celebration held in different villages has its own distinctive local flavor.

In some instances a celebration is an annual event set on a specific date. On other occasions there is no exact date, but rather a seasonal time. Check with Chet Schmidt at Nature's Way Guest House in Punta Gorda or the Toledo Visitors' Information Center on Front Street at the Punta Gorda wharf about activities during the period you're in the area. If an observance is planned, you won't regret the effort it may take to see it.

Cortez Dance: One celebration with elements of both Christian and Mayan traditions is the Cortez Dance, which represents the coming of Christianity to the Mayans. The dance has twenty-eight participants. Some play the parts of Indians; others play the Spanish (wearing black, including the priest) and carry weapons. Two Mayans are clowns who howl throughout the ceremony, and one actor carries a large ceremonial hatchet. The dancing clowns represent insincere Christian converts who submit to Christianity without conviction. The Mayan with the hatchet represents defiance and must be baptized three times before he becomes a Christian. As actually happened in the area, most of the actors representing Mayans submit to baptism with little resistance.

Deer Dance: In San Antonio, the Deer Dance chronicles the activities of a Mayan hunter while incorporating Christian cross-raising. This celebration can be witnessed every August 24 and 25. The marimba is the preferred musical instrument and is carried while it is being played. Of the dozen or more participants, some dress as hunting dogs, two as women, two in black, one as a hunter, and one as a deer. The dance itself is a reenactment of a successful hunt. The Deer Dance is held at the annual replacement of the seventy-foot pole forming the cross that stands in front of the church. On August 24, about three dozen men carry a new pole to the square. The next day a jug of whisky and a bag with a few dollars in it is placed upon the cross at the intersection of the crossbar with the old pole, which is still standing. Three climbers are chosen by the *alcalde* to retrieve these prizes. The one climbing fastest gets them. The old pole is then chopped down and the new one placed in a new hole. As the telephone pole–size cross is being hoisted during the Deer Dance, the "deer" pushes its antlers against the pole to show he is helping to raise it. While the pole is being pulled into place it is jerked and lowered in sudden bursts, giving the impression that it may fall on the "deer," who responds by scampering to safety. This is especially exciting to the village's children. Finally the pole is raised, the community is guarded by a Christian cross, and age-old Mayan hunters ask for a year of successful hunting.

Monkey Dance: Traditionally, the Monkey Dance was performed to protect milpas from monkeys, which were considered to be mischievous if not downright evil. Often seen as the offspring of the devil, monkeys were thought to have the ability to slow the growth of corn and bring about destructive rains — to say nothing of their pillaging of fruit and vegetable crops. The dance was originally performed to ensure well-timed rains and successful crops. To "ape" monkeys, dancers wear red masks and black costumes. Flutes and guitars provide the musical accompaniment. Today the dance is performed primarily for entertainment purposes for villagers and nonobtrusive outsiders.

Blue Creek Cave Hike

I highly recommend this streamside jungle walk, which commences in the Mayan village of Blue Creek. The hike's turnaround point is at Blue Creek Cave, where a large stream literally pours from the cave on its journey to the Moho River and the sea. The Blue Creek Cave is known as Hokeb Ha in Mayan. The walk, with the option of a refreshing swim, takes from two to three hours round-trip. The area around the cave is an excellent picnic spot.

Scenic Drive: The road running left to Blue Creek village from the fork at Roy's Cool Spot Grocery is a rough and rocky 3.8 miles, but the scenery is beautiful. The road travels through jagged and irregular karst limestone country that is exploding in new-growth jungle. This exotic landscape is unfamiliar to people from temperate climates. The flat areas on the drive contain milpas, pasture, new-growth rain forest, and occasional thatch and pole houses. I saw many kinds of birds, including two magnificent king vultures gliding slowly along the side of the road, perhaps honing in on a roadkill. Blue Creek is not always signposted. You'll know you've reached the village when you pass a row of picturesque thatch and pole houses on the road's right side about a hundred yards before the road crosses a rock bridge with multiple culverts. Park on the east side of the bridge. The roadside houses pressed up against the rain forest are excellent subjects for afternoon photography, but be sure to respect the privacy of their shy Mayan owners. Ask them before you photograph.

Trail Description: The trail to Blue Creek Cave starts near the parking area on the east side of the creek. It travels along the watercourse through new-growth plants that are racing skyward in a contest to grab all the sunlight possible. At times the vegetation is so thick that the trail literally becomes a tunnel burrowing through otherwise impenetrable forest. Watch for species of kingfishers and other birds. After about five minutes you'll begin to notice large, buttressed trees. The trail widens and you'll come to a clapboard guesthouse with a large porch that overlooks a long pool suitable for swimming. The guesthouse is owned by International Zoological Expeditions, based in Sherborn, Massachusetts. School groups often use the house during the dry season. Continue past the guesthouse, always keeping the left fork of the creek in sight. (I veered inland past the guesthouse following the dry right fork and became lost for about thirty minutes.) Stay near the left fork and you'll come to a large pool with a waterfall feeding into it. Notice the varieties of fish in this pool. If you climb above the waterfall over boulders you'll find two more large pools and Blue Creek Cave, where the creek flows from the cave. The large pool in the cave mouth is milky blue, which is the reason for the cave's name. The most private pools for swimming — with lush, vegetation-coated cliffs towering overhead — are to the left of Blue Creek Cave.

Caution: Keep in mind that limestone boulders are extremely slippery when wet. Be careful when rock-hopping around the cave.

Access: Blue Creek Cave is about twenty-one miles from Punta Gorda. You head toward San Antonio from the Southern Highway but turn left before reaching it at Roy's Cool Spot Grocery. From Roy's it is 3.8 miles. No buses access the area.

Temash and Moho River Areas

From Punta Gorda to fifteen miles south at the Guatemala border there are no roads. This is a largely inaccessible area of low rain forest and extensive river systems twisting their way through mangroves and jungle. For the adventurer these river systems are highways and can be explored by hiring a boatman with a motorized open boat in Punta Gorda.

Temash River

One of my more memorable adventures in Belize was exploring the Temash River system (with a stop in the isolated Garifuna coastal community of Barranco) in an open fiberglass dory powered by outboard motors. Outings in this area rate as true adventure and can be experienced to varying degrees by anyone who feels at home in an open boat and has the money to pay for a trip. It takes the better part of a full day, minimum, to explore the Temash River region. If you're particularly ambitious you can expand a boat adventure into a cultural interchange and hike that includes traveling up the Temash River to Crique Sarco, a Mayan community on the river reached only by boat. You can hike another three miles to Dolores, the most remote Mayan village on the Belize side of the Guatemala/ Belize border. These communities are far out of bounds of commercial tourism but offer incredibly enriching experiences.

My Temash River tour began at 7:30 one morning at Nature's Way Guest House in Punta Gorda. Proprietor Chet Schmidt had arranged for his stepson Jerry, a young, friendly, Creole man, to guide Tony Rath and me up the Temash, with additional stops planned at the

Garifuna village of Barranco and the Moho River. We packed lightly, carrying a lunch, camera equipment, light rain gear, sunscreen, and large hats. We climbed into a twenty-five-foot fiberglass dory and set off.

From the sea, Punta Gorda appears as a small, sleepy place on a bluff with nothing but mangroves and jungle as far as the eye can see to both the north and south. As the boat planed over the still waters of the Gulf of Honduras, we saw the large Voice of America facility with its twenty antennas just south of town. Soon we were skimming along a coastline of white mangroves and narrow beaches. The white mangroves are thick and about forty feet tall, with distinctive light-colored trunks, in contrast to the more common red and black mangroves seen in other parts of Belize. Up close, the "whites" can be seen to discharge salt from a pore at the base of each leaf.

Fifteen minutes into our journey we passed the mouth of the Moho River, barely distinguishable along the lush, green coastline. Thirty minutes south we passed a single rickety pier with a few dugouts floating near it. This was Barranco, the last coastal town before reaching the Guatemalan border. We would visit Barranco and the Moho River on our return.

After thirty-five minutes, Jerry turned toward shore. He carefully directed the boat around shoals created by the constant silting action of the Temash River. The Temash's headwaters are eighty-five miles to the west in Guatemala. Besides the shallow water, the broad river mouth is highlighted with palms and two sandy spits. On each side of the river mouth are tiny thatched huts on stilts and dugouts pulled up near them. These are the homes of fishermen. As we purred up the river's 200-foot width it became apparent why former Deputy Prime Minister and Minister of Natural Resources Florencio Marin declared 80,000 acres of the drainage basin the Sarstoon-Temash Nature Reserve in 1993. Both banks are lined with very dense stands of red mangroves. Rain forest extends in all directions behind the mangroves. Large wading birds, mostly great blue herons, slowly flapped this way and that along the river, using it as an aerial highway through the forest. We also identified yellow-crowned night herons, green night herons, three kinds of egrets, and parrots in the rain forest trees. About 200 yards up the river we passed a dwarf mangrove forest on the south side of the river. We saw two snakebirds standing motionless in the foliage, looking like two sun-worshipping crucifixes with their wings held straight out from their bodies. These cousins to cormorants must dry their feathers, which become water-logged, an odd burden for a water bird. If you're lucky you'll get to see one of these birds hunt. Snakebirds skewer fish with their sharp beaks, wait for the fish to die, and then gulp it down.

Upriver about a half-mile we passed a hundred-foot-square grassy knoll, a suitable camping spot on dry ground, a rarity on a river lined with mangroves. This is the only picnic or camping spot for miles. We noticed that the white mangroves, so dominant along the ocean, had given way to red mangroves. The red mangroves have pronounced, pendulous roots hanging from outstretched limbs that allow them to colonize new areas. Red mangroves also produce via traditional seeds.

Fourteen minutes up the river we put ashore on the north bank where there is a survey marker left behind by researchers from the University of Edinburgh. The spot was magical. To this point the riverbank's dense and impenetrable foliage offered few places to put one's foot on shore. But where the University of Edinburgh had marked a few trees, we could wade among the mangroves and buttressed trees whose immense branches support bromeliads and orchids. And blue morpho butterflies were everywhere. These unmistakable butterflies have glistening, rich blue, five-inch wing-spans. Apparently, early March, the time of our visit, is an optimum time to see these beauties.

We ate lunch quietly in our boat, which was tied to a river mangrove. Scanning the river and opposite bank, we saw no sign of humankind. The butterflies danced around us, some with jagged tears in their wings — evidence that even something as pretty as a blue morpho is just another meal to insect-eating birds. A hikatee, an endangered river turtle exploited for its meat, surfaced in the main channel and slowly paddled downstream, unaware of us. We saw the backs and dorsal fins of relatively large fish that Jerry identified as tarpon. "They know how to fight like no other fish," he explained.

Later we continued upriver past two large tributaries. Black mangroves about eighty feet high line the banks; behind them stand huge sapodilla trees. These are among the best stands of black mangroves reported anywhere. Parrots flew high overhead, screeching as they passed. Large fishing birds flapped lazily ahead of our boat. We turned off the motor. There were no sounds except for birds and a far-off howler monkey calling in the forest. We drifted slowly down-

Mayan children from Dolores at the local swimming hole, southern Belize.
Photo by Tony Rath.

stream and saw a small crocodile slide from a log. Morlet's crocodile, an endangered species, lives here. We were about fifteen miles
upstream, and this was as far as we could go and still have time to
visit Barranco and the Moho River.

But Tony Rath, my companion this day, has gone farther. In 1989
he went up the river to Crique Sarco, another forty-five minutes from
our present position, and from there to Dolores by foot.

Dolores

Dolores is a community of about 150 Ketchi Mayan Indians that is
usually visited via the Temash River to Crique Sarco and by foot from
there to Dolores. The distance between these two villages is covered
by walking continuously for three hours over a distance of about
seven miles. Tony recalled that the trail was easy to follow, but
muddy. The area receives an incredible 180 inches of rain a year.
Tony found a place to stay in Dolores by talking to the village leader.

A journey to Dolores is as remote as you can get in today's Mayan world. It is Mayan life much as it has always been lived. There are no automobiles, no electricity, no trappings of the twentieth century, discounting a few outboard motors. Houses are classic thatch and pole structures. Corn is the life blood of the village. Men spend time tending crops while women mash corn into flour and tortillas in a process that begins before dawn each morning. Much of the rest of the women's day is spent washing clothes. Typically, the hottest part of the day is spent in hammocks. Infants are carried on their mothers' backs in slings suspended from their mothers' foreheads. Children spend some of each day at their favorite swimming hole in the companionship of others their age. The wild fig trees around the village attract howler monkeys, whose resonating territorial soundings are so loud that the soundest sleeper cannot avoid waking.

During Tony's visit he saw numerous jaguar and tapir tracks and sighted and heard a plethora of exotic and colorful birds. He recalled Montezuma oropendulas, laughing falcons, slaty trogons, green honeycreepers, and several species of parrots. He felt Dolores was perhaps the "purest look" at the traditional Mayan lifestyle and its close relationship to nature. To try to visit Dolores, contact Chet Schmidt at Nature's Way Guest House in Punta Gorda.

Barranco

On our way back down the Temash and up the coast, we docked at the Barranco pier. Barranco is the last Garifuna community connected to the outside world solely by boat. (In actuality, a circuitous dirt track to the village from Punta Gorda via Aguacate exists and can be negotiated with 4WD and luck during the brief dry season.) Barranco means "Red Cliffs" in the Garifuna language, an apt name because the village sits atop fifteen-foot-high red cliffs, visible far out to sea. No doubt the high ground was chosen as a hedge against hurricanes. The village has been in existence since 1862 and was originally settled by a Garifuna turtle hunter. Both Spanish- and English-speaking missionaries have taken on the roles of teachers here, but today's educators are Garifunas who have been certified to teach after studying in Belize City or elsewhere.

Barranco is a dying community. The population has shrunk from about 700 to 200 in the last ten years, as the young and educated

Garifunas head to cities for employment. Still, Barranco is a fascinating place: it offers an unfiltered glimpse of Garifuna life as it was lived two centuries ago. Dugout canoes are the predominant watercraft. Most of the town's modest structures are built in modified Mayan style. Palm fronds are used for roofing, and stilts are used to elevate floors to make the most of cooling breezes and as a hedge against ground-dwelling termites and ants.

The village has a feeling of a paradise lost. Besides the ready source of food in the nearby sea, the town has all kinds of food-producing trees: breadfruit, mango, breadnut, provision fruit, cashew, avocado, fig, citrus, and something called a tropical apple, which has thicker skin than any apple I've seen. The provision fruit is watermelon size. Judging by the immense size of some of the productive trees, Barranco's earliest inhabitants spent time planting fruit-bearing trees, which are now contributing to the gustatory pleasure of their great-great-grandchildren. One villager told us that the area was once rich in pineapples.

Barranco has no formal accommodations or eateries for visitors but has signed on as part of the Village Guesthouse and Ecotrail Program. Inquire at Chet Schmidt's Nature's Way Guest House as to the status of Barranco's guesthouse (both in Punta Gorda, see below).

Moho River

Due to time constraints we were unable to investigate the Moho River farther than a couple of miles. What we saw in this short distance was a lowland watercourse lined with mangroves. The bird life was similar to that on the Temash River and just as abundant. There were also large numbers of blue morpho butterflies. The size of the river mouth and flow from the river was perhaps 75 percent of that of the Temash. The channel was deep and easily navigable.

From an adventure point of view, the Moho deserves comment. Located between Barranco and Punta Gorda, the Moho's drainage is equal to that of the Temash. The Moho's drainage and tributaries include Aguacaliente Swamp (a huge wetlands), several inland lagoons, Blue Creek, and Aguacate Creek, and the Moho itself extends inland fifteen miles and across the border into Guatemala. The Moho has no roads crossing it and no Mayan villages along its banks. With so little human influence it promises to be rich in wildlife. For more details, check with Chet Schmidt at Nature's Way Guest House or Larry Smith of Southern Reef Charters (both in Punta Gorda) or with residents of Barranco. The only motorized watercraft for hire in the area are found at Punta Gorda.

Visiting these remote river areas and villages is a rare experience, giving you a distinct feeling you are treading where few outsiders have ever been.

Be prepared: Have a plan to deal with mosquitoes and sunburn, which can be problems. Take extra liquids to prevent dehydration.

Caution: A visit to Barranco or Dolores should be undertaken only after first consulting a person knowledgeable about these villages.

Accommodations: Barranco is part of the Village Guesthouse and Ecotrail Program. Villagers plan to provide quarters for guests. Dolores is far off the beaten path and not visited often by outsiders. Talking to the village leader about renting a hammock for the night is the way to procure a place to sleep.

Access: These areas are reached by boat. Contact Chet Schmidt, Nature's Way Guest House, 65 Front Street, P.O. Box 75, Punta Gorda, Belize, C.A. (phone 07-22119), or Larry Smith, Southern Reef Charters, Punta Gorda (phone 07-22682).

Offshore

Cayes of Port Honduras

Immediately offshore from Punta Gorda there are many islands, predominantly mangrove-type, but some with enough dry land to maintain healthy coconut palms and other trees. In general, the quality of birding and fishing on these islands far surpasses snorkeling due to the limited underwater visibility caused by river sediments from the constant rains. Frenchman's Caye is privately owned. It has coconut, avocado, and cashew trees and is located about seven miles north of Punta Gorda. The nearby Moho Cayes are a group of five islands with the southernmost island the only sand caye of the group. This island has an attractive stand of coconut palms, a dock, and a small house with a caretaker/fisherman, who is usually out fishing during daylight hours. The island is used by British soldiers as an off-duty, back-to-nature retreat for fishing, sunbathing, philosophizing, swimming, and ale drinking. Western Snake Caye is another attractive island and belongs to a group of cayes about nine miles north of Punta Gorda. There is decent snorkeling around Western Snake Caye provided that heavy rains have not caused nearby rivers to muddy the waters.

Be prepared: Combating bugs (sand flies and mosquitoes) can be a problem on many islands in this area due to a combination of seasonal and meteorological factors. Inquire about bug density before visiting cayes close to the coast.

Access: Nature's Way Guest House (phone 07-22119) in Punta Gorda organizes day trips to Moho Cayes, Frenchman's Caye, and the Snake Cayes. Depending on your island destination, boat hires for one to six people range between U.S. $85 and U.S. $150. Also try Southern Reef Charter (phone 07-22682) in Punta Gorda.

Sapodilla Cayes

Consisting of six main islands, the Sapodillas are among the most beautiful cayes in Belizean waters. They occupy the southern terminus of the Barrier Reef. Located due east of Punta Gorda, the Sapodilla Cayes are offshore about thirty miles.

In the summary of the 1991 publication *The Sapodilla Expedition Report,* authored by Tony Rath (working for the Marine Division of the Programme for Belize), the importance and fragile nature of these islands is made clear: "The Sapodilla Cayes are easily one of the premier locations on the Belize Barrier Reef in terms of biological diversity (reefs), critical habitats (turtle nesting), commercial fisheries, and tourist potential. Most of the marine area is relatively pristine with moderate fishing pressure and some anchoring and trash impacts from tourist boats, but little other exploitation."

The Sapodilla Cayes lie in a north/south orientation and are clustered in a five-mile area. From north to south, here are brief descriptions of each one.

Northeast Caye and Frank's Caye: Separated by a narrow channel, Northeast Caye and Frank's Caye are in unaltered natural states, with intermittently used fishing camps on their northern shores. Frank's Caye is actually three small cayes: a large central caye with two small satellites. Coconut palms dominate the interior of the central island and all of Northeast Caye. Northeast Caye has an excellent sandy beach.

Nicolas Caye: If Nicolas Caye is an example of what is in store for the Sapodillas, these magnificent islands' ecology will surely suffer. The oval-shaped island is about 400 yards across. In fall of 1991 most of the natural vegetation, including a coconut forest, was removed and burned to make way for an ambitious resort with more than twenty-five cabanas, including a large restaurant. This is Toucan Island Resort, which caters to divers and snorkelers. The island has excellent snorkeling and diving directly offshore and a nice beach wrapping around its southern end. Historically this beach was used by nesting hawksbill turtles. Only careful control of visitors will maintain turtle-nesting sites.

Hunting Caye: Hunting Caye is the jewel of the Sapodillas, with a dominant coconut forest, spectacular beaches, and superb snorkeling and dive sites. It's no wonder the British chose it for a token Defence Force Base (three small, wood-frame buildings and a sign with arrows and the names of faraway places) to repel the Guatemalan invaders, who have yet to materialize. This is duty in paradise. There must have been profound disappointment among the half-dozen soldiers stationed here when Guatemala dropped its claim of owning Belize in 1992.

The cove-shaped beach on the east side of the caye is a top candidate for the prettiest pristine beach in Belize. With a backdrop of coconut palms swaying in the breeze, the water colors sparkle brilliantly. Good snorkeling is a few strokes offshore. Hunting Caye's half-mile proximity to high-use Nicolas Caye causes environmentalists serious worry. Hunting Caye's beaches are used by hawksbill turtles to lay their eggs. Too many visitors to these beaches will undoubtedly disturb nesting activities.

In his 1991 expedition for the Programme for Belize's Marine Division, biologist Tony Rath recommended that Hunting Caye be given national monument status. He feels that the scenic beauty of the island alone would justify such a classification. Included in his recommendation are protecting turtle-nesting activities and limiting visits to day use only. He suggested that overnight visitors camp at nearby Lime Caye.

Lime Caye: Lime Caye, also known as Low Caye, is also under pressure from unbridled human use. Freya Rauscher, author of *Belize and Mexico's Caribbean Coast*, described the island after a 1990 visit: "This spectacular jewel of a caye is everybody's idea of what a South Pacific island ought to look like. Nothing could be more appealing than its beautiful soft, sandy beaches bordered by a lovely stand of coconut trees rustling gently in the Caribbean tradewind breezes." A few months later, biologist Tony Rath reported: "Lime Caye is also heavily impacted by tourism . . . Devegetation and beach erosion are ongoing problems, especially along the southern shore and the southwestern end of the island." Huge conch-shell mounds created by Belizean fishermen give testimony to the richness of the fishery in the area.

A Guatemalan tour operator sends tourists to the island from Livingston, Guatemala, a couple of times a month from November to May. Other visitors arrive by boat from Punta Gorda. The "facilities" are found at the center of the island and consist of a couple of driftwood sheds, benches, and a shower. There are posted signs asking visitors to take their rubbish with them. The island is best suited for day visits.

Still, Lime Caye is a very pretty place and worth a visit. Everyone just needs to practice the Sierra Club axiom "Leave only footprints [or bubbles] and take only photographs." The northern end of the island is encircled by a reef that protects a shallow lagoon with superb visibility and snorkeling.

Ragged Caye: Last in the Sapodilla chain is Ragged Caye, the southernmost island on the Barrier Reef. It is also known as South Caye and Sapodilla Caye. The island was transformed from a beautiful caye dominated by coconuts and casuarina trees to a denuded island about half its original size when Hurricane Fifi and other tropical storms swept over it in the 1980s. Honduran fishermen sometimes camp here. Their past presence is evident in the large mounds of conch shells. The beauty of Ragged Caye is best appreciated underwater along its shores.

Crescent Moon Beach, Hunting Caye. *Photo by Tony Rath.*

Dive and Snorkel Sites in the Sapodillas: In his July 1991 marine survey for the Programme for Belize, Tony Rath made six dives in the Sapodillas to assess the health and diversity of the area's underwater world. Following are some generalized summaries of those dives.

Dive 1: Channel between Hunting and Nicolas cayes. Considering how close these islands are to each other, the channel is deep, about 100 feet. The drop-off is fairly close to shore. Species diversity is relatively low. Sea grass dominates the upper slopes near Nicolas Caye, and corals and sand prevail on the upper slopes of Hunting. Conch were fairly abundant at about forty feet on both sides of the channel. There is a healthy colony of garden eels at the bottom of the channel — always a treat for divers. A current of about a half-knot was measured, which is a safety consideration for some swimmers.

Dive 2: Southwest of Ragged Caye (leeward). Ragged Caye may have taken a beating, but the western side of the island's reef system is a superb dive and snorkel site, with depths of five to sixty feet in waters that are generally protected. Tony Rath: "This area was easily the richest in diversity and in the most pristine condition of any of the sites explored in the Sapodillas." The reef is relatively shallow and made up of extensive colonies of lettuce and staghorn corals. The tines on the staghorns were among the longest ever seen by Rath, who has dived throughout Belize for more than a decade. It is assumed that the water clarity is usually good because the area is protected against the prevailing northeasterlies. There is a vast abundance and diversity of fish life. Damselfish and hamlets are especially plentiful. Yellow-tail damselfish, dusky damselfish, three-spot damselfish, blue hamlet, indigo hamlet, and barred hamlet are well represented. Rath feels that the diversity around Ragged Caye is so great that the area should be set aside as a protected marine area.

Dive 3: Outer reef crest of the Sapodilla area, east of Nicolas Caye. The reef drops off in spectacular fashion. The dive was to about ninety feet. There is spur and groove topography and sandy patches. Gorgonians are common to about forty feet, and plate corals dominate deeper areas. Reef fish of many varieties and open-water predators can be seen on this dive. Wind and rough seas can make the outer reef difficult or impossible to access.

Dives 4 and 5: Due west of Lime Caye on the inner drop-off. Surge over the reef and silt from shallow water have affected the corals, which are not as healthy or diverse as in other areas. The bottom (sixty feet) was littered with broken coral put there by the surge. The shallow areas, at about twenty feet, are soft corals and sand. Lettuce coral is prevalent at a depth of thirty feet. Fish are numerous and the diversity is high, but not as impressive as in the areas around Ragged Caye.

Dive 6: West of the white coral sandbar off Ragged Caye. Like Dive 2, which was also in this area, Dive 6 proved to be equal in astounding diversity and pristine-quality reef. This dive went up one side of the reef, over the crest, and down the other side. As with Dives 4 and 5, the inner reef slope is littered with coral debris, created by the ocean surging against the reef. The crest of the reef and shallow areas are "a spectacular solid carpet of lettuce coral with occasional sand-filled depressions." This, coupled with a profusion and diversity of fish, further convinced Tony Rath that "the Sapodilla Caye Range is a prime candidate for a protected area."

Caution: You always snorkel and dive at your own risk. You are far from help should you have an accident. Be aware of currents, dive or snorkel with a buddy, and be aware of your distance from shore. "Look, but don't touch" is the best advice for your own safety in avoiding stinging corals and for preventing damage to the reef. Divers must be NAUI or PADI certified.

For dive equipment information, contact Chet Schmidt at Nature's Way Guest House (phone 07-22119) in Punta Gorda or Larry Smith, owner of Southern Reef Charters (phone 07-22682) in Punta Gorda. Southern Reef Charters is the most complete diving service in Punta Gorda.

Critical Conservation Needs for the Sapodillas: Though the Sapodillas are gems, surrounded by generally pristine reefs, they are also among the most environmentally vulnerable islands in Belize because of their proximity to Guatemala and Honduras. These two countries are the most involved in taking tourists to the islands, and policing the activities of nationals from neighboring countries is, at times, difficult for Belize. Several officers of the Belize Audubon Society voiced their concerns to me about the future impact of tourism on these islands. They cite their remoteness and the tourism activities of other countries as causes for concern in devising effective protection for such ecologically sensitive areas as turtle-nesting sites and magnificent coral gardens.

The fate of the Sapodillas will be decided in the next decade as pressures to develop the islands increase and the leaders of cash-poor Belize wrestle with decisions involving greater riches and establishing standards for environmental quality. If the example of Nicolas Caye is repeated, the natural treasures known as the Sapodillas will be greatly devalued. If, after visiting here, you share this concern and would like to see greater protection of the area, put your thoughts on paper and mail them to the Belize Audubon Society, 27 Regent Street, Belize City, Belize, C.A.

Access: For U.S. $300, Nature's Way Guest House (phone 07-22119) offers a boat hire for one to six people to Hunting Caye, the consensus gem of the Sapodillas. This is an expensive trip for one or two people, but it becomes an economy package when the cost is split four to six ways. There may be other boat operators willing to make the trip, but check on the experience of the operator prior to taking an excursion of this length. Also try Southern Reef Charters (phone 07-22682).

FIVE
CAYO DISTRICT

Overview

The Cayo District is Belize's largest district, encompassing 2061 square miles. This is the western highlands region, where the air is fresh, winter mornings are a tad cool, and flying bugs are seldom seen nor heard. *Cayo,* as the district and its main town of San Ignacio is called, means "island" in Spanish. The name seemed appropriate to the early loggers who set up camp in a clearing near to where the Mopan and Macal rivers converge. The tiny town was bordered by water and accessible only by boat in the early days. The camp grew to become the town of San Ignacio, nestled into dripping green hills in the heart of today's Cayo District as if it had been there from time immemorial.

Traveling west on the Western Highway from Belize City, the Cayo District begins in the flat savanna country near Belmopan, the nation's capital. It ends in the lush, rolling pastures dotted with huge cohune palms and highland jungle at the Guatemalan border at Benque Viejo del Carmen. A quarter of the district's 40,000 people live in Belmopan and the twin towns of Santa Elena and San Ignacio on opposite sides of the Macal River. The rest of the inhabitants are spread over the land in small villages or farms.

There's diversity and adventure aplenty in Cayo. As you head west from Belize City and first enter Cayo, you can visit Guancaste National Park and Blue Hole National Park, two of the nation's oldest protected areas. Both are small and suitable for a short daytime visit. The parks are close to Belmopan, a city that was carved out of jungle in 1971. From Belmopan westward the Western Highway begins to climb gradually.

As you proceed, adventures present themselves. There's Spanish Lookout, a Mennonite community with the appearance of 1930s rural America. It is accessible by a small, hand-cranked ferry across the Belize River followed by a six-mile drive. To the southwest lies Mountain Pine Ridge Forest Reserve, a massive, 3300-foot-high mountainous uplift, part of which is comparable in age to some of the continent's oldest formations. As the reserve's name implies, pine is the dominant tree, creating a rare conifer-dominated ecology with a tropical understory. The reserve has a 1000-foot waterfall, cascading streams lined with ferns and orchids, and caves to explore. Caracol, the largest Mayan ruin in Belize, lies south of Mountain Pine Ridge. The remains of more than 5000 structures have been identified there, making the site as important as any in the Mayan world. Caracol is in the early stages of being partially reclaimed from the jungle.

The district also offers a half-dozen mountain lodges where guests spend their nights in cozy, thatched-roof, plaster-walled bungalows with riverbank and jungle vistas. Guests dine on quality food and spend their days visiting Mountain Pine Ridge, birding, camping, river rafting, canoeing, horseback riding, or exploring ruins.

The district is known for its Mayan ruins. Besides the immense ruin at Caracol, there's Xunantunich, with a temple that is the second-highest human-made structure in Belize. From its top you'll have one of the best vistas in Belize. There are numerous other ruins and a one-day trip can take you to Tikal, in Guatemala, perhaps the most spectacular Mayan ruin of all.

The diversity in Cayo takes many forms. Architecturally speaking, it starts with the drab buildings of the emerging capital. Don't let the architecture fool you. The celebration here is that true democracy has prevailed since the nation was born in 1981. Then there's San Ignacio, the charming little town on a hilly riverbank overlooking the Macal River. Slow-paced San Ignacio is a stopping place for young budget travelers from all points on the globe.

The people of the Cayo District are a varied group. Hispanics are predominant, especially since the latest influx of immigrants from Guatemala. But there are also large enclaves of blue-eyed, blond-haired Mennonites, as well as Mayans, Europeans, North Americans, and Creoles. Among the places and people to visit are jungle lodges owned by former African colonials, a farm owned by herbalists who are working to identify and study the medicinal properties of plants, and the five charming Garcia sisters, whose Mayan art is sold from their humble shop near San Antonio village.

And for the most ambitious of the adventure-travel crowd there are vast stretches of rugged jungle that have seen fewer people in the last hundred years than make up a football team. The newly created Chiquibul Forest Reserve and the untouched areas of the Maya Mountains have undisturbed populations of jaguars, ocelots, mountain lions, tapirs, gibnuts, and avian rarities such as scarlet macaws.

Guancaste National Park

Guancaste National Park is a fifty-acre preserve featuring an immense guancaste tree that survived the logging era. The tree and surrounding remnant tropical forest are located on the banks of the Belize River on the north side of the Western Highway at the turnoff to the Hummingbird Highway and Belmopan. The Belize Audubon Society was instrumental in creating the park, which is staffed by a warden and caretakers between 8:00 A.M. and 4:00 P.M. daily. The park has a well-maintained trail system with eight separately named trails, none of which take longer than thirty minutes to walk. The park is a good picnic spot.

The park's name comes from the giant and spectacular guancaste tree located about a ten-minute walk west on the Guancaste Trail from the parking area. The guancaste is a rapid-growing species and among the largest trees found in Central America, with a height of 130 feet and massive trunk 6 feet thick. The seed pods vaguely resemble a human ear, which accounts for its local name, "monkey's ear tree." Guancaste trees were preferred for making the large dugouts known as pit-pans. Still in use in remote areas, pit-pans were the Toyota truck of water travel in Belize during the colonial period.

The park's immense guancaste tree escaped becoming a pit-pan because, instead of the usual straight trunk, this one divided many times at its base, rendering it useless for fashioning a boat. The multiple trunks make for an even wider guancaste than most. This one harbors more than thirty-five epiphytes, including orchids, bromeliads, cacti, and ferns. Decorated with so many kinds of plants, the tree is simply spectacular. However, there is more to the park than this one unique tree.

Variety of Trees: Guancaste Park offers a glimpse of a wide assortment of mature rain forest trees in a short walk from your car. There's a self-guided botanical map for loan or sale at the visitors' center next to the parking area. Thirty trees are marked on this map. You'll see large raintrees, mammee apple, hog plum, bullhorn, ceiba, cohune palm, bookout, quamwood, and a large cotton tree near the park's northern boundary. There's a nice specimen of a straight-trunked guancaste on the Amate Trail near the intersection of Roaring Creek and the Belize River. An extraordinary ceiba tree can be found on the trail bearing its name. You'll find it near the benches overlooking the river.

Wildlife: For such a small park there's a good chance you'll see wildlife. Among mammals, jaguarundis, kinkajous, pacas, armadillos, agoutis, white-tailed deer, and possums are sighted regularly. Agoutis, squirrels, and coatimundis are often sighted on the Cohune Trail. More than fifty species of birds have been sighted in the park. Among the more spectacular and rare species are the blue-crowned motmot, which is usually seen on the trail bearing the bird's name that departs the featured guanacaste tree toward the parking area. Iguanas are usually plentiful along the Amate Trail. There's a bench on this trail that affords an excellent vista of the Belize River and Roaring Creek; this is a good spot to sit quietly and watch for wildlife. Look for iguanas on the far side of Roaring Creek. The large males are orange in color and measure about four feet in length. Hikatees, rare turtles, can sometimes be seen floating in the Belize River. They are often spotted in March as they nest in the soft mud of riverbanks in the area of the Riverview Trail.

Caution: There have been several armed robberies of tourists and one rape at Guancaste Park in recent years. If no park staff are present at the visitors' center near the parking area, it is not advisable to walk the trails. Discuss your intentions and the trails with the staff, whom I found very helpful and eager to please. During my visit one Mayan caretaker walked the trails with me " . . . because it is safer for visitors this way."

Accommodations: Most visitors explore the park for about two hours. The nearest accommodations are in Belmopan.

Access: Guancaste Park is forty-eight miles from Belize City on the Western Highway and two miles from Belmopan on the Hummingbird Highway. Bus service from Belize City, Belmopan, and San Ignacio stops at the park several times daily. Try Batty Brothers, 15 Mosul Street, Belize City (phone 02-72025) or Novelo's Bus Service, 119 George Street, Benque Viejo del Carmen (phone 093-2054).

Belmopan

Belmopan, Belize's capital, is located at the geographic center of the country. Still known as the "new capital," it was bulldozed out of lowland jungle in 1971 after Hurricane Hattie devastated Belize City in 1961. The thinking of the British, who moved the capital, was that a capital in the interior would be spared the kind of devastation caused to Belize City and other coastal areas that are periodically ravaged by hurricanes. It was also thought that moving the capital to the center of the country would help open up the interior. It turned out that declaring a new capital doesn't necessarily mean people will move there. More than twenty years after Belmopan was created, Belize City is still the business hub of the country and preferred urban center. To this day many Belizeans who are elected or appointed to serve in the national government commute daily to Belmopan rather than live there.

The capital, featuring no-frills architecture of two- and three-story concrete buildings, lies on the Hummingbird Highway two miles southeast of the intersection of the Hummingbird and Western highways. It is about fifty miles from both Belize City and Dangriga and has a population of about 3000 civil servants and city workers. Belmopan is in the first phase of a twenty-year development program, which when completed will include new, more spacious government houses, green belts, industrial parks, schools, a hospital, and other amenities of a modern city. That's the plan; getting the money to pay for all this is the problem. When passing judgment on the Belizean capital, however, keep in mind that the nation has only been in existence since 1981.

The backdrop for the emerging capital consists of the rugged Maya Mountains to the west and lowland savanna to the east. The area around Belmopan is mostly devoted to agriculture.

The atmosphere in Belmopan is laid-back, and officials are accessible providing you make an appointment and have something worth their while to discuss. I was able to meet with then Prime Minister George Price and then Attorney General and Minister of Tourism and the Environment Glenn Godfrey, as well as longtime

Permanent Secretary, Minister of Tourism and the Environment, and former president of the Belize Audubon Society Dr. Victor Gonzalez on a single afternoon. All three men were candid, warm, efficient, and helpful.

The opportunity I had to meet with high-ranking government officials made clear the unique qualities at work in a small democratic country. Where else could villagers regularly meet with a governmental minister like Glenn Godfrey to design the development of their area? Due to Belize's small size, there is an intimacy between leadership and citizens that is more akin to the ancient Greek city-states than to the modern, multilayered, monolithic governments that dominate today's world stage.

The best thing about Belmopan is that it houses one of the few truly democratic governments operating in Central and South America. The government operates on the British model, with the Prime Minister and his Cabinet coming from the party with the majority in the House of Representatives. The Prime Minister and his Cabinet form the executive branch. The legislative branch is made up of the eight-member Senate and the twenty-eight-member House of Representatives. The judicial branch has a Supreme Court and a Court of Appeals. Each district also has separate civil courts. Justices are appointed and operate independently of political parties. The Queen of England is the titular head of state and is represented by a Governor General who is Belizean. As mentioned, the highest-ranking leaders in Belize are uniquely accessible to their people. Former Prime Minister George Price set aside one day a week to meet with citizens about anything concerning the government, and his Cabinet did the same. Manuel Esquivel, who was elected Prime Minister in 1993, is expected to keep this tradition alive. This is only possible because of Belize's relatively small population, and because the government is committed to staying in touch with the populace. On a personal level, I found George Price to be warm and engaging. I talked to a number of Belize Zoo employees whom Price sometimes picked up hitchhiking on their way home from work on the Western Highway. "If he knows your face, he'll pick you up," one explained to me in admiration of his Prime Minister. Esquivel is no less caring. Price and Esquivel are the only Prime Ministers Belize has had.

Department of Archaeology: Probably the place most visited by tourists in Belmopan is the Department of Archaeology. The vault in the basement of this building holds many priceless Mayan artifacts. The public is allowed to view the artifacts a couple of times a week. The department is located at 25 Mahogany Street. For information, phone 08-22106.

Plans for a National Museum: In the future there will be a national museum in Belmopan. A National Museum Committee has collected approximately BZ $1,000,000 toward building a 32,000-square-foot museum that will house a dozen or more exhibits. The project is estimated to cost BZ $7,000,000. Jorge Espat, who heads the committee, says, "The project will add to the rich diversity of our nation. It will contribute greatly to the tourism industry, the education of the community, and more importantly nourish and preserve our culture and identity." In an interview in *Belize Today,* Espat outlined six main exhibits his committee would like to include in a national museum. The largest will be a historical exhibit that covers the formation of the continent to the present, encompassing both geological and human history. According to Espat, few people realize that Belize has some of the oldest soils on earth in Mountain Pine Ridge Forest Reserve. The Mayan civilization will be featured in great detail in an exhibit that should rival any Mayan exhibit in the world. The historical exhibit will also showcase Belize in the Americas, the Spanish and British eras in Belize, slavery, the coming of the Garifunas, and the influx of refugees from the Caste Wars. It will also explain the emergence of the merchant class, which traded illegally with the Confederate states during the U.S. Civil War, how British colonialism worked, and the growth of Belize's nationalist movements, which eventually led to independence.

Key Ministries, Departments, and Emergency Contacts: Department of Archaeology (for viewing Mayan artifacts), phone 08-22106; Belmopan Hospital, phone 08-22263/22264; Information Office (for general inquiries), P.O. Box 60, Belmopan, Belize, C.A., phone 08-22019/22159 and fax 08-23242; Lands and Survey Department, Ministry of Natural Resources (for topo maps), phone 08-22249/22231; police, phone 08-22222/22223; Printing Department (for official documents and publications), phone 08-22293.

Consulates and Embassies: British High Commission, 34/36 Halfmoon Avenue, phone 08-22146/22147; Panamanian Embassy, 79 Unity

Boulevard, phone 08-22714; Venezuelan Consul General, 18/20 Unity Boulevard, phone 08-22384. (*Note:* The U.S. Embassy and sixteen other consulates or embassies are located in Belize City.)

Shopping: El Caracol Gallery and Gift Shop, located at 32 Macaw Avenue (phone 08-22394), has a selection of stone carvings, ceramic pottery, baskets, and Mayan musical instruments for sale.

Accommodations and Eateries: The Belmopan Convention Hotel (M, E) (phone 08-22130/22340; fax 08-23066) caters to visiting business and government leaders. It is not luxurious, but functional, with all the modern conveniences, including a swimming pool. It's easy to find at 2 Bliss Parade, the second right off Constitution Drive as you enter Belmopan. Major credit cards are accepted. My favorite place in Belmopan for "atmospherics" and good prices is the Bull Frog Inn (M, E) at 25 Halfmoon Avenue (phone 08-22111; fax 08-23155). From the United States and Canada, bookings can be made through Winter Escapes, P.O. Box 429, Erickson, Manitoba, Canada ROJ OPO (phone 204-636-2968). Credit cards are accepted. To find the Bull Frog Inn, locate East Ring Road (the road circling the capital). The Bull Frog has a Casablanca-style garden bar and restaurant with both foreign and Belizean dishes. It is a favorite of government officials. Owner John D'Silva says he can arrange tours to nearby Mayan ruins. Practically next door you'll find the Circle A Lodge (M) at 35-37 Halfmoon Avenue (phone 08-22296). Only cash is accepted here for payment. Out of town, but nearby off the Western Highway at mile 47, is Banana Bank Ranch (M), a unique lodge experience on the Belize River. The ranch is owned by John and Carolyn Carr, who came to Belize from Montana thirty years ago. You'll be ferried across the Belize River to your bungalow-style lodging. The Carrs have a private zoo, which includes a jaguar. Carolyn's wildlife oil paintings are very high quality and are sold as prints throughout the country and abroad. Horseback riding and canoeing are offered to guests. Traveler's checks are accepted. Contact Banana Bank Ranch, Mile 47 Western Highway, Cayo District, Belize, C.A. (phone 08-3180). For economy foodstuffs, you'll find an open-air market near the bus terminals on Bliss Parade in Belmopan.

Access: Buses from Belize City, Dangriga, and San Ignacio (near the Guatemalan border) connect to Belmopan daily. Contact Batty

Brothers (phone 02-72025) or Novelo's Bus Service (phone 02-77372). If you're driving, the approximately fifty-mile distance from both Belize City and Dangriga takes a little more than an hour under normal conditions.

Caution: The Western Highway, which is paved, is deceptively treacherous, especially after a rain, when the limestone-surfaced screenings become as slick as ice. At all times, drive slower than you would in North America on a similar-looking surface. Cars traveling too fast have a tendency to slide from the roadway, which I experienced twice and witnessed on another occasion when a driver was killed.

Blue Hole National Park

Blue Hole National Park is a 575-acre preserve located twelve miles southeast of Belmopan off the Hummingbird Highway. The principal attractions are the Blue Hole and St. Herman's Cave. The Blue Hole is a collapsed karst sinkhole where underground river water on its way to the Sibun River comes to the surface in a verdant jungle setting before continuing on its journey into an underground cavern. The sinkhole is 37 feet deep, kidney-shaped, and about 80 feet by 300 feet. The water is an uncommonly rich sapphire blue color and suitable for a refreshing swim.

The Blue Hole is directly off the highway. Reaching it after parking your car amounts to walking down a flight of steps. Having been underground, the water is cool, making a swim here particularly refreshing on a humid, hot day. There is a changing room, but not everyone uses it. During my second visit here, three French women tourists took the plunge au naturel, which brought a bashful smile to the face of the conservative-minded Mayan warden, whose brain I was picking about wildlife in the area. "Europeans," he offered as an explanation. The best swimming area is at the east end of the pool. The changing room and toilet are near the top of the stairs.

St. Herman's Cave: The cave is about 400 meters from the Hummingbird Highway, but you aren't supposed to park where you see the cave signposted from the road. This becomes a point of confusion to most visitors approaching from Belmopan. Your car is at risk if you park there, because it will not receive the protection that is offered at the Blue Hole, which is a short distance southeast from the signposting of St. Herman's Cave. The cave is normally reached by taking a rugged hiking trail from the Blue Hole that heads west. This trail over very uneven karst limestone has many ups and downs and covers about two miles before reaching the cave. The cave entrance has steps, and you'll need a light inside. It can be explored for a distance of about a mile. The cave is noted for its cool air, a rare and welcome sensation in the tropics. A great many Mayan artifacts — mostly pottery, spears, and torches — have been recovered from the cave. Archaeologists have identified a distinct type of pottery here known as *zuh uy ha,* which roughly translates to mean "virgin water from cave drippings." Mountain Cow Cave and Petroglyph Cave, just outside the park boundary, can be visited only if a permit is granted from the Department of Archaeology in Belmopan.

Wildlife: For a small park, Blue Hole National Park boasts sightings of practically every mammal and a healthy percentage of the 500 bird species living in Belize. Jaguarundis, ocelots, and jaguars have been seen on numerous occasions. Kinkajous, brocket and white-tailed deer, white-lipped peccaries, tamanduas (anteaters), coatimundis, pacas, and armadillos have also been seen regularly. Reptiles include the iguana, green snake, boa constrictor, and the deadly fer-de-lance.

Birds are plentiful, with more than a hundred species having been recorded. Some of the more exotic and rare species include the keel-billed toucan, slaty-breasted tinamou, king vulture, white hawk, spotted wood quail, black-hawk eagle, blue-crowned motmot, slaty-tailed trogon, and nightingale wren.

Trails: The trail to the Blue Hole from the road is a series of steps. The trail to St. Herman's Cave starts near the changing cabana. This trail cuts through secondary-growth, low-dense forest over rough terrain that continually climbs and drops. The walk is strenuous but beautiful and offers a glimpse of many kinds of plants and possibly sightings of animals. For those wanting to visit the cave, but with minimal excursion, take the road by the pasture on the southeast side of the park. Ask the warden, who is usually found in the parking area, where the pasture route starts.

Be Prepared: Juan Choc, the warden at Blue Hole National Park when I visited there, suggests that anyone walking to the cave should take a light of some sort, liquid to avoid dehydration, and a light pullover top to stay warm if planning a lengthy visit in the cave. Having binoculars and a bird book will increase your appreciation of wildlife.

Caution: As with Guancaste National Park, Blue Hole National Park should not be visited unless staff members are on duty. These two parks seem to have crime-related problems not often experienced elsewhere in rural Belize. The park is open from 8:00 A.M. to 4:00 P.M. daily. However, it's wise to inquire about the hours to see if they've changed, before visiting.

Hundreds of people a month visit this roadside park without incident, but there have been a few ugly incidents with tourists being victimized. I stopped here once at about 5:00 P.M. for a quick dip and returned to my rental car ten minutes later to find two men siphoning gas from my tank. The men looked Guatemalan and were carrying machetes (a bush tool as common as trousers, and not necessarily a sign of hostile intent). I diffused the situation with humor in Spanish. "*¿Ustedes tienen sed? Yo tengo agua.*" (You're thirsty? I have water.) The response was a series of retreating bows and sheepish smiles that lasted for a distance of about twenty-five yards, after which both men turned heel and sprinted down the road and into some bushes. My guess is that the two were probably from Ringtail Village, a resettlement village for recently arrived Guatemalan refugees located a few miles south of the park. Due to their befuddlement I was left with their hose and gas can. I dropped the can near where they disappeared but kept the hose. The point of telling this story is that there was no sign of danger when I stopped. There were no other vehicles nor was anyone in sight, which meant the men were lying in wait nearby. This was my only such experience in Belize, but it left a strong impression and was not the only such incident I heard of involving foreigners at Blue Hole. "Stopping and leaving your car unattended here should only be done when the warden is around. It is safe with us, but not so safe without us," says Juan Choc.

Accommodations: There are no accommodations at Blue Hole. Overnight camping is neither wise nor permitted. Belmopan has the closest accommodations.

Access: Buses run regularly between Belmopan and Dangriga. Blue Hole National Park lies twelve miles southeast of Belmopan on the Hummingbird Highway. Let the driver know you want to get off at Blue Hole or he may not stop. From Dangriga, the park is forty-three miles northeast on the Hummingbird Highway.

Spanish Lookout and Other Mennonite Communities

Signposted on the Western Highway in the area of a government agriculture station known as Central Farm, Spanish Lookout is the most accessible and modern Mennonite community in Belize. Spanish Lookout Mennonites are representative of the "progressive" (or modern) Mennonites, of which there are several communities. The progressives, who also call themselves the Evangelical Mennonite Mission Church, have embraced modern devices such as electricity, tractors, mechanized farm machinery, and motor vehicles, unlike more conservative Mennonites. Other such communities in Belize are found at Blue Creek, Rosita, and to a lesser extent Georgeville, Orange Walk Town, and Hattiesville.

The Spanish Lookout community, which numbers about 1400 individuals, is laid out on a spacious, homogeneous-looking grid that is viewed by the Mennonites who live there as seven different villages: Gnadenfeld, Gruenfeld, Shoental, Rosenhof, Rosenort, Talheim, and Edental. The homes are modest, and the cattle and chickens are plump and well cared for. Visually, you'll think you've stepped back in time a half-century to the farms of the U.S. Midwest. By Belizean standards, Spanish Lookout is clearly a prosperous community. The entire community, including miles of grazing land, was hacked out of jungle by pioneer Mennonites who moved from either Mexico or Canada into the region in the 1950s.

Nearby Barton's Creek, a much smaller Mennonite community, is an example of the more conservative wing of the faith, known as Old Colony, or Kleine Gemeinde Church. The Old Colony Mennonites don't interact with Belizean society a great deal and practice a more spartan lifestyle, forgoing electricity, making use of draft horses and human labor for agricultural work, and relying on the horse and buggy for transportation. The buggies are typically outfitted with car tires instead of fragile, rigid, wooden-spoked buggy wheels. When you come across Old Colony Mennonites you'll notice that the men dress in long-sleeved cotton shirts, straw hats, and pants with suspenders, while the women's attire consists of long dresses and bonnets. They also usually look weathered beyond their years and are characteristically very shy toward outsiders. Besides Barton's Creek, Old Colony Mennonites are found at Shipyard and Little Belize. Some communities have both progressive and Old Colony Mennonites living in the same region. The Barton's Creek Mennonites, who live in a remote area south of the Western Highway, can be visited, but only through an intermediary.

Spanish Lookout, Barton's Creek, and other Mennonite communities are self-sufficient. They aren't set up for tourism nor are they particularly interested in it. However, the Spanish Lookout Mennonites have successful chicken, dairy, and beef cattle operations that put them in constant contact with greater Belize. Driving through Spanish Lookout is not seen as intrusive, though don't expect to be greeted warmly unless you arrive with a purpose in mind other than gawking. This is a working community. Idle time is not in vogue. I found the Spanish Lookout Mennonites friendly and conversant when I engaged them on topics related to agriculture. Most spoke English, a second language to their primary language, a centuries-old German dialect that dates back to the 1500s, when the religious order got its start during the Reformation. In recent years, Belizean Mennonites have increased their ranks with the conversion of Belizean nationals of Hispanic and Mayan backgrounds. Mennonites of European origins are taught in German and English, while Mennonite converts from within Belize are taught primarily in English by Mennonite teachers.

Meeting Mennonites: On the ferry crossing the Belize River on the way to Spanish Lookout, I began talking with Ernest Reimer, who runs a successful poultry operation in Spanish Lookout. I own livestock in the United States, so we had some common interests. Ernest had a friendly innocence about him. He drives a shiny new Chevy pickup and was clearly proud of his success in the poultry business. Over lunch, at a small counter restaurant in Spanish Lookout, he explained the ins and outs of making a profit in Belize's poultry market. I bid Ernest farewell and, thanks to his knowledge of the community, tracked down the source of life-size sewn replicas of toucans and macaws that I'd seen in gift shops around Belize. Mary Reimer (no relation to Ernest) and her daughters made the expertly sewn replicas of tropical birds that I had seen. When I parked my car and knocked on their door, the family looked a bit surprised. Mary's two teenage daughters behaved in an incredibly shy manner, avoiding eye contact and giggling quietly with each other when I entered the house. Mrs. Reimer offered me a glass of water and explained that her daughters' behavior was due to my being the first non-Mennonite ever to visit their home. Mary's husband eyed me suspiciously at first but began to open up when I asked questions about livestock diseases. I bought a stuffed toucan, which made the visit worthwhile for everyone.

The lesson here is that, as with people everywhere, a meaningful exchange is possible, as long as you act naturally and speak to your hosts about the business of their everyday lives. Showing up in a Mennonite community with a camera, as if you're visiting Disneyland, may net you a few photos of scowling Mennonites or the tops of their hats as they look downward to foil your photos. I didn't take a picture but went away with a vivid memory.

Historical Perspective: The Mennonites were one of the many Christian groups that broke with the Catholic Church during the European Reformation in the 1500s. For centuries the Mennonites were persecuted (primarily over their pacifist views, religious interpretations, and refusal to participate in local governments) in a succession of countries until they emigrated to Canada, the United States, and Mexico. They came to Belize in the 1950s. Since arriving, they have cleared more than 150,000 acres of lowland jungle, making their land into the most productive agricultural property in Belize. Internally, the Mennonites of Belize have split among themselves many times, but most fall into either the progressive or Old Colony camps. Most recently a group of Old Colony Mennonites from Blue Creek (which is mostly progressive) moved to Bolivia to practice their religion in the manner they preferred.

If the Mennonite story in Belize interests you, buy a copy of *Pioneer Years in Belize,* by Gerhard S. Koop. The author is a Mennonite living in Spanish Lookout, so the story is told from the Mennonite perspective. Koop, who came from Manitoba, Canada, chronicles overcoming hardship in Belize and the constant, singular drive to establish productive agriculture in a place where Mennonites can practice their brand of religious and social freedom. The last few lines of the book may well capture the Mennonite view of the larger world and their role in it: "Observing the courage and endurance of the Mennonites in general, there is no doubt of their progress. But the world's political unrest clearly indicates that the end times may not be pleasant. We praise God for all the blessings we have received. Without Him we can do nothing and nothing good has been done without His help."

Accommodations: Mennonite communities do not offer accommodations to tourists. San Ignacio and numerous jungle lodges are within short drives of Spanish Lookout and Barton's Creek.

Access: There is no public transportation to Spanish Lookout or Barton's Creek. To reach Spanish Lookout, watch for signs pointing north from the Western Highway in the area of Central Farm. You must cross the Belize River by a hand-cranked, cable-connected ferry. The distance to the community from the Western Highway is six miles. If you're heading to Belize City after visiting Spanish Lookout, take the road to Iguana Creek. This route offers a scenic alternate route that intersects the Western Highway farther east than the Central Farm approach. Barton's Creek is not suitable for a casual drive-up visit. Work through Mountain Equestrian Trails (see "Mountain Lodges" below) if you wish to visit. M.E.T. is close to Barton's Creek, and co-owner Marguerite Bevis has a long-standing relationship with this community.

San Ignacio and Santa Elena

San Ignacio and Santa Elena are often described as the twin-town hub of the Cayo District. Santa Elena is located on the east side of the Macal River about seventy-two miles from Belize City. San Ignacio lies across the river from Santa Elena. The one-lane Hawkesworth Bridge connects the two towns. This is the longest suspension bridge in Belize and requires that you make sure it is free of vehicles heading in your direction when you drive across it.

Santa Elena is a nondescript sprawl, including gas stations and small businesses. San Ignacio, on the other hand, is charming and is built on sharply jutting hills with narrow, irregularly laid out streets and storefronts reminiscent of the old-time American West. The town also has plenty of characters to enhance its frontier image. San Ignacio is the administrative center for the Cayo District, and the two towns have a combined population of about 7000 people. Compared to Belize City, the hustler element is nonexistent. I never had an unpleasant human interaction in San Ignacio, nor did I witness any.

San Ignacio was established by Europeans as a logging center well over a century ago. The combination of oxen pulling huge mahogany logs to the river, where they were bound together to be floated to Belize City, and the gathering of chicle (the sap of the sapodilla tree once used widely in chewing gum) in the region by tough and independent *chicleros* helped mold the town. Today, the town relies on cattle ranching, tourism, and small retail businesses.

For visitors traveling independently (rather than as part of a tour run by one of the nearby mountain lodges), San Ignacio is the place to rent a hotel room and spend a few days visiting the many attractions in the region. The Mountain Pine Ridge Forest Reserve and the Mayan ruins at Xunantunich, Cahal Pech, Pilar, Caracol, and Tikal in Guatemala are all possibilities. Canoeing and swimming in the Belize River are also popular activities.

Depending on your pocketbook and tastes, there are two directions to consider after you cross the bridge into San Ignacio. For economy travelers, turn right (or get off the bus) and walk down Burns Avenue. This is the main drag. On the left side you'll find Eva's Restaurant and Bar, a sort of informal meeting place for travelers

1. EVA'S BAR AND RESTAURANT TOURIST INFO

2. BUDGET HOTEL

3. POST OFFICE AND POLICE

4. SAN IGNACIO HOTEL

5. TOWN SQUARE

6. SAN IGNACIO HOSPITAL

SAN IGNACIO

from all over the world. The food is good and reasonably priced, and Eva's owners, Bob and Nestora Jones, are very helpful. Bob is a former British soldier who couldn't get Belize out of his blood. Now he's a beacon for young travelers, clueing them in on what's in the area and the best places to get a cheap hotel room or rent a canoe.

If you want a more self-contained experience, turn left after crossing the bridge and drive up the hill a hundred yards to the San Ignacio Hotel (see "Accommodations"), which is on the outskirts of town. This is a well-run, moderately priced hotel with an excellent restaurant. It has a comfortable atmosphere and is among my favorite places to stay in Belize.

The Basics in San Ignacio: Market day is held by the Cultural Center east of Burns Avenue on Saturday. All shops are closed on Wednesday afternoons, and a few may be closed on Saturday mornings. Only eateries and hotels are open on Sunday. You'll find the Belize Bank at 16 Burns Avenue (phone 092-2031) and the Atlantic Bank across the street at 17 Burns Avenue (phone 092-2596). The police (phone 092-2202) are located in the large white building on the south side of the town square, adjacent to the east end of the Hawkesworth Bridge. There's also an interesting outdoor mural here that chronicles Belizean history. For medical problems requiring a doctor, go to the San Ignacio Hospital (phone 092-2066) on Hospital Street. The town boasts three nightclubs: the Blue Angel on Hudson Street (phone 092-2080); Le Brilliant Nightclub on Burns Avenue (no phone); and the Cahal Pech, at the top of the hill near the ruins (phone 092-2736). Club life doesn't generally start until about 9:00 P.M.

Canoe Rentals: Besides Cosmos Camping (see "Camping"), there's Canoe Rentals (phone 092-2188), owned by Dan Montgomery.

Accommodations: Sitting high on a hill overlooking the Macal River is the San Ignacio Hotel (M). This is the best place to stay in San Ignacio. Owner/manager Mariam Roberson has put together the most complete accommodation in western Belize. The rooms are small, but Mariam offers all the extras of an expensive hotel: air-conditioning, laundry service, restaurant (try the chicken dishes), gift shop, conference room, bar, and a very nice swimming pool. This is the favorite haunt of business and government officials traveling in the region. There's even a security guard to watch over your vehicle. This may be the only hotel in San Ignacio where you can make international calls from your room. All major credit cards are accepted. Contact San Ignacio Hotel, P.O. Box 33, San Ignacio, Cayo District, Belize, C.A. (phone 092-2125/2034; fax 092-2134).

The downtown area of San Ignacio mostly offers budget accommodations with shared bathrooms. Most of them are tidy. The Jaguar Hotel (B), 19 Burns Avenue (phone 092-2320), has a 20 percent discount for students, three rooms to one bathroom, up to three in a room, fans provided; cash and traveler's checks only. The Belmoral Hotel (B), 17 Burns Avenue (phone 092-2024), accepts cash and traveler's checks only. At the Central Hotel (B), 24 Burns Avenue (phone 092-2253), owners Neville and Vera "Charlie" Collins and manager Tony Wells are usually around to help with bus schedules and basic information. The rooms are clean, baths are shared, and there's a friendly atmosphere. Only cash and traveler's checks are accepted. Lastly, for its name if nothing else, you might try the Hi-Et Hotel (B), 12 West Street (no phone), which accepts cash and traveler's checks only.

Camping: Try Cosmos Camping (B) on Branch Mouth Road. You can rent a hammock here if you're traveling light. A young Austrian/Belizean couple runs Cosmos. It's on the river and is walking distance from town. If you can't find Cosmos, ask at Eva's Restaurant on Burns Avenue. A popular spot among the young Europeans hanging around Eva's is Black Rock (B), a place where you can rent an already-standing, large tent on a remote section of the Macal River. Food is prepared in an open hearth. Activities include horseback riding, swimming, sunbathing, hiking, and canoeing. Access is by footpath once you get to the footpath by car. Inquire at Eva's for more information.

Access: Bus service runs hourly from Belize City to San Ignacio. Buses also run regularly from the Guatemalan border, which is eight miles away. Novelo's Bus Service (phone 092-2054/02-77372) has a yard in nearby Benque Viejo del Carmen to assure a steady stream of buses. Batty Brothers (phone 02-72025) also serves San Ignacio. By car, the seventy-two-mile trip from Belize City takes about two-and-a-half hours. Air travel isn't offered yet, though there's quite a bit of talk about putting in a commercial strip for light planes at Central Farm, which is ten miles away.

Xunantunich ("Maiden of the Rocks") Ruins

Xunantunich, which means "Maiden of the Rocks" in Mayan, is a moderate-size site, but an important ceremonial center with a spectacular central structure, El Castillo (the Castle), which rises 130 feet and affords one of the best vistas in all of Belize. The turnoff for the site is just off the Western Highway at San José Succotz, which

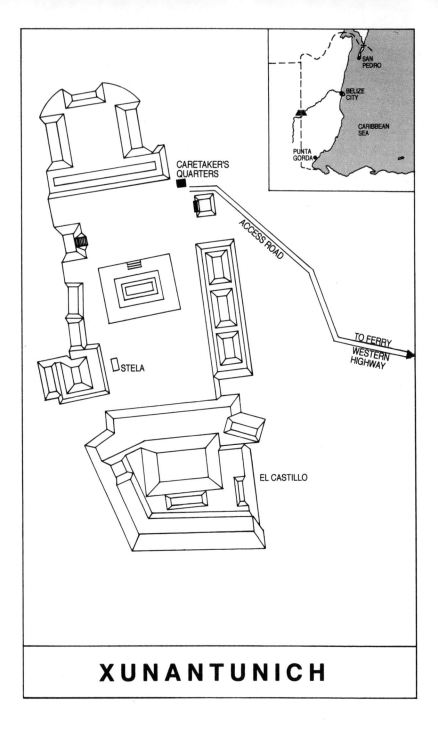

CARETAKER'S
QUARTERS

ACCESS ROAD

TO FERRY
WESTERN
HIGHWAY

STELA

EL CASTILLO

SAN
PEDRO

BELIZE
CITY

CARIBBEAN
SEA

PUNTA
GORDA

XUNANTUNICH

is six-and-a-half miles west of San Ignacio and only one-and-a-half miles from the Guatemalan border. The site offers a peaceful setting enclosed by an island of remnant jungle that's surrounded by a patchwork of pasture and farms. Climbing El Castillo is the preferred activity here. The climb starts on the east face, veers left, and circles around the back. You must climb steep stairs without a railing and scamper up a short ladder to reach the summit. The view, which takes in much of Belize and miles of Guatemala, is tranquil and awe-inspiring. You'll be able to make out villages, large patches of jungle, and agricultural areas. The view from the top also allows you to scan the smaller temples and three plazas that make up the immediate site.

The site was occupied during the Classic Period (A.D. 250–900) and abandoned about A.D. 850. Much of the early archaeological work amounted to pillaging or incompetence, resulting in much of what could have been known about the site being forever lost. Other than knowing that the site was damaged by an earthquake during the Late Classic Period (about A.D. 1100), not much is known about Xunantunich. There are a number of large stelae that have been collected and placed under a thatched roof in the central plaza. The obvious restoration work on the side of El Castillo about halfway through the climb was undertaken in 1972. The frieze here depicts the days of the week and lunar observances. There is also a figure of a headless man on this frieze, likely connected to the fact that the execution of prisoners and people chosen for sacrifice was a common practice among the ancient Mayans here. On the site's west flank is a ball court where Mayan rulers watched contests that often resulted in death to the losing team—also a sign of the times. Archaeologists from southern California are presently beginning a long-term study of the site, so perhaps the history of Xunantunich will become known in years to come.

Elfego Panti, the longtime Mayan warden at this site, is as good a source as any about the history of Xunantunich. He's also knowledgeable about plants and animals. His office is a traditional thatched-roof structure near the parking area. Elfego is worth engaging in conversation about the site and is eager to share his knowledge. There is a fee of U.S. $1 to visit the site, with Elfego or a replacement on duty from 8:00 A.M. to 5:00 P.M. every day. For safety reasons, Elfego suggests visiting the site only when he is there.

Accommodations: Camping is not permitted. Many of the mountain lodges are in the area, as are the towns of Benque Viejo del Carmen and San Ignacio. The towns have moderate and budget accommodations.

Access: You can ride a bus to San José Succotz, take the ferry across the Mopan River, and walk two miles (mostly uphill) to the site. Most people visit as part of a tour group (see "Mountain Lodges") or in a rental vehicle. If it's been raining, the current may be too strong to safely run the hand-cranked, cable-connected ferry. Rain also makes the uphill portion of the dirt road to the site difficult to negotiate for two-wheel-drive vehicles. Though it's not mandatory, tipping the underpaid ferry operator is appreciated.

Other Mayan Ruins

Cahal Pech ("Location of Ticks")

Cahal Pech and El Pilar are two smaller sites in the general vicinity of San Ignacio. In fact, Cahal Pech is in town. It's up the hill as you leave town and within easy walking distance of downtown. The first time I tried to visit it I ended up at a nearby hilltop bar and dance hall by the same name. Cahal Pech translates as "Location of Ticks," a somewhat ominous name. The site has not enjoyed a great deal of protection, and its close proximity to San Ignacio has resulted in much looting over the years. There are several structures, the tallest being about eighty feet. Seven plazas and thirty-four structures have been identified, including an ancient sauna. USAID and the University of Trent in Canada are beginning excavations here to get a picture of the role Cahal Pech played in the area. It appears to have been abandoned around A.D. 850. Cahal Pech isn't the most dramatic site you'll find, but it is worth a look if you're staying down the street at the San Ignacio Hotel or elsewhere in town. If you're in town on a weekend you can visit the ruins and the dance hall (there's sometimes a tough crowd) in a single evening.

Access: The site is about a ten-to-fifteen-minute walk from town and a shorter drive. The site is not well signposted, so you may have to ask locals how to find it once you turn off the paved road.

El Pilar

El Pilar is a large, unexcavated (except for looters) site of about fifty acres on private agricultural property just east of Xunantunich. Archaeologists are especially interested in studying the site's large defensive walls, which may have been built when the Mayan population centers began to collapse. The site is mostly a mystery.

Access: To visit El Pilar, you can either drive or take a cab from San Ignacio to Bullet Tree Falls and from there locate a trailhead for a short walk to the site. Locals can direct you to the trail. Mountain Equestrian Trails (see "Mountain Lodges" below) and possibly other mountain lodges offer tours to El Pilar.

Mountain Pine Ridge Forest Reserve

Mountain Pine Ridge Forest Reserve is an immense, 300-square-mile area that features cool pine forests and bracken ferns instead of Belize's usual strictly tropical varieties of plants. There are also cascading streams, impressive waterfalls, and caves you can walk through. On the northern base of this immense formation, which is 3300 feet high along its crest, are the Mayan villages of Cristo Rey and San Antonio. Close to San Antonio you'll find the famous Garcia Sisters Museum (actually an art gallery). In the southern portion of Mountain Pine Ridge lie Augustine and a logging camp and farther south are the Vaca Plateau, Chiquibul Forest Reserve, and Caracol. (The only way to reach Caracol is through Mountain Pine Ridge.) Parts of this massive uplift are ancient, comparable in age to Canada's Laurentian Shield and Venezuela's Angel Falls, which are among the oldest geological formations in the Americas, dating back 600 million years. There is no evidence to suggest that the Mayans occupied Mountain Pine Ridge on a permanent basis.

Hidden Valley Falls: These falls are spectacular. A single ribbon of water similar to the falls in Yosemite Valley drops more than 1000 feet from pine forest into jungle. There is a picnic table and a forestry building at the parking area and vista point. The falls are one of the farthest destinations in Mountain Pine Ridge from the Western Highway. From Georgeville on the Western Highway, the falls are reached by turning south, proceeding to mile 11 on the dirt road into the region, turning left at mile 11 (signposted), traveling four more miles, and turning left again where the falls are signposted. After a steep descent on the final leg, the road will dead-end at the overlook to the falls. The terrain is very steep and not suitable for doing much besides snapping a few photos and picnicking. Hiking to the base of the falls is hazardous and would require technical mountain-climbing skills. All roads are dirt, and keep in mind that the final steep vehicular descent becomes an ascent that may be impossible to negotiate on the return in a two-wheel-drive vehicle if it's been raining.

Rio On: This is a cascading river that pours over some of the oldest rock in the Americas. There are numerous large pools for bathing. The water is cool, but the air temperature is usually warm enough to tempt a swim or soak. There are also interconnecting pools. Steep steps descend from a picnic area to the base of the pools. The most private pools are upstream and require climbing over treacherous slick rock surfaces. In some areas, the natural water slides connect one pool to the next, creating the opportunity for an exhilarating experience. You must exercise good judgment about where to climb and where to swim and which natural water slides are safe. The river becomes an unsafe torrent when it has been raining. Rio On is reached by driving eight miles from the intersection that is the turnoff to Hidden Valley Falls. Instead of taking the left to the falls, go straight. The route should be signposted. You'll come to a series of creeks before reaching the pools of the Rio On.

Rio Frio Cave: Past the headquarters for the Western Division of Forestry (in Augustine), at mile 22 from Georgeville, you'll find Rio Frio Cave. The road to the cave through Augustine is hard to follow.

If you lose your way, usually someone is around to ask. The cave's hangar-size entrance is masked in vines and trees. Though there's enough light inside the cave to see unaided, you're best off with a flashlight because the surface is slippery and uneven in places. The cave is nearly a mile in length. After a while you'll see the light from the other entrance. A stream runs through the cave, and there are both stalagmites (extending vertically from the floor) and stalactites (extending vertically from the ceiling), with more of the latter. With the aid of a flashlight you'll see bats hanging from the ceiling. Almost always, the formation of stalactites, which is caused by dripping moisture to the cave floor, precedes the formation of stalagmites. Both icicle-shaped structures are made from carbonate of lime, a substance in limestone that is held in solution until water drips or evaporates. Much of Belize is riddled with cave systems similar to the one at Rio Frio Cave.

There's a good-quality nature walk with numbered trees and two smaller caves within a short distance of the parking area at Rio Frio Cave.

Caution: You will be traveling on miles of dirt roads in Mountain Pine Ridge, which is easy enough if you keep your speed down. It's a good idea to pack extra food and water in case of a breakdown. Generally, the roads to the sites listed above can be visited safely in a two-wheel-drive vehicle in a matter of hours. However, if it rains, retreat from the area if you're not in a four-wheel-drive vehicle, which is preferable for the area. Other hazards include fogs that sometimes engulf the mountain, making getting lost a distinct possibility should you miss a signpost or wander down a logging track. The meager signposting should be watched for. Do not drive down dirt tracks that suddenly appear unless you're reasonably sure where they go. There are many surveying and logging roads that will surely lead you to an empty gas tank far from the Western Highway, where the nearest filling station is located. Start with a full tank. Look out for logging trucks. Mountain Pine Ridge is a reserve, which allows carefully managed logging. Logging trucks always have the right of way, especially a fully loaded truck coming downhill. Don't assume that a logging truck will stop. After all, gravity may have more to do with a truck's downhill motion than the truck's driver. Lastly, along the road to Rio On and Rio Frio Cave, creeks can swell and engulf the roadway, making the road impassable during prolonged rains. If you get in a jam and can't get out, seek help at the forestry camp at Augustine or stay with your car.

Access: There is no public transportation to Mountain Pine Ridge. You should be in and out during daylight hours. There is a gate-keeper who monitors traffic. There are two roads from the Western Highway that converge on the main dirt road into Mountain Pine Ridge. Coming from Belize City or Belmopan, the first turn is at Georgeville at mile 65. The second is in Santa Elena at mile 72. All the roads into the region are dirt. These two access points converge near the Mayan village of San Antonio.

Garcia Sisters Museum

The Garcia Sisters Museum, located at the base of Mountain Pine Ridge Forest Reserve near the Mayan village of San Antonio (called Ta Nah in Mayan), is one of the more celebrated sources of artwork made by today's Mayans. The five Garcia (Mesh) sisters — Maria (Mai), Sylvia (Che), Piedad (Ocol Ix), Aurora (Lol), and Carmelita (Kaior Nin) — are members of the Uxawall Mayan tribe, which has its roots in Mexico. The Garcia sisters have been producing stone carvings in Mayan motifs and replicating ancient Mayan art or modern themes for years. The "museum" might more accurately be called an art gallery. It's what's for sale that attracts people, not what isn't. Much of the stone work is of jungle animals, which have important symbolic significance for Mayans past and present. I bought a highly stylized vulture figure carved from gray slate. It is now displayed in my living room. Some of the work is nicely done, and some may appeal to less discriminating tourists, especially the pendants. The Garcias appear to keep all price ranges in mind.

The Garcia sisters are personally charming, able self-promoters, and an interesting mix of liberated women and advocates for the resurrection of traditional Mayan ways. They are different from any Mayan women I met anywhere else in Belize. Just talking with the lively and articulate Garcias is worth the trouble of visiting their museum. "Okay, so you're a journalist. I'm going to help you educate people. I'll write down our Mayan names [in parentheses adjacent to each sister's Spanish name in the above text] and list some Mayan words you can share with your readers. This way people from where you live can know about Mayans," offered Aurora Garcia, who ended each burst of words with melodic laughter.

Aurora often serves as spokesperson for the group, but don't let any shyness exhibited by any of the other sisters fool you. When it comes to bargaining, Aurora and her sisters can hold their own with any New York street vendor. The price for the good art isn't cheap, and there's a nominal charge to visit the museum. The actual museum pieces were hard to remember a week after my visit, but the newly created work done in the "Garcia Sisters motif" is what sticks. I still remember a large, beautifully proportioned jaguar figure that was out of my price range.

According to Aurora, she and her sisters work year-round producing carvings that take as long as four months each to create. They transform slate from rough river rock into art by using hacksaws, Exacto knives, and plenty of elbow grease to get the glossy sheen that characterizes most of their art. The slate carvings depict ancient Mayan gods and symbols. "This way we honor our culture and share it with outsiders," said Aurora.

The Garcia sisters grew up in the nearby village of San Antonio (not to be confused with San Antonio in the Toledo District) and were educated there and brought up as Catholics. They now talk about the sorrow of being taught to forget about their historical beliefs and are strong advocates for keeping their traditions alive. Aurora says she and her sisters were inspired by their father, who was among the area's best *chicleros*. The *chicleros* used to spend their lifetimes deep in the forest locating sapodilla trees and bleeding them for chicle, once the key ingredient in chewing gum. "My father always wanted the best for us," explained Aurora. "He never imagined we would be able to make money from art from our little museum on a dirt road off the highway. We were confident our love for art and our heritage would prevail."

The actual museum is a fairly humble-looking structure and should not be taken as an indication of the efforts and marketing savvy of the Garcia sisters. The last line on the sisters' promotional pamphlet captures their unbridled enthusiasm: "Art is old as time itself and beautiful as no one can imagine." You can get in touch with the Garcia sisters by writing to the Garcia Sisters Museum, P.O.

Box 75, San Ignacio, Cayo District, Belize, C.A. (no phone). They take orders and send art abroad.

Access: There is no public transportation to the museum, which is located eight miles from the Western Highway. Turn south at mile 72 in Santa Elena onto Cristo Rey Road (dirt). You'll see Maya Mountain Lodge within the first three-quarters of a mile. If you don't, you're on the wrong road. You can also reach the museum via the turnoff from Georgeville, but it's a longer dirt-road drive. If you're headed to Mountain Equestrian Trails, this route makes the best sense. Most mountain lodges offer visits to the museum, though a few have been feuding with the Garcias about increased visitor fees. Don't miss the museum if you're interested in what Aurora and her sisters have to offer.

Mountain Lodges

The Cayo District is the highland region of Belize, and many visitors access the natural wonders of Cayo through its mountain lodges. Westward on the Western Highway past the intersection of the Hummingbird Highway is the heart of the district. The road begins to climb gradually. To your left the rugged highlands of Mountain Pine Ridge climb to 3300 feet, and close to the Guatemalan border lies the Vaca Plateau. This is an area of sharply plunging terrain, endless jungle, pine forests, occasional rolling pastures with mature cohune palms, large river systems, rushing mountain streams, waterfalls, and bountiful wildlife. In this setting you'll find the lovely town of San Ignacio and the mountain lodges.

The lodges, or resorts, offer highly personalized service for a relatively small number of guests at any one time. Typically, guests stay in thatched-roof bungalows and eat meals in a common dining area. Meals are usually included in room costs. Each day a choice of activities or a set itinerary is laid out for guests. In most cases each excursion is an additional cost, unless you've prepaid your entire stay. The lodges may appear to offer similar services, but I found differences between them in terms of quality of service and prices for identical activities. It pays to shop around by making inquiries via the mail. The range of activities includes visiting Mayan ruins at Tikal in Guatemala or at Xunantunich, Caracol, and Cahal Pech in Belize, canoeing, horseback riding, birding, photographic safaries, wilderness treks, wilderness camping, swimming, and sightseeing in national parks and wilderness areas. The lodge operators are among the better promoters and advertisers in Belize's tourism industry. The price symbols listed below for the lodges — budget (B), moderate (M), and expensive (E) — refer to room rates and in most cases don't include daily activities.

Mountain Equestrian Trails (M, E): This is my favorite mountain lodge because it has the best balance of the bunch. There's an appealing combination of reasonable price, expertise, quality of activities, setting, genuine enthusiasm, and a willingness to please. Owners Marguerite and Jim Bevis have put together an attractive small lodge in low jungle at the foot of the immense and largely pristine Mountain Pine Ridge escarpment. The thatched-roof cottages are artistically built, private, and cozy. The cantina/restaurant is the meeting place for guests, who are served home-grown fruits and vegetables, Texan-style barbecues, and Italian and stir-fry dishes. Guests are a mixed bag. In one evening I met a French couple, two British commandos on R&R, a woman and her daughter from Virginia, and two members of a Canadian film crew who had been in Belize making a nature film. I awoke to a crescendo of bird calls, ate a hearty breakfast, climbed aboard a docile horse, and spent the day riding past lush pasture and through milpas and jungle creeks that cascade downward from Mountain Pine Ridge. The horses were trail-wise and easy to handle. M.E.T. has the deserved reputation of having the best wilderness horse rides in Belize. One- to six-day trips are possible.

However, where Mountain Equestrian shines brightest among the competition is in breadth and quality of the "soft" and "hard" itineraries it offers guests. In a three-day period with the Bevises, I took an all-day horseback ride through a variety of pristine environments (carry binoculars and a bird book), floated through an immense cave in an inner tube, and visited the magnificent ruins at Caracol. Along the way we saw a great deal of jungle wildlife and had a genuine good time. There is something for everyone with the Bevises — even the over-the-edge adventure types can find a kindred soul in Jim Bevis. When I met Jim, he was recovering from a nasty injury that

Jim Bevis of Mountain Equestrian
Trails in the Cayo District.
Photo by Eric Hoffman.

had deadened the nerves in three fingers. He sustained the injury
during a grueling two-week Maya Mountains traverse, which he led
through the trailless heart of the most rugged portion of the Maya
Mountains. The rigors of the journey also resulted in the loss of
twenty pounds for Jim and the first ever recorded walking expedition across the entire Maya Mountains. Near their lodge, the Bevises
also have been instrumental in creating the Slate Creek Preserve,
a 3500-acre sanctuary for the many creatures of the lowland forest.

M.E.T. has developed unique packages that include visiting Barton's Creek Mennonites, rafting through immense caves in inner
tubes, visiting Caracol and Xunantunich, camping in the Chiquibul
Forest Reserve, and visits to such well-known destinations as the Belize Zoo, Crooked Tree Wildlife Sanctuary, the Cockscomb Basin
Wildlife Sanctuary, and the natural sights on Mountain Pine Ridge.
M.E.T. also coordinates its efforts with Rum Point Inn in Placencia
and other companies with excursions to Tikal. For a price, M.E.T.
will meet you at Belize City's international airport or in San Ignacio
if you arrive in the region by bus. Major credit cards are accepted.
Contact Marguerite and Jim Bevis, Mountain Equestrian Trails, Mile
8 Mountain Pine Ridge Road, Central Farm Post Office, Cayo District, Belize, C.A. (phone 082-3180/3310; fax 082-3235/3505).

Maya Mountain Lodge (M, E): Located close to the Western Highway, Maya Mountain Lodge is among the longest-standing mountain lodges in operation. The layout and structures are much like M.E.T.'s, but the closeness to the highway (three-quarters of a mile) and surrounding activities takes away some of the wildness found at other lodges. However, this is one of the few lodges that can be reached by bus. Maya Mountain Lodge is five minutes from San Ignacio by car (for a price, staff will also meet guests at Belize City's international airport) and five minutes by foot from the bus stop at the Esso Station across from Cristo Rey Road (a few miles east of San Ignacio) on the Western Highway. I saw a wide range of bird life around the lodge, including arcani toucans in the fruiting trees.

Owners Suzi and Bart Mickler have compiled impressive reading material about the local environment for their guests. Meals are painstakingly prepared, and the ambience is quiet and usually alcohol free. Maya Mountain offers a host of activities to guests, including visits to Mayan ruins (including Tikal), Mountain Pine Ridge, the Garcia Sisters Museum, market day in San Ignacio, Blue Hole National Park, and Guancaste National Park. The Micklers are also set up to coordinate a lodge stay with coastal destinations in Placencia and elsewhere. Major credit cards are accepted. Contact Bart and Suzi Mickler, Maya Mountain Lodge, 8 Cristo Rey Road, Box 46, San Ignacio, Cayo District, Belize, C.A. (phone 092-2164; fax 092-2029).

Nabitunich Lodge (B, M): Located on a 400-acre horse and cattle operation between San Ignacio and the Guatemalan border, Nabitunich (which means "Stone Cottage") may offer the best deal for the price. The setting is beautiful: lush pastures with cattle, egrets, horses, and large cohune palms. Owners Rudy and Margaret Juan are an interesting couple. He's a Belizean national; she arrived in Belize decades ago from England as a nurse for the United Nations. Margaret has spent much of her life setting up health clinics for rural people outside the reach of medical help. In fact, the lodge itself grew out of a small guesthouse built by the Juans to accommodate groups of doctors who were coming from North America to work in clinics in the area. After a number of years, the Juans decided to expand their accommodations and cater to specialized groups. The thatch and mortared-rock bungalows are tastefully done.

Nabitunich does not have as wide a range of activities as some of the more high-profile lodges, but for someone wanting to meet interesting owners and stay put, this is the place in terms of natural beauty and price. Still, horseback riding, canoeing, swimming, birding, and trips to local ruins are part of most stays. The birding here is excellent, especially along the river bordering the property. "We're mostly known for our friendly hospitality, good food, and country setting," explains Margaret. Only traveler's checks and cash are accepted. Contact Rudy and Margaret Juan, Nabitunich Lodge, San Lorenzo Ranch, Benque Viejo del Carmen, Cayo District, Belize, C.A. (phone 093-2309; fax 093-2096).

Duplooy's Riverside Cottages and Hotel (E): Duplooy's is located on the Mopan River on the south side of the Western Highway west of San Ignacio near the Guatemalan border. Judy and Ken Duplooy have carved out a lodge with an outstanding river view. Judy leads horse rides to the remote Vaca Plateau, where she has located caves with undisturbed Mayan artifacts. Ken has collected a great number of live orchids from nearby forests for his guests' appreciation. The deck that doubles as a dining area and observation platform looks down on jungle foliage that is rich in bird life. Terrestrial wildlife, such as tayras, coatimundis, jaguarundis, and kinkajous are occasionally sighted from the deck. The Duplooys offer many of the same excursions as the aforementioned lodges. The canoe trip to San Ignacio from here is a must. Kingfishers, a number of other water birds, and usually parrots are seen. Ken, a former English colonial from Africa, rates with the best of them as an entertaining storyteller. Major credit cards are accepted. Contact Judy and Ken Duplooy, Duplooy's Riverside Cottages and Hotel, Bid Eddy, San Ignacio, Cayo District, Belize, C.A. (phone 092-2188 or, in the United States and Canada, 1-800-359-0747; fax 092-2057).

Chaa Creek Cottages (E): Located near Duplooy's on the south side of the Western Highway, Chaa Creek is perhaps the most photogenic and best-known lodge in the area. Owners Mick and Lucy Fleming started from scratch more than a decade ago. They are well connected with media types in Belize City, and their prices reflect their stature among the lodges. Chaa Creek is aesthetically stunning, with tastefully built thatch and stucco bungalows overlooking the Macal River. The Flemings' employees take visitors on excursions throughout Mountain Pine Ridge and the ruins at Xunantunich, Caracol, and Tikal. Chaa Creek is also next door to the Panti Trail, on which renowned medicinal plant expert Rosita Arvigo conducts nature walks. The lodge also offers customized tours to all parts of Belize, including the Cockscomb Basin Wildlife Sanctuary, Bermudian Landing Community Baboon Sanctuary, Belize Zoo, and Crooked Tree Wildlife Sanctuary. The Flemings have traveled and lived in remote parts of Kenya, Europe, and North Africa and apply what they've learned about running lodges in other parts of the world to their operation. The cuisine was noted as among the best in Belize by *Belize Review* editor Meb Cutlack. Major credit cards are accepted. Contact Mick and Lucy Fleming, Chaa Creek Cottages, P.O. Box 53, San Ignacio, Cayo District, Belize, C.A. (phone 092-2037; fax 092-2501).

Hidden Valley Inn (E): This small inn may be among the most intriguing of all. It is located in the northern Maya Mountains near Mountain Pine Ridge on an 18,000-acre private estate in an area of pine woodlands and crisscrossing streams lined with orchids, bromeliads, and wildflowers. The inn boasts more than ninety miles of its own trails and an exceptional amount of wildlife. Among bird species here are the endangered ocellated turkey, orange-breasted falcons, and rare congregations of king vultures. The vultures are known to frequent the top of a particular waterfall. Coatimundis, kinkajous, bush dogs, and tayras are common. All five wild cat species living in Belize have been spotted.

Each room has its own fireplace and bath. Freshly cut flowers in your room and a shared reading room are also part of the hospitality. The inn had just taken on a new manager, Neil Rogers, formerly the manager of highly rated Chaa Creek, when I visited. Rogers is a personable Brit. He was busily designing an expanded itinerary for guests when I met him. Among his new ideas was a mountain bike trek that stops at swimming holes every few miles or so. Major credit cards are accepted. Contact Hidden Valley Inn, P.O. Box 170, Belmopan, Belize, C.A. (phone 08-23321; in the United States and Canada, 1-800-334-7942).

Other Lodges: There are a dozen other lodges and camping areas in the highlands around San Ignacio. There are also more conventional and often much less expensive places to stay in San Ignacio. (See "San Ignacio and Santa Elena" and "Benque Viejo del Carmen.") For a full listing of lodges, contact the Belize Tourist Board, 415 Seventh Avenue, New York, NY 10001 (phone 1-800-624-0686 or

212-268-8798; fax 212-695-3018). Ask for a copy of *Belize, the Adventure Coast, Travel Industry Sales Planner*. In Belize, the Belize Tourist Board is located at 83 North Front Street, Belize City, Belize, C.A. (phone 02-77213/73255).

Access: In general, public transportation does not reach the lodges. Buses do run regularly from all points in Belize to San Ignacio and Benque Viejo del Carmen, which are the two towns within a short drive of most of the lodges. For a price, the lodges will pick you up at these towns or even at Belize City's international airport. Always inquire about the cost of this service.

Ix Chel Farm and Panti Mayan Medicine Trail

Ix Chel Farm is located right next to Chaa Creek Cottages on the Macal River. The farm's purpose is to identify medicinal plants and learn all that can be understood about their healing powers. The farm's owners, Rosita Arvigo and her husband, Greg Shropshire, are certified naprapaths from the Chicago National College of Naprapathy. According to *Webster's New Twentieth-Century Dictionary, Unabridged,* "Naprapathy is a system of treatment based on the theory that disease symptoms are due to strained or contracted ligaments and disorders of the connective tissues and can be cured by massage." Arvigo and her husband also refer to themselves as holistic practitioners and herbalists. Visitors to Ix Chel Farm are introduced to a number of plants whose leaves, bark, roots, and juices are thought to have medicinal value.

Arvigo has based much of her knowledge of medicinal plants on the long relationship she's developed with Don Eligio Panti, a ninety-year-old Mayan medicine man from the relatively nearby village of San Antonio. Panti is one of the very few remaining indigenous bush doctors who bases his knowledge and cures on an accumulation of traditional knowledge passed on to him by earlier Mayan medicine men.

Arvigo is representative of a growing number of people who see the importance of recording what men like Panti know. She is also part of an increased awareness that salvation for rain forests may lie in understanding medicinal applications of plants whose healing powers are yet to be understood. Plants such as yew trees and periwinkle from other parts of the world have proven themselves useful in arresting or curing terminal diseases. Staff at the New York Botanical Garden have asked Arvigo to send them plants that she feels have medicinal qualities. She has also been sending plants to the National Cancer Institute. In 1989 Arvigo and her husband developed the Panti Mayan Medicine Trail, where she leads walks for visitors explaining the medicinal uses of plants that Don Eligio Panti has identified as having curative powers. The Panti Trail is among the most popular two- to three-hour outings in the Cayo District.

Arvigo also has founded Rosie's Original Mayan Herb Company, which sells packets of "wild-crafted, hand-chopped, and sun-dried" herbs. According to Arvigo, each packet contains complete instructions for use. Most packets retail for about U.S. $12 for six ounces of remedy. Rosie's offerings include Blood Tonic Tea (for rheumatism, arthritis, toxicity, and fatigue), Balsam Bark Tea (for conditions of the kidneys, bladder, and liver), Billy Webb Bark Tea (for diabetes and hypoglycemia), Female Tonic Tea (for menstrual problems or irregularities and uterine conditions), and Jackass Bitters Tea (for parasites, amoebas, malaria, fungus, ringworms, and yeast infections). Arvigo also conducts seminars on natural healing, healthful living, and herbology.

Access: Most visitors walk the Panti Mayan Medicinal Trail in conjunction with daytime activities from nearby Chaa Creek Cottages, Duplooy's, and other mountain lodges. You can also visit on your own. After leaving San Ignacio on the Western Highway in the direction of the Guatemalan border, look for the turnoff to Chaa Creek and Duplooy's. Follow the dirt road until you come to Chaa Creek. Ix Chel Farm is about a hundred yards southeast of the lodge. To contact Ix Chel Farm, write to Dr. Rosita Arvigo, Ix Chel Farm, San Ignacio, Belize, C.A. (phone 08-23180).

Caracol ("Snail") Natural Monument

Thanks to archaeologists Arlen and Diane Chase, the importance of Caracol as an ancient Mayan center on par with Copan, Palenque, Chichen Itza, and Tikal has become known in the last few years. A visit to Caracol feels like stepping onto the movie set of *Raiders of the Lost Ark*. Only at Caracol it's the real thing, and instead of Harrison Ford and a host of villains, you'll meet a renowned husband and wife archaeology team and their supporting cast of archaeologists, students, and staff (many of them Mayan) camped in the jungle. This team is entirely consumed with pursuing discoveries about the Mayan world. In this regard, Caracol has already paid great dividends. Discoveries here are causing scholars to rewrite previous interpretations of the ancient Mayans.

Caracol is an immense ruin with as many as a hundred archaeologists and support staff hacking and sifting on a daily basis during the dry season through a city center measuring thirty-one square miles. The site is surrounded by remote jungle teeming with wildlife. During the wet season the site is abandoned. Located deep in the interior near the Guatemala border in Chiquibul National Park, Caracol has always been difficult to visit, which accounts for the delay in archaeological efforts.

My memories of Caracol will always be vivid because of the wild setting and pioneer feeling that permeates the place. The site has some spectacular temples. Caana (Sky Palace) is the largest temple among many smaller temples that jut skyward from the jungle floor. It's the most massive and tallest human-made structure in Belize today. It stands 140 feet high, which is 10 feet higher than El Castillo at Xunantunich, the frequently visited ruins near Benque Viejo del Carmen on the Guatemalan border. The Chases predict that Caracol will most likely become the number-one archaeological destination for tourists visiting Belize in the years to come.

Monumental Discoveries: Discovered in 1938 but not explored until 1950, Caracol was initially thought to be one of many small cere-

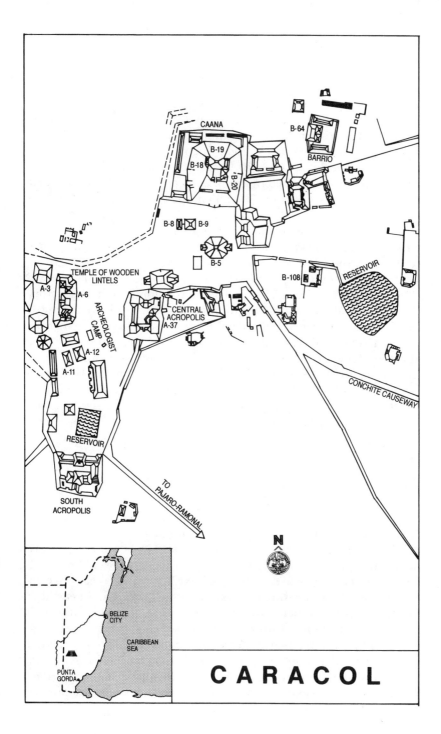

CAANA

B-19

B-18

B-20

B-64

BARRIO

B-8 B-9

B-5

B-108

RESERVOIR

TEMPLE OF WOODEN LINTELS

A-3

A-6

ARCHEOLOGIST CAMP

CENTRAL ACROPOLIS
A-37

A-12

A-11

RESERVOIR

CONCHITE CAUSEWAY

SOUTH ACROPOLIS

TO PAJARO-RAMONAL

N

BELIZE CITY

CARIBBEAN SEA

PUNTA GORDA

CARACOL

monial sites reclaimed by the jungle. When the Chases began work here in 1985, they soon found they were scratching the surface of an immense Mayan center with a metropolitan area measuring seven miles across that was connected to satellite communities by causeways. The Chases conservatively estimated the population of Caracol and its outlying areas at 180,000, which is roughly the population of modern-day Belize. Only in Caracol the population was highly centralized and organized to live in an overall area of less than fifty square miles. This was in A.D. 700, about when Europe was entrenched in the Dark Ages.

In 1986 the Chases' team unearthed a carved stone altar with extensive hieroglyphics that described Caracol's victory over Tikal, once considered the most powerful Mayan center in the entire region. This was an astounding discovery, creating shock waves that are still ricocheting in academic circles. The hieroglyphics told of a victory in A.D. 562 that marked the beginning of 140 years of unchallenged dominance by Caracol of its neighbors, extending over much of Belize and Guatemala. During this period Tikal went into a decline and Caracol experienced a building boom and population explosion probably fueled by the flow of tribute to Caracol. The discovery of Caracol's role in Mayan history helped fill in an important part of the Mayan story, explaining the shifts in power in the region. Among other things, the inscriptions on the stone altar help explain the decline in the quality of construction techniques that had occurred in Tikal after the date of its defeat.

Emphasis on Excavation: Presently the emphasis is on excavation at Caracol, not tourism. Restoration is proceeding, but at a slow pace. Still, there is much to see for anyone vaguely interested in the Mayans, wildlife, or archaeology. The special excitement of visiting Caracol lies in that it is a site whose treasures and important secrets are being interpreted daily by archaeologists from all over the world.

At Caracol you won't see the parklike setting with extensive restored temples and residences like those at Tikal. The unearthing of Caracol is in the beginning stages. You'll see teams of archaeology students from many different countries, camp workers, and the Chases busily at work reconstructing the civilization that once thrived here. The setting is in both primary and secondary tropical forests. Interaction with the archaeological team is stimulating. During my stay I met a Mayan expert from Germany who was wearing a miner's hat as he was being lowered by a rope into a newly discovered tomb. He carried a sketch pad and a machete to dispatch, if necessary, a deadly fer-de-lance that had been seen slithering into the tomb by a student. Later in the day he returned to camp headquarters covered with dirt to exclaim exuberantly that he had found a calendar in the tomb and many important artifacts. For our party of four he took the time to interpret the hieroglyphics on a large stone altar near where our vehicle was parked.

In a long, hutlike structure known as the "lab," the Chases sometimes show visitors the many figurines and pottery that have been collected from the ruins. Some of the finds are astounding. Arlen Chase showed us a jade head that had rested in a stone box filled with liquid mercury. He explained that the contents were so perfectly preserved that cloth that had been locked in the box for more than 2000 years still had its color. What the ritual deposit symbolized could only be guessed at.

In the afternoon an archaeology student took our group for a three-hour walk around Caracol. We investigated a few recently unearthed tombs, walked down an ancient causeway wide enough for two semitractor trailers to drive side by side, watched wild ocellated turkeys (an endangered species) perform their colorful mating rituals, and climbed to the top of Caana, the Sky Palace (carry something to drink if you do this). The Chases found a royal burial of a woman near the temple's top. It is thought that the woman was either a ruler or the wife or mother of a ruler. As far as is known, burying women in royal-type tombs was relatively rare among the Mayans. From the temple's top there is a stunning treetop view of miles of jungle that takes in much of the Vaca Plateau and Chiquibul Forest Reserve. Wildlife was plentiful during our walk. Keel-billed toucans, parrots, hummingbirds, and bright green tree snakes were some of the creatures we came across.

Metropolitan Marvel: The Chases have pieced together a picture of Caracol that makes the metropolis the marvel of its time. All areas between houses and clusters of houses were terraced for agriculture, with crops of corn, beans, squash, and cotton being grown. Rainfall was painstakingly collected in elaborate catchments and channeled to reservoirs with waterproof clay plaster membranes to prevent seepage. One of the ancient reservoirs still holds water that is used by archaeologists and camp workers during the dry season. Caracol had about twenty miles of plaster-coated roads that linked parts of the city together. Roads radiated outward, often to dead ends where market check stations stood. There goods coming and going from the city could be monitored and possibly taxed. Caracol's epicenter, where ball courts, the huge Caana temple, and an acropolis are located, were coated in colorful plasters, depicting the exploits of rulers and successes in battles.

Large Middle Class: The Chases also discovered that a sizeable middle class lived in Caracol, which is contrary to the conventional view of the Mayans as having a small elite of dynastic god/kings with the rest of the society serving them. By assessing garbage left behind by the middle class, Arlen Chase concluded that "Wealth was shared here. A sizeable middle class lived much like the dynastic upper class associated with most centers."

Theory on Mayan Demise: Though many ancient Mayans enjoyed a bountiful and peaceful coexistence with their surroundings, the Chases have also pieced together a great deal of evidence from their work at Caracol and other sites that points to increasingly violent warfare as the reason that Mayan cities were abandoned. "There was a common belief that persisted that the ancient Mayan cities were benevolent places. For periods of time the average Mayan probably felt protected and secure. However, public blood-letting and humiliation through the use of torture were part of what happened to losing rulers," explained Arlen. It is believed that Lord Double Bird, a ruler from Tikal captured in combat about A.D. 562, was kept in a cage and ritualistically bled and tortured in public for several years to commemorate Caracol's victory over Tikal. In the important ball court games, the heads of prisoners were sometimes used instead of balls. Losers in these contests were sometimes sacrificed in hideous ways. The Chases believe that ritualistic torture and the sacrifice of defeated leaders were not disruptive to Mayan society because they usually affected the ruling elite, not the general populace.

However, in the Late Classic Period (A.D. 900–1200), warfare changed. Warfare had been somewhat benign during the Classic Period (A.D. 500–900). Defeated rulers were slain ceremonially and their subjects made to work for the victors. About the time the use of the *atatl*—a throwing device used to propel a spear great distances and with tremendous velocity—came on the scene, the emphasis changed to killing, not taking, prisoners. Suddenly the *tzompnatli* — a rack with skulls displayed — begins to appear in ceremonial centers. "Now they're beheading the commoner, not just the ruler," explained Arlen. "Instead of captive laborers, the object became head-hunting. Murals at other sites show houses being sacked with thatched roofs in flames. The terror of this kind of total warfare raises fundamental questions about leadership and faith in the religious order that was the glue to the social fabric of ancient Mayan society. The civilization's governmental foundation erodes. The Mayan civilization doesn't entirely die. It merely disperses into the bush and becomes more benign." Why the bloody escalation between population centers occurred is not known, but depletion of the soil, drought, and too many people in too small an area may have been contributing factors that fueled the quest to conquer and annihilate competing centers of power.

Tourist-proofing: As the excavations come to a close in an area, restoration is undertaken. So far, only three areas in Caracol's center have undergone restoration, which Arlen refers to as "tourist-proofing." Included in the effort is A Group, a major plaza that once was an observatory area; the South Acropolis, once a residential area for the wealthy; and Caana, the immense, pyramidlike temple that has tombs and former residences for high-ranking officials on its flanks. "Someday we hope to have a great deal more of Caracol tourist-proofed, including some of the outlying areas, so visitors will get a sense of the size and complexity of this place," explained Arlen, who pointed out that the will to open the treasures of Caracol to the outside world is limited by funding, which has been sporadic.

Special Permission Requirement: It is imperative to contact the Department of Archaeology and/or the Western Division of Forestry prior to a visit for permission and advice on accessibility.

Accommodations: Camping is allowed, but only with a special permit issued by the Department of Archaeology in Belmopan. Most people visit Caracol in a day trip from one of the Cayo District's mountain lodges (see "Access" and "Mountain Lodges").

Access: Getting to Caracol used to be a major challenge, possible only in dry spells in a very solid four-wheel-drive, providing you could get a permit from the Department of Archaeology. Today, if you show up without a permit you may be asked to go get one, and in the process you'll lose two days or more time. For years a special German-made, all-terrain, indestructible mechanical marvel called a Unimog was the vehicle of choice for tour groups attempting to reach Caracol. Horses were also used. The Unimog days seem to be over. The road has been improved. Now, reaching Caracol as part of an organized adventure-travel group has a better than average chance of succeeding during the dry season.

The route to Caracol is through Augustine in the Mountain Pine Ridge Forest Reserve. (If you're driving, be sure you start out with a full tank as there is no gas in Augustine. The nearest gas is on the Western Highway.) The site is thirty miles from Augustine, but the road can be extremely treacherous and slow. Generally, the road is regarded as impassable during the wet season. The government has hired Mennonite heavy-equipment operators to widen the road, hoping this will offer longer periods of access. Most visitors arrive in a four-wheel-drive as part of a travel package of one of the Cayo District's mountain lodges. Mountain Equestrian Trails provides reliable service and good company for competitive prices. Contact Jim and Marguerite Bevis, Mountain Equestrian Trails, Central Farm Post Office, Cayo District, Belize, C.A. (phone 082-3180/3310; fax 082-3235/3505). (See also "Mountain Lodges"; most lodges listed there offer trips to Caracol.)

Chiquibul Forest Reserve and National Park

The Chiquibul Forest Reserve has been an unknown region, not much more than a place name on the map, even to people in the Western Division of Forestry in Belmopan. But new knowledge about the area's biodiversity and endangered bird life resulted in the government splitting the reserve and redesignating much of it in December 1991. More than half of the Chiquibul was declared a national park. The original Chiquibul Forest Reserve covered 714 square miles (or 456,000 acres). The new Chiquibul National Park of 265,894 acres enjoys the most protection possible under Belizean law.

The reason for the national park designation is to safeguard the remote region's natural treasures, which are only beginning to be catalogued and understood. The entire Chiquibul region is uninterrupted rain forest, and the new national park carved out of it contains some rare natural gems. Caracol Natural Monument, which is enjoying ever-increasing significance among the Mayan ruins of Mesoamerica, and the identification of endangered bird species contributed to the upgrade to park status. Two birds living here rate high in beauty and rareness. Wildlife Conservation International scientists Bruce and Carolyn Miller found the very rare and endangered keel-billed motmot, a graceful bird with the cackle of a chicken, sleek lines, a rufous forehead, and a rich green crown. The area also harbors the endangered scarlet macaw, a spectacular red, gold, and blue, three-foot-long member of the parrot family that has been eliminated throughout most of Central America due to habitat destruction and the pet trade. About a dozen other endangered species enjoy the solitude of these forests.

The national park came into being after a strong lobbying effort by Bruce and Carolyn Miller, the Belize Audubon Society, the Belize Zoo and Tropical Education Center, and other serious conservationists in Belize. The Millers believe the Chiquibul region is among the richest places they've surveyed in terms of bird and plant life. A biodiversity study of all creatures and plants is in the works. Shrouded in rain forest, the area is crisscrossed with watercourses and deep, twisting canyons, which guarantees that traipsing through the area to figure out what's there is the challenge of a lifetime.

The new national park is bordered on the north by the Vaca Forest Reserve, on the east by the remainder of the Chiquibul Forest Reserve and the Maya Mountain Forest Reserve, on the south by the Columbia Forest Reserve, and on the west by the Guatemalan border. Since Chiquibul National Park isn't designated on most maps, you can find its general vicinity by locating Caracol on a map.

Still, maps of the region are deceptive. They show a number of place names south of Augustine where the park is, including Caracol, which is occupied during the dry season when archaeological efforts are under way. But other places on the map—such as Millinario, San Pastor, and Reforma—are names of abandoned logging camps. For the most part, the Chiquibul region is void of people.

Getting around in this area in the dry season is accomplished by the Cayo District's mountain lodge operators using four-wheel-drive vehicles or horses. Chaa Creek Cottages, Duplooy's, and Mountain Equestrian Trails are among those who take people into this region. Aside from Caracol, each of these lodges is fairly secretive about exactly where they take their clients—and for good reason. If they were to share their destinations with competitors, truly unique experiences would be lost for future clients. For example, when I interviewed Mick Fleming, co-owner of Chaa Creek Cottages, he described an uninhabited rain-forest river system where customers stand a good chance of seeing a tapir and are sometimes kept alert at night by the cough of a jaguar. Seeing a tapir with any kind of regularity is a coup in the adventure travel business. Judy Duplooy, of Duplooy's Riverside Cottages and Hotel, discovered caves with rows of Mayan pottery that have been sitting where they were left during the peak of the Mayan civilization more than a thousand years ago. My only foray into the region was during a visit to Caracol, which possessed an impressive variety of wildlife despite the presence of human beings. The Chiquibul area will become better known in years to come. It is a region with great promise for the naturalist and adventure traveler.

Accommodations: There are no accommodations in either the Chiquibul National Park or Forest Reserve. Camping should be attempted only through one of the mountain lodges.

Access: Contact the mountain lodges. Trying to operate on your own in this region would be foolhardy at the least and possibly life-threatening.

Benque Viejo del Carmen

Benque Viejo del Carmen is a tiny border town that does nothing to improve the image of border towns. The place looks a little run-down and sleepy. If you find yourself there overnight waiting for the border to open or buses to run, there are places to eat and stay. George Street is the main street. One of the better places is El Indio Perdido (B, M), located out of town at Collar Creek. In town, try Hotel Central (B), on the corner of Churchill and Diaz streets (phone 093-2080), or Maya Motel, 11 George Street (phone 093-2116). With the exception of El Indio, these are cash-only operations. They offer continental breakfasts. If you can, get down the road eight miles to Burns Avenue in San Ignacio. This is where the memorable social and aesthetic atmosphere is.

Crossing the Border into Guatemala: You need a valid passport; a visa is issued on the spot. Usually the border is open from 6:00 A.M. to 12:00 midnight. Often there's an undeclared delay around lunch that extends to 2:00 P.M.. The first time I tried crossing, I was in a rental car. The Guatemalans had no problem taking my fifty quetzales (about U.S. $9) for departure tax after informing me I couldn't take a rental car into Guatemala. I had been in Guatemala for about sixty seconds. There is no charge to enter Guatemala, but you are charged fifty quetzales upon departure.

The history between Guatemala and Belize has been tense, but less so in recent years due to Guatemala finally recognizing Belize's sovereignty. Crossing is usually efficiently handled, taking only about fifteen minutes unless it's crowded. Both countries take turns processing you and seem to enjoy stamping your passport many times. There's a no-man's-land of about a hundred yards between the two customs stations. You'll be approached by money changers both on the Belizean side and in the no-man's-land. You may want to exchange a little money here because Belizean currency isn't honored far past the border. You'll also be approached by mini-car drivers wanting to take you to Tikal (about U.S. $60 both ways for the 170-mile round trip). We rented a mini-van driven by Angel, a sometimes preacher, hunter, and tour guide. He turned out to be fine.

As for buses, both countries turn them around at the border. There usually isn't a long wait between transfers from one bus system to the next. Check with Novelo's in Benque Viejo del Carmen (phone 093-2054). The town on the Guatemalan side, Melchor de Mencos, is a ramshackle border town with innumerable cheap tourist shops in clapboard structures. You can take a cab to Melchor de Mencos and try to find something to buy, though it's mostly a low-end-oriented place. There are some nice prints of ancient Mayan art that are of good quality. Being able to speak Spanish will make a foray here worthwhile.

We were not stopped in our mini-van further along the road to Tikal, but we saw buses being pulled over often at army checkpoints. On one occasion tourists were being searched at gunpoint by the army. Angel, the driver of our van, passed all such unpleasantries with a wave. "They know me," he assured us as they waved back. We made it to Tikal without a single stop.

Caution: Guatemala has a poor human-rights record. There was a coup there in May 1993. Coups are commonplace, as are highway bandits and abuses of Guatemalan citizens by the army. It's not wise to investigate remote areas without a local to interpret events. Be aware that due process is a fleeting concept in Guatemala. Tourists who are detected carrying dope or acting "dopey" find themselves in a heap of trouble fast. A slovenly personal appearance can also cause you problems. If you're a journalist, it's not wise to have this fact typed onto your temporary visa. The army has checkpoints manned by teenage soldiers, all of them armed with automatic weapons. At night, the road between Melchor de Mencos and Tikal is a virtual foot highway used by humans, horses, pigs, and cattle. Driving, even as a passenger, should be avoided at night.

Tikal National Park, Guatemala

"Tikal is overwhelming. The magnificent temples in a rich jungle setting teeming with wildlife overloads the senses like nowhere else I've been. As I investigated the pyramids and palaces, monkeys played in the giant trees above my head. While I walked down a jungle path, three scarlet macaws screeched past me," recalled longtime world traveler and friend Mike Larrabee after his visit to Tikal. Larrabee's curiosity about humankind's past has taken him to dozens of the best-known ancient ruins in Mesoamerica and on many other continents during the last forty years. His sentiments are echoed by practically everyone who visits Tikal, including this author. Tikal—a Mayan name whose meaning has been lost — is simply an astounding, unforgettable place. You'll be struck by architectural grandeur, artistic refinement, and still unsolved mysteries of the ancient Mayans, and you'll be doing this in a rich lowland and rain forest setting that is part of an immense sanctuary containing thousands of kinds of plants and animals. Many of the creatures seen around the ruins today are depicted in the ancient Mayan art found at Tikal. The conclusion is that not much has changed here, environmentally speaking, since the days when ornately dressed priests stood on the steps of the great temples before the Mayan throngs, which numbered around 55,000 when Tikal was at its zenith.

National Park: Today the creatures living in and around Tikal enjoy total protection in Tikal National Park, the 222-square-mile preserve surrounding the ruins. The park is managed by the Director of National Parks, who operates under the Institute of Anthropology and History of Guatemala. The director is responsible for maintaining roads and trails, consolidating and restoring the ruins, and protecting wildlife. Hunting and molesting wildlife is forbidden.

The park boundary is located in Guatemala about 85 miles west of the Belize border or 190 air miles north of Guatemala City. Tikal is famous the world over for its ruins; however, the pristine jungles surrounding the ruins support a healthy web of wildlife in great profusion, adding a dimension to exploring these ruins that you won't find in many other places.

The ruins are celebrated for two basic reasons. First, the techniques and aesthetic sense of the ancient building of Tikal is on a scale and refinement rivaling any other site. Second, these ruins have undergone lengthy and expensive excavation, consolidation, and restoration (see "Nomenclature" below), allowing much of their full grandeur to be seen and appreciated in their superb natural setting.

Nomenclature: When talking about Tikal there is a nomenclature that deserves mention. In park literature and from the lips of park guides you will hear the terms *consolidation* and *restoration.* Consolidation deals with reclaiming an existing structure from the forest and securing its structural integrity by strengthening masonry with new plaster or merely cutting away invasive roots. Restoration goes a step further than consolidation. It involves partially rebuilding an existing structure by bringing in materials (bricks, lintels, etc., often from the remains of different structures) and reconstructing a portion of a structure to bring about a more complete appearance. Another term I initially found confusing was the use of the term *temple*. In the Tikal lexicon, a temple is a huge pyramid structure standing above 125 feet in height. The smaller pyramids are simply called pyramids or shrines. There are five major temples in Tikal and numerous smaller pyramids and shrines.

Scope of Archaeological Effort: The ruins exposed and maintained for public viewing cover about six square miles, though the metropolitan area was much bigger during Tikal's heyday, about A.D. 550. Much of the excavation, consolidation, and restoration at Tikal occurred during an intensive eleven-year effort by the University Museum of the University of Pennsylvania during the 1950s and early 1960s, though Europeans had been working at the site as far back as the 1800s. The earlier work ranged from pillaging in the name of science to serious academic and scientific efforts to record and save what was found. More recently, the Guatemalan-run Tikal National Project has been responsible for expanding the area restored for the public.

The six square miles that have been reclaimed from the forest, sifted, analyzed, and restored have yielded a great volume of knowledge. The more than 2800 constructions that have been explored consist of temples, residences, ceremonial platforms, ball courts, tombs, plazas, sweat baths, palaces, marketplaces, dumps, terraces, and causeways. The unique Mayan monuments known as stelae (vertically displayed stones, often covered in hieroglyphics and weighing many tons) and altars (round, drumlike stones also usually weighing tons) are found here in abundance, usually one paired with the other. There are also numerous carvings, often in rot-resistant wood placed in lintels over doorways. Many of these lintels have been removed and now reside in various museums around the world; a few remain.

Often the ruins reclaimed from the forest rest on top of previous structures. Even after archaeologists have spent decades tunneling through temples to figure out how many structures have been built underneath the ones visible today, it's estimated that lying beneath the mapped buildings are more than 1000 structures that will never be excavated. Construction went on at the site for 1100 years without interruption and for another 600 years with only a few lulls prior to the civilization's collapse. Hundreds of burial chambers and entombed offerings have been found, as have strange tunnels known as *chultuns*. More than 100,000 smallish artifacts, such as personal jewelry, gardening tools, weapons, ceremonial pendants and knives, pottery, carvings, and the like, have been unearthed and recorded.

An aspect of Tikal that is sometimes difficult to grasp is that today's ruins and artifacts span a human occupation that exceeded 1600 years, not counting the post-collapse period, which accounts for a few more centuries. In this great expanse of time, changes occurred in pottery and building techniques and in the culture itself. There are three basic eras. The Pre-Classic Period started about 600 B.C. and lasted until A.D. 250. The Classic Period is divided in two stages here: Early Classic, from A.D. 250 to 550, and Late Classic, which followed until Tikal's fall in about A.D. 900. Most of the buildings visible today are from the Late Classic, when Tikal was at its largest and most impressive. The third era is the Post-Classic Period, from A.D. 900 to 1200, which commenced after the culture's collapse. During this period the Mayans remained here, worshipping and living, but with a neglectful and even destructive bent toward the works of their ancestors.

The Ruins

Enjoying the ruins is done by walking down ancient Mayan causeways (named after modern-day archaeologists) that crisscross the site. Most tourists spend from one to three days in Tikal. Depending on your priorities you can easily spend a week in Tikal just visiting all the major ruins and attempting to absorb the significance of each temple, altar and stela, or acropolis. However, you can come away satisfied and awestruck in just a one-day visit, which is one of the most popular ways of visiting the park, especially from Belize.

Great Plaza: This is the impressive center of the ruins. It is located on a footpath about a mile from the parking area and museum. You'll first notice Temple I rising 145 feet above the trees and other ruins. Temple I sits at the east end of the Great Plaza facing Temple II, an equally imposing pyramid. Flanked by Temples I and II on the east and west, the Great Plaza is further surrounded by the North

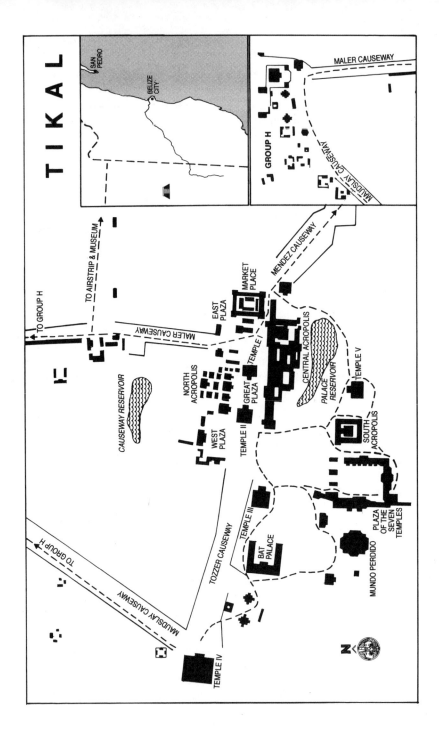

Acropolis and the Central Acropolis, two immense labyrinths of buildings. The plaza itself takes up about two-and-a-half acres. Excavations have revealed four plaster floors that were laid down as early as 150 B.C. and as late as A.D. 700.

Today the Great Plaza consists of mostly grass with stelae and altars whose inscriptions tell of the past glories of Tikal's rulers. At the plaza you are surrounded by temples, palaces, and other structures. This is a great place for a picnic lunch.

Temple I: Known as the Temple of the Giant Jaguar, this 145-foot-tall structure is a classic Mayan temple. A steep stairway goes up the center of the structure, which was used by ancient priests to carry out ceremonies and rituals. The pyramid has nine sloping terraces. In Mayan architecture nine is a reoccurring number that is thought to have had religious significance. Temple I was built over centuries with succeeding generations building atop an earlier edifice. Limestone plaster and rock were the primary building components. The present temple was completed in the Late Classic Period around A.D. 700.

One of the richest tombs unearthed at Tikal was found in Temple I. Known as "burial 116," the tomb was that of a large man, thought to have been a leader. Buried with him were 200 pieces of jade jewelry, pearls, seashells from the Pacific Ocean, and a headdress weighing about fifteen pounds. The tomb produced a great deal of knowledge about trade routes and customs. Scientists date the burial to about the time of the last construction phase in the Late Classic. For me (a nonarchaeologist), the most interesting object to be found in burial 116 is an entirely delightful piece of carved human leg bone depicting a canoe being paddled by two gods with stylized passengers who are jungle creatures. Though it may not have been so intended by the ancient artist who created it, this carving of passage to another world projects a warm, appreciative feeling toward the creatures of the forest and humankind's relationship with them. The carved bone is found in the Museum Sylvanus Morley, one of the two on-site museums. Enlarged prints of this carving can be purchased throughout Guatemala. It is believed that the burial of an important person, such as burial 116, was conducted at the base of the temple just prior to commencement of construction, or when construction was begun anew on an existing structure. In this case the burial may have coincided with a renewal of construction.

Temple I in the Great Plaza
at Tikal, Guatemala.
Photo by Mike Larrabee.

Temple I is impressive, but not as awesome a sight as during its days as an active Mayan shrine. Plaster and paint remnants suggest that the entire temple was coated in red plaster, with its roof comb at the top coated in blues and greens. Highly ornate friezes added embellishment. Priestly leaders dressed in ornate and cumbersome costumes slowly ascended and descended the steep stairs to carry out their ritualistic and astronomical duties. There are chambers inside each temple that were used for ritualistic purposes. The temples were for the ruling priestly elite to use and for the commoners to observe. There is a small ball court on the immediate south side of Temple I.

Temple II: Temple II faces Temple I from the west end of the Great Plaza. This temple is also known as the Temple of the Masks because of the large stone masks at the foot of the stairway leading to the top of the temple. Temple II is 125 feet high and has three terraces instead of nine like its counterpart. Its roof comb is missing, which decreases its height a great deal. Temple II balances the Great Plaza as a nearly equally imposing bookend to Temple I. With its comb, Temple II may have been the same height as Temple I. The temple was completed in its present form in about A.D. 700. It was used for the same kinds of rituals practiced at Temple I.

To casual visitors, the excitement about Temple II is that you are permitted to climb it. The fifty-one steps to the top are very steep — the incline is forty-five degrees. Descending from this temple is more of a challenge than going up. There is no guard rail; so if you take a tumble, you may go quite a distance. From the top you'll find an excellent view of the plaza and nearby acropolis, ball courts, and palaces. On the temple's upper platform are ancient Mayan graffiti thought to have been etched in the stone during the Late Classic and Post-Classic periods. Unfortunately there's also some twentieth-century graffiti as well. There are scenes of a bound prisoner being run through with a spear. The largest stela (uncarved) found in Tikal was found at the base of Temple II.

Stelae and Altars: Throughout Tikal you'll come across pairings of a large, multi-ton, tombstone-like stone standing vertically before a large, cylindrical stone with a face measuring perhaps four feet across. The vertical stela and the cylindrical altar are often ornately carved. The carvings usually depict a historical event as it pertains to a powerful individual. The inscriptions and artwork are stylized and representative of sometimes individualistic and usually intricate hieroglyphics associated with all time periods of the ancient Mayans. There are more than 70 such altars and stelae in the Great Plaza and nearby North Acropolis. In all, more than 250 altars and stelae have been recovered. Not all stelae have hieroglyphics. The stories told on stelae and altars are often about victorious battles and are frequently dated, which helps archaeologists understand what occurred during particular periods of time.

Oddly, succeeding generations often smashed the faces on stelae, destroying the caricatures of the previously glorified individuals. You'll notice such stelae with damaged faces. Even more puzzling is that even though many of the altars and stelae that you'll see were found in their present positions, archaeologists have determined that many of them were moved at great effort by Mayans living during the Post-Classic Period. In some instances, an altar from the Pre-Classic

Period was found neatly placed next to a stela from the Late Classic Period — each with carvings that tell of events that took place centuries apart. Why Mayans living around A.D. 1200 undertook this task is not known. Perhaps it was some sort of attempt to revive their culture. Today, each altar and stela is marked with a red numeral that will help you identify it and read about its history in literature you can purchase at the park. For more details about the origins of Tikal's stelae and altars, buy a copy of *Tikal: A Handbook of the Ancient Mayan Ruins,* by archaeologist William Coe. Not all stelae and altars are described, but many are. Coe's book is published by the University Museum of the University of Pennsylvania. It can be purchased at the Tikal Museum (see below) or in the United States or Canada.

North Acropolis: This is an immense and elaborate two-and-a-half acres of ruins sitting atop a hand-filled platform directly north of the Great Plaza. Building started here in 100 B.C. What you see is merely where it ended in A.D. 900. Temples are the dominant structures. Still, this area has the greatest concentration of architecture from the Early Classic Period. You'll see buttressed walls and large stone faces. Many of the artifacts recovered here are found at the on-site Tikal Museum. The area has also produced some of the more notable tombs. One particularly bizarre burial took place here. A tomb from the fifth century A.D. yielded what has been surmised to have been a priest accompanied in death by nine servants, nine crocodiles, and nine turtles. Everyone except the priest was killed to be part of the entombment.

Central Acropolis: This acropolis is twice as large as the North Acropolis and, like the North Acropolis, was built over centuries before it arrived at its final form. It is primarily known for its six ball courts and its palaces, the latter having served as either living quarters for the power elite or administrative offices. There is still disagreement among archaeologists as to what these stone edifices with family-size sleeping platforms were used for. There are few food preparation areas and no signs of garbage, which would normally be associated with residential blocks.

Temple III: Also called the Temple of the Jaguar Priest because of a carving found here of a hideously obese priest wearing a jaguar-skin robe, Temple III is found on the causeway between the Great Plaza and Temple IV. Temple III stands 180 feet tall and contains three ceremonial rooms, not the usual two found in the other pyramids. The temple is still mostly covered in dirt and vegetation, but the rooms have been somewhat restored. You can reach the rooms and view the carving of the priest by scrambling up the east side of the temple.

Bat Palace and Twin Pyramid Complex: If you continue along the tree-shrouded causeway from Temple III to Temple IV, you will pass the Bat Palace (a series of rooms, most likely for day-to-day living) and the Twin Pyramids (two identical, middle-size pyramids on an east-west orientation). Two side-by-side, smallish pyramids is a reoccurring theme at Tikal. Built in A.D. 711, the stelae and altars at these pyramids are particularly well preserved and contain a great deal of information that has allowed dating of the site. One altar depicts two priests in discussion surrounded by human bones!

Temple IV: This is the largest pyramid of all. To the top of its roof comb, this gargantuan pyramid measures 212 feet high, making it a candidate for the tallest standing human-made structure in the Americas prior to the European conquest. Considering that its construction was managed without draft animals or machines, the temple, like the rest of Tikal, is a phenomenal feat. Ancient Mayans transported more than 250,000 cubic yards of material to build Temple IV, according to William Coe, who also points out in his book that the only pre-Conquest temple that may have been higher is the Pyramid of the Sun at Teotihuacán, near Mexico City. Temple IV was built in about A.D. 750.

This temple is a lot of fun to scale. From the top, vistas of endless jungles of the Peten area of Guatemala and beyond stretch out in all directions. The only breaks in the treetop view are other temples poking above the canopy. The most immediate great temple to the south is Temple V, which is part of the South Acropolis and very near the Plaza of Seven Temples. You can also see Temples I, II, and III.

The route up Temple IV requires a degree of athleticism and will power. You must scramble up steep paths and occasionally hang onto branches to stop from sliding back down. Near the top on the temple's south side you can scale a ladder with rungs spaced more for a giant than normal-size people. This will put you at the base of the building's magnificent top comb.

Temple V: The fifth great pyramid of Tikal is located east of the South Acropolis. It is immense and measures 190 feet high. It is unique because despite its size it has only one tiny, hallway-like room (instead of the normal two or three average-size rooms) for priests to carry out their ceremonies. People are not allowed to climb to the top of Temple V.

Other Ruins: Other areas that are particularly interesting include the Twin Pyramid Complexes P and M, the Temple of the Inscriptions, the Lost World Complex (featuring a 100-foot pyramid), the Pyramid of Perishable Temple, the East Plaza (a five-acre marketplace), the Plaza of the Seven Temples, the Group H buildings, numerous ancient reservoirs, and the four ancient causeways that connect the ruins.

Wildlife

Walking the trails around Tikal is a treat, especially at dawn or dusk, when the creatures of the forest are most active. Many of the causeways are shaded by towering, 150-foot ceiba trees and other rain forest species. There are numerous spider monkey troops in the forests within the ruins. They usually stay high in the canopy and are first noticed when seed pods and bits of fruit dropped by them suddenly appear on the jungle floor. There are plenty of other animals as well. Around the parking area, museums, and restaurants you're likely to see ocellated turkeys, which prefer the open, grassy areas near the trailheads leading to the ruins. The ocellated turkey is a spectacularly colorful large bird that is easy to photograph. The resident flock of scarlet macaws is also usually in this area; the birds often land in trees near the restaurants and museums in hopes of handouts or leftovers from somebody's lunch. Terrestrial jungle creatures and birds of the rain forest are often sighted on the trails. I saw spider monkeys, a jaguarundi, two foxes, a tayra, a green snake, toucans, motmots, parrots, tinamous, and hummingbirds. I talked to people who had seen jaguars, deer, and peccaries during the week of my visit.

Museums

Two excellent museums are maintained at Tikal. As you near the parking area you'll notice the Tikal Museum (or Museo Litco) on the left side of the road across from the Comedor Maya restaurant. The Tikal Museum was completed in 1964 and has a scale model in relief of most of the ruins of Tikal. This excellent miniature model is worth studying before heading out to walk the ruins. The museum also houses objects recovered by the Tikal Project, a Guatemalan-managed group working with the Director of National Parks and the University Museum of the University of Pennsylvania. On exhibit are stelae, altars, pottery, shell, jade, and stone objects that were artistically crafted by ancient Mayans. Numerous publications can be purchased here as well. For me, the best was William Coe's *Tikal: A Handbook of the Ancient Mayan Ruins,* which costs U.S. $10. Coe is an archaeologist who knows Tikal well. His book is detailed, a little dry, but very readable, and includes a map of the ruins.

The second museum, Museum (or Museo) Sylvanus Morley, is named after a famous archaeologist. It contains a stela with a Mayan calendar, a reconstructed burial, ceramic pottery from different eras, jewelry, weapons of war, and the famous stylized canoe scene carved on a human leg bone. This museum is on the right near the hotels as you head toward the Great Plaza.

Additional Information

Guides, Entrance Fees, and Shopping: You can hire a guide for about U.S. $30 a day. Ask at the Tikal Museum. There is a fee of less than U.S. $10 for entering the park and charges for visiting the museums. The hotels sell weavings from the interior of Guatemala and prints of ancient Mayan art.

Be Prepared: The best time to visit Tikal is during the dry season, from February into May. December through February can be surprisingly cool. June into November is a time of regeneration, which includes the rainy season. March to May are the hot months, when trees lose leaves. However, many trees also flower during these months. Take along rain gear. And always have sunscreen, a hat, comfortable walking clothes, and insect repellent, though usually you can get by without it most of the time. Carry a snack and fluid on your tour of the ruins. Once you walk into the ruins it's a fairly long way back out to get food and something to drink.

Caution: See "Benque Viejo del Carmen" for my views on some of the harsh realities of traveling in Guatemala. Basically, Tikal National Park is very well run. However, Guatemala has a shaky human-rights record, which means if you do something stupid, such as carry dope or disobey directions at a roadblock, you may be treated harshly. The road to the park is bumpy, dusty, often shared with livestock and people, and sometimes aggravatingly slow due to army checkpoints. It also gives you a glimpse of rural poverty, in case you haven't seen what is meant by "sub-subsistence" living. You should avoid driving the road at night for about a dozen reasons. Pedestrians and livestock on the road are difficult to see. The army can be intimidating when teenage soldiers stop your vehicle, ask you to get out, and then go through your papers with machine guns at the ready. They are usually courteous and serious. Their directions and requests are generally in Spanish. Rebels and bandits also sometimes operate along the highway, but only a few incidents involving tourists are reported each year. Thousands of people travel the road without incident.

To play it safe, I recommend entrusting your journey to seasoned Guatemalan tour operators and mountain lodge operators in Belize's Cayo District who know the dangers and changing conditions along this stretch of highway. If the road in and out of Tikal is a bit too adventuresome for you, fly to Flores and take a cab or bus to Tikal. Inside, Tikal National Park is reportedly quite safe, and my experiences there were relaxed and entirely trouble-free.

Accommodations and Eateries: There is an assortment of places to stay at Tikal, all of them small operations with minimal impact on the park's idyllic setting and well-maintained grounds. Hotel Jaguar (B) has cabana/tents for U.S. $8 per night and accepts cash or traveler's checks only. The Jungle Lodge (M) has thirty-two individual bungalows, each with a private bath and electricity. The lodge serves three meals a day for reasonable prices. For advance reservations, contact Antonio Ortiz, Jungle Lodge, 29 Calle 180-01, Zona 12, Guatemala City, Guatemala, C.A. (phone 768775/770570; fax 760294).

For price and quality, this was the best deal. Practically next door is the Tikal Hotel (M). It has a cozy restaurant and nice rooms. You can also stay in nearby Flores at the Hotel El Camino Real (M, E). I had an excellent fried chicken lunch at the Comedor Maya (B), a small outdoor restaurant across from the Tikal Museum. This was the best place for the price.

Access: Tikal is about eighty-five miles west of the Belize/Guatemala border. Many of Belize's mountain lodges in the Cayo District can arrange a trip for you; in fact, many offer a one-day Tikal excursion in package deals (see "Mountain Lodges"). Regardless of how your trip is arranged, you must have a valid passport. If the lodge operator has advance notice, he or she can arrange for your visitor's pass ahead of time and will provide for your transportation. You can also take your chances at the border by hiring a Guatemalan with a minivan. If you take this route, you can cut costs by joining with others going in the same direction. After some bartering, we split the all-day rental of $130 among five people. The drive took a little more than two hours, and we didn't have to go through the lengthy stops and searches to which bus travelers are often subjected at numerous Guatemalan army checkpoints. Note that rental cars from Belize are not allowed to cross the border into Guatemala. Commercial bus is very cheap, but it takes longer and may involve those extra checkpoint hassles. Taking your own vehicle into Guatemala is not something I can recommend, but if you insist, have an international insurance policy that covers all contingencies.

Air travel is the fastest and most trouble-free way of visiting Tikal in one day from Belize. Tropic Air has regularly scheduled flights to Tikal from Ambergris Caye and Belize City's international airport. The fare is about U.S. $200 for a round-trip ticket. Contact Tropic Air in the United States or Canada at 1-800-422-3435 or in Belize at 02-45671. Island Air also provides this service but sometimes only seasonally; phone 02-31140/026-2180. You can also schedule a visit to Tikal through Aerovias Airlines directly from the United States or Canada. In North America, phone 305-885-1775; in Belize, phone 02-75445.

SIX

ORANGE WALK DISTRICT

Overview

Located north-northeast of the Belize District, the Orange Walk District is Belize's second-largest district, encompassing 1790 square miles. The district is landlocked between the Belize and Corozal districts to the east, Guatemala to the west, and Mexico to the north. It is sparsely populated, with about 10,000 people in Orange Walk Town, the district's largest town. The rest of the population lives in small villages in the eastern half of the district. Most of the district is involved in agriculture, primarily sugar cane. Prior to sugar cane, logging was the primary source of income. The western half of the district is mostly uninhabited, ecologically diverse, and wildlife-rich rain forest that can be accessed by visiting either Chan Chich Lodge or the Rio Bravo Conservation and Management Area (known as the Rio Bravo Project). The district is a mix of Creole, Mennonite, Mayan, but mostly Hispanic residents. Though there is no citified hub worth a great deal of time and no coastline, the Orange Walk District should not be overlooked. It offers some of the best natural destinations in Belize, and in the case of Chan Chich, possibly in all of Central America.

Three destinations in the Orange Walk District loom as extremely worthwhile: the Lamanai ruins on the New River (easily accessible by boat), the 202,000-acre Rio Bravo Project run by Programme for Belize (not for everyone since it's more difficult to access and has spartan accommodations), and Chan Chich Lodge, a top contender for the best jungle lodge experience in Central America. Chan Chich is located in the middle of 140,000 acres of privately owned and managed rain forest on property adjoining the Rio Bravo Project.

Orange Walk Town

Orange Walk Town is the hub of Belize's second-largest district. Located on the west bank of the New River on the Northern Highway, the town is sixty-six miles (or ninety minutes by car) from Belize City. Its 10,000 residents are mostly Hispanic, with more Spanish spoken here than in any other hub in Belize. Orange Walk Town is sometimes referred to as the "breadbasket" of Belize, because most of the district derives its living from agriculture, mostly sugar cane. The town is not geared to tourism, yet has all the basics in terms of accommodations, gas station, public transportation, restaurants, food stores, and clothing. For tourists or travelers, Orange Walk Town usually amounts to a gasoline or food stop, possibly a hotel room, but not much more. Most needs can be met simply by finding the appropriate store on the Northern Highway through town. A Shell Station is located at the south end of town.

History: Orange Walk Town was originally known as a logging center and later as an area whose residents, living on milpas, made their livelihood as *chicleros* and maize farmers. With a large sugar cane factory just south of town, the entire area is now primarily involved in the seasonal harvesting and processing of sugar cane.

Historically, Orange Walk Town was the scene of ongoing warfare between the Spanish and the Mayans, who resisted being subjugated to European powers. The last skirmish was in 1876, when the famous Mayan leader and pillager Marcus Consul attacked the military garrison at Orange Walk Town. Archaeological work at the nearby small Mayan ruin of Cuello places Mayans in the area as long ago as 1000 B.C.

Emergencies: In emergencies, dial 90. For the Orange Walk Town Hospital, phone 03-22143.

Accommodations and Eateries: There are several hotels on the main street. Most hotels also provide meals. Mi Amor Hotel (B) (phone 03-22031) and Baron's Hotel (B, M) (phone 03-22847) are on Victoria Avenue (the name for the Northern Highway in Orange Walk Town). Cash only for these two hotels. Lamanai Outpost Lodge (B, M), Indian Church (phone/fax 02-33578), is located near Lamanai ruins and is the best accommodation near town. Maruba Resort and Jungle Spa (E), near Maskell village (phone 03-22199, or in the United States and Canada, 1-800-627-8227), is a luxury operation offering massage and seaweed wraps. These two hotels accept most credit cards.

Access: Orange Walk Town is linked to the rest of Belize by the Northern Highway, which passes through the center of town. Buses are the most common means of public transportation. For a schedule, phone Batty Brothers at 03-22858.

Cuello Ruins

Cuello is a small Mayan ruin of great importance to archaeologists. Prior to excavations here it was believed that Mayan civilization began about 600 B.C. Cuello produced evidence that pushed back the starting date to 1500 B.C. This discovery astounded archaeologists involved in the study of ancient Mayans. The site deserves mention, but as an experience it is much less visually exciting than nearby Lamanai, or La Milpa, Altun Ha, and the many other spectacular ruins described in this book. Cuello is located four miles from Orange Walk Town on Yo Creek Road on property owned by Belize's most successful rum distiller, whose name became the site's name.

Permission to Visit: Permission must be granted before visiting the ruins. The Cuello brothers, Hilberto and Oswaldo, makers of Belize's well-known Caribbean Rum, own the property. I met with Hilberto Cuello, and it turned out that Hilbert's story was, in some ways, more interesting than the visually unimpressive ruins that had put me in contact with him. He started his operation in 1959 with a homemade still while working as a *chiclero*. "We were very poor, but I knew people like rum. It was pretty much trial and error," explained Hilberto with a shy shrug about how he became Belize's leading rum distiller. Hilberto's liquor is sold under the Caribbean Rum label and is highly regarded throughout Belize and other parts of the Caribbean for its reasonable price and smooth taste. You'll find a retail outlet for Hilberto's rum in Orange Walk Town.

Lamanai ("Submerged Crocodile") Ruins

With the possible exception of Caracol, Lamanai (which translates as "Submerged Crocodile") is arguably Belize's most exotic and stimulating ancient Mayan ruin. The extensive ruins are among the largest in Belize and possess the most unique post-Conquest history of all Belize's Mayan sites. Visiting Lamanai involves a thirty-minute river trip in a small, open boat that glides up the New River. The river is especially rich in bird life. The site is located on the shore of an immense lagoon system. The ruins are near the shore and surrounded by lowland rain forest, which hides most of the huge stone and rubble edifices from view from the river. Howler monkey troops live in the high trees around Lamanai, further enriching the experience. A visit to Lamanai gives you the feeling of having stumbled across ancient ruins in a pristine jungle far from civilization. Because the natural world surrounding the site is intact, you'll go away with a sense of the rich relationship the Mayans must have had with their lowland jungle world.

History: Lamanai is one of Belize's largest ruins and was occupied for 3200 years, starting in 1500 B.C. and extending until after the Spanish arrived. This makes Lamanai unique in two ways: its extremely lengthy period of continuous habitation and the fact that large numbers of Mayans lived here long after most metropolitan centers had been abandoned throughout the Mayan world. Both these aspects of Lamanai's history intrigued Dr. David Pendergast and his Royal Ontario Museum colleagues, who came to Lamanai in the 1970s to try and discover why Mayan life lasted so long here after it had disintegrated elsewhere.

Pendergast pinned down the length of occupation by identifying domesticated pollen from ancient corn crops in lagoon sediments. Lamanai's early beginnings can be seen clearly in a single man-size statue of a human face that is ancient Olmec in design. The Olmecs were centered to the north in the centuries preceding the rise of the Mayans. The Olmecs were on the wane as the Mayans were solidifying their culture, and apparently the Olmec and Mayan cultures overlapped at Lamanai. During the Pre-Classic Period the Mayans developed astronomy, architecture, and sophisticated mathematics, which launched Lamanai into the Classic Period, which ran from A.D. 250 to 900. At Lamanai's zenith, Pendergast estimates the population to have been between 20,000 and 50,000 Mayans.

Put in perspective, Lamanai flourished fifteen centuries before the United States was created. While Europe entered the Dark Ages, citizens at Lamanai cultivated crops, dug interlocking canals, perfected the calendar, and used mathematics in their daily lives. Architecture took on grandiose dimensions, murals decorated immense temples, and priestly astronomers and mathematicians used their superior understanding of the constellations to direct the pragmatic and religious activities of the ancient Mayans.

In about A.D. 1200, most of the Mayan world fell apart due to internal problems most likely related to drought, depletion of food supplies, and rebellion against the upper classes, but this didn't occur in Lamanai. For some reason, Lamanai forged on after the great Mayan centers at Caracol, Tikal, Copan, and Palenque were abandoned and reclaimed by the jungle. David Pendergast believes the answer may never be known for certain, but is probably due to a combination of factors. The ready food supply in the nearby lagoons may have helped sustain the population here, whereas centers without nearby waters as an alternate food source were disrupted by drought and the depletion of soil associated with growing crops.

Spanish Driven Out: Pendergast focused on Lamanai after reviewing old Spanish documents describing the region in the sixteenth and seventeenth centuries. The Spanish found a large population living in and around Lamanai. They set up missions, which indicate to Pendergast that the concentration and size of the Mayan population were sufficient to justify building a church, something the pragmatically religious Spanish would do only when they believed the potential for large numbers of converts was great. The Spanish missionaries didn't fare too well at Lamanai, indicating that the Mayans in this area still had a fair degree of confidence in their own belief system. Missionizing efforts were started twice, but on both occasions the Mayans living at Lamanai made martyrs of their Christian friars by killing them and burning their churches to the ground in order to reestablish their traditional beliefs.

In fact, in Lamanai at the site of the churches, Pendergast and company dug out Mayan figurines that told the story of what had occurred. All that remained of the first church was a large mound. Digging in the mound, Pendergast unearthed the foundation of a small Mayan temple surrounded by the Spanish church's foundation. When Pendergast began sifting through the second church site, he found offerings of crocodile and frog figurines and a stela set upright.

Pendergast interpreted the sequence of these findings as evidence of the religious tug of war that went on sometime between 1450 and 1650. Apparently a late Post-Classic Mayan town was thriving, and at least one important temple was standing when the Spanish first arrived. The Spanish, as was their custom during the Conquest, pulled down the shrine and replaced it with a church at the very place the shrine had stood. The church was eventually destroyed. In the ruins of the second church Pendergast found a ceramic crocodile with gaping jaws at both ends and a deity emerging from a mouth. This figurine is thought to be the Mayans' way of saying that attempts to eradicate Mayan beliefs would meet with the same fate as the church.

The Site: From the point the tour boat bumps the grassy shore, the actual site lies about 400 yards inland from the western shore and parallels the river in a north/south orientation for about two miles. The Mayan caretaker/warden is usually found near the thatched hut near the beginning of the forest. He is an excellent source of information and may have maps of the ruins. The highest temple, which is unmistakable soon after you enter the jungle past the caretaker's hut, is 112 feet tall. Known as "Lag" by archaeological students, or structure N10-43 on site maps, this is the third-tallest temple in Belize. It was probably the tallest temple for centuries, because it has been dated to the Pre-Classic Period, which is before the two taller temples found at Xunantunich and Caracol were created. The temple was enlarged over time to accommodate new styles and new rulers. Its core is filled with stone rubble, as are the ruins of many Mayan temples. The climb up the forty-five degree incline to its top is a reward worth the sweat. The temple pokes above the nearby treetops, affording a spectacular view of the New River, the rain forest, nearby lagoons, and the rest of the site.

During my visit to the temple, about a dozen howler monkeys occupied the upper foliage of nearby trumpet and allspice trees, where they dined on the leaves and lolled about in the heat of the day. As you look out across the jungle you'll see large guancaste, cedar, and mahogany trees poking above the cohune palms and lower foliage. If you're on top at day's end, the forest will come alive with a plethora of bird calls and most likely the unforgettable bellowing of a male howler monkey. With a little imagination and knowledge of traditional Mayan building techniques, you can envision the area as it once was. The temples were well maintained and coated in fresh, colorfully painted murals depicting battles and other significant events. In the surrounding areas thousands of average Mayans lived in tightly clustered one- and two-room thatched dwellings that look much like modern-day Mayan structures made from materials chopped from the jungle. The upper classes occupied more permanent structures neatly surrounding well-defined city squares, or plazas. The area immediately around the temple was probably thinly populated, reserved for the priests' activities and ceremonies. Over centuries the city continually changed. In general, temples were often built over, making increasingly larger temples that sometimes engulfed lesser structures that are now partly exposed. Good stone was not abundant in the lowland areas, so Lamanai's many large stone edifices were constructed with rubble interiors and exteriors held together by lime cement coated in garish murals commonly in green and red colors.

Of the more than 740 structures identified by Pendergast and his team, the structure known as "Fut," or N9-56 on site maps, is perhaps the most interesting. It lies on the east side of the main trail heading north near the largest temple. This middle-size temple has two huge stone faces, each the size of a person, which are clearly Olmec in origin. One of these faces is fully excavated and partially protected under a thatched awning. The face has an elongated, Oriental appearance, with eyelids half shut, mouth agape, and two prominent front teeth protruding downward behind the top lip. This characteristic buck-toothed face is common to the Olmec civilization but is not normally found in Mayan ruins. The Olmecs were in decline when Lamanai and the rest of the Mayan world was on the rise. The face is evidence that the Olmec culture had influence on the Mayans of northern Belize.

Accommodations: Staying at the sight overnight is not permitted. The nearest accommodations are in Orange Walk Town, where most hotels are in the budget category. Tastefully laid out Maruba Resort and Jungle Spa (E) (phone 03-22199), near Maskall village, is also in the area and offers guests trips to Lamanai for a fee. Also try Lamanai Outpost Lodge (B, M) (phone 02-33578). Most credit cards are accepted at both Maruba Resort and Lamanai Outpost Lodge.

Access: Lamanai is normally reached via a small boat on the New River from the bridge just south of Orange Walk Town. Boats can also be hired at Guinea Grass and Shipyard. Guinea Grass is about a half-hour drive, and Shipyard about a forty-five-minute drive, from Orange Walk Town. Arrangements can also be made through Maruba Resort, which is about forty minutes south of the bridge. Many tour companies and resorts rely on boat owners Antonio and Herminio Novelo, who are good naturalists and will go to great lengths to point out birds, Morlet's crocodiles, hickatee turtles, and other wildlife as you make your way up the New River to the ruins. If you're in the area on your own, you may save some money by dealing directly with the Novelo brothers. Their company, Jungle River Tours, Eco-tourism, can be contacted at 20 Lovers Lane, Orange Walk Town, Belize, C.A. (phone 03-22293; fax 03-22201). The thirty-minute trip by water gives you a glimpse of the riverine world of the ancient Mayans. You can also reach Lamanai in a four-wheel-drive vehicle during the dry season (October through April) from San Felipe, a village near the Mennonite community of Blue Creek. Occasionally, boat hires from as far away as Ambergris Caye make the trip to Lamanai.

Rio Bravo Conservation and Management Area

The Rio Bravo Conservation and Management Area is an immense, 202,000-acre expanse of tropical moist forest located in the remote northwest corner of Belize. The area is a pristine environment packed full of jungle plants and animals. There is no public transportation into the region, but it can be visited by the adventuresome traveler. The Programme for Belize, whose office is located in Belize City, manages the area. If you want to visit, make arrangements through the 1 King Street office before traveling to the field station and modest, no-frills dormitory. Reached only by dirt road via the Mennonite community of Blue Creek, the Rio Bravo Conservation and Management Area is north of and adjacent to the 140,000 acres of jungle owned by Chan Chich Lodge. So, from the perspective of the region's wildlife, the habitat available is 342,000 acres. The area's eastern boundary is the Peten region of Guatemala and the Quintana Roo region of Mexico.

The Rio Bravo area will undoubtedly become a magnet for amateur naturalists when it becomes better known and its managers develop easier access into the region and around the site. The area contains great tracts of jungle and extremely diverse and abundant forms of plant and animal life. Human intrusion is minimal and hunting is forbidden. Presently only the fringes are readily visited by outsiders. Besides providing a haven for the wildest of creatures, including the jaguar, the Rio Bravo area has La Milpa, a previously unexcavated (except for looters) major Mayan ruin hidden under immense trees and other broadleaf jungle plants.

Unique Conservation Program: The area is known simply as the Rio Bravo Project, or by the acronym RBCMA. The Programme for Belize's management of the Rio Bravo Conservation and Management Area is unique and innovative. In some ways the project is a high-stakes experiment, designed as a prototype for developing countries who must integrate the economic needs of their citizens into management of vast areas that possess natural treasures such as the intricate and fragile ecosystems found in the Rio Bravo area. The Programme for Belize is a private, nonprofit Belizean corporation that acts as a bridge between private and public sectors. With seed money from mostly U.S. sources, the agency has raised U.S. $6 million to buy the land, which will be held in trust for the people of Belize in perpetuity.

Like the Cockscomb area, Rio Bravo is as healthy a jungle environment as can be found in Central America. Both areas boast five species of wild cats, and Rio Bravo may surpass anyplace in Belize for its diversity of birds. But, unlike the Cockscomb, which is off-limits to all kinds of human exploitation, the Rio Bravo Project seeks to manage and protect itself with funds generated by activities and by-products from the forest, such as nontimber forest-product extraction (chicle harvesting, medicinal plants, etc.), eco-tourism, scientific studies, and sustained-yield selective timber harvesting.

According to Joy Grant, the Belizean native who heads the Programme for Belize, the first priority is to catalogue the plants and animals living in the management area. This may not sound innovative, but in other protected places throughout the world, biodiversity assessments are usually undertaken long after exploitation has occurred. After-the-fact studies skew findings and complicate effective management. This won't be the case with Programme for Belize. Rio Bravo is practically a pristine environment, harboring the same plants and animals that have been there for centuries. Among the working scientists are ornithologists Nicholas Brokaw and Elizabeth Mallory, who have conducted studies of flowering plants and climate and assessed permanent and transient bird populations. Wildlife biologists from the University of Florida and University of Idaho are studying large mammals, and archaeologist Norman Hammond from Boston University plans to learn as much as possible about the Mayans who once dwelled here.

Why not set aside the whole area and call it a national park, prohibiting exploitation of any kind? The reason is money. Industrial nations such as the United States and Canada, with multibillion-dollar budgets and multifaceted taxing mechanisms, have the ability to set aside large tracts of land and pay for their upkeep through a number of revenue sources. In underdeveloped countries such as Belize, where the average annual income is U.S. $1500, that option doesn't exist.

How to implement a bona fide, self-sustaining management plan without government funding is the crux of the experiment the Programme for Belize is attempting to address. The charter for the RBCMA seeks to include all segments of society in directing the management plan. Soon after Joy Grant took over the Programme for Belize from a North American director, she was credited with winning the support of key fellow Belizeans, who had been generally skeptical when the program was largely seen as a North American scheme that put nature before the needs of Belizeans. There had been little local support for a program that put a vast area off-limits to most Belizeans, whose daily toils to feed their families precluded them from ever visiting the area on a vacation. Now, a greater number of Belizeans see the wisdom of proceeding carefully in developing low-impact human activities in a region that is recognized as a bastion of plant and animal life. Members of the Programme's board of directors include leaders from the sugar industry, conservation groups, and government officials. The Programme for Belize operates under a charter that holds biodiversity and animal habitat needs as top priorities. "This is the entire society's project, not just a segment. It's about educating people as to how ecological systems work and how people can operate successfully without upsetting the apple cart. It's about understanding different perspectives," says Grant. "Our basic tenet is accepting that our main purpose is to link economic development and conservation of the country's wildlife, forest, and marine areas." Grant believes that including local people in management of the area (as *chicleros,* loggers, guides, naturalists, etc.) builds support among people who might exploit the area in harmful ways were they excluded from the economic part of the formula. "Economic and ecological needs are linked and must be addressed as a whole," she says.

Grant is a force to be reckoned with. She holds an M.B.A., was once second in command at the Belizean embassy in Washington, D.C., and was offered the second-highest position in the Central Bank of Belize. Instead, she took the director's post for the Programme for Belize. Grant sees women as important contributors to the worldwide conservation movement because, as she says, "women are nurturing in all societies."

Wildlife: The Rio Bravo area is in elite company with the wilds of adjoining Chan Chich Lodge, the Cockscomb Basin, and the Chiquibul Forest Reserve as the most pristine and biodiverse ecosystems in Belize that are accessible to people. The combination of no hunting, vast size, few people, and remoteness had added up to a de facto sanctuary long before the Programme for Belize purchased the property. As many as sixty species of bats live in the area. Preliminary assessments by jaguar experts concluded that there is a greater potential for large cats here than in the famous Cockscomb Basin Wildlife Sanctuary. In fact, jaguars have been sighted in the region (including Chan Chich to the south). Ocelots, margays, pumas, and jaguarundis are also present, which indicates an abundance of prey species such as white-tailed and brocket deer, two species of peccaries, and numerous other creatures. Tapirs, kinkajous, anteaters, coatimundis, and foxes are often seen, and both black howler and black spider monkeys are common.

While I was exploring some Mayan ruins with other visitors, a particularly territorial male spider monkey dedicated to protecting his females and their young descended to within forty feet of us. The monkey shook branches, chattered incessantly, and threw twigs at us. When this failed to drive us off, he threw his own excrement and hit three of us squarely in the face. I'll never forget Programme for Belize's on-site manager, John Masson, standing beneath the monkey swearing at it while the monkey bared its teeth and tossed a steady stream of harmless projectiles in our direction. "From one primate to another, you are a little bastard!" yelled John, while the rest of us doubled up in laughter.

If birds are an indicator of natural wealth, Rio Bravo is a gold mine. An incredible 355 species were recorded in a study ending in November 1991. Among them are the ocellated turkey, king vulture, crested guan, great curassow, ornate hawk eagle, and species of tinamous, parrots, and a remarkable 26 migrant species of warblers. Some species, such as the spectacular ornate hawk eagle and strong-billed wood creeper, nest here because they need old-growth forests.

Plant Life: Tropical moist forest is the general type of rain forest found here. More than 250 species of trees live in it, along with hundreds of other kinds of plants, including multitudes of orchids and bromeliads. Within the general forest type there are a dozen recognizable plant communities that are usually identified as belonging to five classifications: upland broadleaf forest, swamp forest, palm forest, savanna, and marsh. Each area of distinctly different vegetation attracts different animals. Most of Rio Bravo is upland broadleaf forest, containing mahogany, cedar, and other commercially viable hardwood species. In general, the forest gets taller as you head south, due to better soils and increased precipitation. The wetter forests are also known as mesic forest, characterized by canopies of more than 100 feet and a richness in figs and other fruiting tropical trees. Annual rainfall is about sixty inches with most of it falling between June and January.

La Milpa Ruins: Wrongly named "Las Milpas" on maps, this archaeological site is near the Rio Bravo Project's field station and dormitory. Not much is known about what went on here. Educated guessers postulate that La Milpa flourished for several centuries and reached its peak during the Late Classic Period, around A.D. 900. Today, except for looters' tunnels, La Milpa has been reclaimed by the jungle, with immense trees growing directly out of pyramids adorned in philodendrons and ferns. Renowned Mayan archaeologist Eric S. Thompson identified La Milpa as the third-largest site in Belize in the 1930s. One pyramid stands seventy-five feet tall. More recently, archaeologists Annabel Ford and Scott Fedick identified eighteen plazas and sixty structures, most of them between fifty and seventy-five feet high. Unfortunately the site was reputedly visited by the notorious Mayan site looter Jackie Vasquez prior to a serious archaeological attempt to excavate the area. Vasquez died a few years ago, so what he and his cohorts found will probably never be known. Most of the tunnels through the stone pyramids show that the looters were systematic, precise, hard-working, and in possession of a fair understanding of where tombs were likely to be found. In one case, during my visit, a plundered tomb lay exposed, its shiny red plaster interior exposed to the elements. Stelae, storage areas, ball courts, and reservoirs can also be seen. Since the site is sprawling and overgrown with hundred-year-old mesic forest, having a guide such as John Masson is the sensible approach to finding your way around. Ask for John or someone with comparable knowledge if you organize a group to visit La Milpa.

Accommodations: The field facilities are spartan and suitable for the seasoned field biologist, nature-oriented traveler, birder, graduate student, or guided student groups who stay in dormitory quarters in a clearing near the La Milpa archaeological site. There is talk about building some bungalows for eco-tourists. Arrangements to visit the Rio Bravo Project must be worked out with the Programme for Belize office prior to driving to the site. Contact Programme for Belize, 1 King Street, P.O. Box 749, Belize City, Belize, C.A. (phone 02-75616; fax 02-75635). You can also stay at Chan Chich Lodge and visit the Rio Bravo area (see "Chan Chich Lodge").

Access: Visiting the Rio Bravo Project is a major commitment requiring a two-hour, one-way drive on dirt roads from Orange Walk Town (plus another two hours on pavement if you're starting from Belize City). Top off your tank before leaving the Northern Highway near Orange Walk Town. You may be able to buy gas at Blue Creek during daylight hours. The final leg of the drive consists of turning west from the Northern Highway onto any of a number of dirt roads (the one from Orange Walk Town to Cuello and Yo Creek is easy enough to find) that will take you to Blue Creek. Turn south a mile or so after Blue Creek at the T before you come to Tres Leguas. (*Note:* Some maps show two roads heading south. You want to proceed in the direction of Gallon Jug and Chan Chich Lodge.) Continue on until about ten miles south of the village of Blue Creek and you will see Rio Bravo's field station on the right side of the road.

Driver's advisory: You are definitely off the beaten path and should not attempt this trip at night. Your car must be in top mechanical condition as it will be subjected to hours of dust (or mud) and bumpy roads. Check the condition of your tires and make sure gas, oil, and radiator levels are topped off before heading out. Make sure your spare tire and car jack are ready to do their jobs. The road is negotiable in muddy conditions but best attempted in a four-wheel-drive. If you try the trip at night you may get lost; you'll run a good chance of missing Rio Bravo's field station entirely and wind up at Gallon Jug or Chan Chich Lodge, which is farther south on the same dirt track. There's a checkpoint set up north of the Rio Bravo Project that may turn you back if you aren't a scheduled visitor.

If you're headed for Chan Chich Lodge by car, visiting the Rio Bravo Project is a matter of stopping during your journey. Set aside about two hours for your visit, maybe longer, depending on your interest. You should travel with enough food to meet your needs for a day or so. If you run low on food you can also buy very basic foodstuffs at the Mennonite store in Blue Creek. If you fly to Chan Chich, visiting Rio Bravo is an activity that's sometimes offered to guests.

Chan Chich Lodge

Simply put, Chan Chich Lodge is among the elite jungle experiences anywhere in the world. This is the kind of place that leaves an indelible impression on your memory. To many visitors, time spent here is a visual, auditory, and spiritual experience that taps the primeval thread that ties all of us to our ancestral beginnings in the tropics, where theory has it that humankind got its start eons ago.

Chan Chich Lodge can provide this primeval connection as well as anywhere because it is located in the middle of 140,000 acres of verdant rain forest. This immense area is surrounded by much larger areas of uninterrupted jungle, putting Chan Chich in the heart of the Belizean rain forest. It is protected by its remoteness, size, and management decisions. For example, the hunting ban is enforced, not just written. Most guests arrive in light aircraft from Belize City's international airport after a forty-five-minute flight. Getting here on the ground from Belize City is an all-day event requiring driving hours north to Orange Walk Town before bumping along for hours more on dirt roads.

Waking up at Chan Chich Lodge was unforgettable. I was serenaded during the predawn hours by dueling male howler monkeys who expressed their insults to each other in deep, throaty, territorial bellowing matches from the trees surrounding the lodge. I dozed off and was awakened at dawn by an indescribable combination of bird calls. Peering out from the window slats of my thatched-roof bungalow, I saw a dozen endangered ocellated turkeys wander within ten feet of where I lay cozily in bed. Either the birds didn't know I was there or they didn't care. I showered and walked to breakfast under the casual gaze of a troup of spider monkeys dangling high above the ground as they feasted on the fruit in a huge amate fig that stood near the compound.

The lodge's twelve bungalows are nestled among immense grass-covered, pyramid-shaped mounds, which are Mayan ruins. As we ate and discussed the day's activities, parrots screeched and unseen birds let loose their contributions to the morning's ever-changing melody. Later in the day on the lodge's many trails, I saw otters in a stream and dozens of species of colorful birds. That night I saw two ocelots, a crowning moment for anyone seeking an intimate relationship with nature. This was in the first twenty-four hours—I had forty-eight to go.

The lodge is the brainchild of Barry Bowen, Belize's beer (Beliken) king and leading entrepreneur. Bowen once owned 250,000 acres in the area, but he sold 110,000 acres to the Programme for Belize to become part of the Rio Bravo Conservation and Management Area. On the 140,000 acres he kept for himself, Bowen went to work creating the tiny village of Gallon Jug, where he has an experimental farm, horse stable, residences, and school for the more than 150 people employed in various capacities on his land. The

Chan Chich Lodge is about ten miles south of Gallon Jug near the Chan Chich River and situated in the plaza of a Mayan ruin. From the tops of the middle-size pyramids there you can peer out over the jungle. With the exception of the lodge, Gallon Jug, and the tiny village of Sylvester in the vicinity of the Guatemalan border, the jungle stretches out of sight in all directions. The idea of creating a big resort is not what Bowen and his on-site partner/managers Tom and Josie Harding had in mind. "The idea is to provide an intimate experience with minimal impact, which means staying small," explained Tom Harding. This is why Chan Chich is popular with top birders, conservation groups, and embassy officials assigned to Belize from abroad.

Wildlife: The rain forest here is similar to that of the Rio Bravo Project to the north, but the trees are generally taller with many mature specimens evident. You'll notice in older forests (which are hard to find) such as these that ground vegetation is not as tangled and impenetrable as in secondary forests. Older forests (as well as other types of forest) often attract forms of wildlife that you won't find elsewhere. The presence of the Chan Chich River meandering through the jungle near the lodge adds to the diversity of the already astounding amount of wildlife found in the entire region.

Five felines—jaguars, ocelots, pumas, margays, and jaguarundis—occur here in great enough numbers to have been sighted. Finding tracks of the felines is fairly common. Tapirs and river otters are sometimes seen along watercourses. Red brocket deer are common, as are white-tailed deer. This is the only place in Belize I sighted red brocket deer, which are delicate-looking creatures about half the size of deer in North America. Watch for them crossing roads and trails into thick brush. Both large white-lipped and smaller collared peccaries root through the underbrush. Middle-size terrestrial and aquatic predators are also numerous. I saw dozens of gray foxes, a lone river otter, and the aforementioned ocelots. You'll notice that the foxes are much smaller than their brethren in North America. They also seem more at home in the trees. Coatimundis, kinkajous, and tayras are also sighted. Agoutis and pacas, the two distinctly large Central American rodents that look something like oversize guinea pigs, are often seen darting across trails and dirt roads in explosions of speed. These two similar-size species are easy to confuse with each other. The agouti is solid in color and comes in hues of brown and red.

When alarmed, the agouti often makes the hair on its rump stand on end, giving it a larger appearance. The paca is light brown with white spots.

Black howler and spider monkeys are seen regularly, but telling them apart is not always easy for the first-time visitor. Often you'll catch a glimpse of a primate high in a tree and not know what kind it is. Though the two monkeys look quite different close up, differences in behavior separate them from afar. Spider monkeys are high-speed aerialists, seemingly reckless leapers that charge through the upper canopy, jumping and scrambling as they go, in an impressive acrobatic display. Sometimes you'll see babies clinging to their mothers in what must be an exhilarating ride to any youngster. Howlers are usually slower-moving and less prone to go airborne than their acrobatic cousins. There's no doubt which monkey is the howler when a male howler begins his deafening territorial vocalizations, usually to another male whose troup is in the area.

If you see a gold-colored, monkey-size creature with a round face and round ears climbing through the forest on a fairly low to the ground "arboreal highway," chances are you're looking at a kinkajou, a harmless and cute vegetarian related more closely to a raccoon than to a primate. Its nickname is "honey bear" because of its alleged fondness for sweet-tasting fruit.

Birders' Paradise: The bird life is phenomenal. It's no wonder birders from as far away as Europe come here to add to their lifetime lists. In the nearby Rio Bravo area, more than 355 different species have been recorded. The true number is probably higher. See "Rio Bravo Conservation and Management Area" for an idea of the variety you'll find here. Ocellated turkeys regularly enter the compound. Predatory birds and parrots seemed especially prevalent during my visit.

It's no accident that ornithologists Carolyn and Bruce Miller, working for Wildlife Conservation International, have been conducting bird surveys from nearby Gallon Jug for the better part of two years. Wildlife Conservation International is recognized as one of the world's premier conservation organizations in providing accurate data about species populations that is used by international bodies such as the International Union for the Conservation of Nature (IUCN). The Millers' book, *Exploring the Rainforest, Chan Chich Lodge Belize,* is one of the best source books on bird species, plants, and mammals in Belize. It presents general information and scientific

The ocellated turkey in northeastern Belize. *Photo by Eric Hoffman.*

details in an interesting, conversational manner. The sixty-five-page publication was created to sell to guests at Chan Chich Lodge but is available to others by mail. It also has detailed information on each of Chan Chich's hiking trails, discussing particular trees along the trails and the kinds of wildlife associated with them, thus giving readers a greater understanding of the intricate relationships that make up the rain forest community. The book has four very thorough appendixes listing the birds, amphibians, reptiles, mammals, and trees of Belize. If you plan a visit to Chan Chich, I strongly suggest purchasing this book ahead of time (see "Accommodations" for address). As of this writing, it retailed for U.S. $10.95 plus mailing costs. This publication, combined with hiring a guide (U.S. $10 per hour) and the occasional slide show (compliments of the Millers), makes the Chan Chich birding experience extremely educational for the novice and hard-core birder. If you hire a guide, I suggest contacting Gilberto, who is very knowledgeable and helpful. He's lived in the area his whole life and has a very good eye for spotting wildlife. He works for Chan Chich.

Plant Life: This alone is worth walking the trails, even without the wildlife. You'll see hundreds of rain forest species, and if you take along the Millers' book, you'll learn a great deal about the trees on each of Chan Chich's seven trails. Even without this printed aid you'll recognize pointsettias, only here they are five feet tall. You'll see philodendrons descending fifty feet or more, strangler figs engulfing other trees, giant fruiting buttressed figs twenty feet across at the base, and flowering trees you've never seen before. The local names for many of the trees tell you something about their qualities and provide something to talk about in cases where the odd names remain a mystery. Some of the more colorful local names (listed along with their scientific names in the Millers' book) include custard apple, bastard grand betty, chicle macho, mylady, bastard rosewood, monkey apple, drunken bayman wood, boy job, old william, axe-master, give-and-take, monkey-tail palm, stinking toe, wild pigeon plum, bullet tree, male bullhoof, silly young, and knock-me-back.

Trails: There are seven trails leading from Chan Chich Lodge. You'll find that they are quite wide and free of debris, which means you won't accidentally stand on a deadly fer-de-lance snake taking refuge under leaves. The trails are from one-quarter mile to two-and-a-half miles in length and offer a great deal of variety, including a riverine jungle environment, Mayan ruins, old-growth forests, dry forests, and a wide range of plant communities. Looters' trenches cut directly into some of the Mayan tombs appear fresh, though they were dug prior to 1988. Many of the trails have marked and numbered stops that coincide with explanations found in the Millers' book.

Your tastes and the time of the year you visit will partially determine which trails you will enjoy most. I liked all of them for different reasons. Silent walking is the best policy. The trails along Little Chan Chich Creek were the longest and most rewarding, though they can be subject to seasonal flooding. I saw an otter along one of these and signs of tapirs. Bird life seemed prevalent on all of the trails in the mornings and evenings. Several of the trails take in unexcavated Mayan ruins. One of the shortest walks is to the top of an unearthed temple that affords a stunning view of the surrounding rain forest.

If you have a particular mission in mind, such as seeing an ocelot or a rare bird, check the guest book in the lodge. Past visitors often record comments about special experiences they've had. I noted that two guests had seen an ocelot in the evening on one of the lodge's service roads. I went there around dusk with two other visitors and sat quietly waiting. As if on cue, two ocelots appeared at sunset.

Mayan Ruins: Your bungalow and the entire lodge rest on a grassed-over Mayan plaza, and the large, grassy mounds surrounding your accommodation are the remains of ancient temples. Archaeologist Dr. Tom Gruderjan visited the site in 1988 and left notes that Carolyn and Bruce Miller worked into the text of their book. Gruderjan said the ruins around the lodge are remnants of a mid-size Mayan community. Plaza A, where the lodge is, was built during the Late Classic Period (A.D. 600–900). Gruderjan speculates that the large structures on the west side of the plaza may have played a part in marking winter and summer solstices. Plaza B and its structures (mounds) south of the lodge were probably built in the Early Classic (A.D. 300–600). These buried stone remains of the long-dead culture that dwelled here were probably used for ceremonial purposes, not for daily living. As in most Mayan centers, the regular folks lived in thatch and pole houses much like Mayans today. In years to come, attempts by archaeologists to piece together the story of Chan Chich's temple will tell more about the people who lived here.

Other Activities: Horseback riding is available with horses kept at Gallon Jug. There are a number of good swimming holes. Canoeing in a nearby lake, Laguna Verde, and trips to the Rio Bravo Project can also be arranged. A lecture/slide show by the Millers is well worth it, if they are available. Their tropical bird slides, especially of rare species, are world class. You can also go on night walks with high-powered lights to see the cast of nocturnal jungle characters, including bats (about sixty species), cats, and owls. Tom and Josie Harding have also added Tapir Hole nature observation and Punta de Cacao Mayan ruins to their offerings. You're charged extra for activities involving guides and transportation.

Be Prepared: Reading about what lives here prior to your arrival will enhance your experience. Take along bug repellent, a water bottle, bird book, field glasses, light rain gear, and a good hat.

Caution: Chan Chich Lodge is a professionally run operation staffed by people who know the rain forest. They give sound advice. Stay on the trails. Getting lost here can be life-threatening. There are a number of plants that defend themselves through releasing skin irritants or thorns, so touch plants at your own peril. The rainy season usually runs from June through August. Summer can be oppressive due to excessive heat and humidity. The fall and winter are wonderful times to visit.

Accommodations: Chan Chich Lodge (E) consists of twelve bungalows, each with two queen beds and private bathroom facilities. There is a spacious main lodge where meals and drinks are served and a small library is kept. The ambience is casual. Tom and Josie Harding are more than managers. They are knowledgeable about the rain forest, and Tom supervised building the lodge. Each structure was fashioned entirely from wood harvested from the forest. Anyone vaguely knowledgeable about construction and architecture will appreciate the skillful blending of traditional Mayan and modern techniques that bring together the best of both in this exceptional lodge. Major credit cards are accepted. Contact Chan Chich Lodge, P.O. Box 1088, Vineyard Haven, MA 02568 (phone 1-800-343-8009; fax 508-693-6311). Or in Belize, contact Chan Chich Lodge, 1 King Street, P.O. Box 37, Belize City, Belize, C.A. (phone 02-75634; fax 02-76961).

Access: Most people arrive at nearby Gallon Jug via light aircraft from Phillip Goldson International Airport. This flight takes about forty-five minutes and is arranged as part of your package at Chan Chich. You can also drive, which takes much longer and necessitates procuring a vehicle. See the "Access" section of "Rio Bravo Conservation and Management Area" for details on driving.

SEVEN

COROZAL DISTRICT

Overview

The Corozal District is Belize's smallest and northernmost district, encompassing a mere 718 square miles. To the north is Mexico and immediately across the border is the city of Chetumal, which has a population greater than all of Belize. Belizeans go to Chetumal to shop.

The Corozal District is primarily Hispanic, with most citizens speaking both Spanish and English. However, you may run into individuals who speak Spanish only. The district's economy is based largely on sugar cane, though there are efforts under way to diversify the economy and enhance the region as a tourist destination. At present, tourism is less important here than in the districts to the south, where more natural destinations are located.

The Shipstern Nature Reserve and Butterfly Breeding Centre is the most outstanding destination for naturalists. Of the two Mayan ruins that are regularly visited — Santa Rita (in Corozal Town) and Cerros (remote coastal ruins reached by boat) — the latter is the more pleasant to visit. Adventure Inn, located north of Corozal on the coast, is the only resort I found with a warm, private ambience integrated into the natural surroundings. The average tourist passing through the Corozal District will likely recall it as a peaceful, fairly nondescript place between the Mexican border and the exceptional natural destinations farther south.

Corozal Town

This is Belize's northernmost sizeable town. Only tiny Consejo, Chan Chen, Remate, and Santa Elena on the border are farther north. Corozal Town is located on Corozal Bay nine miles south of the Mexican border and the large Mexican city of Chetumal. Corozal Town is the administrative hub for the district. The town's population is estimated at 7500. The waters here are warm and good for swimming and fishing, but snorkeling isn't of the quality you'll find on the cayes.

The town is laid out on a grid around a central square where you'll find groceries, banking, gas stations, and all basic necessities. As you enter town on Santa Rita Road (the old highway, now a loop off the Northern Highway), turn west on First Street South (next to the bus terminal and across from a gas station) to find the square. The town-hall mural depicting the area's history is a true work of art and very informational. It carries a spiritual message as well as a historic one. I found myself photographing it and talking with the town's mayor, Mario Narvaez, who happened to be standing nearby when I visited the mural.

Corozal Town was settled in earnest in 1858 by refugees from Quintana Roo province, just over today's border in Mexico. The refugees were fleeing the bloody Caste Wars (1847–1863). To this day, most of the Corozal's inhabitants are Hispanic.

The town's economic base is agriculture, primarily sugar cane. "Economic growth through diversification is important. We see tourism playing a much larger role in the future," said Mayor Narvaez, who explained that there are several coastal resorts in the talking stage that may become a reality in years to come.

Hurricane Janet destroyed most of Corozal Town in 1955, following which the town was rebuilt around a central square. The Corozal Hospital (phone 04-22076) is north of town at Santa Rita Hill near the intersection signposted to Chetumal. For emergencies of all kinds, dial 90. For the most part, Corozal Town serves as a rest and refueling stop for travelers headed to and from Belize from Mexico. With the exception of Adventure Inn at Consejo and Tony's Inn and Beach Resort, there isn't much resembling the resorts or offerings found in the cayes or mountain lodges to the south.

Accommodations: Adventure Inn (M), located a few miles north of town at Consejo, is the only rurally situated resort around Corozal Town. Cozy bungalows on the bay are rented to guests. Windsurfers and light sailcraft are available for rental. Meals are tasty local dishes that are reasonably priced. The resort has a laid-back, total escape atmosphere. Owner Bill Wildman is a longtime transplant to Belize from Canada and one of Belize's foremost cave explorers. Major credit cards are accepted. Contact Adventure Inn, Consejo Shores, P.O. Box 35, Corozal Town, Belize, C.A. (phone 04-22187; fax 04-22243).

Another sure bet is Tony's Inn and Beach Resort (M, E). Owner Dahlia Castillo runs a clean place with all the amenities. Major credit cards are accepted. Contact Tony's Inn, South End, Corozal Town, Belize, C.A. (phone 04-22055; fax 04-22829). Hotel Maya (B, M) has clean rooms for reasonable prices. Major credit cards are accepted. Contact Hotel Maya, P.O. Box 112, Corozal Town, Belize, C.A. (phone 04-22082; fax 04-22827).

Access: Most people reach Corozal Town by private car or bus. Contact Batty Brothers (04-23034) for bus schedules and fares; the station is located at the corner of 7th Avenue and Santa Rita Road in North Corozal Town. Venus bus line also has scheduled routes between Chetumal, Corozal Town, and Belize City. Venus shares the terminal with Batty Brothers at the corner of 7th Avenue and Santa Rita Road.

Crossing the Mexican Border

If you're a citizen of the United States, Canada, and most other nations, you need a valid passport but no visa to cross the border in either direction. If you're from China, Taiwan, India, Colombia, Libya, Pakistan, Peru, or South Africa, you must get a visitor's permit to enter Belize by applying to the Immigration and Naturalization Office in Belmopan before entering the country.

The border is open twenty-four hours a day, and it normally takes about fifteen minutes to clear Belizean customs. Upon entry, you're automatically allotted a thirty-day stay. If you want to visit longer, you must apply for an extension (which costs U.S. $12.50) at the Immigration Office, 115 Barracks Road, Belize City, Belize, C.A.

Belizean customs authorities often search the luggage of inbound travelers. They also may ask for proof that you have the means to spend U.S. $50 per day. A credit card and traveler's checks are usually sufficient proof.

If you're driving your own vehicle into Belize, you must show a valid driver's license and the vehicle's registration. You must get a permit for your vehicle that is surrendered when you leave Belize to avoid the possibility of paying expensive customs fees. You also must buy temporary insurance that covers your stay.

The border crossing between Belize and Mexico is located where the Northern Highway crosses the bridge over the Río Hondo, just past Belize's most northerly town of Santa Elena. Chetumal, the Mexican city on the other side of the border, has a population of 200,000 — more people than live in all of Belize. Belizeans often shop in Chetumal because of greater selections and better prices. The open-air market, which is most active on Saturdays, is especially popular.

If you're driving your own car from the United States, the trip is 1300 miles from Texas and takes from two to seven days, depending on your desire to push yourself. Add a day or two to this travel time if you start at the California/Mexico border.

Two Belizean bus lines, Batty Brothers (phone 02-72025) and Venus (phone 02-73354), run regularly between Belize City and Chetumal, a distance of 116 miles. There is a bus terminal in Corozal Town, nine miles south of the border. The bus fare between Belize City and Chetumal is less than U.S. $10. The buses are converted U.S. school buses, so expect a no-frills trip.

You can also arrange to get to Belize from Cancun or other destinations in Mexico. If you decide to head to Belize from Cancun, contact the Belize Tourist Board, Hotel Parador, Avenida Tulum No. 26, Cancun, Quintana Roo, Mexico. Or phone the Belize Transfer Service (phone 415-641-9145 in Mexico) for information on fares and schedules. The distance to Belize City from Cancun, Mexico, is 344 miles, including a boat transfer.

Cerros Ruins

Cerros was an important Mayan trading center in the Late Pre-Classic Period (350 B.C.–A.D. 250). It has half a dozen structures and three plazas to explore, the tallest being a sixty-five-foot pyramid. *Cerros* means "hills" in Spanish, a name thought to refer to the nearby low hills. There are also some ancient structures right on the water — and some underwater. Archaeological evidence was found here of an elite ruling class that thrived much earlier than most archaeologists thought. The site is believed to have been a maritime trading center that facilitated the movement of goods between the sea and the interior via the New River into what is now central Belize and via the Río Hondo into the Yucatán. The site is located on an uninhabited part of the coast across Corozal Bay from Corozal Town.

Cerros is usually visited via a twenty-minute ride from Corozal Town in an open boat. Boat rental runs about U.S. $100 per trip, so sharing the ride with any new friends who'll help pay this cost will make this an affordable undertaking. From January to April, which is the dry season, the site can be reached by four-wheel-drive via the sleepy and photogenic villages of Chunox, Progresso, and Copper Banks. This route passes by extensive tropical wetlands that are home to many kinds of birds. For either the sea or land approach, inquire at Adventure Inn (phone 04-22187). The best deal I could find for the boat trip to Cerros was offered by Ediberto Escalante, who would make the trip for U.S. $75 in his Boston whaler. He can be found by asking around in the village of Consejo.

Santa Rita Ruins

Corozal Town is built around and on top of the Late Classic (A.D. 1350–1530) ruins known as Santa Rita (named by a Spanish map maker). It was still an active trading center when the Spanish arrived in the 1500s. It was occupied intermittently starting around 1800 B.C. Santa Rita, like Lamanai to the south near Orange Walk Town, was among the Mayan areas in northern Belize and southern Mexico that were still being occupied in an organized citylike existence when the Spanish arrived. Attracted by the gold jewelry worn by local Mayans (gold was a rarity among Mayans), the Spanish conquered the town in 1531, but they were driven out of the area by the Mayans a few years after. Centuries later, in 1858, survivors of the bloody massacres known as the Caste Wars (1847–1863) settled here, which was the start of today's Corozal Town. The site is strategic in that it is near the area's two river systems: Río Hondo and New River. Archaeologists Arlen and Diane Chase excavated tombs here that contained a burial of a man covered in jade, but most of the entombed contents were lost forever due to cavalier treatment by locals during the last hundred years. Bricks from the site were used to build houses and pulverized to make roads.

My attempt to visit the one fifty-five-foot high, partially restored temple open to the public was memorable. With only slight trepidation I parked my car in the run-down residential section of town that surrounds the ruin. As I was contemplating the modern-day litter that had collected at one end of the site and a few seminaked children playing in the street, a malnourished horse dragging his tether rope ambled up the street and began chewing on my windshield wipers. When I waved my hand at his head, he spun defiantly, pulling a wiper from the car. Then he kicked feebly in my general direction, hitting the door of my car and denting it as he ambled off. A moment later an aggressive beggar approached me and demanded money or food. It occurred to me that the timing of these two unlikely back-to-back scenes seemed choreographed. I remember staring at the disheveled six-footer's well-developed biceps and broad shoulders while he repeated semicoherent utterances, his hand outstretched and his eyes bloodshot. I gave him a can of beans and retreated into my car. I was happy the car started on the first try and even happier to drive away with only one windshield wiper missing.

These two incidents and the state of the neighborhood, no doubt, affected my assessment of Santa Rita. I only got a glimpse of the temple. I was told afterward that groups fare better because of "safety in numbers" and that the caretaker keeps the downtrodden at bay. He didn't work on Sundays, the day of my visit. Of all the Mayan ruins listed in this book, only Cuello was less impressive than Santa Rita, but at least it had been safe.

Shipstern Nature Reserve and Butterfly Breeding Centre

Located on a remote lowland peninsula in the Corozal District, the Shipstern Nature Reserve is a unique 22,000-acre sanctuary. It is the only area in Belize that protects coastal mangroves, semideciduous lowland hardwood forests, and vast saltwater wetlands in a single reserve. The reserve is managed by International Tropical Conservation, which is based in Switzerland. The area is not as readily accessed by visitors as other reserves in Belize. In part this is because Shipstern is off the beaten track, taking an hour one way on a dirt road from Orange Walk Town or close to two hours from Corozal Town. In the right (dry) weather conditions, the trip is well worth it. The Visitors' Centre and Butterfly Breeding Centre are open daily from 9:00 A.M. to 12:00 noon and from 1:00 P.M. to 5:00 P.M., except for Christmas, New Year's, and Easter Sunday. All visitors should stop at the Visitors' Centre and check in with the manager. There is a nominal admission fee.

Wildlife: Shipstern Lagoon is a vast shallow area that is habitat to practically every wading bird species in Belize. During winter months, migrant species from North America mass here. The combination of wetlands, savanna, and extremely diverse lowland forests is home to a surprising range of wildlife. In a one-day visit I saw two species of toucan, white hawks, ospreys, flocks of small parrots, and frigate birds. More than 200 species of birds have been recorded here, including rarities such as reddish egrets, white-winged doves, yellow-lored parrots, and Yucatán jays. Except for Belize's two monkey species, most major mammals living in Belize can be found here. Tapir, jaguar, ocelot, jaguarundi, and white-tailed and brocket deer tracks are found often on the trails and mudflats in the reserve. Sighting a wild cat of any species or a tapir is rare, but it does happen.

There is no shortage of reptilian and amphibian life forms — more than 60 species live here. The largest is the endangered Morlet's crocodile. Tree frogs are especially plentiful.

Butterflies: Shipstern is perhaps best known for its 200 species of butterflies. The Butterfly Breeding Centre concentrates on breeding 25 species. The large blue morpho butterfly is bred here, along with a great number of members of the Heliconius family that occur throughout Central and South America. The butterflies are most active when the sun is out. One of the primary aims of the Butterfly Breeding Centre is to provide, for photographic purposes, rare species that are very difficult to find in the wild. Many of the species living in the captive breeding area normally live in the rain forest canopy and are rarely seen by people. The center also sells pupae to European and Japanese butterfly houses. The profits help pay for managing the reserve. The reserve also undertakes the task of showing nearby citizens of the fishing village of Sarteneja that an unmolested forest can become economical if a resource — in this case, butterflies — is carefully managed.

Chiclero Botanical Trail: Near the Visitors' Centre a trail with markers (corresponding to a guidebook's identifications) has been hacked out of the jungle to educate visitors about the kinds of plants living here. At last count the trail had forty-two numbered species of plants with explanations as to the identity and role of each plant in the makeup of the forest. The trail takes from twenty to sixty minutes to complete.

Mayan Artifacts: The Mayans lived here in great numbers. Remnants of more than thirty buildings have been identified; however, very little excavation has taken place. Instead, villagers and opportunistic collectors wander off with what they find. Mayans lived in the area until the late 1700s.

Admission Fee and Contact: Admission is free. However, a guided tour of the botanical trail costs U.S. $12.50 for up to four people. If you have questions that you'd like answered by mail, contact Shipstern Nature Reserve, P.O. Box 1694, Belize City, Belize, C.A.

Be Prepared: Carry a hat, long pants, raincoat, insect repellent, binoculars, and food and liquid refreshment. Mark your route on a map before setting out for the reserve. There's a good chance you won't find anyone to help guide you for much of the trip.

Accommodations: There are no accommodations in the reserve, but nearby Sarteneja has budget accommodations. Try Diani's Hotel (B) (phone 04-32084), which accepts cash only for payment. Sarteneja is a scenic little Hispanic fishing village settled at the time of the Caste Wars during the last century. See "Orange Walk Town" in the preceding chapter and "Corozal Town" for other places to stay.

Access: Venus bus line has a daily route to Sarteneja from Orange Walk Town. You can also arrange for a visit by boat via Adventure

Inn in Corozal Town or on Ambergris Caye. The roads into the region are dirt and especially slow-going if it's been raining.

If you attempt this trip on your own from Corozal Town, get directions at your hotel or from someone who knows the area. There are several dirt roads not on any map (and a hand-cranked ferry) that will allow you to cut a half-hour off your journey by avoiding a longer route through Orange Walk Town.

From Orange Walk Town it's about an hour's drive to the Visitors' Centre at Shipstern under normal conditions. You'll pass through San Estevan and head toward Progresso. However, before you reach Progresso, follow the signposting to the Mennonite community of Little Belize until the Little Belize turnoff. Don't turn off here but instead continue on the main dirt road until you reach the nature reserve. The Visitors' Centre is three miles before the town of Sarteneja.

Bibliography

Books and Articles

Arvigo, Rosita. "Don Eligio's Pharmacy." *Sanctuary, Journal of the Massachusetts Audubon Society,* September 1988.

Ball, Joseph, and Taschek, Jennifer. *Late Classic Lowland Maya Political Organization and Central-Place Analysis.* San Diego: Department of Archeology, San Diego State University, 1991.

Belize Audubon Society. *Belize: A Guide to the Country and the Wildlife.* Belize City: Belize Audubon Society, 1992.

Belize Department of Archaeology. *Interested in the Maya Ruins of Belize?* Belmopan, Belize: Department of Archaeology, Ministry of Education and Culture, 1985.

Belize Tourist Board. *Belize: The Adventure Coast.* New York: Belize Tourist Board, 1993.

Bevis, Jim, and Bevis, Marguerite. *Slate Creek Preserve.* Cayo District, Belize: Mountain Equestrian Trails, 1991.

Bevis, Marguerite. *Maya Mountain Traverse.* Cayo District, Belize: Mountain Equestrian Trails, 1992.

Boo, Elizabeth. *Ecotourism: The Potential and the Pitfalls.* Washington, D.C.: World Wildlife Fund, 1987.

Bowman, W. A. J. *Citrus Culture in British Honduras.* New Orleans: Franklin Printing Company, 1955.

Carter, Jacque; Gibson, Janet; and Sammon, Rick. *The Hol Chan Marine Reserve, Belize.* Croton-on-Hudson, N.Y.: CEDAM International Press, 1988.

Chase, Arlen F., and Chase, Diane Z. "Mixing Archeology and Touristic Development in Caracol." *Belize Today,* vol. 5, no. 5, 1991.

Coe, William. *Tikal: A Handbook of the Ancient Maya Ruins.* Philadelphia: University Museum, University of Pennsylvania, 1990.

Education Task Force. *A History of Belize, Nation in the Making.* Belize City: Sunshine Books, 1991.

Environmental Education, Curriculum Development Unit, Ministry of Education. *Land Use.* Belmopan, Belize: Government Printery, 1991.

Foster, Byron. *The Baymen's Legacy: A Portrait of Belize City.* Benque Viejo del Carmen, Belize: Cubola Productions, 1987.

Foster, Byron. *Heart Drum, Spirit Possession in the Garifuna Communities of Belize.* Benque Viejo del Carmen, Belize: Cubola Productions, 1986.

Garrett, Wilbur E. "La Ruta Maya." *National Geographic,* October 1989.

Gibson, Janet. *The Coral Reef.* Belize City: Belize Audubon Society, 1986.

Glassman, Paul. *Belize Guide.* Champlain, N.Y.: Passport Press, 1987.

Godfrey, Glenn D. *The Sinner's Bossanova.* Benque Viejo del Carmen, Belize: Cubola Productions, 1987.

Greenberg, Jerry, and Greenberg, Idaz. *The Coral Reef.* Miami: Seahawk Press, 1990.

Greenberg, Jerry; Greenberg, Idaz; and Greenberg, Michael. *Beneath the Tropical Seas.* Miami: Seahawk Press, 1986.

Greenberg, Jerry; Greenberg, Idaz; and Greenberg, Michael. *Fishwatcher's Field Guide.* Miami: Seahawk Press, 1979.

Greenberg, Jerry; Greenberg, Idaz; and Greenberg, Mimi. *Reefcomber's Guide.* Miami: Seahawk Press, 1982.

Greenberg, Jerry; Greenberg, Idaz; and Greenberg, Simba. *Marine Invertebrates of the Tropical Atlantic.* Miami: Seahawk Press, 1980.

Guderjan, Thomas. "New Information from La Milpa, the 1990 Field Station." *Mexicon: Aktuelle Informationen und Studien zu Mesoamerika,* vol. 13, no. 1, 1991.

Hammond, Norman. *The Discovery of La Milpa.* Boston: Department of Archeology, Boston University, 1990.

Hecker, Ann Prince. "A Guide to Belize's Reserves." *Sanctuary, Journal of the Massachusetts Audubon Society,* September 1988.

Hoffman, Eric. "Land of Five Cats." *Pacific Discovery,* September 1993.

Hoffman, Eric. "Land of the Jaguars." *Animals,* May/June 1993.

Hoffman, Eric. "Women for a Wild Belize." *Animals,* September/October 1992.

Hoffman, Eric. "Wonder Woman of Belize." *International Wildlife,* November/December 1992.

Horwich, Robert, and Lyon, Jonathan. *A Belizean Rainforest, The Community Baboon Sanctuary.* Gays Mill, Wisc.: Orang-utan Press, 1989.

King, Emory. *Emory King's Driver's Guide to Beautiful Belize.* Belize City: Tropical Books, 1990.

Konecny, Michael. *Movement Patterns and Food Habits of Four Sympatric*

Carnivore Species in Belize, Central America. Gainesville, Fla.: Department of Zoology, University of Florida, 1986.

Koop, Gerhard S. *Pioneer Years in Belize.* Spanish Lookout, Belize: Gerhard S. Koop, 1991.

Krohn, Lita. *Readings in Belizean History.* Belize City: Belizean Studies, St. John's College, 1987.

Krohn, Lita. "13 Artists." Benque Viejo del Carmen, Belize: Belize Arts Council, 1991.

Lemmon, Alfred. *Maya Music and Dance.* Belize City: Bliss Institute, 1967.

Mahler, Richard, and Wotkyns, Steele. *Belize: A Natural Destination.* Santa Fe: John Muir Press, 1991.

Mallan, Chicki. *Belize Handbook.* Chico, Calif.: Moon Publications, 1991.

Marin, Vildo, ed. *Characters and Caricatures in Belizean Folklore.* Belmopan, Belize: Ministry of Education and Culture, 1991.

Matola, Sharon. *Hoodwink the Owl.* London: Macmillan Caribbean, 1988.

Matola, Sharon. "The People's Zoo." *Sanctuary, Journal of the Massachusetts Audubon Society,* September 1988.

Meerman, Jan. *Birds of Shipstern Nature Reserve.* Shipstern Nature Reserve, Belize: Shipstern Nature Reserve, 1991.

Meyer, Franz. *Diving and Snorkeling Guide to Belize.* Houston: Pisces Books, 1990.

Miller, Carolyn. "A Home for Howlers." *Sanctuary, Journal of the Massachusetts Audubon Society,* September 1988.

Miller, Carolyn, and Miller, Bruce. *Exploring the Rainforest at Chan Chich Lodge, Belize.* Gallon Jug, Belize: Chan Chich Lodge, 1991.

"Museum in the Making, A." *Belize Today,* vol. 5, no. 5, 1991.

Nicolait, Lou. "Frontier Economy." *Sanctuary, Journal of the Massachusetts Audubon Society,* September 1988.

PADI Open Water Diver Manual. Santa Ana, Calif.: Professional Association of Diving Instructors, 1988.

Perkins, Judith. *The Belize Barrier Reef Ecosystem.* Bronx, N.Y.: New York Zoological Society, 1983.

Peterson, Roger Tory, and Chalif, Edward. *A Field Guide to Mexican Birds.* Boston: Houghton Mifflin Company, 1973.

Programme for Belize. "Management Plan for the Rio Bravo Conservation and Management Area, Belize." Belize City: Programme for Belize, 1990.

Rabinowitz, Alan. *Jaguar.* New York: Doubleday, 1991.

Rabinowitz, Alan. *Jaguar Predation on Domestic Livestock in Belize.* Bronz, N.Y.: New York Zoological Society, 1986.

Rabinowitz, Alan, and Nottingham, Ben. *Mammal Species Richness and Relative Abundance of Small Mammals in Subtropical Wet Forest.* Bronx, N.Y.: New York Zoological Society, 1989.

Rabinowitz, A. R., and Nottingham, B. G. *Ecology and the Behavior of the Jaguar* (Panthera onca) *in Belize.* Bronx, N.Y.: New York Zoological Society, 1985.

Rath, Tony. "Cockscomb Basin Expedition Final Report." Belize City: Environmental Studies, 1989.

Rath, Tony. "Sapodilla Cayes Expedition Report." Belize City: Programme for Belize, Marine Division, 1991.

Rausher, Freya. *Cruising Guide to Belize and Mexico's Caribbean Coast.* Stamford, Conn.: Wescott Cove Publishing Company, 1991.

"San Pedro Blessed with Chamber." *Barracuda Divers' Newsletter,* 1991.

Showman, Assad. *Party Politics in Belize.* Benque Viejo del Carmen, Belize: Cubola Productions, 1987.

Stevens, Katie. *Jungle Walk, Birds and Beasts of Central America.* Belize City: Angelus Press, 1988.

Stuart, Gene S., and Stuart, George E. *Lost Kingdoms of the Maya.* Washington, D.C.: Book Division of National Geographic, 1993.

Thompson, J. Eric S. *The Maya of Belize.* Benque Viejo del Carmen, Belize: Cubola Productions, 1991.

VanKirk, Jacques, and VanKirk, Parney. *Creatures and Critters You Might See on the Trail.* Nobleton, Fla.: Film Team International, 1989.

Wood, Scott; Leberman, Robert; and Weyer, Dora. *Checklist of the Birds of Belize.* New York: Carnegie Museum of Natural History, 1986.

Daily and Monthly Publications

Amandala, 3304 Partridge Street, Belize City, Belize, C.A. (Weekly independent newspaper in Belize with the greatest number of subscribers.)

Belize Review, News, Views and Ecotourism (Meb Cutlack, ed.), 7 Church Street, Belize City, Belize, C.A. (Bimonthly, independent, investigative, environmentally oriented magazine.)

Belize Times, P.O. Box 506, 3 Queen Street, Belize City, Belize, C.A. (Newspaper presenting the views of the People's United Party.)

Belize Today, Belize Information Service, P.O. Box 60, Belmopan, Belize, C.A. (Bimonthly publication with accurate information on important current events in Belize.)

Belizean Tourism News, Belize Tourist Board, 415 Seventh Avenue, New York, NY 10001. (Tourist-related news publication.)

Centre Forum, Belize Centre for Environmental Studies, P.O. Box 666, 55 Eve Street, Belize City, Belize, C.A. (Independent newsletter that discusses and investigates key environmental concerns facing Belize.)

People's Pulse and Beacon, 7 Church Street, Belize City, Belize, C.A. (Newspaper that presents the views of the United Democratic Party.)

INDEX

Aberdeen Restaurant-Bar-Hotel, 119, 123
Accommodations. *See also individual establishments*
 at Altun Ha, 88–89
 on Ambergris Caye, 110–112
 in Barranco, 247
 in Belize City, 64–69
 in Belmopan, 264
 in Benque Viejo del Carmen, 301
 at Bermudian Landing Community Baboon Sanctuary, 85
 at Blue Hole National Park, 268
 boating operations and, 25
 at Caracol National Monument, 297
 on Caye Caulker, 122–123
 on Caye Chapel, 126
 at Chan Chich Lodge, 339
 at Chiquibul Forest Reserve, 300
 at Cockscomb Basin Wildlife Sanctuary, 197
 in Corozal Town, 344–345
 at Crooked Tree Wildlife Sanctuary, 77–78
 in Dangriga, 156–158
 at Gales Point, 100
 on Glover's Reef, 142
 in Hopkins, 169
 in Laguna, 233–234
 at Lamanai, 325–326
 on Lighthouse Reef, 139–140
 in Mennonite villages, 271
 at Mountain Pine Ridge Forest Reserve, 284–290

 in Orange Walk Town, 320
 in Placencia, 209–212
 in Possum Point Biological Station, 176
 price ranges, 41
 in Punta Gorda, 219–220
 at Rio Bravo Conservation and Management Area, 331
 on St. George's Caye, 128
 in San Antonio, Toledo District, 235–236
 in San Ignacio, 274–275
 scuba diving operations and, 22–23
 at Shipstern Nature Reserve and Butterfly Breeding Centre, 350
 on South Water Caye, 163–164
 at Tikal National Park, 314–315
 on Tobacco Caye, 166
 on Turneffe Islands, 133
 at Xunantunich, 278
Admiral Barnaby Art Gallery and Coffee Shop, 61
Adventure Inn, 344
Agouti, 334–335
Agriculture, 12, 45, 295, 320
Air travel
 to Belize, 28–29
 within Belize, 31
 to cayes, 101
 charter, 32
 to Guatemala, 315
 private, 31
Alcoholic beverages, 47, 154, 321
Altars, 309–310

Altun Ha (ruin), 27, 86–89
Ambergris Caye, 101–115
Amigo Travel, 105
American crocodile (*Crocodylus acutus*), 130–131
Animals. *See* Wildlife
Antelop Trail, 192–193
Arawak Indians, 10
Archaeological excavation, 294–295, 304–312
Art galleries, 61, 149, 282–284
Artists, 119, 148–149, 282–284
Arvigo, Rosita, 289, 290–291
Atolls, 14–17, 21–22
    in Belize District, 52, 129–142
Auil, Alan, 33–34, 55–56
Automobiles, 30–31. *See also* Driving
Automobiles, rental, 33–34
    in Belize City, 55–56
    in Dangriga, 158
    in Guatemala, 301, 315

Baboons. *See* Black howler monkey
Baird's tapir, 47, 182
Bamboo, 174
Banana Bank Ranch, 264
Banking. *See* Essential services
The Barge, 108
Baron's Hotel, 320
Barracuda, 115, 162, 204
Barranco (village), 231, 245–246
Barrier Reef, 14–15, 44, 145–146
Barton's Creek (village), 269
Bat Palace, Tikal, 311
Battle of St. George's Caye, 9–10, 127
Batty Brothers Bus Service, 275, 345
Baymen, 9, 126
Begging. *See* Panhandling
Belizean Rain Forest: The Community Baboon Sanctuary, A, 84–85, 97
Belize Audubon Society, 61–62
    Bermudian Landing Community Baboon Sanctuary and, 84
    black howler monkeys and, 81
    reef conservation and, 17
    as tourist information source, 38
Belize Biltmore Plaza, 34, 64, 68–69
Belize Center for Environmental Studies, 58

Belize City, 52–72
    market, 59–60, 63–64
    Municipal Airport, 56
    North Side, 54–59
    South Side, 59–63
Belize Diving Service, 120
Belize Guest House, 65–66
Belize High Commission to Canada, 37
Belize Tourism Industry Association (BTIA), 57
Belize Tourist Board (BTB), 23, 37, 56–57
Belize Zoo and Tropical Education Center, 89–93
Bellevue Hotel, 67–68
Belmopan, 261–265
Belmopan Convention Hotel, 264
Belmoral Hotel, 274
Beni, Alejo, 11, 150
Benque Viejo del Carmen (village), 300–302
Ben's Bluff Trail, 193–194
Bermudian Landing Community Baboon Sanctuary, 78–86
Big Creek, 201
Biodiversity studies, 328
Biosphere and Oceanic Society, 133
Bird Caye Bird Sanctuary, 98–99
Bird watching. *See also individual birds*
    at Chan Chich Lodge, 335–336
    at Cockscomb Basin Wildlife Sanctuary, 183
    at Crooked Tree Wildlife Sanctuary, 73–75
    on Lighthouse Reef, 135
    at Possum Point Biological Station, 175–176
    at Rio Bravo Conservation and Management Area, 330
    on Temash River, 242–243
    on Turneffe Islands, 131
Black-bellied whistling duck, 74
Blackbird Caye Resort, 133
Black Carib. *See* Garifuna culture
Black Creek, 75
Black howler monkey (*Alouatta pigra*), 80–81, 187, 335
Blackline Marine, 57, 67, 99

Black mangrove, 243
Black orchid, 47
Black Rock, 275
Bladen Nature Reserve, 228
Bliss, Henry Edward Everest Victor,
  58–59
Blue Creek Cave, 239–241
Blue Hole, Lighthouse Reef, 107, 134,
  137–138
Blue Hole National Park, 257, 265–268
Blue Marlin Lodge, 163
Blue morpho butterflies, 243
Boating, 24, 125. *See also* Canoeing;
  Kayaking; Sailing
Boats, charter, 33, 70, 124
  at Cerros Ruins, 347
  at Crooked Tree Wildlife Sanctuary,
    76
  at Lamanai, 326
Boats, private, 31
Bob's Hilltop Hotel, 235–236
Boca Ciega Blue Hole, 114
Bonefish Hotel, 157
Border crossing, 301–302, 345–346
Bowen, Barry, 47, 62, 333–334
British Commonwealth, 45
Brodie (store), 60
BTB. *See* Belize Tourist Board
BTIA. *See* Belize Tourism Industry As-
  sociation
Budget Rent A Car, 33–34, 55–56
Bull Frog Inn, 264
Burial, in Tikal, 307–308
Business hours, 40
Bus service
  to Belize, 30
  within Belize, 32
  in Belize City, 62–63, 70
  to Belize Zoo and Tropical Educa-
    tion Center, 92
  to Belmopan, 264–265
  to Bermudian Landing Community
    Baboon Sanctuary, 85
  to Blue Hole National Park, 268
  to Cockscomb Basin Wildlife Sanctu-
    ary, 198
  to Corozal Town, 345
  to Dangriga, 158
  to Guancaste National Park, 260

  into Guatemala, 301
  into Mexico, 346
  to Nim Li Punit, 226
  to Placencia, 212
  to Punta Gorda, 220
  to San Antonio, Toledo District, 236
  to San Ignacio, 275
  to Shipstern Nature Reserve and
    Butterfly Breeding Centre,
    350–351
Buttercup tree, 182
Butterflies, 243, 349–350

Caana (Sky Palace), 292
Cabs. *See* Taxi service
Cahal Pech (ruin), 278–279
Camping, 41
  at Caracol Natural Monument, 297
  at Gales Point, 100
  in Placencia, 211
  in San Ignacio, 275
  on Temash River, 243
Canadian Consulate, 56
Canoeing, 25, 107
Caracol Natural Monument, 27, 258,
  292–298
Carib Indians, 10
Carnival, 106
Carrie Bow Caye, 159–161, 165
Cars. *See* Automobiles
Cassava bread, 154
Caves, 16
  at Blue Hole National Park, 265–266
  on Caye Caulker, 120–121
  at Gales Point, 95
  near Mayan villages, 232–233
  at Mountain Pine Ridge Forest
    Reserve, 280–281
  in Toledo District, 239–240
  underwater, 114
Caye Caulker, 115–125
Caye Chapel, 125–126
Caye Corker. *See* Caye Caulker
Cayes, 14–17, 44. *See also individual
  cayes*
  in Belize District, 52
  in Stann Creek District, 159–166
  in Toledo District, 247–254
Cayetano, Pen, 148

Central Acropolis, Tikal, 310
Central Hotel, 274
Cerros Ruins, 346–347
Chaa Creek Cottages, 288–289
Chan Chich Lodge, 62, 319, 332–339
Chase, Arlen and Diane, 292–298
Chateau Caribbean, 66
Chau Hiix (ruin), 75–76
Chau Hiix Lodge, 77
Chetumal, Mexico, 343, 346
Chicleros, 272, 283
Chiquibul Forest Reserve and National
    Park, 298–300
Chucil Baalum (ruin), 178
Chun Bus Service, 236
Circle A Lodge, 264
Climate, 36–37
    at Chan Chich Lodge, 339
    at Cockscomb Basin Wildlife Sanctu-
       ary, 177
    at Crooked Tree Wildlife Sanctuary, 76
    at Tikal National Park, 313
    in Toledo District, 215
Clothing, 37, 71
Coast Road. See New Road
Cockroach Wall, 108, 132
Cockscomb Basin Wildlife Sanctuary,
    145, 177–198
Coco plum, 116
Cohune palm, 19–20
"Coloured class," 10
Colson Caye, 203
Comedor Maya (restaurant), 315
Conservation, 91
    in Cockscomb Basin Wildlife Sanctu-
       ary, 179
    economic needs of citizens and,
       327–329
    of iguanas, 174
    of rain forests, 19–21
    of reef system, 16–17
    on Sapodilla Cayes, 253–254
Conservation groups
    information sources on, 61–62
    Rio Bravo Project, 326–332
    as tourist information source, 38
Coot, 74
Coral Gardens, 108

Corals, 15
    at Hol Chan Marine Preserve,
       113–114
    off Lighthouse Reef, 139
    off South Water Caye, 162
Coral snake, 43
Corn, 245
Corozal Town, 343–345
Cortez Dance, 238
Cosmos Camping, 275
Cottage Colony (resort), 128
Crawl Caye, 132
Credit cards, 38–39, 65
Creole culture, 40, 72–73, 79–80
Crime
    in Belize City, 70–72
    at Blue Hole National Park, 267
    on Caye Caulker, 118–119
    at Guancaste National Park, 259–260
Crocodiles, 130–131
Crooked Tree Hotel and Cabanas,
    77–78
Crooked Tree Resort, 78
Crooked Tree Wildlife Sanctuary,
    72–78
*Cruising Guide to Belize and Mexico's
    Caribbean Coast,* 68
Cuello Ruins, 321
Cultural diversity, 8–12
    on Caye Caulker, 117–118
    in Cayo District, 258
    in Orange Walk District, 319
Culture shock, 53, 151–152
Curassow Trail, 190–192
Currency exchange, 38–39, 301

Dairy farming, 12
Dances, Mayan, 238–239
Dangriga, 11, 146–159
Dangriga Art Center, 149
Deep-sea fishing, 26
Deer Dance, 238–239
Dehydration, 42
Department of Archaeology, 262–263,
    297
Development issues
    on Ambergris Caye, 104
    in Belmopan, 261

on Gales Point, 95–96
in Placencia, 198–200
Diani's Hotel, 350
Dive services, 21–23, 109, 120
Diving. *See* Scuba diving; Snorkeling
Dolores (village), 244–245
Dory's Channel, 108, 131
Driving
    to Belize, 30–31
    in Belize City, 69–70
    cautions, 35–36, 92–93, 281–282
    in Guatemala, 302, 314
    into Mexico, 345–346
    at Rio Bravo Conservation and Man-
        agement Area, 332
Drugs, illegal, 45–46, 72, 119
Drums, 11, 152–153
Dugu (healing rite), 11, 152–153
Dumb cane, 194
Duplooy's Riverside Cottages and
    Hotel, 288

Eagle ray, 132, 204
Earl's Cafe, 64
Economy, 44–45, 327–329
Ecosystems, 13–20
Eco-tourism, 6, 14. *See also* Tourism
Education, 91, 167
Elbow, The, 132
El Caracol Gallery and Gift Shop, 264
El Castillo, 275–277
El Indio Perdido, 301
Elkhorn coral, 141, 206
El Pilar (ruin), 279
El Salvador, Mundo Maya program
    and, 27
Elvi's Kitchen, 105
Embassies/consulates, 37, 56, 263–264
Emerald Forest Reef, 141
Emerald House (store), 106
Emergency facilities. *See* Essential ser-
    vices
English colonists, 8–10, 126–127
Entertainment
    on Ambergris Caye, 106
    in Belize City, 57
    in San Ignacio, 274
Entry requirements, 37

for Guatemala, 301
for Mexico, 345
Environmental concerns. *See* Conserva-
    tion
Esquivel, Manuel, 262
Essential services
    on Ambergris Caye, 105–106
    in Belize City, 58
    on Caye Caulker, 119
    in Corozal Town, 344
    in Dangriga, 146
    in Mayan villages, 235
    in Placencia, 202
    in Punta Gorda, 218
    in San Ignacio, 273–274
Ethnocentricity, 168, 234
Eva's Restaurant and Bar, 272–273
*Exploring the Rainforest, Chan Chich
    Lodge Belize*, 335–336
Exports, 45

Fairweather and Noble Rose (resort),
    166
Farming. *See* Agriculture
Fax facilities. *See* Essential services
Felines, 183–186, 334
Fer-de-lance snake, 42–43, 188
Ferries, 31, 221
Fish
    as export, 45
    at Hol Chan Marine Preserve, 114
    at Laughing Bird Caye National
        Park, 206–207
    off Lighthouse Reef, 139
    off Placencia, 204–205
    off St. George's Caye, 127
    off Sapodilla Cayes, 252
    off South Water Caye, 161–162
    off Turneffe Islands, 132
Fishing, 25–26
    off Ambergris Caye, 110
    off Caye Caulker, 121
    operations from Belize City, 57
    off Placencia, 207–208
    off Turneffe Islands, 132–133
Flag, national, 46
Fort Street Guesthouse, 65
Fox, Kitty, 207, 210–211

Frangipani House, 164
Frank's Caye, 249
Frenchman's Caye, 247
Frigate bird, 102–103, 135
Fruit trees, 246
"Fut" (N9-56), Lamanai, 325

G & G's Inn, 218–219
Galeria Hicaco (store), 119
Gales Point, 94–100
Gallon Jug (village), 333–334
Garcia sisters, 282–284
Garifuna culture, 145, 149–150,
    245–246
  cuisine, 154
  history, 10–11
  language, 40
  villages, 166–170
Garinagu. See Garifuna culture
Geography, 44
Geology, 16
  of Caye Caulker, 116
  of Mountain Pine Ridge, 279–280
  national museum and, 263
Georgetown, 170
G.G.'s (restaurant), 63
Gibnut Loop Trail, 192
Gibson, Janet, 17, 115, 140
Gill, Emma, 118, 121–122
Give-and-take palm, 42, 182
Glover's Reef, 21–22, 140–142
Glover's Reef Resort, 142
Godfrey, Glenn, 94–95, 105, 261–262
Goff's Caye, 128
Gon's (restaurant), 64
Government, 45–46
  at Belmopan, 261–262
  as British colony, 10
  Cockscomb Basin Wildlife Sanctuary
    and, 179
  departments of, 263
  Gales Point development and, 95–96
Grant, Joy, 328–329
Gray fox, 334
Gray lizard (Anolis allisoni), 136
Great Britain, 46, 249
Great Plaza, Tikal, 305
Green iguana (Iguana iguana), 83

Green moray, 114
Grouper, 115
Guam Bank, 178
Guancaste National Park, 257, 259–260
Guancaste tree, 259
Guatemala
  crossing into, 301–302
  Mundo Maya program and, 27–38
  refugees from, 12, 267
  tourists from, 250, 253–254
  transportation to Belize, 30
  travel connections to, 221
Guides
  at Chan Chich Lodge, 336
  at Crooked Tree Wildlife Sanctuary,
    76
  fake, 83–84
  at Tikal National Park, 313

Habitat loss. See Conservation
Half Moon Caye Natural Monument,
    107, 134–136
Haulover Creek, 54
Hawksbill turtle, 135
Health concerns, 41–43
Herons, 73–74, 242
Hidden Valley Falls, 280
Hidden Valley Inn, 289
Hieroglyphics, 294, 309
Highways. See individual highways;
    Roads
Hiking
  at Bermudian Landing Community
    Baboon Sanctuary, 82–83
  at Blue Hole National Park, 266–267
  cautions, 196–197
  at Chan Chich Lodge, 337
  at Cockscomb Basin Wildlife Sanctu-
    ary, 190–195
  at Crooked Tree Wildlife Sanctuary,
    75
  at Shipstern Nature Reserve and
    Butterfly Breeding Centre, 350
  at Tikal National Park, 312
  in Toledo District, 239–241
History, 8–12
  of Ambergris Caye, 101–102
  of Caye Caulker, 116

of Cockscomb Basin Wildlife
Sanctuary, 178–180
of Corozal Town, 344
of Dangriga, 148
Guatemala and Belize, 301
of Hopkins, 168
of Lamanai ruin, 322–324
Mennonites and, 270–271
national museum and, 263
of Orange Walk Town, 320
of Placencia, 200–201
of Punta Gorda, 216–218
of St. George's Caye, 126
of Seine Bight, 170
Hol Chan Marine Preserve, 16, 107,
113–115
Holiday Hotel (restaurant), 105
Holidays, 40
March, 9, 59, 106
November 19, 150–152
Honduras
Mundo Maya program and, 27
tourists from, 253–254
Honey bear. *See* Kinkajou
Hopkins (village), 166–169
Hortence's Market, 202
Horwich, Robert, 80, 94–96
Hospitals. *See* Essential services
Hotel Central, 301
Hotel Jaguar, 315
Hotel Maya, 345
Hotels. *See* Accommodations
House of the Rising Sun, 111
Hub Guest House and Restaurant,
157
Hummingbird Highway, 34–35
Hunting Caye, 249
Hurricane Hattie, 130, 170, 261
Hurricanes, 36, 180, 250
Hut (restaurant), 105

I and Jah International Outrigger Sail-
ing Club, 121–122
Iguana (*Iguana iguana rhinolopha*), 83,
135, 173–174, 187–188, 260
Immigration offices, 37, 218
Immigration problems, 12, 181
Independence (town), 228

Indigenous Experience/Host Family
Network, 230–231
Inner Lagoon, 202–207
Inner-tubing, 25
Inns. *See* Accommodations
Inoculations, 42
Insect pests, 42, 122, 248
International Expeditions, 37–38
International Tropical Conservation,
349
International Zoological Expeditions
(IZE), 165
Islands. *See* Cayes
Ix Chel Farm, 290–291

J&L Grocery, 119
Jabiru stork, 74
Jaguar, 185–186, 329
Jaguar Hotel, 274
Jaguarundi, 185
Journey's End (resort), 112
Judicial system, 262
Jungle Hut, 158
Jungle Lodge, 315
Jungle River Tours, 326

Karen's Fast Food, 202
Katie House (restaurant), 64
Kaway tree, 194
Kayaking, 25, 207–208
Keel-billed motmot, 299
Keel-billed toucan, 47, 223
Ketchi Mayans, 229–230
King, Emory, 61
Kingfishers, 73
Kingfisher Sports Ltd., 208
King vulture, 289
Kinkajou, 335
Kitty's Place, 208–211

"Lag" (N10-43), Lamanai, 324
Laguna (village), 231–234
Lamanai (ruin), 27, 319, 322–326
Lamanai Outpost Lodge, 320
Lambey, Pablo, 149–150, 154
La Milpa Ruins, 330–331
Language, 39–40, 229
Laughing Bird Caye, 16, 203, 205–207

Law enforcement, 45–46
Lighthouse Reef, 21–22, 134–140
Lighthouse Reef Resort, 134, 139–140
Lime Caye, 250
Livingston, Guatemala, 221
Local Guest House, 77
Lodges. *See* Accommodations; Mountain lodges
Loggerhead turtle, 135
Logging, 19, 178–179, 257, 272
Logwood tree, 9, 19
Long Caye, 108, 136
Low Caye. *See* Lime Caye
Lubaantum (ruin), 222–224

Macy's Cafe, 63
Mahogany tree, 19, 46–47
Manatee Lagoons. *See* Gales Point
Manatee Road. *See* New Road
Manatees. *See* West Indian manatee
Mango Creek, 201, 228
Mangrove ecosystem, 17
Man-of-War Caye (near Dangriga), 159
Man-of-War Cayes, 203–204
Manta Reef Resort, 142
Maps, 34–35
   of Belize, 30
   of Belize City, 70
   of Chiquibul Forest Reserve and National Park, 299
   of Placencia, 202
Marco Gonzalez archaeological site, 101
Margay, 184
Marine Parade, Belize City, 58
Markets
   in Belize City, 59–60
   in Placencia, 202
   in Punta Gorda, 218
   in San Ignacio, 273–274
Martinez Restaurant, 119
Maruba Resort and Jungle Spa, 78, 320
Mary Ellen's Little Italy (restaurant), 105
Matola, Sharon, 90–92
Maya Airlines
   to Dangriga, 158
   to Placencia, 212
   to Punta Gorda, 220

Maya Center, 178, 180–181
Maya Motel, 301
Maya Mountain Lodge, 287
Maya Mountains, 44, 145, 177, 227
Mayan culture
   architecture, 307
   art, 282–284
   decline of, 296–297, 323
   engineering, 222, 311, 325
   history of, 8
   language, 40
   modern, 229–239
Mayan ruins
   on Ambergris Caye, 101–102
   near Belize City, 86–89
   in Cayo District, 275–298
   at Chan Chich Lodge, 338
   at Cockscomb Basin Wildlife Sanctuary, 178
   in Corozal District, 343
   at Crooked Tree Wildlife Sanctuary, 75–76
   in Orange Walk District, 321–326
   at Rio Bravo Conservation and Management Area, 330–331
   in Toledo District, 215–216, 222–228
   visiting, 26–28, 297
Melchor de Menos, Guatemala, 301–302
Mennonites, 12, 268–271
Mexican Birds, 76
Mexican Corner (restaurant), 63
Mexican Rocks, 108
Mexico
   Caste Wars refugees, 11, 172, 344
   Mundo Maya program and, 27–38
   transportation to Belize, 30
Mi Amor Hotel, 320
Middle Caye, 141
Miller, Bruce and Carolyn, 335–338
Minerals, 227
Mira Mar (hotel), Caye Caulker, 123
Mira Mar Hotel, Punta Gorda, 219–220
Mohammed's (restaurant), 64
Moho Caye (Belize City area), 129
Moho Cayes, 247–248
Moho River, 246–247

Mom's Triangle Inn, 57, 64, 67
Monkey Bay Wildlife Sanctuary, 93–94
Monkey Dance, 239
Monkey ear tree. *See* Guancaste tree
Monkey River Mayan Ruins, 226–228
Monkey River Town, 228
Monkeys, 79
Mopan Mayans, 229–230
Morlet's crocodile (*Crocodylus morletti*), 131
Morning Glory (restaurant), 219
Mosquito Caye, 207
Mosquitoes. *See* Insect pests
Motels. *See* Accommodations
Motion sickness, 42
Mountain cow. *See* Baird's tapir
Mountain Equestrian Trails (lodge), 271, 285–286
Mountain lion, 185
Mountain lodges, 284–290, 300, 315
Mountain Pine Ridge Forest Reserve, 18, 257, 279–282
Mundo Maya (Mayan World) program, 27–28
Muscovy duck, 74
Museums, 263, 313
Museum Sylvanus Morley, 313
Music, 11, 152–153
    Mayan, 233–234, 237–239

Nabitunich Lodge, 287–288
Naprapathy, 290
National parks
    in Cayo District, 257
    Chiquibul Forest Reserve, 298–300
    Guatemalan, 303
    information sources on, 61–62
    Laughing Bird Caye, 205–207
Nature's Way Guest House, 218–219, 254
New River, 322
New Road, 35
Nicolas Caye, 249
Nightclubs. *See* Entertainment
Nim Li Punit (ruin), 225–226
North Acropolis, Tikal, 310
Northeast Caye, 142, 249
Northeast Marine Environmental Insti-

tution, Inc. *See* Possum Point Biological Station
Northern Caye, 138–139
Northern Fisherman's Cooperative, 119
Northern Highway, 34, 51, 54–55
Northern jacana, 73
Northern Lagoon, 94, 98
Northern Turneffe, 131–132
Novelo's Bus Service, 30, 62–63, 275

Obeah, 152–153
Ocellated turkey, 312
Ocelot, 184–185
Olmecs, 322–323, 325
Orange Walk Town, 319–321
Orchida House (restaurant), 64
Osprey's Nest (resort), 164
Out Island Divers, 109

Paca, 334–335
Package deals. *See* Tour/charter operations
Pal's Guest House, 157
Panhandling, 70–72, 347
Panti Mayan Medicine Trail, 288–289, 290–291
Paradise Resort Hotel, 111
Paradise Vacation Hotel, 211
Parker, Larry, 108–109, 112
Parrotfish, 115
Paz, Changa, 107–109, 132, 138
Pelican Beach Resort, 148
    accommodations, 156
    Gales Point and, 99–100
    restaurant, 154
    tour/charter operations, 155
Pelican University (resort), 164
Pendergast, David, 322–324
Peregrine falcon, 74
Pescador Caverns, 108
Petty Shop, 154
Phillip Goldson International Airport, 31
Photography
    on Caye Caulker, 120
    in Garifuna villages, 168
    in Mayan villages, 234
    in Mennonite villages, 270

of wildlife, 189
Pinelands ecosystem, 18
Pirates, 8–9
Pit-pans (boats), 100, 259
P.J.'s Gift Shop, 149
Placencia, 198–212
Placencia Dive Shop, 207
Plantains, 154
Plant life. *See also individual plants*
    at Chan Chich Lodge, 337
    at Cockscomb Basin Wildlife Sanctuary, 181–183
    dangerous, 42, 182
    on Lighthouse Reef, 135
    near Mayan villages, 233
    medicinal, 290–291
    at Rio Bravo Conservation and Management Area, 330
Poisonwood, 42, 182
Political parties, 46, 262
Port Honduras, 247–248
Possum Point Biological Station, 174–176
Post offices. *See* Essential services
Pottery, 266
Poultry farming, 12, 270
Price, George, 261–262
Programme for Belize, 62, 326–332
Provisioning
    in Belize City, 60
    on Caye Caulker, 119
    in Dangriga, 146
    in Placencia, 202
Puerto Barrios, Guatemala, 221
Puma. *See* Mountain lion
Punta Gorda, 216–221, 241–242
Punta rock music, 11, 152
Pyramid Island Resort, 126

Rabinowitz, Alan, 179
Raddison Fort George, 68
Ragged Caye, 250
Rainbow Hotel, 123
Rain forest ecosystem, 13, 18–21, 177
    at Chiquibul Forest Reserve, 299
    at Guancaste National Park, 259–260
    at Rio Bravo Conservation and Management Area, 330

Ramon's Village Resort, 111–112
Ran's Villas, 211
Rath, Therese and Tony, 148–149, 155, 203–204, 248
Rattlesnakes, 43
RBCMA. *See* Rio Bravo Conservation and Management Area
Recompression chamber, 22, 43, 109
Red brocket deer, 334
Red-eyed tree frog (*Smilisca phaeota*), 180, 188
Red-footed booby, 134–135
Red mangrove, 114–115, 243
Reef Divers Ltd., 112
Reef ecosystem, 14–17
    in Belize District, 52
    off Placencia, 204
Reef End Lodge, 166
Reef fishing, 26
Regattas, 59, 100
Religion, 62, 268–271
    Garifuna, 150–153
    missionary efforts, 237–239, 323–324
Rendezvous Point, 108
Restaurants. *See also individual establishments*
    on Ambergris Caye, 105
    in Belize City, 63–64
    in Belmopan, 264
    on Caye Caulker, 119
    in Dangriga, 154
    in Orange Walk Town, 320
    in Placencia, 208–209
    price ranges, 41
    in Punta Gorda, 218–219
    at Tikal National Park, 314–315
Rio Blanco Santa Elena Nature Reserve, 236–237
Rio Bravo Conservation and Management Area (RBCMA), 319, 326–332
Rio Frio Cave, 280
Rio Mar Inn, 157
Rio On, 280
River boating, 96, 196
River Overlook Trail, 194–195
River Path, 190–192
Roads, 34–35
    in Belize District, 51

dirt, 281–282
Mayan, 295
Rosado's Tours, 155
Roseate spoonbill, 73
Roy's Cool Spot Grocery, 235
Rubber Tree Trail, 190–192
Rum Point Inn, 200, 208–210
Ruta Maya. *See* Mundo Maya

Safety. *See* Crime; Health concerns
Sail Belize, 129
Sailing, 24
  off Ambergris Caye, 110
  off Caye Caulker, 121
  off Placencia, 207–208
  off St. George's Caye, 128
St. George's Caye, 9–10, 126–129
St. George's Island Cottages, 128
St. Herman's Cave, 265–266
Salt-water crocodile. *See* American
  crocodile
San Antonio, Toledo District, 235–236
Sandborn Caye, 138–139
Sandburg Canyon, 107
Sand flies. *See* Insect pests
S and L Tours and Rentals, 57
Sandy Beach Lodge, 169
Sandy Point, 108
San Ignacio, 258, 272–275
San Ignacio Hotel, 274
San Pedro, 102–107
San Pedro Holiday Hotel, 111
Santa Cruz Village, 236
Santa Elena, 272–275
Santa Rita Ruins, 347–348
Sapodilla Cayes, 248–254
Sarteneja (village), 350
Savanna ecosystem, 18
Scarlet macaw, 299, 312
Scuba diving
  off Ambergris Caye, 107–115
  cautions, 21, 109
  off Caye Caulker, 120–121
  off Caye Chapel, 125–126
  climate and, 37
  essential information, 21–24
  off Glover's Reef, 141
  off Hunting Caye, 252
  off Lighthouse Reef, 136–139

off Lime Caye, 252–253
off Nicholas Caye, 252
at night, 115
operations, 23, 57
off Placencia, 207
off Ragged Caye, 252–253
off St. George's Caye, 127
off Sapodilla Cayes, 252–253
off South Water Caye, 162–163
off Turneffe Islands, 131–132
Sea Flame Restaurant, 154
Sea grass, 114
Seaing is Belizing, 120
Seaside Guest House, 65
Sea urchins, 162
Seine Bight (village), 169–170
Serpon Sugar Mill. *See* Sittee River Sugar Mill
Settlement Day (November 19), 11,
  150–151
Shaiba's (restaurant), 219
Sharks, 42, 138
Shipstern Nature Reserve and Butterfly Breeding Centre, 348–351
Shopping, 40–41
  on Ambergris Caye, 105–106
  in Belize City, 60
  in Belmopan, 264
  at Cockscomb Basin Wildlife Sanctu-
    ary, 197
  in Dangriga, 149
  at Tikal National Park, 313
Sittee River Sugar Mill, 171–172
Sittee River tour, 173–175
Slavery, 9–10
Snail kite, 74
Snakebird, 242–243
Snakes, poisonous, 42–43
Snorkeling
  off Ambergris Caye, 107–115
  off Caye Caulker, 120–121
  off Caye Chapel, 125–126
  climate and, 37
  essential information, 24
  off Glover's Reef, 141
  off Hunting Caye, 249
  off Lighthouse Reef, 136–139
  operations, 57
  off Placencia, 202–207

off St. George's Caye, 127
off Sapodilla Cayes, 252–253
off South Water Caye, 161–162
off Turneffe Islands, 131–132
Sonny's Resort, 211
Southern Highway, 35, 51
Southern Lagoon, 94, 98
Southern Turneffe, 132
South Stann Creek, 196
South Water Caye, 159
Southwest Caye, 142
Spanish colonists, 8–9, 126–127
   driven from Lamanai, 323–324
   at Santa Rita, 347
Spanish Lookout, 257, 268–271
Spider monkey, 79, 330, 335
Spiny-tailed iguana (*Ctennosaura similis*),
   83, 135–136
Split Reef, 141–142
Sponges, 162
Sprat, 204–205
Staghorn coral, 252
Stalactites/stalagmites, 137–138, 281
Stelae
   at Nim Li Punit, 225–226
   at Tikal National Park, 309–310
   at Uxbenka, 224
Steve Tillet and Sons Enterprises, 78
Stinging coral, 42, 253
Stingray, 42
Stone carvings, 40, 282–284
Storks, 74–75
Strangler fig, 182
Sugar cane, 11, 45, 172
Sun Breeze Hotel, 105, 111
Sunburn, 42
Swimming
   at Blue Creek Cave, 240–241
   at Blue Hole National Park, 265
   off Caye Chapel, 125
   at Cockscomb Basin Wildlife Sanctu-
      ary, 192
   off Lighthouse Reef, 136
   near Mayan villages, 236–237
   at Mountain Pine Ridge Forest
      Reserve, 280

Tapir. *See* Baird's tapir
Taxes, 39

Taxi service, 32–33
   in Belize City, 69
   in Dangriga, 155
Tayra, 186–187
Telephone facilities. *See* Essential ser-
   vices
Temash River, 241–244
Temples
   at Altun Ha, 86–88
   at Caracol, 292–294
   at Lamanai, 324–325
   at Tikal National Park, 302–312
Tentacles Restaurant, 201
Thomas's Hotel, 110–111
*Tikal: A Handbook of the Ancient Mayan
   Ruins*, 310
Tikal Hotel, 315
Tikal National Park, Guatemala,
   26–27, 302–315
   Caracol and, 294, 296
Tinamou Trail, 195
Tino's Taxi Service, 155
Tipping, 39
Tobacco Caye, 159, 165–166
Tombs
   at Altun Ha, 88
   at Caracol, 295
   at Tikal National Park, 307, 310
Tony's Inn and Beach Resort, 345
Toucan Inn, 211–212
Toucan Island Resort, 249
Toucan Too (store), 105–106
Tour/charter operations
   in Dangriga, 155
   from mountain lodges, 286
   from Pelican Beach Resort, 155
   from San Pedro hotels, 104–105
   from South Water Caye hotels,
      163–164
Tourism, 45
   Garifuna culture and, 167
   information sources, 37–38, 56–57,
      105
   Mayan ruins and, 297
   in Mayan villages, 230–234
   Mennonites and, 269
   in Toledo District, 215–216
Tradewinds (resort), 211
Trading, Mayan, 227, 346–347

Transportation, 28–36. *See also individual methods*
Traveller's Inn, 219, 220
"Traveller's Reference Map of Belize," 35
Trees. *See individual trees; Plant life*
Tropical Paradise (restaurant), 119
Tropical Paradise Hotel, 169
Tropical Travel, 38
Turneffe Diving Lodge, 133
Turneffe Flats (resort), 133
Turneffe Islands, 21, 130–134
Turtle Inn, 209, 211
Turtles, 135, 249
Twin Pyramid complex, Tikal, 311

United States
　aid to Belize, 45
　Civil War immigrants, 11, 171–172
　Drug Enforcement Agency (DEA), 46
　embassy in Belize, 56
Universal Travel, 57, 105
Uxbenka (ruin), 224

Vaca Plateau, 284
Vegas' Far Inn, 123
Venus Bus Lines, 63, 345
Victoria Peak, 44, 177, 196
Village Guesthouse and Ecotrail Program, 230–234
Visa requirements, 37
　for Guatemala, 301
　for Mexico, 345

Warfare
　Mayan, 296–297
　Spanish against Mayan, 320
Wari Trail, 194–195
Waterfalls
　at Cockscomb Basin Wildlife Sanctuary, 193
　near Mayan villages, 236–237
　at Mountain Pine Ridge Forest Reserve, 280

Weather. *See* Climate
Wee Wee Caye, 176
Western Highway, 34, 51, 92–93, 265
Western Snake Caye, 248
West Indian manatee (*Trichecus manatus*), 97–98
Wetlands ecosystem, 17–18
White ibis, 73
White mangrove, 242
Wildlife, 19. *See also* Bird watching; *individual animals*
　at Bermudian Landing Community Baboon Sanctuary, 80
　at Blue Hole National Park, 266
　at Chan Chich Lodge, 334–336
　at Cockscomb Basin Wildlife Sanctuary, 182–189
　dangerous, 42, 162, 188
　at Gales Point, 96–97
　at Guancaste National Park, 259–260
　at Mountain Pine Ridge Forest Reserve, 288
　at Possum Point Biological Station, 175–176
　at Rio Bravo Conservation and Management Area, 329–330
　at Shipstern Nature Reserve and Butterfly Breeding Centre, 349
　at Tikal National Park, 312
Wildlife Conservation International, 335
Wildlife sanctuaries, 51–52, 134–135.
　See also individual sanctuaries
Windsurfing, 25, 207–208
Wood stork, 74–75

Xunantunich (ruin), 27, 258, 275–278

Yellow-jaw. *See* Fer-de-lance snake
Young's Bus Service, 85

Z-Line Bus Service, 63, 159
　to Placencia, 212
　to Punta Gorda, 220
Zuh uy ha pottery, 266